Deliberative Freedom

Deliberative Freedom

Deliberative Democracy as Critical Theory

CHRISTIAN F. ROSTBØLL

State University of New York Press

Published by
State University of New York Press, Albany

Printed in the United States of America

For information, contact State University of New York Press, Albany, NY
www.sunypress.edu

Production by Eileen Meehan
Marketing by Michael Campochiaro

Library of Congress Cataloging-in-Publication Data

Rostbøll, Christian F.
    Deliberative freedom : deliberative democracy as critical theory / Christian F. Rostboll.
        p. cm.
    Includes bibliographical references and index.
    ISBN 978-0-7914-7459-4 (hardcover : alk. paper)
    ISBN 978-0-7914-7460-0 (paperback : alk. paper)
    1. Democracy.   2. Liberty.   I. Title.

JC423.R6176 2008
321.8—dc22   2007036638

10 9 8 7 6 5 4 3 2 1

For Kathrin, Leo, and Siri

Contents

Acknowledgments

I began this book as a graduate student at Columbia University and I would like to begin by expressing my gratitude to my teachers there. I owe a special debt to Jean Cohen, who has been a continued source of inspiration, encouragement, and critical comments. I also feel extremely fortunate to have had Jon Elster as a reader. His analytic clarity and astute comments have helped me avoid many invalid arguments. I am immensely grateful to them both for their invaluable advice. Other teachers at Columbia who have inspired me by their teaching and/or commented on my work and whom I wish to thank are Robert Amdur, Brian Barry, Bernard Berofsky, David Johnston, Philip Pettit, Jeremy Waldron, and Nadia Urbinati.

Many friends have commented on my work over the seven years or so I have worked on this project. I would like to thank Pablo Gilabert, Tore Vincents Olsen, Reidar Maliks, Andreas Kalyvas, Daniel Cordes, Hans-Martin Jaeger, and Scott Morison. A special thank you goes to Chris Zurn, who did much more than what one could expect from a reviewer and who gave me a lot to think about. I thank Laura Inman and Katherine Pettus for diligent copyediting, and Theresa Scavenius for her help in composing the index. At SUNY Press, I thank Michael Rinella and Eileen Meehan.

I also would like to thank my students at Columbia and Wesleyan during the period 2001–2004. At Wesleyan, I was fortunate to be able to teach two courses directly related to my research, one on deliberative democracy and one on freedom. At Columbia, teaching contemporary civilization helped me situate my thinking in the tradition of great books.

I have presented a number of papers that in some form or another found their way into this book at different conferences and seminars, including the Annual Meeting of the American Political Science Association in Boston in 2002 and in Philadelphia in 2003; the 11th Annual Critical Theory Roundtable, Stony Brook University, 2003; the 61st Annual National Conference of the Midwest Political Science Association, Chicago, 2003; the Colloquium on *Philosophy and the Social Sciences*, hosted by the Institute of Philosophy, Academy of Sciences of the Czech Republic, in cooperation with Charles University, Prague, in 2001 and 2003; and the Thirty-fourth Annual Meeting of the Northeastern Political Science Association, Providence, 2002. I would like to thank the participants in these events, in particular, Susan Bickford, Elizabeth H. Ellis, Cathrine Holst, Arto Laitinen, Michael Lipscomb, and Brent D. Lollis.

I dedicate this book to my wonderful wife Kathrin and to our children Leo and Siri.

I thank Sage Publications for permission to reprint and rework parts of the following articles:

"Preferences and Paternalism: On Freedom and Deliberative Democracy." *Political Theory* 33:3 (June 2005): 370–96. (© Sage Publications, 2005)

"Emancipation or Accommodation? Habermasian vs. Rawlsian Deliberative Democracy." *Philosophy & Social Criticism* 34. (© Sage Publications and David Rasmussen, 2008)

Introduction

[E]very democracy, they say, has liberty for its aim.

—Aristotle, *Politics* 1317a40

Democracy and freedom are clearly related in the popular imagination. Political actors often use them synonymously— promoting democracy is seen as identical to promoting freedom. This is true both of governments and among protest movements.[1] When the United States, under the Bush administration, initiated "Operation Iraqi Freedom" in March 2003, it was taken for granted that bringing freedom to Iraq meant bringing democracy to Iraq.[2] Assessing the progress of the operation in his 2004 State of the Union Address, George W. Bush said, "As *democracy* takes hold in Iraq . . . the Iraqi people will live in *freedom*."[3] When Chinese students demonstrated against the authoritarian Communist regime on Tiananmen Square in Beijing in May 1989, they called their statue resembling the Statue of Liberty "the Goddess of Democracy." For the protesters there would be no meaning in distinguishing between fighting for freedom and fighting for democracy; it was one and the same struggle.[4] In the history of Western political thought a connection between democracy and freedom also has been drawn since its beginnings in Plato and Aristotle.[5] However, even if it is agreed that every democracy has liberty for its aim, as Aristotle claimed, we are no wiser, since both "democracy" and "freedom" have been understood in very different ways, both in theory and in practice. What exactly is it about democracy that makes citizens free? Which conception of freedom

1

does democracy promote? And which model of democracy makes citizens most free? Remarkably, these questions have not been addressed in the discussions of *deliberative democracy*, the most prominent theory of democracy today.[6]

In most, if not all, models of democracy we find, explicitly or implicitly, both a theory of what freedom means, a conception of freedom, and some theory regarding why and how democracy is needed for the sake of this freedom. Thus a model of democracy encompasses both a conception of freedom and a theory about the relationship between democracy and freedom. This book is about the conception of freedom presupposed by deliberative democracy and about the connection between democracy and freedom in this model of democracy. Deliberative democracy refers to the ideal of increasing citizen participation in public deliberation and making collective decision making responsive to public deliberation rather than to economic and social power. Even though this model of democracy has been the object of extensive debate over the last two decades, no one has systematically addressed the issue of which conception of freedom it is committed to. It is therefore unclear what makes it a distinct model of democracy in terms of freedom. Does deliberative democracy promise to make people more free or free in a different and better sense than other models of democracy? Only when we have answered this question will we be able to judge whether it is an ideal worth striving for.[7]

By bringing together writings on deliberative democracy and on conceptions of freedom, this book seeks to clarify the possible connections between democracy and freedom and the meaning of each notion. It is a starting point for my argument not only that every democracy has liberty for its aim but that we fruitfully can differentiate different models of democracy in terms of which conception of freedom they are committed to. Different models of democracy—elitist, pluralist, participatory, protective, and so on[8]—can of course be distinguished in terms of other differences than their view of freedom, but the latter concept gives us a particularly valuable way of distinguishing them. It is not the aim of this book to show this for all the different models of democracy that we may think of but rather to show that the uniqueness and the attractiveness of the deliberative model of democracy can be better assessed by explicating the conception of freedom it presupposes. Actually there is no single, clearly defined model of deliberative democracy but many different versions, so I also will develop and demarcate my version of the model from the others, which I do via a discussion of different conceptions of freedom as well.

The main argument advanced in this book is that *deliberative democracy presupposes a complex and multidimensional conception of freedom*. The theory as well as the practice of democratic deliberation is dialectically interrelated with multiple dimensions of freedom. The multidimensional conception of freedom is the theoretical foundation and normative justification of deliberative democracy. Moreover, the different dimensions of freedom are what make actual deliberation possible; the former are the condition of the latter. But it works the other way too; democratic deliberation is needed in order to understand, justify, and realize the different dimensions of freedom. The relationship between deliberative democracy and the different dimensions of freedom, thus, is dialectical and coconstitutive. It is a relationship of mutual justification and reciprocal reinforcement.

Among the authors endorsing deliberative democracy we find normative commitments to a wider range of dimensions of freedom than we do among proponents of other models of democracy. From living in a deliberative democracy citizens should expect to experience a fuller freedom than they would under the other models. It is this normative commitment to multiple dimensions of freedom that demarcates deliberative democracy as a distinct model of democracy. As the theory has advanced up until now, however, even though we do find examples of commitments to several different dimensions of freedom, they are not all made explicit, nor does any one author refer to them all, and no attempt has been made to integrate them. What this books attempts, therefore, is to develop a theory of freedom and democracy that clarifies the different dimensions of freedom that deliberative democracy should be committed to and to show how, if at all, they can be integrated, and where they cannot be integrated to make manifest the tensions that have to be negotiated. I call this multidimensional and complex conception of freedom *deliberative freedom*.

The theory of deliberative freedom developed in the following chapters seeks to incorporate four conceptions of freedom that have emerged in the history of democratic theory and practice. In doing so the relationships between democracy and freedom and the meaning of the freedom aimed at in earlier models of democracy are not merely incorporated, they are reinterpreted. The contention is not only that deliberative democracy as a theory should be normatively committed to multiple dimensions of freedom but also that the *practice* of public deliberation entails, expresses, and develops the different dimensions of freedom.[9] As a theory, deliberative democracy is in my formulation a regulative ideal that in terms of dimensions of freedom suggests what we should aspire to and in light of which we can see the deficiencies of present conditions and institutions.[10] But it is only in the actual practice of public deliberation, which attempts to mirror the ideal, that we fully develop and understand the different dimensions of freedom. Deliberative democratic practices do not merely aim at protecting existing freedoms but also at interpreting and justifying the freedom that should be protected. In addition, they aim at doing so in a way that itself is not coercive but that respects the freedom of each and everyone not merely in a negative manner but also positively as participants in a common enterprise.

So what are the "dimensions of freedom" to which I am referring? Two dimensions are familiar, namely, public autonomy and negative freedom, or the freedom of the ancients and that of the moderns.[11] Deliberative democrats have attempted to reconcile these two dimensions,[12] but even if these attempts are judged successful, another challenge remains. A third dimension of freedom is neglected by the concern for reconciling public autonomy and negative freedom—and in the closely related discussion of the relationship between democracy and constitutionalism.[13] This dimension concerns free (noncoerced and nonmanipulated) formation of political opinions, what I shall call "internal autonomy." Internal autonomy has played a crucial role in the development of the theory of deliberative democracy. It has been a key argument in this development that the formation of preferences and opinions is endogenous to social conditions and political institutions. It is mainly for this reason that we should go beyond seeing the democratic process merely as one of aggregating preferences. This dimension of freedom gets very different formulations in the "Ideologiekritik" of Frankfurt School critical theory and in theories of adaptive preference formation. Both lines of inquiry have influenced the development of the theory of deliberative democracy, and the dimension of freedom they emphasize must be included in any analysis of it. When the facet of internal autonomy is revealed and restored, the full potential of deliberative democracy, as a theory of emancipation becomes clear.

The idea of the "liberty of the ancients," as it is most often used, obscures a distinction between two different dimensions of freedom. The liberty of the ancients often is seen as referring to a Rousseauist idea of popular sovereignty or public autonomy. But Rousseau's notion of freedom as public autonomy is a modern one, as it is closely connected to the modern idea of sovereignty. A different understanding of freedom—one that is independent of the modern idea of sovereignty—is the idea of freedom as status. The freedom interest at issue here is not making the laws to which one is subject but to enjoy a certain status among others and within a political structure. Freedom as status is associated with the republican tradition in political theory but gets very different formulations in, for example, Hannah Arendt's participatory version and Philip Pettit's more recent and democratically minimalist version. For Arendt, freedom as status is a form of freedom as praxis, and it is concerned with *experiencing a form of activity that is without constraints*.[14] Pettit's status conception of freedom is more passive and more concerned with security than with praxis. I shall later develop a deliberative democratic interpretation of freedom as status. The status dimension of freedom has not been given as prominent a place among deliberative democrats as the other three, but I shall argue that it is indispensable both in terms of checking the other dimensions and because it is presupposed by them. In short, it is required because the processes in which we learn what our political opinions are (internal autonomy), in which we determine what individual freedoms we should give each other, and in which we give ourselves laws must themselves be an expression of freedom—or at least not violate freedom.

Thus we arrive at four main dimensions of freedom. In addition to (1) public autonomy or collective self-rule, and (2) negative freedom or freedom as noninterference, we have (3) autonomous opinion formation or internal autonomy and (4) freedom as status. None of these dimensions of freedom is exclusive to deliberative democratic theory, but I shall argue that the latter has a unique ability to incorporate all four dimensions, and that the theory as well as the practice of deliberation can supply new and valuable interpretations of them. The four dimensions of freedom come together in the overall conception of freedom that I call deliberative freedom.

It is not only deliberative democracy that is dialectically related to deliberative freedom, but the four dimensions of freedom that together form the conception of deliberative freedom are closely related among each other as well. They are so in two different ways. First, they are needed to *balance* each other. Too much concern for one dimension of freedom can undermine the prospects for freedom along another axis. A classic example of this is when public autonomy is used to limit negative freedom: democratically formed majorities can interfere in citizens' private sphere. Another example is when the concern to promote the experience of freedom in political participation (freedom as praxis) threatens the negative freedom to decide one's own conception of the good; this happens when people are forced to participate even if they would prefer not to. A third example is when the aim of transformation into autonomous persons turns into paternalism and a threat to privacy. Conversely, a one-sided concern for negative freedom can be used against both public and internal autonomy: if we think that freedom is only about being left alone, then democratic politics cannot be seen as contributing to freedom, nor can learning from others and developing our internal autonomy in intersubjective practices of deliberation. I argue that the simultaneous concern for and systematic inclusion of several dimensions of freedom, first, make clearer the normative basis and importance of these tensions; second, they give us a unique way of analyzing them; and, third, they open up avenues of sometimes overcoming them and at other times negotiating the appropriate balance between the different freedom interests that they express.

Interestingly, even if the different dimensions of freedom sometimes compete and are in tension with each other, they also *presuppose* each other. No dimension of freedom is complete in itself. Freedom cannot be protected before it has been defined, interpreted, and justified, hence, negative freedom cannot stand alone but presupposes the more social freedoms involved in the deliberative process. The laws that set the boundaries of our negative freedom must be given by ourselves, otherwise the limits of coercion are determined coercively, which is contradictory, thus negative freedom presupposes public autonomy. And the process of determining the meaning and boundaries of freedom must itself be an expression of our freedom; otherwise, the way in which we aim at freedom would itself be a negation of freedom, which also is contradictory. Thus public autonomy presupposes freedom as praxis and status. Finally, the acceptance of the laws defining and conditioning our freedom must not be coerced but must be products of free processes of opinion and will formation: public autonomy presupposes internal autonomy.

Deliberative freedom, as I have said, incorporates four dimensions of freedom. These four dimensions are deliberative democratic reinterpretations of conceptions of freedom that we can find in the history of political thought, namely, popular sovereignty, negative freedom, personal autonomy, and freedom as praxis. I also claimed that most models of democracy not only encompass a conception of freedom but also a theory of how democracy relates to that conception of freedom. In earlier models, democracy has been seen as *connected* to the four traditional conceptions of freedom in the following way:

1. *Democracy as popular sovereignty*: The only way in which we can be free in society is to be authors of the laws to which we are subject. Democracy aims at *converting* an inevitable dependence into freedom (Rousseau).[15]

2. *Democracy as instrumental to negative freedom*: Democracy is required in order to protect a form of freedom that in itself is prepolitical or outside political activity. Democracy aims at *protecting* an already understood and demarcated freedom (the liberal view).[16]

3. *Democracy as instrumental to personal autonomy*: Participation in democratic politics creates citizens with autonomous characters. Democracy aims to *transform* individuals into autonomous persons (Rousseau, Mill).[17]

4. *Democracy as intrinsic to freedom as praxis*: Participation in democratic politics is a form of freedom. Democracy aims at *creating a new experience* of being free (one republican view).[18]

In the first of these democracy is seen as conceptually or definitionally connected to freedom; the definition of democracy is the definition of popular sovereignty, which is (a form of) freedom. But democracy also is seen as having the causal effect of turning a form of slavery into freedom. The relationship between democracy and freedom in both (2) and (3) is purely instrumental, and in (4) it is intrinsic. The idea that democracy is instrumental to freedom means that the enjoyment of that freedom is a *consequence* of democracy. For freedom to be intrinsic to democracy it must be *part of* democracy. I shall in this book show how these relationships and conceptions are reinterpreted in and by deliberative democratic theory and practice.

The need for a clarification of the normative commitment to a wider and more complex theory of freedom is especially urgent if we see deliberative democracy as a critical theory, as I argue we should. Critical theory is both intrinsically linked to a multidimensional conception of freedom—because of its concern with emancipation from all forms of oppression—and committed to clarifying the standards in light of which social criticism is made.[19] As a critical theory of contemporary society, deliberative democracy should contribute to analyzing which aspects of contemporary society limit our prospects for enjoying the multiple dimensions of freedom, which it presupposes. But it also should investigate whether it is possible to free ourselves from certain forms of oppression without creating new ones. Thus it is not only deliberative democracy that needs critical theory, it is also the other way around. The concern of critical theory with, for example, ideological delusion very easily turns into paternalism if emancipation from ideological domination is not integrated with respect for (some understanding of) negative freedom, public autonomy, and discursive status. But democratic theory also needs critical theory and ideology critique to remind us that there is more to freedom than constitutional rights. In addition to the liberties of the ancients and the moderns, there is a dimension of freedom that was not theorized until after Constant: the freedom from ideological domination.

Other proponents of deliberative democracy have recently noted and lamented the uncritical direction the theory has taken and urged a return to critical theory.[20] But none has discussed how their complaint relates to the understanding of freedom emphasized in different versions of deliberative democracy, and none has noted the connection to the neglect of internal autonomy in the later theoretical developments.[21]

It is not only the aim of this book to demarcate my version of deliberative democracy from other models of democracy by discussing which dimensions of freedom they aim at but also to differentiate between different versions of deliberative democracy from the same perspective. I address the differences between various versions of deliberative democracy developed hitherto and argue that none of them has developed a sufficiently multidimensional and coherent theory of freedom. The one- or two-dimensionality of earlier versions of deliberative democracy leads either to a neglect of theorizing the other dimensions or, more seriously, to suggestions that promote one or two dimensions at the cost of the others. My aim is to remedy this deficit and to develop a theory of deliberative democracy that integrates the different dimensions of freedom.

There are two dominant versions of deliberative democracy: a version with roots in Habermasian critical theory and a version based on Rawlsian political liberalism. The main contrast between Habermasian critical theory and Rawlsian political liberalism, I argue, is their different understandings of freedom. Critical theory is based on a belief both in the importance of learning processes for freedom and in a concern for emancipation from ideological domination. Political liberalism reduces the concept of freedom to a more modest concern for accommodation of people with different worldviews or comprehensive doctrines. This important difference has been ignored because of lack of self-reflection regarding which dimensions of freedom the two traditions build on. The version of deliberative democracy that I propose seeks to retrieve the critical thrust of Habermas's earlier writings. It does so, however, in a way that is not blind to the importance of the dimension of freedom stressed by political liberalism. It is exactly for this reason that deliberative democracy must be seen as committed to a number of different dimensions of freedom. The version of deliberative democracy that I argue for, then, should be distinguished both from Habermasian and Rawlsian versions and from the convergence between the two.

Why "Dimensions" of Freedom?

Why speak of "dimensions" of freedom and not the more common "conceptions" of freedom?[22] In fact, I will be concerned with *both* dimensions and conceptions of freedom. Some disputes over how best to understand freedom refer to different dimensions of freedom, while others are based on different conceptions of freedom. It is important to distinguish between these different discussions. In addition to dimensions and conceptions of freedom, there also are various "concepts" of freedom. In this work I will be concerned with only one concept of freedom (political freedom), while I will discuss several dimensions and conceptions of freedom. Now what are the differences between concepts, conceptions, and dimensions? The most instructive way to approach this question is to consider the thesis of "essentially contested concepts." The idea of "dimensions of freedom" is not a rejection of the essential contestability thesis but complements and refines it in important ways.

Concept and Conception

The concept refers to the overall idea or the core meaning of a term; conceptions are rival ways of understanding, applying, and/or specifying the concept.[23] John Rawls, for example, sees his "justice as fairness" and utilitarianism as rival conceptions of the same overall concept of justice.[24] The distinction (but not the terminology) lies at the heart of W. B. Gallie's original formulation of the notion of "essentially contested concepts." Essentially contested concepts are characterized by having a "general use" (the concept) and "a number of mutually contesting and contested uses" (the conceptions) of the former.[25] If there were no general use or core meaning to which the contestants all referred, then it would not be a common or single contest. Moreover, without a common uncontested concept, we would have vagueness, ambiguity, or confusion and not essential contestability.[26]

The concept under discussion in this book is not "freedom" as such but "political freedom." If we were concerned with freedom as such we would need to include a discussion of free will, which I do not do. I see the distinction between political freedom and free will *not* as a matter of interpersonal or social relations versus intrapersonal or psychological ones.[27] Rather, discussions of political freedom are concerned with what could be different, what could be affected by collective human action and political institutions. The dimension of political freedom that I call "internal autonomy" is in a sense intrapersonal, but it is political insofar as it depends on socioeconomic and political-institutional conditions. Philosophical discussions of free will, in contrast, concern what is and what cannot be otherwise. This also means that there is an inevitable normative and practical dimension to issues of political freedom that is absent from the free will debate. Our understanding of political freedom has consequences for how to act. Admittedly, the distinction between free will and political freedom is not complete; rather, conceptions of freedom are primarily of one kind or the other.

Conceptions

It is not part of this book to evaluate the intricate discussions about the validity of the thesis that some political concepts are essentially contested. I shall accept the general idea (as outlined below), but my main aim is to argue that there can exist a *different type of relationship* between different formulations of "freedom" than the one suggested by the notion of essential contestability. This different type of relationship we find among the various "dimensions" of freedom. In order to see the distinctiveness of the type of relationship that exists between the multiple dimensions of freedom that I argue that deliberative democracy should incorporate, we must first understand the relationship that often is believed to exist between different "conceptions" of freedom. I characterize this relationship by highlighting five aspects that are usually (if not always) accepted by the proponents of the essential contestability thesis.

First, different conceptions are put forth as *rivals* that are *competing* about giving the best formulation of a concept. Thus in Gallie's words, "To use an essentially contested concept is to use it against other uses . . . [it] means to use it both aggressively and defensively."[28] Or, as Jeremy Waldron puts it in a recent article, "Each conception is put forward as an attempt to *outdo* others in capturing an elusive sense, that we all share, a sense that *somewhere* in the midst of this contestation there is an important ideal that social and political systems should aspire to."[29]

Second, a conception "arises out of and operates within a particular moral and political perspective."[30] Thus the contest between different conceptions does not only concern disagreement over that particular concept but is indicative of a more profound dispute over how to understand a whole range of other normative and theoretical concepts. It is a contest regarding entire "conceptual frameworks" or "world-views." In short, it is an "ideological dispute."[31]

Third, the thesis of essential contestability entails that *one must take sides.* Gallie uses the illustration of competing sport teams, where each team has its supporters. The supporters not only want acknowledgment of their team as champions but just as importantly acceptance of it as expressing "the proper criteria of championship."[32] Thus each person must take sides not only in terms of who should win but also regarding which criteria for winning should be accepted.

Fourth, the contestation between competing conceptions is unsolvable and endless.[33] No conception will ever achieve success in its attempt to outdo the rest.[34] It is because the contest "inevitably" is endless that it is an *essential* contest and not merely a contingent one. Conceptual contests are endless and hence essential when there are "no logically coercive reasons" for preferring one conception to another.[35]

Fifth, contestedness is part of the very meaning of an essentially contested concept. More precisely, a concept is essentially contested when its users understand that it is contested, that is, when they understand that others inevitably will have different and competing conceptions of the same concept. Gallie's idea is (in Waldron's words) "that someone who does not realize that *democracy,* for example, or *art* are sites of contestation really doesn't understand the concept he is invoking."[36]

Dimensions

When I speak of "dimensions" of freedom it is, as mentioned, in order to emphasize that these dimensions stand in *a different type of relationship to each other* than do conceptions of freedom. To see what this means more specifically, let us compare the idea of dimensions of freedom with the idea of conceptions of freedom, relating the former to the five aspects of conceptions explained in the previous section.

First, the different dimensions of freedom are not rivals but stand in a *complementary* relationship to each other. Earlier I described how the multiple dimensions of freedom both balance and presuppose each other. Formulating and advocating a specific dimension of freedom *do not necessarily* entail an attempt at outdoing other dimensions—though it can, contingently, entail such an attempt. I do not see negative freedom and public autonomy, for example, as different and competing conceptions whose aim necessarily is to outdo each other—that some partisans advance as if the latter was the case is accidental. To be sure, there can be conflicts between claims of public autonomy and claims of negative freedom, but they are not necessarily conflicts over the true meaning of political freedom, but rather over which dimension of freedom should be given most weight. Thus there can definitely be contests between the various dimensions of freedom, but they are not essential conceptual contests.

Second, dimensions of freedom *do not necessarily* belong to different and competing moral and theoretical perspectives. To be sure, some ideologies are committed to only one dimension of freedom, but this is neither a conceptual nor a normative necessity. There are other moral and theoretical perspectives committed to more than one dimension of freedom; consider Rousseau or Kant, for example, both of whom are committed to negative freedom, public autonomy, and ideals of personal and moral autonomy.

Third, when discussing dimensions of freedom there is no requirement that one "take sides" for one specific dimension. Rather, it is my contention in this work that deliberative democratic theory makes it possible to adhere to various dimensions of freedom simultaneously. There is nothing contradictory in a democratic theory incorporating and a citizen being attracted to and enjoying, say, both liberal and republican dimensions of freedom. As a theorist, therefore, I also do not take sides, for example, *for* freedom as status *against* negative freedom. My aim is to show that the adherents of different "understandings" of freedom should not see each other as competitors but as developing different aspects of a common aspiration, namely, maximally free citizens. Or, to put it differently, some formulations of "freedom" can be put forward either as conceptions or as dimensions; I aim to show the value of the latter alternative.

Fourth, since there is no necessary competition between the different dimensions in the way there is between rival conceptions, we obviously cannot speak of resolving a contest in the sense of finding a winner. There is, however, a different form of competition between the various dimensions of freedom. This is not one of giving the best definition or theory of the same concept but rather of how much weight each dimension should be given. Previously I mentioned well-known balancing acts. Based on experience—not conceptual analysis—this balancing will never find a resolution. The relationship between the different dimensions is not, however, only a matter of balancing them in practice. There also might be definitional disputes involving different dimensions of freedom. For example, as I show in Chapter 1, some liberals want to define public autonomy as a form of negative freedom and thus collapse what I take to be two different dimensions of freedom. This admittedly muddies the waters. But liberals also want to balance individual rights and political rights, negative freedom and public autonomy. So I maintain the value of distinguishing between disputes over competing conceptions of freedom and disputes over how to balance different dimensions of freedom.

Fifth, the *meaning* of a dimension of freedom does not lie in its competition with other dimensions, as follows logically from what has already been said. However, I shall argue that we cannot gain a full understanding of any dimension of freedom without in some way engaging the other dimensions. The argument for this is complicated and will be given in due course, but earlier I gave some indications of the idea in the discussion of how the different dimensions of freedom presuppose each other.

What I have said might lead to the impression that I take sides with the adversaries of the essential contestability thesis, so note that my main aim is to distinguish discussions regarding dimensions of freedom from discussions of conceptions of freedom. The reason for doing this is not to defend some of the important targets of the thesis of essential contestability. My aim is *not* to remove definitional issues from the contested field of politics to some theoretical neutral level.[37] However, I maintain that the different dimensions of freedom stand in a different type of relationship to each other than do conceptions of freedom. This leads to my second disclaimer: I am *not* claiming that the way in which I formulate the different dimensions of freedom is final and unchallengeable. That would go against some of the basic assumptions of deliberative democracy as I see it: fallibilism, that no one has privileged access to truth, and that justification also of definitions must happen discursively, to name a few that will be explained later.

To summarize, different "understandings" of freedom can be understood either as conceptions of freedom or dimensions of freedom. I do not reject the idea that there are competing conceptions of freedom, but the idea of dimensions of freedom is an important addition to this. Conceptions of freedom relate to my dimensions of freedom as follows: There can be different and competing theories of how best to understand each of the four dimensions of freedom. The characterizations of the four dimensions of freedom that I give in this book are rivals to other conceptions of the same dimensions. In a deliberative democracy the exact meaning of the different dimensions will and should be determined by citizens themselves. Fortunately, the political theorist also is a citizen and can contribute to public deliberation. "Deliberative freedom" is the overall conception of freedom advanced in this book, and it includes multiple dimensions of freedom; of course, there will be competitors to this conception, which might include any number of dimensions of freedom.

Overview of the Book

Deliberative democracy often is seen as a model of democracy based on the transformation, rather than the mere aggregation, of preferences. Chapter 1 presents several arguments against demarcating deliberative democracy in this way and suggests, rather, that deliberative democracy involves a distinctive theory of freedom. This theory of freedom can most clearly be demarcated by contrasting it to a tradition in the history of political thought that sees the aim of democracy as being limited to the aim of protecting negative freedom. A one-dimensional focus on negative freedom does not exclude the transformation of preferences but rather the idea that democracy should aim at a specific type of preference formation. Deliberative democracy is not aimed at transforming preferences *as opposed to* merely aggregating them, but at securing the transformation of preferences in a *free* manner as opposed to under conditions and processes that distort the free exchange of reasons and information. The focus on multiple dimensions of freedom also makes it clear that negative freedom requires a positive counterpart both in order to give meaning and justification to the negative freedom we aim to protect and in order to do so in a noncoercive manner.

The republican tradition offers the main historical alternative to the liberal understanding of freedom and democracy and the relation between those ideas. Some thinkers have associated the republican tradition with deliberative democracy. Chapter 2 discusses Philip Pettit's comprehensive and ambitious contemporary attempt to reconstruct a republican theory of freedom and democracy. Even though Pettit's republicanism has some clear advantages over the liberal theory discussed in Chapter 1, it does not supply us with the multidimensional theory of freedom that deliberative democracy presupposes. In particular, it fails on two levels. First, it misconstrues how democratic processes of political opinion and will formation play an important epistemic role for freedom. Not only is insufficient room given for the dimension of learning and internal autonomy, it also is ignored that freedom as nondomination for its own definition and justification is parasitic upon the epistemic dimension of public autonomy. Second, in rejecting more participatory versions of republicanism, Pettit disregards the importance of the intrinsic properties of the democratic process for freedom. He overlooks that the process employed to determine the meaning and bounds of freedom might itself constitute a violation of freedom if it does not have the right properties.

Both the liberal and republican traditions focus on the external dimensions of freedom or freedom of action. From the perspective of deliberative freedom, we see that this is insufficient. Deliberative democracy is a model of democracy that also must be—and has been—concerned with the free formation of the political opinions that form the basis of democratic decision making. Chapter 3 discusses one approach to the notion of free preference formation, an approach beginning with the idea of adaptive preference formation. (Chapter 5 discusses another, based on the critique of ideology.) In analyzing and discussing Jon Elster's and Cass Sunstein's important contributions to this approach from the perspective of deliberative freedom, it becomes clear that the idea of autonomous preference formation must be checked by other dimensions of freedom, in particular to avoid turning into paternalism. While deliberative democracy must reject the idea that people can never be wrong about their own interests, or if they are, any and all ways of dealing with the issue would be a violation of their (negative) freedom, we should not fall into the opposite camp of paternalistically imposing independent standards of what is good for people. If we see deliberative democracy as also being committed to two other dimensions of freedom, freedom as discursive status and freedom as being a participant in self-legislation, then it is possible to avoid the paradoxical situation where in attempting to make people more autonomous we simultaneously violate their freedom. It is argued that public deliberation properly understood entails a commitment to all these three dimensions of freedom. I also suggest that the deliberative democrat as a critical theorist can initiate processes of self-reflection about adaptive preferences without paternalistically substituting her or his own judgment for those of others. But the latter point is not fully elaborated on until Chapter 5.

Whereas Chapters 1–3 begin from conceptions of freedom and relate them to democracy, Chapters 4 and 5 begin with theories of democracy, deliberation, and public reason and consider which conceptions of freedom they imply. Chapters 4 and 5 are devoted, respectively, to Rawlsian and Habermasian models of deliberative democracy. By making a sharp distinction between these two traditions, I go against what I see as an unfortunate tendency to convergence between Rawlsian political liberalism and Habermasian critical theory. To some extent my own project can be seen as part of this alliance insofar as I attempt to show that deliberative democracy can be committed to both the dimensions of freedom emphasized by the Rawlsians and those underlying the Habermasian versions of deliberative democracy. But the union has been an unbalanced one, moving more in the direction of the Rawlsian pole—stressing freedom as accommodation (a conception of negative freedom)—and away from Habermas's roots in critical theory—focusing on freedom as emancipation. This means that the dimension of freedom stressed by the earlier Habermas and other critical theorists is neglected. When conceptions of freedom are discussed as dividing the two traditions, the focus is exclusively on the weight given to negative freedom and public autonomy, respectively. This discussion leaves out the notion of internal autonomy or free formation of political opinions, which informs the ideology critique of earlier critical theory. The result is a convergence around an understanding of freedom with less critical potential.

Rawlsian deliberative democracy is more concerned with accommodation of citizens with different comprehensive doctrines than with public deliberation as a process that aims at emancipation through learning and enlightenment. Chapter 4 shows how Rawls's idea of public reason entails a protection of citizens from having their fundamental ideas discussed and hence *excludes* seeing public deliberation as a learning process. I argue that this can be connected to a lack of normative commitment to freedom as internal autonomy. I agree with the proponents of political liberalism, that autonomy should not be promoted as constituting the good life; to impose a uniform conception of the good violates an important dimension of freedom. But we need to distinguish between autonomy as constituting the good life and autonomy as the source of our moral and political obligations. I do not think that deliberative democracy can escape, or should try to escape, from a commitment to the latter view.

The notion of internal autonomy has been deemphasized in later writings on deliberative democracy, also by Habermas(ians). In order to clarify and rehabilitate this dimension of freedom I show in Chapter 5 how it informs the theory of ideology, as the earlier Habermas and other critical theorists formulated it. Connecting deliberative democracy to ideology critique changes the main aim of deliberation from one of overcoming fundamental moral disagreement to one of politicizing self-imposed forms of coercion and challenging instances of unreflective acquiescence.

While I think internal autonomy is a crucial dimension of freedom, I also argue that it must be checked by other dimensions. Chapter 6 reveals that a commitment to internal autonomy is compatible with the protection of important negative freedoms. The first step here is to show that internal autonomy is not based on an untenable perfectionism but should be limited in its application to the formation of political opinions or relations of justification. Second, I counter the argument that transformative dialogue is a threat to privacy. The deliberative perspective, however, must reject the idea that any form of dependence or interference is wrong and violates freedom. The deliberative conception of freedom requires that we be able to distinguish between forms of dependence that limit freedom and forms of dependence that are neutral to or even enhance freedom. Deliberation itself implies dependence or, better, interdependence; we need each other to learn and to gain internal autonomy and to exercise public autonomy. But deliberation also requires the freedom to say no. I therefore introduce the idea of procedural independence, a notion that allows for the required distinctions between different forms of dependence and independence.

Chapter 7 analyzes the relationship between freedom, reason, and political participation. The main aim is to clarify the relationship between the intersubjective epistemology that informs my view of public deliberation, on the one hand, and deliberative freedom as a "procedural epistemic conception of freedom," on the other hand. The chapter responds to two opposing objections to deliberative democracy, both of which concern participation and elitism. On the one hand, the focus on reason and rationality has been charged with leading to an elitist politics where only the participation of the wisest is needed. I counter this objection by showing that the epistemic aims of deliberative democracy actually depend on the participation of everyone. In making this argument I show that deliberative freedom is a form of what I call "procedural epistemic freedom." What characterizes this freedom is both that it stresses individual learning over collectively getting it right and that what makes us free is not being right but, rather, forming our opinions and giving laws following procedures with epistemic value. The response to the first objection gives rise to the second, namely, that deliberative democracy is elitist exactly because it requires that everyone participate (and that they do so in a certain way), while many people would prefer not to participate (or to do so in some other way than through public deliberation). The second objection thus holds that deliberative democracy is not neutral between conceptions of the good but is committed to participation as a good. I show that this is a misunderstanding, while I accept that deliberative democracy, of course, is not neutral with regard to its own normative content. The latter *does* mean that participation in deliberation must be seen as a (moral) obligation in a deliberative democracy committed to multiple dimensions of freedom. This obligation, however, has nothing to do with a commitment to a certain view of the good but with a certain view of the right and of practical reason.

The final chapter, Chapter 8, summarizes and elaborates on the four dimensions of freedom that comprise deliberative freedom. It also briefly suggests some institutional implications of the idea of deliberative freedom.

CHAPTER ONE

Deliberation, Aggregation, and Negative Freedom

Despite the large quantity of writings on deliberative democracy over the last two decades, it is not clear what exactly distinguishes deliberative democracy as a model of democracy from other models in terms of freedom. This chapter is an attempt to clarify this issue. In the first section, I begin by making some qualifications to the most common way of demarcating deliberative democracy, namely, the idea of seeing it as a matter of transforming rather than merely aggregating preferences. The second section argues that deliberative democracy can be contrasted to a specific tradition in political theory that reduces freedom to noninterference with private interests and sees democracy as merely instrumental to securing this freedom. Freedom should not be seen merely as the end of democracy, as something to which democracy is only a means, but as what democracy *is*. Democracy is a form of exercising freedom, as well as a way of understanding and protecting freedom. It is my contention that deliberative democracy can be seen as a theory of freedom, and that this can demarcate it as a unique model of democracy.

Beyond the Aggregation and Transformation Dichotomy

It is tempting—and the attempt has often been made—to set up a sharp dichotomy between deliberative democracy and aggregative democracy.[1] But, for several reasons, this is an unfortunate dichotomy, especially when the contrast is drawn as one between transforming preferences versus aggregating preferences.[2] This way of demarcating the theory of deliberative democracy has led to many misunderstandings of what the deliberative project is about and also of what and who its targets are. The idea that deliberative democracy can be understood as being essentially about transforming rather than aggregating preferences goes against the conception of deliberative freedom developed in this book. The exclusive focus on transformation is too outcome oriented and risks sacrificing dimensions of freedom intrinsic to the deliberative process. Thus it does not do justice to the multidimensional understanding of freedom to which deliberative democracy, in my view, should be committed.

I suggest six reasons to go beyond the sharp dichotomy between transformation and aggregation. In discussing these, I hope to counter—while learning from—some objections to deliberative democracy and simultaneously make a preliminary clarification of what I think deliberative democracy is and what it is not.

1. First, the point of the theory of deliberative democracy, as I see it, is not that we need more proper deliberation *in order* that preferences can be changed. Because of the stress on the endogenous change of preferences by deliberative democrats, it is sometimes thought that the argument is that in other forms of democracy preferences are not changed and we need deliberative democracy in order that preferences can be transformed. But that, I think, is a misunderstanding. Preferences are malleable and subject to change in any model of democracy, indeed, under any form of government. It is on the basis of this insight that we must develop a theory of *how* preference and opinion formation can happen in a nondistorted and free manner. That is part of what the theory of deliberative democracy should attempt to do.

    Some criticisms of deliberative democracy seem to rely on a failure to recognize this point. Adam Przeworski and Susan Stokes, for example, both think that deliberative democracy is especially susceptible to manipulation of preferences. But the reason they think so is that deliberative democracy according to their definition is a theory of democracy, which posits the change of preferences as the *aim* of the political process.[3] Both critics go on to accuse deliberative democrats for not having considered the danger of manipulation in public communication. The latter claim is no less than absurd.[4] One of the main proponents of deliberative democracy, Jürgen Habermas, has since the early 1960s been concerned exactly to point to the dangers of manipulation in communication.[5] Since this is so often overlooked—and since it has moved to the background of even Habermas's own later writings—I argue for reviving some of the earlier concerns of critical theory (see especially Chapter 5).

The criticism of being particularly susceptible to the problem of manipulation if directed at deliberative democracy as a *theory* is therefore unfair. As a theory, one of the main concerns of deliberative democracy has been to distinguish between forms of public communication that are manipulative and undermine freedom and autonomy and forms of communication that are undistorted and hence enhance freedom and autonomy. But the criticism also could be directed at deliberative democracy as *practice*. The objection would then be that promoting deliberation would open up for more manipulation. But this objection also would miss the point of the deliberative project, or at least of the project as I conceive it. What deliberative democracy should be calling for is *not* more communication in some uncritical fashion.[6] Rather, the call should exactly be for more deliberation. And to call for more deliberation is to call for less distorted communication. Deliberation should not be defined as "the endogenous change of preferences resulting from communication," as Stokes does,[7] since this definition excludes the possibility of differentiating different forms of communication and hence overlooks the very point of the deliberative model. Rather, deliberation should be seen as a process of mutual reason giving and reason seeking that gives people the opportunity to form their opinions on the basis of insights gained intersubjectively. The call for more deliberation, however, is not (or at least not mainly) a moralizing call to individuals to communicate in a specific way; it is, rather, a matter of calling attention to the socioeconomic and institutional features of contemporary society that inhibit proper deliberation. Deliberative democracy should, among other things, be a critical theory that addresses the aspects of contemporary society, which limit deliberation and which affect or transform preferences in a nonautonomous manner.[8] It should not merely be considered a call for the transformation of preferences but rather of going from one mode of transforming preferences to another.

This argument suggests that it is unhelpful to characterize deliberation as a matter of changing preferences as opposed to just aggregating them. Preferences are always being transformed in the political process and in society in general. What is important is *how* and under what conditions they are changed. Deliberative democrats' quarrel with other models of democracy does not mainly concern the constructedness of preference but what we should do about this fact. After all, Joseph Schumpeter—who if anyone must be placed in the opposite camp than deliberative democrats—agrees with and emphasizes the idea of endogenous preference formation.[9] The point on which deliberative democrats differ from a minimalist democrat such as Schumpeter is not the malleability of preferences but what to do about it. According to Schumpeter, the will of the people is constructed from above, by political elites. The conclusion he draws from this is, roughly, that since the people have no will independently of the elites, then popular sovereignty is impossible, and we should let the elites rule. Deliberative democrats disagree with this so-called realist and uncritical conclusion. It might be true that "the popular will" today is fabricated from above, but that does not have to be the case; it is not a natural, unalterable fact about all politics. It makes a difference under what conditions and in what processes citizens form their opinions and will, and deliberative democrats are—or should be—concerned to show how opinion and will formation can happen as freely and autonomously as possible. Also, it is important to see that deliberative democrats are not committed to a view of democratic legitimacy that requires that the opinions that are expressed in political decisions not be affected by political institutions.[10] Rather, the point is to give an account of *which* institutions and conditions are and are not conducive to free opinion and will formation. It is an untenable view of freedom and popular sovereignty that sees them as requiring that each citizen is entirely independent from other human beings and political institutions.[11]

From the perspective of deliberative democracy, the problem with, for example, minimalist and liberal models of democracy is not that they see preferences as given in ontological or methodological terms, but rather that the models of democracy that they propose are ones that *treat* preferences as given. Some of these models of democracy agree that preferences are constructed but do not want to do anything about it. As I argue in the next section, this connects these models of democracy to the negative freedom tradition in the history of political thought.

2. A second reason to go beyond the sharp transformation and aggregation dichotomy is that the transformation of preferences in deliberation is often taken to be a matter of moving from disagreement to agreement, and it is thought that if there is agreement, then there is no reason for concern. If this were the deliberative democratic view, then it would be right to criticize it.[12] And deliberative democrats do, at least from a cursory reading, give us reason to believe that the aim of deliberation is always to go from disagreement to agreement. A clear example of this is Gutmann and Thompson, for whom deliberation is meant to deal with moral disagreements.[13] But also Habermas's emphasis on reaching agreement or understanding (*Verständigung*) and Joshua Cohen's emphasis on consensus could lead us to believe that deliberation always is aimed at turning disagreements into agreements, and that the existence of agreement is the same as the absence of anything to be concerned about. Yet such a conclusion is the product of confusion. It is a consequence of the failure to distinguish, first, between empirically existing consensus and rationally motivated consensus, and, second, between consensus as regulative ideal for deliberation and consensus as good in itself. It is one thing to say that deliberation should have consensus as its regulative ideal, but it is quite another to say that any existing consensus is good. Clearly, deliberative democrats should be committed only to the first of these two positions. Moreover, the key issue from the perspective of deliberative democracy, as I understand it, is neither that a consensus exists nor what the content of the agreement is but *how* the agreement was reached.

   Under certain conditions, I shall argue, deliberation should aim not at creating consensus but at breaking an existing consensus, at least as the initial step. Critics of deliberative democracy think this idea does not sit well with the aim of reaching consensus.[14] While I agree that proponents of deliberative democracy have paid too little attention to the value of breaking up an existing consensus,[15] I think this conclusion builds on a misunderstanding of what is involved in the aim of reaching agreement. Sometimes deliberation with the aim of reaching agreement can actually lead to undermining an existing consensus. Or, more precisely, the aim of reaching a consensus based on the best available information and reasons, that is, a rationally motivated consensus, might require that an existing, empirical consensus first be challenged.

The objection I wish to counter is that the aim of reaching understanding in deliberation makes it impotent in face of illegitimate forms of consensus. For example, from a Marxist perspective it might be argued that the interests of workers and capitalists are irreconcilable, and therefore that any existing consensus must be a false or an ideological consensus and, hence, the aim of political struggle cannot be to go from disagreement to agreement but rather to make the conflict apparent and to fight it out.[16] Or, to take a more fashionable example, the multicultural character of contemporary society might make every consensus seem to be an expression of the majority culture and hence oppressive and exclusionary. Both of these examples raise important concerns, but I shall argue, first, that these concerns are actually *parasitic* upon an idea of reaching agreement and do not constitute counterexamples; and, second, if the conflict of interests is not seen as one that comes about in the actual processes of deliberation, then the theorists who speak about them must operate with a paternalistic view of objective interests or objective identities.

When a given consensus is regarded as illegitimate, as a "false" consensus, by political theorists, it is often because it is seen as one that represents the interests, identity, or values of a *particular* group as the general interest, the common identity, or the shared values. This is how Marxists view bourgeois ideology under capitalism. Similarly, multiculturalists lament "the universalization of a dominant group's experience and culture, and its establishment as the norm."[17] And, according to some feminists, the great problem in contemporary society is the idea embedded in law, that "to be human ... means to be a man."[18] In these cases we have an empirical consensus if the dominant point of view is generally accepted, but for it also to be a rationally motivated consensus it would have to be a product of a free, open process of deliberation. The criticisms made by Marxists, multiculturalists, and feminists amount to saying to (or about) the dominant group that what it presents as universal (or general or common) is not really so: it is not shared by everyone. But this is exactly what the logic of nondistorted and free communication does, as Habermas has shown.[19] In communication aimed at reaching understanding, participants ask whether what is presented as true or right really is so; or as critical theorists, we aim to show when the conditions necessary for such deliberation are missing. Deliberation takes place when listeners ask for the reasons behind the claims raised by speakers (when they do not understand them or find them objectionable), and when speakers redeem this request in a way that is meant to convince the listeners (as opposed to just manipulating them). By inherently being concerned with reasons or grounds, deliberation makes visible or public the underlying assumptions—cultural meanings, normative principles, factual assumptions, and so on—of our shared culture and makes them the object of reflection, consideration, and evaluation. The very core of deliberative democracy thus is a concern with the possibility of criticizing ideologies, biases, conventions, and the like. Questioning the validity of an utterance is to break the consensus, even if the aim is always to restore it later.

The problem with doing away with the aim of reaching understanding is that it becomes difficult to explain how people (in our examples traditionally oppressed groups such as workers, minorities, or women) realize that they do not share interests with the oppressors or indeed what it means not to agree. In, for example, Iris Young,[20] it is "surprising to find reproachful accusations of 'bias' set alongside assertions of the impossibility of impartiality. If we dispense with any notion of impartiality, how can we condemn, or even identify bias?"[21] There is confusion here between the ideological use of ideals such as impartiality and agreement and the ideal itself. It is one thing to criticize the "hypostatizing [of] the dominant view of privileged groups into a universal position"[22]; it is quite another to reject the idea of following an impartial procedure in order to find universal agreement. Indeed, one cannot make the criticism if one rejects the idea of impartiality. The idea of impartiality guides deliberation, but what in a given case is the impartial outcome can only be known as the result of an actual process of deliberation. It is only by questioning with the aim of understanding what the interests and the reasons behind the hegemonic culture are that one can see oneself as being in conflict with it. One cannot begin with the disagreement. By engaging in deliberation with someone, I might learn that I did not agree with him anyway, that we do not share interests, for example. I could not come to this insight if my aim was to disagree, unless we assume some prepolitical insight into what my interests and those of others are and how they relate. Disagreement is parasitic upon the idea of agreement.

What someone like Przeworski overlooks when he argues for putting "the consensualist view of politics where it belongs—in the Museum of Eighteenth-century thought—and observe that all societies are ridden with . . . conflicts"[23] is that the participants in these conflicts are animated by the desire to be understood. They appeal to justice or some other value that they believe all can share. Conflict might be the order of the day, but it grows out of the aim of reaching understanding, and it is the inherent normative potentials in this aim that should be exploited.

My second reason for defending the regulative ideal of reaching understanding against the focus on conflict is the danger of paternalism. An important advantage of deliberation aimed at reaching understanding is that it connotes a process in which the person herself comes to an awareness of whether or not she can accept something as being in her interest. Those theorists who present interests or identities as given are taking a paternalistic observer's perspective. One critic of deliberative democracy draws the conclusion that "often what is needed is not widespread deliberation but firm action from above to protect the vulnerable."[24] And another critic notes, "I am not entirely against deliberation. But I am against it for now: I think it is premature as a standard for American Democrats, who are confronted with more immediate problems."[25] But here it is assumed that they, as theorists, know what is right, and that state action does not need to be discursively justified. Or, it is assumed that first all the conditions for perfect deliberation must be in place and then one can begin implementing the practice. The deliberative perspective, on the contrary, is a participant perspective, by its nature a nonhierarchical perspective. It is as participants in societal processes of deliberation that citizens learn whether or not they share existing values. We might need firm action to protect the vulnerable, but such action must go hand in hand with discursive justification if it is not to turn into paternalism. The claims of the oppressed are sometimes presented as self-evidently just and right. But even if the fight against oppression is just, there will never be agreement on what it requires in concrete cases or even regarding what constitutes oppression. And, more importantly, the deliberative commitment to fallibilism—the idea that any claim to truth or rightness could be wrong and should be open to contestation—has to be extended to the claims of the oppressed. There are no predeliberative truths about what it is right to do, and even the results of deliberation should always be open to critique and revision. (This is a central epistemic point in this book, and I develop it further in later chapters.) Those who argue against the merits of deliberation and in favor of more forceful and antagonistic means of politics seem to me all too confident that they have the right on their side.[26]

3. It may create confusion to speak of deliberation as aimed at changing *preferences*. "Preferences" have unfortunate individualistic connotations that seem more valid for understanding market behavior than political action; it is a too-simplistic notion to capture what deliberation is aimed at. Deliberation is not necessarily aimed at changing private preferences. In many instances it is aimed at setting up rules within which people can act with the preferences they already have. Deliberation is aimed at reaching agreements concerning which rules or laws are legitimate, not at changing private preferences. I can be convinced of the rightness of laws establishing freedom of religion without changing my religious preferences.[27] I might even prefer to live in a society in which all share my religion and still accept freedom of religion, because I realize that I can give no convincing reasons for why people who do not share my religious views should be forced to live in such a society. Or, to take a very different example, I can be convinced of a law securing pluralism in the media even if I prefer to watch only one TV station. The private person chooses what she prefers, but the citizen must also be concerned with what is available to others.[28]

   Preferences may sometimes change, because people realize that their preferences were based on insufficient information or bad reasoning, but this is not the main aim of deliberation. The deliberative process is not aimed at convergence of preferences but at coming to an agreement on certain principles, despite differences in personal preferences.[29] In other terms, deliberation is primarily aimed at reaching agreements about what it is *right* to do, not on what we *like* to do. This point is important from the perspective of a theory committed to multiple dimensions of freedom, because the idea of changing preferences very easily turns into paternalism or disrespect for the freedom to choose one's own conception of the good. To be sure, a dimension of freedom that deliberative democracy should be committed to does concern the free formation of political opinions, or what I later shall refer to as "internal autonomy." But this dimension of freedom is not concerned with our private preferences.[30]

Rather than changing preferences, the aim of deliberation should be gaining insights and forming opinions and judgments. We might gain insights and form judgments on many different levels, about others and about ourselves (about needs, interests, and desires), about the world (facts and causal relationships), and about possible arguments (normative as well as theoretical). These insights and judgments may affect us in different ways; they might affect our fundamental values, our beliefs, or our derived preferences, where the latter are products of the first two.[31] I shall go into more detail on these issues in Chapter 7, but here I want to point to the fact that changing preferences may refer to many different ideas. For example, the fact that after a process of deliberation I no longer support the proposal I set out supporting need not mean that I have changed my fundamental preference for it (here in the sense of desiring or valuing it); it might be a consequence of finding no good reason why others should also support it. I have learned that it is unreasonable to ask for my desire to be satisfied, which does not necessarily lead to a change of the preference for having it satisfied. To be more precise, it is unreasonable for me to ask for a political decision that will lead to the satisfaction of my desire, because I have learned in deliberation that it imposes heavy burdens on others, is unfeasible, or whatever. What should be stressed here is that there are many instances in which the aim of deliberation is not to change our fundamental preferences but to come to a better understanding of the perspectives of others, facts about the world, and consequences of different policy proposals.

4. A fourth problem with seeing deliberation in contrast to aggregation is that it might give the impression that there is no concern for the satisfaction of needs, interests, or desires. One dimension of deliberative freedom concerns the ability to have one's needs and desires fulfilled. Deliberation should not be seen as a way of transforming people into noumenal selves without needs, interests, and desires. One of the main advantages of deliberative democracy over Kantian ethics is exactly that it gives us a way of combining a concern for universalization with our particular and different interests, needs, and desires. The reason we need intersubjective dialogue and not internal monologue is exactly that we are different and have different interests, needs, and desires, and we need to know what these are to come to decisions that are in the equal interest of all. This is crucial for the theory of freedom that I am developing. In Kant, as is well known, there is a problem of combining the freedom of the noumenal self with the heteronomy of the empirical self. Because deliberation happens between real people and does not rely on the dichotomy between the intelligible world and the world of sense, it does not run into this Kantian problem.[32]

In relation to interests, it also is common to think that aggregation must be of egoistic interests and deliberation must be about transforming narrow self-interest into an altruistic concern for the common good.[33] But this dichotomy overlooks the possibility that the effects of deliberation may point in different directions, and also that aggregation can be of altruistic preferences. Indeed, one aim of deliberation should be for citizens to become more aware of and concerned with the satisfaction of their own interests. As Jane Mansbridge has argued, "Greater awareness of self-interest is absolutely required for good deliberation when a hegemonic definition of the common good makes less powerful members either unaware of their own interests or convinced that they ought to suppress those interests for the common good even when others are not doing their just share."[34] It is possible for someone to be too altruistic or to lack understanding of what is in her own interest. Deliberation ideally helps one clarify one's interests, knowing how they can be met, and ascertaining to what extent it is just for one to have them satisfied. Injustice is not always the consequence of people being partial to themselves but also can be a result of being so *against* themselves. I should caution here that I am not speaking of objective interests, which others can know better than the concerned person herself. I am claiming that people can be (1) mistaken about what their interests are, (2) lack knowledge of how to fulfill their interests, and/or (3) be too little concerned about their interests than is good for justice. And I am claiming that deliberation (under the right conditions) may help these deficiencies, not as a process where the truth is imposed on some by others but as a process where we learn from each other.

5. The contrast between aggregation and transformation can lead to the idea that we can set up the two in a simple manner as alternative ways of solving a problem. It also might be thought here that transforming opinions works on the same time frame as does aggregation. But if we construe deliberation as a matter of gaining insights or as a learning process, then this means that deliberation cannot be seen as a simple alternative that can substitute for aggregation. One of the aims of deliberative democracy is to broaden the focus of democratic theory from the political process narrowly construed to a concern for all the factors that play into the formation of political opinions. This also means that deliberation should not only be evaluated on the basis of its local but also on the basis of its global effects. Thus when Ian Shapiro, for example, notes that deliberation might lead to hardening of opinions and increasing conflict, he is too focused on its local effects.[35] In a deliberative democracy citizens are both participants in and observers of different sites of deliberation. One cannot merely study one site or occasion of deliberation in order to judge its effects. What matters are the overall and long-term effects of living in a society with widespread opportunities for participating in processes of public deliberation in formal as well as informal institutions. Deliberation should be seen and evaluated as a society-wide learning process. Deliberative democracy is for this reason a theory concerned with much more than the decision-making process in formal institutions.

To be sure, circumscribed instances of deliberation aimed at making decisions, for example, in legislative bodies, are essential for democracy. But it is crucial to see that these instances are embedded in a larger context of deliberative practices. A legislator might not change his mind or be willing to learn when confronted with her opponent on the floor of Congress or Parliament, but this does not prevent her from learning from her broader participation in and observance of public deliberation in civil society.

6. Finally, deliberative democracy cannot do without aggregation. No proponent of deliberative democracy believes that we can do away with mechanisms of aggregation in complex modern societies. Because of contingent constraints, especially the time constraint to decide, deliberation can never be any more than a supplement to aggregation.[36] However, it is important to see that aggregation does not constitute a definitive end to the political process. Aggregation or voting might be necessary to come to a decision, but this does not mean that deliberation about the issue has come to an end. Everyone should remain free to criticize any decision made and to attempt to change it. Deliberation should not be a part only of the process before aggregation (turning unreflective preferences into reasoned judgments) but also after aggregation (probing whether former decisions are valid).

The Negative Freedom Tradition and Democracy

Rather than differentiating deliberative democracy from aggregative democracy as a matter of transformation versus aggregation, I contrast the former to a tradition that is characterized by a specific conception of freedom. I suggest that deliberative democracy should be seen in contrast to a tradition of models of democracy that reduces freedom to a matter of noninterference with private interests and desires. This tradition is one that focuses on private interests and pleasures and hence is concerned either with the protection and/or the satisfaction of these. On the protective side, political freedoms (the rights to speak, assembly, and vote) are seen merely as a means to the protection of private interests (in particular, the right to private property). On the satisfaction side, the democratic process is indeed seen as one of aggregation. However, aggregation is not emphasized because preferences are seen as given but rather because of the negative conception of freedom. Whether or not preferences are given or constructed is really outside the concern of this model of democracy; indeed, it is off-limits. Preference formation is part of the sphere of negative liberty, as it is construed by this tradition.

Deliberative democracy should not be seen in contrast to this tradition because the latter is concerned with interests and preferences but rather because it views these in an uncritical manner. Due to its one-dimensional commitment to negative freedom, this tradition sees interests and preferences as merely a private and subjective matter. It *treats* people as if they have clear ideas about what their interests and preferences are and as if they cannot be mistaken about their interests and preferences.[37] And popular sovereignty is reduced either to a matter of being able to protect these interests or as a matter of having the opportunity to have one's preferences counted in the aggregative process. There is no room for freedom either as something intrinsic to political participation or as a matter of collective self-legislation. In contrast to this tradition, I see democracy as a form of exercising and experiencing freedom. Deliberative democracy, I think, should be formulated in terms of a theory of freedom. This theory does not reduce freedom to *one* dimension but sees deliberative democracy as committed to and expressing *multiple* dimensions of freedom. It does not deny the importance of some degree of negative freedom, but it sees this as only part of what deliberative freedom requires and as dependent on other dimensions of freedom for being interpreted and justified as well as for being implemented in a way that itself does not undermine the concern for overall freedom.

The negative freedom tradition begins with Thomas Hobbes and includes most notably Jeremy Bentham, James Mill, Isaiah Berlin, F. A. Hayek, Joseph Schumpeter, Anthony Downs, and William Riker. Clearly there are great differences between these writers, but I believe that they share an uncritical (or a defeatist) attitude to people's existing interests and preferences and still see them as the center of what politics is about. I argue that this is a tradition that has resulted in a combination of an understanding of democracy as a procedure for protecting and aggregating self-interested or private preferences and a conception of negative freedom or freedom as noninterference *with private interests as understood in some sense subjectively and prepolitically*. Moreover, it is a tradition that neglects to theorize how to determine the meaning and boundaries of negative freedom in a noncoercive manner. As a theory that focuses on noncoercion, this latter omission makes it incomplete and unstable.

It might come as a surprising claim that this tradition combines freedom and democracy, since it is a tradition that explicitly rejects the idea that there should be any "necessary connexion between individual liberty and democratic rule."[38] But my claim is not that the combination of negative freedom and aggregative democracy is conceptual or necessary. Nor is it my claim that everybody in the tradition shares the idea that negative freedom connects to aggregative democracy. Rather, the contention is that the tradition *historically* has resulted in a view of a free and democratic society as one that combines aggregative democracy and negative freedom. The combination of negative freedom and aggregative democracy, however, is not entirely fortuitous. Aggregative democracy and negative freedom have the same aim: the protection of private interests or preferences. In aggregative democracy voting is seen as the assertion of private interests with the aim of the self-protection of self-interested individuals against the state.[39] Negative freedom is, correspondingly, seen as freedom from interference with private interests as subjectively conceived. A distinction between protecting and promoting self-interest is obscured here. The tradition under discussion tends to take the idea of a private sphere as a given and hence to regard negative freedom and the vote as ways of protecting what we already rightfully have. As such, it obscures that a specific understanding of how the private sphere should be understood and demarcated is promoted.

Note that I am not making a conceptual point about aggregative democracy and negative freedom but trying to identify how they have been conceived in a specific, influential tradition in political theory.[40] This tradition deserves our interest not merely because of its influence in academia. More importantly, some of the key features of this tradition have a strong hold on the public mind in existing democracies. Part of the resistance to a more deliberative democracy comes from an ideology based on a too-narrow focus on the idea that the only freedom interest we have is to be free from interference with our private goals. From this perspective even beginning to discuss the idea that people do not always know and vote what is best for them is seen as a threat to freedom and democracy. Showing that this is an unfounded (or at least exaggerated) concern is an important aim of this book's focus on multiple dimensions of freedom and the idea of their mutual dependence.

Because there is an obvious similarity between what I say here and a well-known argument that goes back to C. B. Macpherson and has been elaborated on by David Held, let me differentiate my point from theirs. Macpherson and Held also note the connection between negative freedom and what they call "protective democracy," but their focus is on how this relates to the emergence and protection of the market and capitalism.[41] From my perspective, the connection to capitalism, even if important, is not the focus. The focus of the present book is rather the fact that this tradition blocks the possibility of seeing public deliberation as a precondition and exercise of freedom. When freedom is seen as negative and democracy as protective, then any idea of public, intersubjective learning and justification is seen at best as unnecessary and at worst as a threat to individual freedom.

My theory of deliberative freedom does not reject everything that comes out of this tradition of self-interest liberalism. The mechanisms of aggregation still play a role in deliberative democracy. And the idea of negative freedom is certainly not rejected tout court, though we shall see that the concept of negative freedom is more complicated than it is presented in this tradition. What deliberative democrats must reject is the idea that overall freedom can be understood in terms of negative freedom and the protection of self-interest. I argue that deliberative freedom cannot be patterned on negative liberty, as it is understood in the tradition of self-interest liberalism. Public autonomy, moreover, cannot be understood as having the same meaning, structure, and purpose as negative freedom. Most importantly, negative freedom is parasitic upon an intersubjective exercise of public autonomy, both for determining the former's meaning, significance, and boundaries and in order to do so noncoercively.

In what follows, I discuss the negative conception of freedom, show how some of the elements of negative liberty connect to aggregative democracy, and make a criticism of them from the perspective of deliberative freedom.

The Negative Conception of Freedom

Negative freedom in its Hobbesian-Berlinian formulation may appear a very simple idea. It is a mechanistic notion according to which freedom means the absence of external obstruction to or interference with motion or activity.[42] Negative freedom in its simplistic formulation is seen as a matter of protecting an "area within which a man can act unobstructed by others."[43] It is interesting to note, however, that both Hobbes and Berlin quickly move beyond the simplistic formulation of the concept of negative freedom. They both move toward something that relates to the satisfaction of given, individual, and private desires. Thus Hobbes says that a free man is defined by not being "hindered to do what he has a will to"; a free man "finds no stop, in doing what he has the will, desire, or inclination to do."[44] And Berlin says that a person lacks negative liberty if "prevented from attaining a goal."[45] Coercion—the antithesis of negative liberty—for Berlin is that which frustrates "my wishes"[46] or "frustrates human desires."[47]

It should be clear that there is a difference between being obstructed in one's movements and being prevented from attaining one's goals or in doing what one has a desire to do. We might see the latter category of obstructions as a subset of the former. Not all our movements are aimed at attaining some goal, and not all our acts are expressions of our desires. Some of our acts are random or unwilled, and obstructions to these acts would not count as a hindrance to what we have the will or desire to do.[48] If I am about to drive off the road in the mountains and am prevented from doing so by the railing, then my movement is obstructed, but I am not prevented from doing something I want to do, assuming I am not on a suicidal mission.

These remarks open up a wide range of issues to be answered by proponents of negative liberty, all of which I cannot go into. The point to emphasize here is that the Hobbes-Berlin conception of negative freedom is closely related to the satisfaction of desires and to the protection of private interests. This view represents a *specific* understanding of negative freedom; it is one conception of an overall concept of negative liberty.[49] The general formula of negative freedom as noninterference requires that we answer the question of "obstruction to what?" "The absence of interference with what *aspect* of myself constitutes freedom?"[50] In Hobbes and Berlin (and Bentham), the answer to this question is "private desires and interests." This view of freedom holds that I am free when no one obstructs me in satisfying my desires or interferes with my interests. There is a clear, positive dimension to this view. Hobbes and Berlin give an answer to what it is we should be free *to* do, namely, to act on our desires.[51] It is not a mere accident that Berlin and Hobbes move beyond the simplistic, mechanistic definition of negative freedom. That conception of freedom is absolutely uninteresting in a political context when it is not related to some idea of what it is we should be free to do, and some positive idea of what it is to be a free human agent.

Freedom, also in its negative dimension, is an essentially moral notion. Ronald Dworkin argues that a conception of liberty fails the test if "[i]t declares a violation when a violation is no wrong, and it therefore does not show us what the special importance of liberty is." "A conception of liberty is an interpretive theory that aims to show why it is bad when liberty is denied, and a conception of liberty is therefore unsuccessful when it forces us to describe some event as an invasion of liberty when nothing bad has happened."[52] My point is similar, but Dworkin's formulation is not sufficiently precise. While we, in formulating a conception of freedom, will be guided by norms of what we believe it would be bad to deny people, this does not mean that the definition of freedom on which we settle will be so perfect that an infringement of freedom so understood will always be wrong. Freedom is inevitably an incomplete moral notion.[53] We will tend to define freedom in a way that makes it *usually* wrong to limit freedom, but we must accept that in certain circumstances infringements can be justified. Furthermore, if we see freedom as involving more dimensions, it is sometimes justified to limit one dimension for the sake of another if the overall freedom of each is thereby augmented.

It should be emphasized that I am making both a conceptual and a historical argument. The conceptual argument is that the idea of freedom as the absence of obstruction or freedom as noninterference is parasitic upon an idea of "obstructions to what?" or a specification of interference "with whom?" or "with what?" and "by whom?" or "by what?" The historical argument is that there is an important tradition in the history of political thought that has defined the "with what?" as private interests and desires. The answer to "interference with whom?" is the self-regarding private person who is concerned with fulfilling his private desires, not the political person or the citizen who also is concerned with how his private desires affect others and with coming to an understanding with them. And the answer to "by whom?" is the state, not other private actors. The historical point is perhaps most clearly expressed by Benjamin Constant in his description of the liberty of the moderns: "The aim of the moderns is the enjoyment of security in *private pleasures*; and they call liberty the guarantees accorded by institutions to these pleasures."[54] My criticism is mainly of the contingent answer given by the liberal self-interest tradition. It is clear that the answer we give to the question of "obstruction to what?" has great political implications. The point to stress at this juncture is the inadequacy of negative freedom as a basis for a conception of overall freedom insofar as it sees freedom as the freedom of the private person, of "le bourgeois" and not of "le citoyen." When freedom is reduced to its negative dimension, as it is in the tradition under scrutiny, it is impossible to speak of the freedom of the citizen as a participant in the political process, because freedom is tied to private pleasures. According to this negative conception of freedom, freedom is external to politics; it is seen "as beginning where politics ends, especially in various forms of private life."[55] "[L]iberalism," as Hannah Arendt puts it, "has done its share to banish the notion of liberty from the political realm."[56]

The conceptual point also is important. It is so because the tradition I have tried to identify speaks as if it follows naturally from the concept of negative freedom, that it is a freedom against interference by the state with the interests and desires persons identify for themselves when they see themselves as private persons concerned only with furthering their own good. But this answer is a contingent one and in no way natural or neutral. It can therefore not be treated as prepolitical and without need of democratic justification.

There are two main reasons negative freedom cannot stand alone but rather should be regarded as a *dimension* of freedom that is parasitic on other dimensions of freedom.[57] First, there are no neutral or obvious answers to the following questions: (1) Who should be protected against interference? Only mature human beings or also children, or animals? (2) What constitutes interference? Arguments, manipulation, threats, or only overt violence? (3) What and who can exercise interference? The state, private persons, the market, ideology? Any idea of negative freedom depends on a *positive* specification and justification of its meaning and boundaries. Second, because negative freedom and its meaning cannot be seen as a given, it is parasitic upon collective forms of justification and decision making.[58] In order for this decision-making process itself not to be coercive and violate the freedom it attempts to define, it must itself be a process whose intrinsic properties are expressions of freedom.

My purpose thus is not a crusade against negative freedom as such because it makes the citizen "the servant of egoistic man," as Marx's was.[59] It is important not to mistake the liberal ideology of the negative freedom of bourgeois man with the idea of individual rights as such, as Claude Lefort convincingly argues Marx did.[60] But this does not mean that we should not be critical of the liberal ideology, which is still with us, and which too often determines how individual freedoms function in society. My point is not that we should give up on the protection of negative freedom per se, but rather that it is not an uncontroversial question what that means and that it therefore must be subject to deliberative scrutiny and democratic legitimation.

In the negative freedom tradition it is assumed that by defining certain limits to the scope of political decisions or to protect a certain area from political interference, people are equally free to lead their lives as they like. This strategy leads to the depoliticization of certain spheres of life. In these spheres people are free to make private choices. The importance of this type of freedom should certainly not be underestimated. The problem emerges when it is thought that we can define prepolitically or once and for all which spheres or which practices should be privatized. From a social-theoretical perspective, it is evident that historical demarcations of the private sphere have had a tendency to protect the individual freedom of the powerful at the expense of the oppressed. This is clear in the protection of the patriarchal family and the capitalist economy as part of the sacred private sphere. Women and workers have found that their path to emancipation was and is to challenge earlier definitions of what is private and protected by negative freedom.[61] Both in cases of women's emancipation and in the case of workers' rights and social justice, proponents of negative freedom (private property and privacy) will find that negative freedom, as they understand it, is violated. But what is happening in these struggles is in fact that oppressed groups are claiming that they do not enjoy equal freedom. To be sure, the protection of the private sphere does not always protect the powerful and privileged, as is evident from, for example, the privacy protection that *Roe v. Wade* (the 1973 Supreme Court decision that protects the right to abortion) affords women in the United States. This is just to illustrate that boundaries of negative freedom, in order to afford equal freedom, must be subject to continued discursive justification.

Thus it is a specific conception of "negative freedom," a specific answer to the question of "obstruction to what?" that lies at the heart of the liberal self-interest tradition and that, perhaps beginning with Bentham, has been connected to the aggregative model of democracy. Four core elements to this conception should be emphasized in order to see its relationship to aggregative democracy. First, desires, interests, and preferences are seen as brute and given facts about individuals.[62] They are seen as something individuals possess as atomistic or isolated individuals.

Second, individuals have *immediate access* to their desires and interests. What my interests and desires are is a matter for me to determine privately, and no one can say that I am mistaken about what I want without interfering with my negative liberty. Third, it follows from this that freedom is limited to a matter of freedom of action. My freedom is limited only if others prevent me from doing what I want to do. Finally, because each individual alone can determine what her interests and desires are, all individual preferences are seen as being of equal value. Consequently, all interests and desires should be equally accommodated.

Negative Freedom and Aggregative Democracy

Let us consider how the aggregative model of democracy relates to the four elements enumerated in the last paragraph of the preceding section. First, like the theory of negative freedom, the aggregative model of democracy sees individual preferences as given, not ontologically but normatively. Preferences are regarded as data exogenous to the political process that can be collected and aggregated into something that suffices for legitimizing political decisions. The preferences and interests that serve as input into the aggregative mechanism are the preferences and interests that citizens bring from their protected and allegedly coercion- and power-free private sphere. Through voting, citizens assert their interests or express their private preferences vis-à-vis the state. They are seen as protecting something natural, not as promoting a certain view of what freedom means and requires.

Second, according to the aggregative model, the interests and preferences of citizens are the interests and preferences that each citizen by herself thinks she has. Determining interests and preferences is a purely subjective and private matter.[63] Voting is seen as an expression or assertion of each citizen's privately determined interests and preferences.

Third, popular sovereignty on the aggregative model is basically a matter of having the opportunity to choose between different alternatives, that is, between different competing candidates and parties.[64] This is a form of freedom of action. The aggregative model of democracy is not concerned with how citizens have come to have the preferences on the basis of which they make their choices but only with the freedom to choose.[65]

Finally, because only the citizen herself can judge what her interests and preferences are, all votes must be counted and weighted equally.[66] In the aggregative model, there is no room for arguing that some claims have greater merit than others; all we can do is see which claims get the greatest quantitative backing in the aggregation of purely private and subjective preferences.

To avoid misunderstanding and to show that I am not attacking straw men, let me expand on two points made in the previous simplified enumeration. I shall expand first on the point that preferences are seen as given, and second on the point that the aggregation of these preferences is seen as sufficient for the legitimacy of political decisions. Regarding the first point, while Hobbes perhaps sees desires as brute facts about us, this clearly is not the case with someone like Schumpeter, for whom it is important to emphasize that they are manufactured. My point is that no matter how this issue is construed, immediate and expressed preferences are still uncritically accepted as the only possible legitimate input to the aggregative process; for purposes of the democratic process, they are treated *as if* they were unchangeable. I argue that this is the result of a respect for the negative freedom of the private person who is construed as aiming at protecting her own interests as she sees them. The disagreement I am articulating is not concerned with the ontological status of preferences but with how they should be treated practically and normatively.[67]

The second point—that the aggregation of preferences is seen as sufficient for legitimizing political decisions—requires a little more elaboration. It is most important to stress that it is hard to find anyone in the tradition I have identified who thinks that the aggregation of preferences can be used to identify the popular will. The fact is, this tradition is very critical of the idea of popular sovereignty. Indeed, thinkers in this tradition have been in favor of democracy only insofar as they have seen it as being instrumental to the protection of the freedom of the private and prepolitical person. The aggregation of preferences that takes place in elections is in general not seen as a matter of creating a popular will but rather limited to electing rulers.

Among some of our protagonists the protection of interests is seen as embedded in the vote itself. The idea of the vote as self-protection is placed at the center of what democracy is about by James Mill,[68] but also accepted by his son, John Stuart Mill, who however does not see this as all democracy is about.[69] An interesting contemporary example of this view is William Riker's. Riker is best known for having argued (using insights from the social choice literature) that voting cannot reveal the popular will, and that the idea of populist democracy therefore is incoherent. This is not the place to go into that argument, but note that Riker's critique is directed not at any and all models of populist democracy but at aggregative democracy when it is seen as embodying the idea that "the will of the people is the liberty of the people."[70] In response to this view, Riker makes a move that is typical for the tradition of which he is part. He says that we do not have to worry about the fact that aggregative mechanisms cannot reveal the will of the people, for there is an alternative conception of freedom that does not think the will of the people is their liberty. "[L]iberals," Riker writes, "can cheerfully acknowledge that elections do not . . . reveal popular will."[71] They can do so because of their adherence to the negative conception of freedom and a purely instrumental view of political participation when they see the vote as a popular veto against tyranny. "Suppose freedom is simply the absence of governmental restraint on individual action. Then the chance to engage in vetoing by rejecting officials and the chance that the rejection actually occurs are the very essence of this freedom, which is substantially equivalent to liberal democracy."[72] On Riker's understanding of liberal democracy, popular sovereignty as voting is reduced to having the same purpose as individual rights: protection against state interference. On this view there is no way in which state action can be seen as either an expression of political freedom or as helping to enhance freedom. It is not only that the state is seen *only* as a threat to freedom, but the democratic process also is given no value whatsoever as a process in which we can learn from each other in a noncoercive way which forms of interference limit freedom and which might actually enhance freedom. All interference is seen in the same light and the vote is seen as a way in which we can minimize it. Moreover, it is neglected why liberals wanted a state in the first place: to protect everyone's equal freedom not against the state (it was not there yet) but against the encroachments from other human beings.

These views of democracy entail a narrowly instrumental and individualistic view of politics.[73] I argued earlier that in the negative liberty tradition, freedom comes to signify the freedom to act on one's individual desires or personal preferences. In the models of democracy related to this tradition, this idea translates into the idea of freedom to have one's preferences or interests counted in the aggregative process. These views involve an individual-instrumental conception of freedom. The individual-instrumental conception of freedom entails a view of the individual as standing over and against the world, and whether this individual is free or not depends on whether "the world" blocks the possibility for the individual of satisfying her preferences and protecting her interests. This also is how politics and government are seen, as institutions that either threaten the interests of the individual or as being instrumental to the satisfaction of desires that are determined prepolitically in a private sphere free from intervention.

Three aspects of the instrumentalism of these models of democracy distinguish them from deliberative democracy, as the latter is seen in this book. First, politics is seen as only a matter of protecting interests or satisfying desires and not as a matter of interpreting them. It is hereby disregarded that an important part of the political process concerns interpreting and clarifying what interests, needs, and desires we have.[74] Much political domination is exercised not by directly denying the protection of the *expressed* interests of the oppressed but by manipulating the way in which the latter *interpret* their interests.[75] I return to this point in Chapter 5.

Second, the instrumental view of politics entails a belief in that the end of government can be identified independently of or prior to the means. This is most explicit in James Mill, who begins his "Essay on Government" thus: "The question with respect to government is a question about the adaptation of means to an end."[76] But it is a more widely shared view within the tradition I am discussing, and it has to do with the prevalence of its specific conception of negative freedom. To be more precise, it has to do with that within the tradition it is thought that its conception of negative freedom is not a specific conception but the natural and neutral view of what freedom is and entails. The end of government is thought to be the protection of the negative freedom of the self-interested man. This idea is not itself thought to be in need of justification, or it is at least not thought to be in need of political or democratic legitimation. From the perspective of deliberative democracy and especially from my emphasis on deliberative freedom, this can be shown to be an untenable view. First, what the ends of government are should be subject to public deliberation and democratic legitimation. Second, I am critical of the idea that freedom can be prepolitically defined, as it is within the negative freedom tradition. I am not arguing against the idea that democracy is about freedom, and hence I am not arguing against democracy relying on some substantial value, but I am arguing against the specific, one-dimensional view of freedom advanced by these writers. As already argued, negative freedom is parasitic upon some positive idea of "freedom to what?" Enjoying private property is, for example, a quite substantive and by no means natural answer to this question.[77] It is therefore necessary to consider a dimension of freedom that fills out the answer to the question "freedom to what?" Freedom should not be seen merely as the end of democracy but as what democracy *is*. Democracy is a free, noncoercive way of determining what freedom means and requires. Since democracy is seen as a form of exercising freedom, the means (the procedures) must themselves embed freedom.

Third, in the instrumentalist view, political participation is seen as a cost that the individual will incur only for instrumental reasons.[78] As Constant says about the moderns, politics is a distraction from private enterprises that they accept only "as little as possible."[79] In the most extreme versions of instrumentalism like James Mill's, if one can gain the advantages of voting in some other way, then one has no reason to want to participate at all.[80] In this view, in Alan Ryan's words, "Politics is dispensable, because politics is a means to an end, in principle replaceable by a more efficient means if one should be found."[81] This, of course, gives a very precarious foundation to democracy.[82] It also exhibits a too-narrow understanding of freedom. I shall argue (mainly in Chapter 2) that there is an important intrinsic value to having the opportunity of participating in the political process, and that this value should be seen as a dimension of freedom. When James Mill argues that all women and men under age forty need not have the right to vote because their interests are taken care of by their husbands or fathers,[83] he neglects the crucial dimension of freedom that has to do with being respected as a full and mature human being.[84] He does not see that freedom has a status dimension.

Deliberative democrats disagree with some of the fundamental assumptions and principles of the negative freedom and aggregative democracy tradition, but the criticisms I have made should not be seen as a wholesale rejection of everything that comes out of this tradition. It is important to remember that the negative freedom view criticized here is not the only possible conception of negative freedom and its consequences. I argue in Chapter 6 that deliberative democracy does involve a respect for individual liberty, which involves certain negative elements, but its specific meaning must be determined in deliberation itself.

Conclusion

I have attempted to identify a tradition that construes negative freedom in a certain way, sees protection of this freedom as the raison d'être of democracy, and consequently overlooks (or rejects) the further dimensions of freedom that are presupposed by public deliberation properly under-stood. Let me conclude this chapter by listing four issues of freedom concerning which I especially find reason for deliberative democracy to go beyond the negative freedom models of democracy. First, the latter models are uncritical of how people have come to have the preferences or interests they have. This excludes any concern with freedom in forming one's opinions, as opposed to either protecting or satisfying given interests or desires. Second, by seeing democracy as, at most, being instrumental to freedom, politics as a process falls out of view, and the dimension of freedom involved in enjoying the status of being a citizen and the in-trinsic value in participation are disregarded. Third, the negative freedom tradition fails to say how we should determine which freedoms to protect and how we can reach agreements about this issue in a noncoercive and free manner. Fourth, to see any and all government interference as a violation of freedom excludes even the thematization of the issue of whether socioeconomic conditions matter for freedom.

CHAPTER TWO

Republican Freedom and Discursive Status

The idea of negative freedom or freedom as noninterference with private interests as understood subjectively and prepolitically was discussed in Chapter 1. I argued that this view of freedom cannot stand alone but needs to be coupled with a positive dimension specifying the question of freedom "to what?" and with a means of determining this positive dimension. That is, freedom as noninterference is parasitic not only on a positive dimension of freedom answering the question of freedom "to what?" but also on a process in which the boundaries of negative freedom can be determined. This process, in turn, is not merely one aimed at protecting interests but also of interpreting them. Finally, this process must not itself violate freedom.

This chapter investigates a republican conception of freedom and connects it to deliberative democracy. The republican conception of freedom is of interest, first because it has been presented as an alternative to freedom as noninterference and thus might be seen as capable of overcoming some of the shortcomings of the tradition discussed in Chapter 1, and second, because it has been presented as a conception of freedom appropriate for the theory of deliberative democracy.[1] Thus it could be regarded as a candidate for what we are looking for.

The specific formulation of republican freedom that I focus on is Philip Pettit's notion of "freedom as nondomination." Pettit's theory is the most elaborate, well-worked-out, and influential contemporary reconstruction of a republican conception of freedom.[2] I am concerned both with whether it is a viable conception on its own terms and whether nondomination is a sufficient condition for the freedom that we should expect from living in a deliberative democracy. Can freedom as nondomination fulfill the role as the conception of freedom deliberative democracy should be normatively committed to? Is it the conception of freedom presupposed by the theory and practice of public deliberation?

Prima facie, there are several appealing features to Pettit's conception of freedom. First, it goes beyond Berlin's problematic dichotomy of negative and positive freedom. Second, it gives a suggestion as to how to avoid the counterintuitive idea that legitimate law compromises freedom in the same way as any other interference. Third, it does not see the ultimate freedom as freedom from other people but rather as enjoying a certain status and recognition among them. Fourth, it sees freedom as connected to democracy, particularly deliberative democracy. However, even if Pettit elaborates a conception of freedom with some features that seem attractive, his conception fails in some essential respects. Indeed, upon closer inspection, some of the attractive features of the conception turn out not to be consistently borne out by the theory. Part of the problem is that Pettit attempts to give a unitary definition of freedom, a monistic conception meant to outdo other conceptions. I aim to show that such an enterprise is bound to fail. We cannot achieve a complete theory of freedom and democracy only on the basis of the ideal of nondomination. Many of the values that Pettit himself advances cannot be derived from the value of nondomination alone but require the addition of other values,[3] or, as I suggest, a more complex, multidimensional theory of freedom.

Domination without Interference

In his *Republicanism*, Pettit presents his view of freedom as "a third, radically different way of understanding freedom," in contrast to Berlin's two concepts of liberty (R, 19). Pettit calls his alternative conception "freedom as nondomination" and claims that it is inherent in the republican tradition of political thought. My aim is not to question his historical claims[4] but rather to discuss how radically different his conception really is and whether he presents a viable alternative theory of freedom.

Pettit, to a large extent, explicates his conception of freedom as nondomination in contrast to freedom as noninterference (Berlin's negative freedom). Freedom as nondomination is, like freedom as noninterference, a negative notion, but it is concerned with absence of domination rather than absence of interference. In focusing on domination, Pettit wants to make two main points against the notion of freedom as noninterference. He claims first that *not all* interference compromises freedom, and second that *not only* interference compromises freedom. The first point is meant to show that there are qualitative differences between forms of interference. Specifically, Pettit wants to show that only arbitrary interference compromises freedom. He draws a distinction between compromising and conditioning freedom; nonarbitrary interference does condition freedom, it limits one's range of choices, but it does not compromise one's freedom (R, 75 ff.).[5] In this way he hopes to avoid what he takes to be an unfortunate consequence of the conception of freedom as noninterference, namely, that any law compromises freedom (a view held by Bentham and Berlin).[6] I return to this point in a later section in this chapter.

Pettit's paradigmatic example of loss of freedom without interference is the subjection of the slave to the noninterfering master. The slave remains a slave even if she has a kind master who never interferes with her. Pettit draws a compelling picture of this possibility. Even if the master does not interfere with the slave, the slave will know that she is "depending on his grace and favor" (R, 33); she will be "in a position where fear and deference will be the normal order of the day" (R, 64). It seems plausible that being under the domination even of a kind master who never actually interferes will have these psychological effects on the slave. But what exactly constitutes this domination? Pettit says, "The fact that in some respect the power-bearer has the capacity to interfere arbitrarily, even if they are never going to do so" (R, 63). "Domination can occur without interference, because it requires only that someone have the capacity to interfere arbitrarily in your affairs; no one need actually to interfere" (R, 23).

It might seem as if Pettit speaks of interference only in the sense of exercised coercion. Thus we would have the idea that domination can occur—and freedom be compromised—without anyone exercising interference (putting in shackles, imprisoning, or the like). But those who favor the notion of freedom as noninterference clearly do not speak of interference only when actual coercion takes place but also of the coercion of the credible threat. When Bentham and Berlin see any law as compromising freedom, they are not just talking about when it is actually used in punishment but also about its function as a credible threat. My freedom, in this view, is compromised not only when I am actually fined or imprisoned but also when the costs of certain acts have been increased by the enactment of the laws.[7] So Pettit must be making a stronger claim, namely, that domination can occur without being accompanied by credible threats. For freedom as nondomination to be different from freedom as noninterference, we must be able to have domination without credible threats. Is it possible to separate the two? Can the master dominate his slaves without interference or the threat thereof? If there is no credible threat against the slave, then why can't she just walk away? How can a slave be dominated without feeling a threat hanging over her head? I do not think Pettit's definition of domination gives satisfactory answers to these questions—which is not to say that they cannot be answered.

For Pettit, freedom is compromised by the presence of some who have the capacity to interfere arbitrarily in others' choices. Thus some have dominating power to the extent that the following three conditions are satisfied (R, 52):

1. they have the capacity to interfere
2. on an arbitrary basis
3. in certain choices that the other is in a position to make.

Nondomination is in place when we have security against such interference; this is the positive aspect of freedom as nondomination (R, 51). So, for Pettit, the move from domination to nondomination is one from lack of to presence of security against arbitrary interference.

I suggest an alternative way of looking at the move from a dominated to a nondominated status. The status of the dominated party is not merely characterized by a lack of something. Pettit's paradigmatic example of a dominated person is the slave, but the slave has a *positive status*, she is a slave. The slave experiences domination because of her position in the social structure. The same is true of Pettit's other examples of dominated persons, the worker in capitalist society, and the wife under patriarchy. These categories of people are dominated because of some of the main structures of contemporary society, the capitalist division of labor and the patriarchal family.[8] What makes the slave, the worker, and the wife subject to domination is not merely lack of positive guarantees against arbitrary interference but the positive privileges that their respective masters have of interfering with them. Domination does not exist by the mere fact that someone has *the capacity* to interfere arbitrarily in others' affairs but in their accepted right to do so. As Henry Richardson has argued, kidnappers have the capacity to arbitrarily interfere with people's lives, but we do not for that reason regard them as dominating their potential victims (all of us).[9] We must distinguish between (1) the mere capacity to interfere arbitrarily, and (2) the accepted right (or authority) to do so with impunity. The first can never be entirely removed. Through law we can raise the cost of arbitrary interference, but legal deterrence cannot create absolute security.[10] It is the second form that constitutes domination in the sense that some are allowed to be masters over others. And, crucially, this accepted right to interfere is, when effective, backed by force.

To clarify, by "accepted right" I do not mean to imply any form of legitimacy, for then the adjective "arbitrary" would not apply. My point is that for masters to be able to dominate without any form of interference, their right to do so must be accepted by their society to some degree. The reason the noninterfered-with slave cannot just walk away is that she knows that society accepts her master's right to arbitrarily interfere with her; the master need not interfere or threaten her. But is there not, then, a threat hanging over her head, perhaps not from anything her master has done or said but from the society of which they are both part?

W. E. B. DuBois notes in a discussion of antebellum America, "The police system of the South was primarily designed to control slaves."[11] The single slaveholder did not need to interfere directly with his slaves, because he knew he had the backing of the coercive force of the police. He could dominate his slaves without threatening them, because there was a threat from somewhere else. Similarly, if women feel dominated by their husbands, this is because they know that the society in which they live accepts—by convention and/or law—that their husbands are their masters; it is because being a wife is seen as a subordinate status. The same is true of the domination that fathers exercise over their daughters in patriarchal societies, as we learn from Virginia Woolf: "If they wished that their daughter should stay at home, society agreed they were right. . . . Should she [the daughter] persist further [in her desire to leave home], then law came to [the father's] help."[12] Regarding workers, Pettit sees them as dominated because they are exposed to interference by their employers (R, 141). But this description ignores the wider economic structure of which both capitalists and proletarians are part. The unfreedom of the workers is not only a product of the personal relationship between employers and workers, as Pettit describes it, but of the economic structure as a whole. The subordinate status of wives and daughters, like the subordinate status of the slave and the laborer, is not only or primarily the product of absence of security against interference but the product of *the presence of another interference regime.*[13] It is because they are part of such a regime that the dominated parties are dominated. And conversely, to be a master is a social position in a certain structure, not an individual attribute.[14] To be dominator and dominated are status positions within a certain social and institutional structure.[15] Domination can exist only in the relationship between superior and subordinate. Only when a hierarchy has been established and accepted does the noninterfering master become a possibility.

The idea of a noninterfering master, then, is incomprehensible without an account of the structures and institutions that determine his position. Pettit is right, that interference need not *directly* take place for freedom to be compromised, but he fails to explain why. There is a sociological—structural and institutional—deficit in his theory.[16] It is only by giving a structural and/or institutional explanation of the positions of the different parties that we can understand why some people may be dominated without experiencing direct interference by their masters. The fact that some dominated people do not experience direct interference from their *immediate* masters does not mean their positions are not determined by interference of some sort. The dominated and dominating parties have come to hold their positions and are kept in those positions only because those positions are in the last instance backed by force. This force might for the dominated parties be one that makes it impossible to do otherwise, makes it prohibitively costly to do otherwise, or makes them *think* that it is impossible to do otherwise, such as manipulation or ideological domination. It should be obvious that the immediate master need not exercise these forms of interference by himself; they could be structural or ideological features of his society. In neglecting such structural and institutional dimensions of coercion—emphasized by Marxists and critical theorists[17]—Pettit is still very close to the Berlinian framework. Like Berlin, he limits his analysis to direct interpersonal forms of compromising freedom.[18] The idea of domination as requiring that someone have the capacity to arbitrarily interfere with others also excludes the possibility of self-imposed forms of coercion, a possibility I discuss in Chapter 5.

There is a further point that has to do with the question of whether a person who is unfree must *know* that she is so. Freedom as noninterference does not seem to require knowledge on the part of the subject. The fact that I do not know that I am not free to do something does not make me free to do it. For example, if I do not know that there is a law against something and do it, then this does not mean that the interference will not materialize, that is, that I will not be punished. But what of the dominated-but-not-interfered-with person, the subject of Pettit's noninterfering master? Imagine a slave who has an extremely kind master and also is ignorant of the world in which she lives, and hence does not know that she is a slave. Will her freedom be compromised according to the idea of freedom as nondomination? It is clear that the psychological consequences of which Pettit speaks will be absent. If the slave does not know that she is a slave, then there is no reason she should be unable to look her master in the eye or would bow and scrape to him. If the master does not interfere with her, then it also seems she can do what she likes and even leave. But if that is the case, then she will clearly not be a slave anymore, nor will the master be a master. The only way the master can make her aware that she is his slave is by interference, actual coercion, or the credible threat thereof. There is no way domination can be upheld if interference is never used and the ability to use it is kept secret.[19] (I discuss the importance of common knowledge later in this chapter).

I have argued that a master can only dominate a slave without interference because of the social positions they respectively hold within certain social structures and institutions, and that these structures and institutions must themselves be coercive if they are to uphold the relationship of domination. In this way, there really is a threat hanging over the head of the dominated party; domination cannot exist without a threat of coercion from somewhere. Pettit might not disagree with this, but if he does his definition of domination is not sufficiently precise. For the purposes of my overall argument, the important point is that we here have what might be called a *status conception of freedom*[20]: To enjoy freedom is to have a certain status within certain social and political institutions, and to be unfree is to have another type of status in different types of institutions. The status conception of freedom sees freedom as intrinsically bound up with the institutional structure of society; it is not merely a matter of direct interpersonal relationships. In the rest of this chapter I shall connect this idea of freedom as a form of status to the institutional structure of a democracy.

Republican Freedom and Demoracy

If the argument in the preceding section is valid, then we can only understand what it means to be dominated with a theory of the structures and institutions that place people in positions of authority and subordination. I shall now argue that we can only fully explain what nondomination means with a normative theory of an alternative set of institutions, namely, deliberative democratic ones. To adequately define nondomination, thus, we need to incorporate a theory of deliberative democracy. The status of being dominated is part and parcel of the existence of hierarchical institutions, while the status of being free is constituted by egalitarian and democratic institutions. This argument, however, will have to reject Pettit's contention that nondomination and democracy are not intrinsically related. Thus we now come to the major concern of this book, the relationship between freedom and democracy. What is the republican view of this relationship?

Pettit joins a wider effort to disentangle republicanism from a positive conception of freedom. As part of this effort it has been argued that political participation is merely a means to the negative freedom that republicans also value the most. Republicans "work with a purely negative view of liberty," it is maintained.[21] In this way, I suppose, republicanism is thought to be more acceptable to us moderns. It could be a response to Benjamin Constant's claim that "the moderns" find the greatest pleasures in private life and hence that is what they seek the liberty to enjoy.[22] And it could be a reassurance to Berlinian pluralists that republicanism is not advocating positive freedom, which, it is believed, can justify oppression. My worry is that this reading of republicanism obliterates some valuable insights regarding other dimensions of freedom. Indeed, I do not understand the urge to find one and only one dimension of freedom in the republican tradition and present it as *the* republican conception of freedom.[23] This reductionistic approach eradicates some valuable aspects of freedom. Freedom should not be equated with democracy, it is claimed. Nor does freedom lie in being a participant in the common enterprise that politics is or was or could be. "Freedom just is non-domination."[24] Why not see nondomination as a *dimension* of freedom rather than a conception attempting to eradicate all others?[25]

Liberalism and republicanism were earlier more commonly contrasted by saying that one is primarily concerned with the freedom of the private individual and the other with the politically active citizen.[26] Quentin Skinner has on a historically informed basis challenged this view,[27] and Pettit follows his lead. The more traditional understanding of republicanism involves two direct and obvious connections between democracy and freedom, both of which have been stressed by republican thinkers but are rejected by Skinner and Pettit. On the one hand, there is the idea that participating in politics affords a unique opportunity to experience a form of activity that is without constraints from either the mastery of other human beings or from the necessity of nature; this view we find in Hannah Arendt's account of ancient Athens in *The Human Condition*.[28] On the other hand, we have the idea that freedom can be equated with subjection only to laws given by oneself; this is the Rousseauian idea of popular sovereignty.[29] Pettit sees both of these as neo-Athenian-inspired forms of populism and communitarianism (R, 8, 27 ff.).[30] He rejects the first view, saying that democratic participation might be a necessary means for promoting freedom, but it does not have any "independent attractions" (R, 8). And he rejects the Rousseauian view: "Democratic control is certainly important . . . but its importance comes, not from any definitional connection with liberty, but from the fact that it is a means of furthering liberty" (R, 30).

I shall argue that Pettit's attempt to avoid positive freedom and to stick to a one-dimensional negative conception of freedom creates unnecessary problems. It makes it impossible to speak of certain crucial concerns of modern society as concerns about freedom, and it negates Pettit's own ambition of seeing freedom as "the supreme political value" (R, 80).[31] In particular, it brings problems with respect to three dimensions of freedom: public autonomy, internal autonomy, and discursive status.

Democracy and Freedom: Tracking Interests

Let us look in greater detail at Pettit's argument about the relationship between freedom and democracy. He explicitly takes a line that differs from other prominent republican thinkers by contending that democracy is only a *means* of furthering freedom as nondomination.[32] In other words, Pettit insists that democracy is *instrumental* and not intrinsic to freedom. But he goes beyond Berlin in seeing the relationship as internal and not merely contingent. What democratic governments do, according to Pettit, is not just add to interference and hence to diminish freedom but rather to substitute one form of interference with a completely different kind. Democratized states represent a lesser assault on republican freedom than nondemocratic ones, and not just contingently but by virtue of being democratized.[33] Only democracies (and only democracies of a certain kind) are institutionally designed to rule in a way that is not dominating. Democracies will, of course, rely on coercive law for implementing collective decisions, but this interference can and should be of a nondominating kind. And, "interference occurs without the loss of liberty when the interference is not arbitrary and does not represent a form of domination" (R, 35). Interference is nonarbitrary when it is "designed to track people's interests according to their ideas" (R, 149). Thus democracy is internally connected to freedom, in Pettit's view, because it is a form of government designed to track people's interests as they see them and to interfere exclusively on that basis. Democratic law is nondominating because it embodies the common interest of the people. Democratic institutions have epistemic value in determining what the common interest is. This is the basis of Pettit's proposition, that not all interference compromises freedom, the second difference to Berlin's freedom as noninterference.

Does Pettit's formula capture all that we can and should say about the relationship between democracy and freedom? Is democracy designed *only* to track self-perceived interests, or are there other aims and ideals that make it important for freedom? What is excluded in terms of the relationship between democracy and freedom when the focus is nondomination as tracking of interests? If tracking interests is important, then how does it take place? And what does it mean to track people's interests according to their ideas? I shall begin with the latter two questions and return to the others later.

In general, I find the terminology of "tracking" unsatisfactory and misleading. The connotation is that *first* we have people's interests and even their common interest, and *then* we have democratic processes aiming at tracking them down. When Pettit speaks of tracking interests, he speaks as if these interests already have been articulated. All democracy is needed for is to "search-and-identify" common interests (TF, 159). This way of looking at democracy overlooks a key insight of theories of deliberative democracy, namely, that a crucial aspect of the political process is the *interpretation* of interests and the *formation* of opinions about the common good. How citizens perceive their interests and the common interest is not independent of mechanisms for identifying them.

In his argument about democracy and freedom, Pettit emphasizes what he calls the contestatory dimension of democracy. He does so because he thinks that the greatest danger is not that all possible common interests are not heard—"There should be relatively little danger of politicians and people failing to detect any matters of common avowable interest" (TF, 161)—but that some interests that are not common become law. From the perspective of nondomination, then, the focus is not the formation of common interest or the democratic genesis of law but rather protecting citizens against laws based on sectarian interests.[34] Pettit reduces the authorial dimension of democracy to a Schumpeterian competition for the vote.[35] This might partly be a realist concession, but the point for us is that he presents it not merely as the only realistic possibility but as all freedom requires. His theory of freedom does not encourage any inquiry into or experimentation with institutional forms that would enable a more participatory form of democracy or ways in which we could approach the ideal that the people are the source of the laws to which they are subject.

Two issues regarding contestatory democracy are of special importance to our discussion of dimensions of freedom. First, it moves the attention away from the authorization and genesis of law to ex post forms of political participation. It is concerned not with the formation of opinions about policies or about the choices people make but with determining whether or not already made laws actually track common interests. Contestation is concerned not with the choices that the people actually have made but with determining whether policies conform to their preferences. Second, mechanisms of contestation do not require common deliberation but can work through channels that limit participation in deliberation and decision making to the few. According to Pettit, we can safely let an impartial body such as an independent court decide whether a certain law or policy is nonarbitrary. For the judges "will be asked to judge on *a factual issue* of whether the policy as identified is supported by common avowable interests and only by such interests" (TF, 165, emphasis added). For Pettit, then, whether or not a policy is arbitrary, and hence whether or not it compromises freedom, is a factual issue that can be determined impartially by a small body of people and, hence, without the participation of the people who are subject to the policy.

There are two difficulties with this position; the first concerns how Pettit views the determination of common interests; the second lies in a disregard for the idea that the intrinsic properties of the process that determines when our freedom is violated matter for that very freedom.[36]

1. Determination of common interests. The shortcoming of Pettit's view is that he presents common interests as *independent of the processes that establish what they are*. It does not matter, on his view, whether courts or people themselves deliberate about what their common interests: the result will be the same. But this view neglects the possibility that people's interpretations of their

needs and interests change in the very process that is meant to discover their common interests. It is a common feature of the literature on deliberative democracy that people's opinions may be transformed in the process of deliberation. This transformation should not be seen as one of discovering a preexisting common interest, I suggest, but of *constructing* a common interest on the basis of new interpretations of interests that are products of the process of deliberation itself. The process of deliberation is just as much a process of individual self-clarification as one of determining common interests, and the latter cannot be seen as being independent of the former.

Pettit sees deliberation as a heuristic device for determining whether or not state action is arbitrary, whether it is sectarian or rather in the common interest. He acknowledges the advantage of people speaking for themselves, but only as sources of information necessary for determining the common interest, not as necessary for learning and constructing a common interest (R, 56 ff.). He sees the tracking of interest almost as a scientific discourse about something in the physical world. But the transformation of opinions in public deliberation about norms cannot be seen as identical to the transformation of scientists' views of the natural world in a process of scientific learning. The social and moral world is dependent on our attempts to determine it in a way the natural world is not. In the very process of determining our common interests, our views of our individual interests change, and we simultaneously create the world of norms that should be recognized.[37] If I am right about this, then it is not possible to establish nonarbitrary laws without the actual participation of the people who are going to live under them.[38] Without actual intersubjective practices of learning, the normative world we are looking for will not even exist.

My argument that the democratic process should not be seen merely as tracking given interests also entails an important dimension of freedom. This dimension, internal autonomy, concerns whether or not people come to see certain policies as being in the general interest and give them their support in a free manner. By free manner, I mean that they are convinced of the intrinsic merits of the policies rather than being forced to accept them by direct coercion, threats, or manipulation. In the language of critical theory, this dimension of freedom is threatened by ideological forms of justification, which are characterized by presenting something as being in the general interest that is not actually so, and it is achieved by excluding some possible common interests from ever being articulated.[39] Pettit should be concerned with political decisions based on ideological justification, since they lead to arbitrary rule in the sense of rule based on sectarian as opposed to common interests. But it is unclear whether he would in fact see such decisions as arbitrary, since he ignores the issue. It appears that it is the attempt to hold on to a purely negative conception of freedom that blinds him to important freedom interests.

To be sure, Pettit *is* concerned with the structure of the public sphere and as such also with the formation of public opinion (R, 165 ff.). My point is that he does not thematize the dimension of freedom that can be seen as entailed by this concern, and that his formula about tracking interests fails to address the issue. All he requires for political decisions not to be arbitrary is that the government must be forced "to track the common, perceived interests of the populace."[40] But this formulation ignores the possibility that what people perceive as being in the common interest could be the product of a distorted process and hence merely a sectarian interest. The fact that Pettit leaves out the question of *how* the people have come to perceive something as a common interest and hence to see its legal implementation as nonarbitrary seems to me a limitation of the conception of freedom as nondomination as Pettit formulates it. If all that is required for an interference to be nonarbitrary is that it conforms to people's perceived interests, then this leaves open the possibility that the interpretations of these interests are the products of domination.

Actually, there is an ambiguity in Pettit's account of whether or not nonarbitrariness requires that the interference be in some objective way in the common interest of the affected parties, or whether it is sufficient that it is *perceived* as being so. It might seem that Pettit wants to build in a certain subjectivism or voluntarism when he speaks of tracking "perceived" interests or tracking people's interests "according to their ideas." The state, if it is to act nonarbitrarily, cannot, it seems, act in ways that *it* thinks should be in its subjects' interest; that is, paternalistic interference would seem to violate freedom as nondomination.[41] In his criticism of deliberative democracy with regard to what he calls the discursive dilemma, however, Pettit says that in his republicanism, "collective rationality is prized over responsiveness to individual views." He sees this as meaning that "the deliberative aspect is given priority over the democratic."[42] Thus for Pettit it is possible to separate the issue of truth or rightness in politics from the procedure that establishes it. There is a tension between the voluntaristic and the epistemic element in his theory, between whether what is required for freedom from domination is that the interference one is subjected to must be: (1) one that one sees as being in one's interest or in accordance with one's preferences, or (2) one that could be seen as being in the common interest from some objective perspective. The advantage of the first perspective is that people themselves determine and know whether or not they are dominated; the advantage of the second is presumably its epistemic quality, that is, that it gets it right. But Pettit does not reconcile the two; they stand as two separate desiderata. My overall argument in this book is that the idea of deliberative democracy should not be seen as aiming to combine two separate desiderata of deliberativeness and responsiveness. The issue of responsiveness cannot be seen as being independent of the process by which the opinions that decisions should respond to are formed. The opinions decision makers should be responsive to are those that result from public deliberation. Decision makers are responsive *and* deliberative when they engage the reasons that are generated in society-wide deliberations. Pettit's view, that there is a collective rationality over and above individual views, entails that some have privileged access to truth.

To recapitulate, for Pettit democracy is related to freedom because it is a form of government forced to track people's interests. But that is too simple and one-dimensional. We do not need only democratic institutions that are forced to track people's interests; we should aspire to a democracy where the common interests on which political decisions are based are themselves products of free interest-interpreting and opinion-forming processes. The latter should be a key reason for promoting a more deliberative democracy, and to understand and emphasize this we need a more complex theory of freedom, one that also includes the dimension of freedom that I call internal autonomy. This theory must include the possibility that freedom can be limited not only by directly interpersonal relations but also by the basic structure of society, as I argued in the first section of this chapter, for different but related reasons.

2. The intrinsic properties of the process. A second objection to construing the issue of whether an interference is arbitrary and compromises freedom as a matter of fact determinable by others on our behalf is that it disregards the *intrinsic* properties of the process that will determine when our freedom is violated. In Pettit's view, what matters for our freedom is that the interference we experience, that is, the laws he admits that condition our freedom, must conform to our common interests. He neglects that the process aimed at determining the latter might itself be seen as violating freedom. And he rejects the possibility that the process of determining what our common interests are, if all affected were able to participate in it, could itself be an important exercise and expression of freedom.

There are several elements to this point. First, if the process of determining which interests are common is not one that includes actual participation by all those affected, then it will not give people the possibility of clarifying their individual interests on the basis of insights gained in free deliberation, and hence to form them freely. Second, without actual participation in determining which interests are common and should become the basis of coercive law, the subjects will not be able to see these as expressions of their own contributions and opinions, and hence as an expression of their own freedom as discursive subjects. Consequently, Pettit's position neglects the intersubjective *status* that can be gained only by being recognized as a person who is not only worth listening to but also whose opinions are given actual influence in determining when her own freedom is violated (see the section "Discursive Status and Recognition"). Third, disregarding the process is to assume that it does not matter for our freedom *who* does the tracking of interests. This third dimension of freedom regards the subject's acceptance of interference: in order not to be an affront to my freedom, an interference must be one that I own, that is, one I can see as self-imposed and not an alien force imposed from without. For Pettit it is sufficient for my freedom that the interference I experience is one that conforms to my interests, but this view underestimates the importance of my ability to determine this and my ability to participate in the justification of interference (see the sections "Which Interests Should Be Tracked?" and "Common Knowledge").

The Intrinsic Relationship between Democracy and Freedom

The objections to the idea of contestatory democracy in the preceding section show, if valid, both that it is an untenable view of democracy and that democracy is not merely instrumental to freedom as nondomination. Let me summarize my argument why democracy is intrinsic to Pettit's own conception of nondomination. First, we cannot separate the common interest from the procedure that establishes what it is. Second, we need a normative theory of which procedures constitute a legitimate way of forming and determining the common interest. Third, this theory itself is part of the conception of freedom. Fourth, this theory should be a theory of (deliberative) democracy. Therefore, since the "not all" part of freedom as nondomination is dependent on an account of the common interest, democracy and freedom as nondomination are intrinsically related.

Thus Pettit's theory of democracy is part of his definition of freedom as nondomination; there *is* a definitional connection between the two. Pettit proceeds as if he has a clear definition of freedom, which is independent of democratic procedures, and it is on that basis that he regards the issue of whether freedom has been violated as a factual issue. But if the definition of nondomination is incomplete without a description of the institutions of the democratic state, then the latter cannot be seen in merely causal terms but must be part of a normative theory.[43]

Now this does not mean Pettit sees a definitional connection between freedom and democracy *in the same way* Rousseau does. Pettit's position seems to be that only the *quality* of the interference and not its *source* matters for republican freedom. In order for interference to be nondominating it must have the quality of tracking the interests of the interferee, but the issue of self-imposition has no internal connection to republican freedom. Pettit is more concerned with government *for* the people than government *by* the people. Democracy does not require that the people be in active but only in passive control, which means their "preferences, if not [their] choices, are privileged."[44] The mechanisms of democratic control that he favors "ensure not that ordinary people dictate what policies will be selected and applied but that the policies selected and applied will conform to people's common, recognizable interests."[45] Participation and self-imposition might help secure that common interests are tracked, the argument must go, but in itself it contributes nothing to freedom. I find that unconvincing. Suppose that state action fails to track common interests because the process is fallible. Is there not a way in which it contributes to our freedom if we in some sense were authors of the interference? Pettit sees freedom as defined by the *security* against arbitrary interference, and this security, he believes, is attained by democratic institutions that track common interests. But clearly there are no perfectly reliable democratic procedures. The epistemic fallibility of democratic procedures is partly mitigated, I think, by the fact that they are the result of our own fallibility.

Think about it this way: We are concerned, respectively, with three different dimensions of freedom, when we ask about the quantity, the quality, and the source of interference. These are the concerns, respectively, of a Berlinian liberal, Pettit's republican, and a Rousseauian. When Pettit denies that republican freedom is definitionally connected to self-government, he reduces the connection between democracy and freedom to a matter of the quality of the interference. One problem with this is that it entails that there is *no* benefit in terms of freedom to being a participant in self-government if it does not secure that the result has the right quality. If our perceived common interests are not tracked, then it makes no difference whether the source of interference was ourselves or a dictator.

Paradoxically, if we applied the same idea to an individual, then we would arrive at a positive conception of freedom (in one of Berlin's senses of the concept[46]). We would have to say that an individual who makes a choice that does not promote her interests as she perceives them would not be free in any sense, that is, the fact that she made the choice does not contribute to her freedom. True, positive freedom usually is seen as promoting not merely perceived interests but objective interests; however, it is possible for a person to make choices that go against even her perceived interests; as such, she may be seen as lacking positive freedom in a sense. It is in this sense that Pettit's account of nondominating interference turns out to entail a positive conception of freedom: One is free if and only if the interference promotes one's interests as one sees them. Paradoxically, if he had accepted that it contributes to the freedom of citizens to be participants in collective self-legislation, then this would have mitigated the paternalist danger of the positive dimension of freedom involved in the exclusive focus on the quality of the interference. The dimension of enjoying public autonomy upholds the importance of willing and choosing, which is lacking in the objectivist idea of tracking interests.

To clarify, I am not criticizing Pettit for suggesting that political institutions be designed so they improve the quality of the laws; obviously that also is the aim of deliberative democracy. And when I say that this implies a positive conception of freedom, it is not a reproach, though it does go against Pettit's claim that republicanism does not promote a positive conception of freedom. My point at this juncture is that this dimension of freedom is not all democracy can and should aim for. Pettit's shunning of positive freedom and his rejection of the idea that public autonomy is a dimension of freedom only create problems. Democracy should not merely be designed to give the laws a certain quality but also to secure that their source in some sense is the people as a whole. The latter is one of the ways Berlin defines positive freedom, but we have seen here that the idea of freedom as public autonomy can substitute for another positive conception of freedom, the idea that freedom means that the government enacts laws of a certain quality. The overall argument of this book is that the aim should be to include both dimensions of freedom: deliberative democracy requires both that the laws are self-given and that they have a certain quality. This distinction shows that we can separate freedom as public autonomy (relating to the source of the law) and freedom as status (relating to the quality of the law); however, as I argue later, status concerns more than the quality of the law. Pace Pettit, even if the quality of the decisions leaves something to be desired, the fact that they are made by those to whom they apply does contribute to their freedom. Thus I see two general reasons citizens would not see state interference as compromising their freedom: they see it as justified because it corresponds to their view of what is in the common interest, and they see it as legitimate because they have participated in the making of the law.

Pettit runs into contradictions by attempting to distance his conception of freedom both from Berlin's noninterference and from positive conceptions of freedom. He claims that nondomination is not merely a matter of *promoting* noninterference, otherwise he would not have an *alternative* conception of freedom, but the composite value of noninterference and security.[47] Pettit distinguishes nondomination from noninterference by insisting that the institutions that secure against arbitrary noninterference are not merely means to an end but part of the simple value of nondomination (R, 46, 73 ff., 86 ff.). However, as we have seen, in order to distinguish his theory from the positive freedom tradition, he claims that *democracy* is only a means of furthering liberty. But if democracy is a main republican institution, then this cannot be right. He cannot have it both ways—either republican institutions are means to an end, or they are intrinsic to freedom. In sum, it is only if Pettit can show that institutions are not merely external safeguards of noninterference that he can distinguish his conception of freedom from Berlin's, but by doing this he also must accept that democracy is intrinsic to freedom as nondomination.

The Status of Living among Others

The only positive dimension to freedom as nondomination that Pettit allows for is the requirement of the *presence of security* against interference on an arbitrary basis; the positive dimensions involved in participating in self-government are rejected as external to the conception (R, 51, 27 ff.). Nevertheless, freedom as nondomination is seen by Pettit as a social or civil freedom; it is "the status associated with living among other people, none of whom dominates you" (R, 66). Pettit thinks this constitutes another contrast to freedom as noninterference, which, he says, may be enjoyed in isolation. But he is smuggling in a dimension that is not part of his definition of nondomination. If I live in complete isolation, then clearly no one will have the capacity to arbitrarily interfere with me, and I might have the greatest possible imaginable security against such interference—a security I could never achieve in society. Pettit seems implicitly to realize the point. "Nondomination, *as that is valued* in the republican tradition, means the absence of domination in the presence of other people, not the absence of domination gained by isolation" (R, 66, emphasis added).[48] Thus he has not shown that the social dimension constitutes a *definitional* difference to freedom as noninterference. A proponent of the latter conception could equally say that she is concerned with and values only the noninterference enjoyed among others (e.g., that gained by having a right against interference in a certain area). Thus Milton Friedman writes, "As liberals, we take freedom of the individual . . . as our ultimate goal in judging social arrangements. Freedom as a value in this sense has to do with the interrelations among people; it has no meaning whatsoever to a Robinson Crusoe on an isolated island."[49] To be sure, someone who values noninterference rather than merely nondomination might be more inclined to prefer the heath to the city, since any and all interference is seen by her as compromising her freedom. For the person who values nondomination, living among other people is not such a threat, since it is possible to live under common laws without being dominated and unfree. This is an important difference, but it does not show that it would be better in terms of nondomination to live in the presence of other people than to live in isolation.

Pettit is promoting a fuller conception of freedom than is presented by his strict definition. This is a conception of freedom that involves not only nondomination or security against arbitrary interference but also the recognition of one's *status* as an equal and a free person who shares a common, human-made world with others. The nondomination that concerns him exists neither by isolation nor by default but "by virtue of social design" (R, 67). The added condition that nondomination must be a matter of social design is not directly explained, but clearly it cannot be derived from the condition of security alone. It could be explained in terms of a conception of intersubjective status and recognition. The person who enjoys nondomination in isolation is perfectly secure, but she does not enjoy intersubjective status or recognition. Being a member of a legal regime designed to protect you against domination, in contrast, does involve recognition of you as a free person with equal social status. But in order to make the last point part of a theory of freedom, we need either a fuller conception of freedom or the addition of other dimensions of freedom, none of which are integrated in Pettit's republican theory.

If Pettit had not decided that Hannah Arendt is not a real republican, then he could have found in her work a valuable distinction between liberation and freedom.[50] One of the distinguishing features of Arendt's understanding of freedom is the idea that we can experience it only among other people.[51] This intersubjective element distinguishes freedom from liberation. Freedom depends on the presence of institutions—on law, a constitution—and on the presence of other human beings, both of which liberation can be without. I can achieve liberation from oppression by fleeing to an uninhabited island, but that does not make me free. Arendt says, "The status of freedom [does] not follow automatically upon the act of liberation. Freedom need[s], in addition to liberation, the company of other men who [are] in the same state, and it need[s] a common public space to meet them—a politically organized world, in other words, into which each of the free men [can] insert himself by word and deed."[52]

For Arendt, thus, freedom is a form of status that we can achieve only in an institutional setting. The best description of what it means to lack such a status we find in the discussion of stateless persons in *The Origins of Totalitarianism*. The stateless person is a person without status. She is liberated from oppression and might be seen as negatively free—and as free from domination. But such a person also is deprived "of a place in the world which makes opinions significant and actions effective."[53] By distinguishing freedom from liberation, Arendt both perceives negative freedom as a necessary condition of freedom and makes the presence of others a precondition or even a part of freedom. She makes clear to us a dimension of freedom that emphasizes the importance of the presence of others. Of course, it is not sufficient that others are present physically; our common presence must be of a specific kind. This kind of presence is one in which we are not merely negatively free to speak and act, but where our speech and action are heard and seen and have an effect upon our common world. In other words, it is a presence of common political action. As such, Arendt explicates a dimension of freedom, freedom as praxis, that shows the *intrinsic* value of political action in terms of freedom. Pettit rejects, as mentioned, that political participation has any such "independent attractions," in addition to its instrumental role in furthering freedom as nondomination. But for this reason he also lacks a reason for seeing freedom achieved in the presence of others as superior to freedom achieved by isolation. The problem here is again Pettit's one-dimensional approach to freedom.

Actually, Pettit does speak of something that comes close to Arendt's conception of freedom. In *Republicanism*, he says, "To be a person is to be a voice that cannot be ignored, a voice which speaks to issues raised in common with others and which speaks with authority . . . to be taken as someone worth listening to" (R, 91). This dimension of freedom is elaborated on in *A Theory of Freedom*, in which freedom as discursive control is described as a form of psychological freedom or as "freedom in the agent." In the political realm, this freedom is respected when citizens enjoy "discursive status," and Pettit claims that freedom as nondomination gives recognition to all as discursive subjects (TF, 91, 103, 139). In the recent "Discourse Theory and Republican Freedom," discursive status is connected to a view of the person as a discursive being. The discourse-theoretic image of persons, which Pettit attributes to Habermas, means that their beliefs and desires cannot be seen as given but "evolve under the influence of discourse with one another."[54] We recognize each other as discursive beings, as persons with discursive status, when we seek to influence each other only through reasons, when we see each other as responsive to reasons rather than to mere force.

My question is whether democracy can be seen as merely instru-mental to discursive status or whether it shows that democratic participa-tion has intrinsic value. To be consistent, Pettit would have to hold the former view. The relationship he sees between democracy and discursive status is as follows: Democracy not only tracks interests but should do so in a way that can be discursively challenged by the citizens; only with democratic governments can one raise claims based on reasons.[55] The nonarbitrary interference of democracies "does not take in any way from their status as subjects capable of commanding a discursive hearing in relationships with others."[56] But is it not rather the case that democracy *gives* citizens such a capability and such a standing? Discursive capability and status are not properties persons have independently of society and that government can protect the individual enjoyment of in a purely external fashion. Rather, discursive capability and status are attributes that can develop only in the presence of others and can only be fully realized when our interaction is guided by rules that are discursively justified. It is by living in a democracy—in particular, a democracy that promotes public deliberation—that we become citizens whose opinions matter and to whom reasons for interference must be given and taken. It is as participators in deliberative politics that we have discursive status in relation to the law; it is part of our public role as citizens. If this is not an intrinsic value of political participation, then no one sees democracy as anything but instrumental.

It might be that Pettit and I understand the idea that democracy is merely instrumental to freedom in different ways. The important point for me is that democracy can be seen as related to freedom in a way that goes beyond the liberal understanding (as a protection of a freedom that is understood, defined, and capable of being enjoyed independently of democratic processes). When Pettit and others reject the dimensions of freedom otherwise associated with republicanism, they eradicate what is distinctive about the tradition and what sets it apart from liberalism. They also obscure the idea that the freedom we enjoy in society is a *transformed* freedom, a freedom the meaning and extent of which we cannot establish and understand except as members of a democratic society. Democracy not merely protects freedom but transforms our understanding of freedom.[57] Deliberative democracy sees this transformation as a learning process that takes place intersubjectively.

My claim is not that we can treat each other only as discursive subjects in explicitly political or official interaction; that would clearly be false.[58] However, only in democracies—and only in democracies where political decisions in the final analysis are based on reasons rather than mere force (bargaining based on threats or voting without prior reason giving)—do citizens *fully* grant each other the status of persons that can be interfered with only for reasons that have been discursively tested. Treating each other as discursive subjects is part of the ethos of a deliberative democracy.

Discursive status clearly goes beyond the quality of the law, beyond both security against arbitrary interference and the tracking of interests, to a matter of the process of justifying and making law. Now the point is not that this is wrong in itself. Indeed, deliberative freedom includes a dimension of freedom that is related to the properties of the process that tracks or, as I prefer, constructs common interests. The point is, this means there *are* independent attractions in terms of freedom to being a participant in self-legislation (of a certain kind), and this involves a commitment to dimensions of freedom often associated with republican political theory but rejected by Skinner and Pettit.

The standard liberal objection to the Arendtian view of freedom—to the idea of freedom as praxis and the intrinsic value of political participation—is that it relies on an untenable perfectionism of political action as constituting a happy and fulfilling life. It is easy to ridicule the idea that going to endless meetings should be a good life, and it is important that individuals be free to define their own conception of what the good life is. But these objections sidestep the more profound point in Arendt. This underlying point is that we can develop our human capacities only in society, and included among these is our capacity for free action. There are a number of different ways in which living in society and specifically a democratic society is required for freedom. The very idea of freedom develops only in society, our capacity for choosing our own conception of the good is a product of society, and only the presence of others makes our exercise of many freedoms meaningful. It would take us too far afield to go into an argument for these assertions here.[59] My point is that they also must underlie Pettit's view, and that they imply that living in a democratic society is not merely a means to freedom but is *part of freedom*. If it is accepted that living in a democratic society is necessary for understanding freedom and acting freely, then it also must be accepted that democratic participation has independent attractions. We cannot separate the idea of freedom from democratic self-rule, as Pettit does when he sees democracy as merely instrumental to nondomination, for living in a democratic society is part of what it means to be free; it is part of the experience of being a free person.

Now all this does not mean that devoting all one's time to participating in politics is the only way to be free, and that this is the highest and only good. I see freedom as praxis as only a dimension or an aspect of deliberative freedom. A society that does not afford this opportunity will be less free than one that does. It is true that this dimension of freedom relies on a certain view of the person, of what it is to be a human being. But that is true of any theory of freedom, as I argued in Chapter 1. The view of the human being that my argument in this book relies upon, however, does not reduce the human being to someone who finds value and freedom only in political participation. However, I do claim that only as members of a society where we see our freedom both as a part and product of discursive interaction with each other and law as based on that interaction can we be free. On this view, political participation is intrinsic to some of our freedom and instrumental to other dimensions. When democracy is seen as being only instrumental to freedom, some of the dimensions of freedom remain hidden—we end up with an impoverished conception of freedom.

Deliberative Democracy beyond Republicanism

In this section I elaborate on the argument that nondomination presupposes a more participatory and deliberative model of democracy than Pettit's favors, and that this model of democracy in turn presupposes more dimensions of freedom than nondomination. The argument refers to three different issues: common interests, common knowledge, and discursive status.

Which Interests Should Be Tracked?

Ealier I noted some problems in Pettit's account of the formation of interests. First, he neglects the possibility of manipulated interests and the importance of internal autonomy. Second, I spelled out a tension between two understandings of common interests: (1) one based on citizens' own views; and (2) one based on some objective perspective. These are issues that the theory of deliberative democracy properly understood is especially well equipped to deal with. Deliberative democracy should be able to overcome the tension between common interests as people see them and some ideal of what is required for an interest to be common or, in other words, to combine some form of voluntarism with an epistemic aim. As I see it, a decision is legitimate if it is the product of the give-and-take of the deliberative process. Such a decision will not be merely the imposition of an arbitrary will, since it is the product of a process where reasons are given and the result is the product of a learning process. The result of the deliberative process is voluntaristic, in the sense that it represents something that the participants actually have been convinced is in their own common interest. It has epistemic quality because the procedure is seen as having epistemic value in being free of any force except that of the best arguments.[60] Thus the result is not merely any perceived common interest but the interest we perceive as being common on the basis of intersubjectively tested reasons.

This reconciliation of a voluntaristic and an epistemic dimension requires that we see legitimate results in a proceduralist rather than a substantive manner. Proceduralism means that we see results as legitimate if they are the results of a certain procedure, as opposed to fitting some objectively given standard. In David Estlund's terms, I am arguing here for "epistemic proceduralism" rather than a "correctness theory." According to correctness theory, outcomes are legitimate if they are correct measured against an already given standard, while epistemic proceduralism "holds that the outcome is legitimate even when it is incorrect, owing to the epistemic value, albeit imperfect, of the democratic procedure."[61] When we submit to a procedure that has epistemic value, it is because we believe it "to be epistemically the best among those that are better than random."[62] In the terms I used earlier, epistemic proceduralism combines a concern for the quality of law with a commitment to the idea that its source must be the people as a whole. The freedom of the people depends on both the epistemic properties of the procedure and the procedure involving a form of self-government. Pettit subscribes to a correctness theory insofar as he thinks that there is a procedure-independent standard that can establish whether interference is arbitrary or not. I have argued for a procedural view not only because it includes a commitment to self-government but also because the result that we are looking for cannot be seen as independent of the procedure that establishes it. Because procedures affect interests, we must be concerned with the former if we are concerned with the latter. *There is no normatively defensible common interest except the one that is created through common deliberative practices aimed at establishing it.*

The procedural view has the advantage of incorporating the other dimensions of freedom that together constitute overall deliberative freedom. First, included in the description of a procedure with epistemic value is what is required for interests to be interpreted and opinions formed in a free manner, for only if the process is free is everything but the force of the better argument excluded (internal autonomy). Second, as participants in this process, we recognize each other as persons worth arguing with, as reasons givers and takers, which I see as the specific status that citizens gain from living in a deliberative democracy (discursive status). Third, only the results of deliberative practices in which we were able to take part will be the basis of law, that is, only those laws we have been able to participate in the creation of are legitimate (public autonomy).

Common Knowledge

Both the statuses of being dominated and being nondominated require that the subject have knowledge of her status (see the first section in this chapter). If the subject of domination does not know that another person has the capacity to interfere with her and that person never exercises that capacity, then it is not clear how it would affect her actions or freedom, and the nondominated person also must know that the laws to which she is subject are not arbitrary. If the citizens do not know whether or not the laws to which they are subject are arbitrary, then one form of interference can be as good as any other *for them*. This point is not integrated in Pettit but requires a theory of freedom and democracy that shows the internal relationship between freedom, participation, and knowledge. Common knowledge goes beyond the three conditions of nondomination, cited earlier. Pettit says only that "non-domination will also tend to connect with common awareness" (R, 70). In contrast, I would say that the common knowledge that is required for enjoying nondomination and the discursive status related to its generation are among the *independent attractions* of being a participant in deliberative processes of self-legislation; they are part of such processes. Again, there is a dimension of freedom that is intrinsic to political participation.

The point that lacking or enjoying freedom as nondomination requires common knowledge is something we can determine only from a participant perspective. And regarding questions of political freedom, it is the participant perspective that has priority. Even if it could be ascertained from an objective perspective whether or not someone enjoys the status of nondomination, this would be inconsequential if the subject, from her own perspective, did not share the knowledge that that was the case. For her there would be no difference between forms of interference that merely condition her freedom and those that compromise it—and the appeal of freedom as nondomination lies exactly in the idea that it does matter how the subject sees her situation. This point gives us a good reason from the value of nondomination to be in favor of deliberative democracy, and not just of any model of deliberative democracy, but one that involves widespread participation in public deliberation affecting the making of law, one that sees the source of law as a crucial dimension of freedom. Only as participants in public deliberation can we gain insight into whether or not the laws to which we are subject are arbitrary, whether or not we are dominated.

The issue of whether or not a law is arbitrary is an epistemic one for both Pettit and me, that is, an issue that has a right and a wrong answer. I suggest that the rightness of a political decision gains its full significance for freedom only if we, the citizens, know it to have this quality. The role of public deliberation in this connection is not merely the best heuristic device for determining which laws are nonarbitrary but is just as much a way in which *each citizen* can get to know this. In other words, it is not merely a matter of the polity getting it right but also of individuals having the opportunity to achieve insights. The latter aspect of deliberation falls out of view in Pettit's account, because he does not see freedom as being intrinsically connected to political participation.

The institutional consequence of my argument is that legislative power should not be given to independent bodies that are not open for political participation by ordinary citizens. A decision made by an independent body would have to be made into law in order to be implemented. But for the citizens who have been excluded from the process of deliberation, and who therefore have not had the opportunity to gain the insights that these laws embody, these laws will present themselves *only* as a coercive force.[63] The *fact* that a political decision is just and wise is not sufficient to make us free. It is not only the content but also the genesis of law that matters for freedom, not only its quality but also its source. A decision that is just would not be an expression of *my* freedom if I did not know it was just, or at least knew why others found it just and justified it as such to me. In the absence of my agreement, a law would be mere force if I were not convinced that the procedure of which it was the product was the best one for determining what is just and for giving the participants insights into what is just. My submission to it would be a submission to an external authority. I have to have the opportunity to learn whether the law is just or not in a process where reasons are given to and by me, if the law is to be anything but an alien imposition upon my will.[64] Only when we have the opportunity to learn in public deliberation—and public deliberation effectively influences lawmaking—will we be able to see the law as more than a matter of outward force, as embodying as well reasons and insights.

Pettit does see the importance of common knowledge, but he believes that it is sufficient that deliberations of official bodies be public so citizens can achieve necessary insights. When he speaks of deliberative democracy, he mainly speaks of the importance of deliberation of *official* bodies, not of society-wide deliberation. And when he does speak of deliberation in society as a whole, he speaks only of these as *reactions* to official deliberations (R, 187 ff.; TF, 168).[65] The purpose of what Pettit calls deliberative democracy, that is, of official deliberations, is to allow for contestation. For people to know whether to contest, they must know the grounds of the decisions made by others (R, 187–90).[66] According to Pettit, then, the decisive factor in order for a law not to feel like an "alien restraint" is not that one has made it but that it has not been challenged in a potential ex post facto process of contestation (R, 253). People are self-ruling not by making law but through their ability to contest law (R, 186).

To be sure, deliberation among public officials is important. But there is a problem with limiting deliberation to this part of the democratic process. As already mentioned, it presupposes that there is a truth that can be determined, and that it is independent of the process that finds it. Now if this truth is the one that *would* have emerged if people had actually deliberated, and hence is the truth about the common interests that *would* have emerged when people had become clearer about what their own interests were, then it is difficult to understand how they would be able to recognize this merely from listening to or reading the proceedings of some impartial body. It is unclear why people would not see laws determined by others as alien restraints if these laws represent common interests that would only exist if the citizens themselves had been through a process of learning, when this process did not actually take place. The clarification of one's own interests and opinions that takes place when one actually participates in public deliberation can hardly be substituted by understanding the grounds of the decisions of others.

Discursive Status and Recognition

Pettit's idea of discursive status entails that there is indeed an independent attraction to the democratic process. However, for Pettit we do not acquire this status from democratic participation. In *A Theory of Freedom*, in which Pettit gives the most elaborate account of what it means to be recognized as a person with a certain status, it becomes clear that the recognition of status happens from above, by the state. The state will "respect the freedom of its citizens, *giving* them a free, undominated status" (TF, 173, emphasis added). From a deliberative perspective, it is especially interesting how Pettit understands *discursive* status. Again, it is in the hands of the state, which he says should "effectively recognize those over whom it claims authority as discursive subjects" (TF, 139). So how does it do that? By securing "that people have discursive reason to endorse [state] action" (TF, 139). But to have discursive reason to endorse something is not the same as having endorsed something on the basis of reasons actually given in a discourse in which one was able to contribute one's own views and to question those of others. Pettit is here formulating a view that comes close to that of some self-described deliberative democrats—the Rawlsians—for whom it is sufficient for public decisions to be based on arguments that we "*could* reasonably expect others *might* endorse."[67] Chapter 4 argues that this view requires people to know prediscursively what is reasonable, and hence the need for public deliberation is preempted[68]; here I focus on Pettit's state-centered approach and its consequences for our status as discursive subjects. In Pettit, it is the state that must give reasons that others can reasonably be expected to endorse. But such an objective, state-centered view is not, I think, sufficient to establish the freedom as discursive status that Pettit himself wants to promote.

In order to establish freedom as discursive status, the status of a person worth talking and listening to, more is required than that the state recognize us as such. The problem with the way in which Pettit views the state and recognition is that he sees them as something external to our own discursive or deliberative practices. For him, citizens are treated as having discursive control if the state gives reasons for the way in which it acts and gives the possibility of contesting its decisions. I, in contrast, do not think we can come to enjoy status as discursive subjects unless we have the opportunity to actually participate in the deliberative practices on the basis of which political decisions are made; discursive status is exactly the type of independent attraction of political participation that republicans have stressed but that Pettit rejects. There are three aspects to this argument. First, there must be actual participation in deliberative processes in which we can show ourselves to each other as subjects capable of giving and responding to reasons. As Pettit himself notes, but without drawing the necessary conclusions, "The more that a person is involved in the exercise of discourse with others, the more will the relational capacity [to discourse] be recognized as a matter of common awareness. And the more it is recognized as a matter of common awareness, the stronger and surer it will become" (TF, 71). Second, these processes must not be a mere charade but must have actual influence on the conditions under which we live. Third, these processes must secure that we live under laws that we have participated in the genesis of, that is, status presupposes being a participant in self-legislation. (The last point does not mean that status is *the same as* being a participant in self-legislation. Neither of the two dimensions of freedom can be reduced to the other.)

These three points are based on the proposition that what is required for discursive status is not merely that you have discursive reason to endorse something (Pettit's view), but that you have actually endorsed something on the basis of an actual discourse in which you were able to take part. Suffice it to give two reasons for this proposition here. First, it is not possible for anyone to *know* what we have discursive reason to endorse without actual processes of deliberation by all those affected. This is the underlying epistemic assumption. Second, the form of recognition that we experience when we are told that we have discursive reason to endorse some policy but do not have the opportunity to take part in the process of formulating that law could turn into state paternalism. We are recognized as being able to understand reasons given by others on Pettit's model, but not as contributors to the deliberations in which reasons are found and decisions are made.

The recognition that takes place under conditions of a more participatory model of deliberative democracy differs from the way in which Pettit envisions the objective recognition by the state. First, there is a recognition that does not involve the state at all. This is the recognition that results from participating in common deliberation about matters of common concern. Such deliberations might have the state as its final addressee, if the state is the agency we wish to implement our demands, but we also might want to solve the issues raised by other means, more local or more global. This is a horizontal model of recognition, as opposed to Pettit's vertical one. Second, the recognition that does involve the state is here seen in a different manner or from a different perspective. We might want to use the state to recognize our equal status as citizens, as bearers of civil, political, and social rights. But the state here is an agency through which we act. We recognize each other through the state. This recognition is an intersubjective and a participatory recognition, as opposed to the objective recognition from without that Pettit envisions.

Conclusion

This chapter has discussed whether or not freedom as nondomination is a viable and sufficient conception of freedom for deliberative democracy. I have shown that without modifications and additions, it is neither. The ideal of public deliberation presupposes in addition to that no one has a capacity to arbitrarily interfere with someone else, dimensions of freedom that are not merely negative, namely, internal and public autonomy.

The main idea I would like to take from republicanism and incorporate into the idea of deliberative freedom is that *freedom is a form of status*, in particular, the idea that it connotes *discursive status*. But I would like to suggest a conception of freedom as status that goes beyond Pettit's formulation. For Pettit, we enjoy an undominated status, that is, the status of being free, when the law has the quality of tracking our interests, and we enjoy discursive status when we have discursive reason to endorse state action: status, thus, is reduced to a matter relating to our role as subjects of law. I have argued that discursive status also must be seen in relation to our role as active participants in making law. Democracy is not merely instrumental to discursive status; rather, it is constitutive of it. Thus it is wrong to see status in merely negative terms while rejecting the dimensions of freedom relating to participating in democratic politics and to being part of processes of self-legislation. These dimensions of freedom must be *added* to a merely negative formulation. When we see that discursive status depends on other dimensions of freedom, the understanding of this status itself also must be modified.

We need a more active or praxis-oriented notion of discursive status than what we find in Pettit. I also have given epistemic reasons for this. Citizens can only enjoy the status of being undominated if they have knowledge of it, and this knowledge they can gain only as participants who not only are given reasons for state interference but who are able to give reasons of their own. Citizens are treated as being capable of giving and responding to reasons only when they have the opportunity of being active participants in self-legislation. Thus I see discursive status as combining an interest in the quality of the law with an interest in how we treat each other as cocitizens and makers of the law.

It is sometimes argued that status is not a conception of freedom at all. Recall that I am not claiming that status is a conception of freedom but rather that it is one dimension of freedom among others that together form the conception of freedom that I call deliberative freedom. It could be argued, however, that it is not even a dimension of freedom. I cannot respond to this objection before I have more fully developed the idea of deliberative freedom; I will return to the issue in Chapter 8.

Like the liberal tradition discussed in Chapter 1, republicanism fails to see the full importance for freedom of the instrumental and intrinsic dimensions of deliberative democratic politics. It is not only that both traditions fail to recognize the different dimensions of freedom, though it is that too, but also that their respective conceptions of freedom are incomplete. As negative conceptions of freedom, both liberal freedom as noninterference and republican freedom as nondomination are dependent on a procedure that can establish what the boundaries of this negative freedom must be. I see it as the epistemic-instrumental dimension of democratic politics to elaborate what negative freedom means and what its boundaries should be in particular cases. But it is crucial that the democratic procedure not itself be one that undermines the freedom of which it seeks to construct shared understanding. The intrinsic properties of the process that determines when our freedom is violated matter for that very freedom. The instrumental dimension of democratic political procedures, therefore, cannot stand alone but must be combined with a concern for their intrinsic qualities. I have argued that procedures of deliberative politics have important intrinsic qualities, qualities that both liberals and republicans to be consistent also should be concerned about. Procedures of public deliberation help identify the justifiable forms of negative liberty in a noncoercive way (something liberalism demands but fails to explain how to obtain). And they give each equal status as a discursive subject (something Pettit calls for but his model of democracy fails to supply). The procedures of deliberative politics must give citizens both the opportunity of gaining and expressing freedom and a way of establishing the epistemic quality of the laws they give to themselves.

CHAPTER THREE

Preferences and Paternalism

*B*oth the liberal and the republican traditions focus on the external dimensions of freedom or freedom of action. Because deliberative democrats are concerned with the *formation* of the opinions that are the foundation of democratic legitimacy, they cannot model their view of political freedom purely on the basis of negative freedom, neither in its liberal or republican formulation. This does not mean that deliberative democracy can do without an idea of negative freedom. Rather, other dimensions of freedom are required, both in addition to negative freedom and in order to determine the meaning and extent of this negative freedom. As we saw in Chapter 1, the negative freedom tradition sees freedom as a matter of absence of interference with what the individual wishes or has a desire to do. Negative freedom is only concerned with whether there are any external obstructions to the individual *acting* on her desires or preferences. How and why the individual has come to have the desires and preferences she has is of no concern from the perspective of negative freedom. The republican conception of freedom discussed in Chapter 2 did not bring us closer to a theory of freedom and democracy that includes an understanding of free preference formation—though it pointed to the idea of status as an important dimension of freedom and thereby took us a step beyond negative freedom. For deliberative democrats, in contrast, the issue of the origins of our political preferences or opinions is of prime importance.[1] The deliberative conception of freedom cannot merely be concerned with freedom of action but must be concerned also with whether the preferences and opinions on the basis of which political decisions are made are formed freely.

An important aspect of the critical edge of the theory of deliberative democracy is that it problematizes the status of the preferences or opinions people happen to have. It does not regard preferences and interests as brute facts that uncritically and unreflectively can serve as input to legitimate democratic decision making. It thematizes both the possibility that preferences can be nonautonomously formed, and that they may be unjustifiable to others in public deliberation.[2] The first issue brings into the picture a dimension of freedom, which has played a crucial role in the development of the theory of deliberative democracy. A main assumption in this development has been that the formation of preferences is endogenous to social conditions and political institutions. It is for this reason we should go beyond seeing the democratic process merely as one of aggregating preferences. But the point is *not* substituting transformation for aggregation of preferences. The point is that transformation is inevitable. What makes the difference normatively is *what kind* of transformation political preferences undergo in the political process. There is an underlying concern here that can best be expressed in terms of a theory of freedom. The concern for how and under what conditions our political preferences are formed is a concern for internal autonomy.[3]

This chapter highlights the importance of the issue of autonomous preference formation, while showing some pitfalls in focusing exclusively on this dimension of freedom. For this purpose, a critical analysis of the works of Jon Elster and Cass Sunstein is most instructive. Elster and Sunstein give the issue of autonomous preference formation center stage. They both explicitly aim to clarify conceptions of autonomy that can be coupled with the theory of deliberative democracy. Not all proponents of deliberative democracy follow either of the two directly, but I believe that the two represent exemplary articulations of the idea that democratic theory should be concerned not merely with aggregation but also with the transformation of preferences that underlies most versions of deliberative democracy.[4] The idea of endogenous preference formation, which is at the center of both Elster's and Sunstein's theories, is the key to that contrast. The connection between this idea and a conception of overall deliberative freedom needs to be clarified.

By analyzing Elster's and Sunstein's theories from the perspective of a theory incorporating multiple dimensions of freedom, we can see that what they regard as necessary in order that preferences are not adaptive runs counter to some other ideas of what freedom requires. I show how Elster's and Sunstein's theories of adaptive preference formation need to be modified and integrated into a complex theory of deliberative freedom, where autonomous preference formation is regarded as only one dimension of freedom among others. I concentrate on two other dimensions of freedom that autonomous preference formation must be seen in relation to, particularly if we want to avoid charges of paternalism. The first complementary dimension of freedom is the status conception of freedom, the importance of which the republican tradition, discussed in the preceding chapter, has pointed to. Freedom as status refers to the treatment of each other as capable of giving and responding to reasons in the process of public deliberation. The other complementary dimension is the freedom of being subject only to laws that are the product of deliberative processes in which one were able to take part, that is, public autonomy or freedom as being a participant in collective self-legislation.[5]

Nonautonomously Formed Preferences

Both Elster and Sunstein have done some important work on autonomous preferences,[6] or, actually, I should say on nonautonomous preferences. There has been much more theorizing about the negative case of adaptive preferences than the positive case of autonomous preferences.[7] The work done on adaptive preference formation is an important step in clarifying one of the dimensions of freedom that public deliberation presupposes and deliberative democracy must be normatively committed to, but it does not bring us far enough. I share with Elster and Sunstein the basic idea that autonomy cannot be identical to want satisfaction because the wants may not themselves be autonomously formed. But neither of their theories gives us an understanding of autonomous preferences that can serve the purposes of a critical theory or that can be combined with a commitment to the other dimensions of freedom. In particular, the theory of adaptive preference formation involves a danger of creating a close tie between deliberative democracy and paternalism, which the commitment to multiple dimensions of freedom requires that we attempt to disentangle.

Nonconscious Preference Formation: Elster's Sour Grapes

Elster's discussion of sour grapes, or adaptive preferences, relates to discussions of deliberative democracy as a critique of the mere aggregation of preferences as the best means to determine just outcomes. The question he poses is, "Why should individual want satisfaction be the criterion of justice and social choice when individual wants themselves may be shaped by a process that preempts the choice? And in particular, why should the choice between feasible options only take account of individual preferences if people tend to adjust their aspirations to their possibilities?"[8] In other words, why care about people's choices if they have not formed their choices freely? Thus Elster is clearly concerned with a problem concerning freedom and autonomy. But it is not clear exactly what the problem for freedom is and whether there is any way around it. I want to consider here what makes adaptive preference formation detrimental to a person's freedom, but I am mainly concerned with what Elster abstains from considering, namely, what it can tell us positively about autonomous preferences.

According to Elster's definition, "*Adaptive preference formation* is the adjustment of wants to the possibilities—not the deliberate adaptation favoured by character planners, but a causal process occurring non-consciously."[9] The characteristic he highlights is that adaptive preference formation is a nonconscious process; it is not intentional but takes place behind the back of the person. Elster contrasts adaptive preference formation to character planning, as advocated by Stoic, Buddhist, or Spinozistic philosophies,[10] and he makes a "distinction between the causally induced and the intentionally engineered adaptation of preferences to possibilities."[11] The latter part of the distinction refers to character planning and is seen by Elster as "much more compatible with autonomy than are either manipulated preferences or adaptive ones,"[12] for "it is better to adapt to the inevitable through choice than by non-conscious resignation."[13]

Is Elster right that consciousness and choice *always* are better and more compatible with autonomy than nonconscious adaptation? They might be so only under certain conditions. At least the requirements of character planning do not take us far enough in order to give a positive account of autonomous preference formation—a point that Elster himself acknowledges.[14] Most seriously, the idea of character planning might be a dead end that can stand in the way of emancipation—hence hardly an idea suitable for a critical theory.

One problem with the idea of character planning is that we might not be satisfied with calling a person's preferences autonomous merely because they are consciously and reflexively formed. Like the contemporary Spinozistic theory of free will advanced by Harry Frankfurt, Elster sees autonomy as characterized by meta-preferences shaping first-order preferences.[15] Meta-preferences are reflexive preferences about which first-order preferences should be one's effective will. While a first-order preference takes the form "I want to x," a meta-preference takes the form "I want to want to x." Now it is possible that something a person does from a meta-preference is something that she was made to do by "irrelevant causal influences," that is, influences that detract from autonomy and rationality.[16] The power structures, the social norms, and even the educational system of contemporary society might be such that they make some people reflexively endorse subordinate positions and unfair treatment. So even if a person consciously endorses her preferences it does not necessarily mean that the endorsement itself is arrived at freely. The mere form of reflexivity does not contribute to freedom if there is no qualitative difference between first-order preferences and reflexive ones.[17] Elster admits that meta-preferences might themselves be adaptive,[18] but then it is not clear why their existence would contribute to freedom at all.

According to Elster, an advantage with character planning as compared to adaptive preference formation is that it makes it possible to "shape one's wants to coincide exactly with . . . one's possibilities, whereas adaptive preferences do not lend themselves to such fine-tuning."[19] Adaptive preferences tend to overshoot; that is, to adapt more than necessary, to make one want even less than is actually possible. It is important to emphasize three points here. First, character planning or adjusting one's wants to the possibilities only matters if one has knowledge of the possibilities. It is true that nonconscious preference formation excludes the possibility of fine-tuning, but being conscious does not change anything unless one has adequate knowledge of the external world. And might it not even be the case that if one is thoroughly ignorant, then one's willing adaptation could be more off the mark than a nonconscious one? Furthermore, pragmatically there is a danger in theories of character planning of becoming more interested in knowledge of the world as it is than in the world as it could be. Of course, the idea of possibilities or feasible set includes what could be the case as much as what is the case, but as my second point makes clear, character planners tend not to focus on how the external world could become if they engaged themselves in it.

Second, character planning is aimed at changing the self, not at changing the external world. As such, it is concerned with an inner freedom that is unconnected to the interpersonal and public dimensions of freedom.[20] Elster holds that character planning "could never detract from" autonomy.[21] But could it not? The Stoic view, where freedom is a matter of controlling one's self by either adapting to the world or

making oneself as independent of it as possible, might I think detract
from the possibility of forming autonomous preferences about the world.
The Stoic view of the relationship between self and external world is
characterized by resignation. Epictetus's *The Handbook*, for example, is in
the main a prescription of how to avoid disappointments. "Do not seek
to have events happen as you want them to, but instead want them to
happen as they do happen, and your life will go well."[22] But anyone who
has been politically active knows that politics is filled with failed hopes.
Deliberate political change has not been achieved by those who are afraid
that their projects might fail but by those who have fought for causes
that at first seemed impossible. The Stoics concentrate on the control of
one's own character because that is something that seems to be "up to
us," as opposed to the organization of the external world, which is seen
as "not up to us."[23] In a sense they are right, political action does, because
it involves a multiplicity of actors, set into motion chains of cause and
effect, the results of which the actors themselves cannot entirely predict
or control. The Stoic ideal of mastership and control of self can only
be achieved by turning away from the unpredictability of acting with
others, of acting politically, and turning inward. In this way it expounds
a view of freedom that is essentially nonpolitical.[24] Of course, it matters how one has come to hold the view that it is better to change the
self than the world. Under certain conditions I could imagine that this
would be the best alternative; sometimes there really are no possibilities
for changing the world to fit one's preferences, and adjusting to this fact
might then be the most reasonable thing to do. My point is that sometimes character planning can detract from autonomy, namely, when it is
not even considered whether the world could and should be different
and is accepted uncritically. Character planning easily becomes a form of
dogma that excludes discussion of whether the world could be different
and whether change should be attempted. The character planner tends
to see the world as independent of herself and hence is foreign to the
possibilities of collective, transformative action.

A character planner who has accepted the status quo as inevitable
and shaped her preferences accordingly, even if she has done so reflexively, will not be open for a change of circumstances that would give
her greater autonomy. She already has endorsed her preference and her
circumstances. The danger is if she *thinks* she is free, because then she
has excluded the possibility that she could become freer, or that there
are other dimensions of freedom. A preference that is consciously ad-

opted, combined with a belief that one is free, might stand more in the way of freedom than an adaptive preference combined with no illusions about being free.

Third, a character planner has accommodationist preferences.[25] An accommodationist preference is distinguished from an adaptive one by being consciously formed. Accommodation is of course the only possibility for the one seeking harmony between herself and the world and only seeks to change herself. The problem here concerns not *how* the preference has been adapted—consciously or nonconsciously—but what it has been accommodated *to*. It seems that accommodation to the circumstances only becomes a problem for freedom when there is in some sense something unfree about the way in which one came to live under those circumstances.[26]

My discussion of Elster has shown some problems in regarding the issue of adaptive preference formation as merely an inner issue. This perspective runs the danger of leading to the idea that freedom can be attained by individually becoming conscious of one's adaptive preferences and reflectively fine-tuning them to coincide exactly with the possibilities. This is a subjectivist view of freedom that is antithetical to any idea that freedom also has intersubjective and public dimensions, as well as to the idea that external circumstances matter for freedom. I do not deny that consciousness of one's preference formation matters for freedom, but the way in which Elster has formulated the issue leads to a dead end where it cannot be connected to the political and external dimensions of freedom, and hence cannot be the basis for social criticism. And there is not any room here for intersubjective processes of learning or for freedom as something that can be attained in deliberation with others. In particular, there is a pitfall in the idea of freedom as character planning insofar as people who reflexively endorse their preferences and their adaptation to their possibilities think that is sufficient for freedom. This view preempts any reflection regarding whether there might be more that is required for being free. But clearly, the mere form of reflexivity, as found in character planning or Frankfurt's "A wants to want to x," cannot be sufficient for freedom. This form of reflexivity does not exclude the possibility that citizens have merely adopted—uncritically or even nonconsciously—their second-order desires from the society in which they live. To be free we also must acquire our reflexive attitudes freely. I have stressed as well that conscious accommodation to the possibilities only contributes to freedom if one has some knowledge of what the possibilities are. This should be knowledge not only of what is, but also of what could be. Furthermore, if one chooses to accommodate one's wants to the status quo, then this is itself a choice and must be arrived at freely. Hence, one must not only have knowledge of the circumstances but also arrive at the choice of whether to attempt to change oneself or the world on the basis of critical reflection.

Analyzing what the idea of public deliberation presupposes in terms of dimensions of freedom gives us a better idea of what internal autonomy means and requires. Participating in public deliberation is, ideally, a way both of going beyond the mere fact of having meta-preferences and of scrutinizing one's possibilities on the basis of the available information. Deliberation triggers self-reflection, not only regarding one's first-order preferences but also regarding one's reflexive preferences. It does so because one must be willing to defend one's opinions and give reasons for them to others, and because one must be willing to listen to the reasons others have for their views. The deliberative process also imparts information about the world because this inevitably will be part of the arguments given for different points of view (see Chapter 7, the section "Learning and the Epistemic Dimension of Public Deliberation"). By participating in common deliberation, our reflexive judgments become products of intersubjective learning. Common deliberation thus achieves the sought-after qualitative difference between acting on first-order desires and acting on reflexive judgment, because the latter alone is based on reasons and knowledge gained intersubjectively. The difference from Elster and Frankfurt is that it is not the reflexivity as such that matters. Rather, what makes a preference autonomous is that it has survived a certain process. And this process is not merely an internal and a subjective one; it is one in which one can check one's preferences against the arguments of others. My preference is autonomous if I still find reasons to hold it after I have heard the relevant arguments and considered the relevant information. We thus get both an intersubjective and a rationality component absent in Elster and Frankfurt.

It might be argued that this does not solve the problem of infinite regress, which often is directed at Frankfurt's account, that is, the problem of how to avoid ascending to higher and higher levels to reach the autonomous self without cutting off the sequence arbitrarily. In one way, this is true. Every result of deliberation is only temporary. I might hear new arguments and learn about new information that make me change my mind, thus I learn that I did not have sufficient reason to hold my former view and hence that it was not fully autonomous. But why should this give rise to an objection? It might be seen as what autonomy is all about: to be continually open to learning, to revise one's views in light of new evidence. This means that we cannot define autonomy as a final state, as in Frankfurt's harmony between different levels of desires. The problem with Frankfurt's view might exactly be to see autonomy as an end state, for seeing it thus might inevitably lead to the infinite regress problem. Rather, we should see *autonomy as a process*. Autonomy, then, is to live under conditions where one can engage with others in deliberative practices that enable one continually to modify one's preferences and opinions in light of arguments.[27]

In order for one's reflexive attitudes to be autonomous, they must not be the result of irrelevant causal influences, to use Elster's terminology. As we go along, I shall argue that reasons qualify as causal influences that are not irrelevant in the sense that they limit freedom. Reasons, however, cannot be the only relevant causal influences on our preferences. As different individuals, we find that some aspects of what we are and what we want are not chosen on the basis of reasons. Most of us do not want to be without these aspects of ourselves, I think, because they are part of who we are as unique human beings. If I could choose my preferences all the way down, I would lack the criteria to do so, and I would lack substance as an individual. I am emphasizing this so as not to make autonomy into an unfeasible ideal and also in order to avoid seeing any and every form of socialization as a limitation of freedom. This is not the place to go into this issue; I simply want to flag the issue.[28] I would like to suggest, though, that whether or not these unchosen aspects of ourselves can be characterized as products of irrelevant causal influences depends on whether or not we find good reasons in common deliberation to reject them. On the Frankfurtian reflexivity model, we lack freedom if we have desires with which we cannot identify, but I think we must say that our freedom is impaired if we do not have the ability to revise or consider whether to reject our preferences in processes of intersubjective learning.

The negative formulation concerning having preferences that we have good reasons to reject is important. We do not rationally choose our identity and desires, and we might not be able to rationally justify them, nor should we be required to do so. The problem for deliberative freedom arises when we have preferences that we have good reasons to disown. We should remember in this connection that reason is permissive;

in some areas of life, it does not command a specific choice but allows a wide range of alternative choices. This is true of what concerns ethical choices, or choices concerning one's conception of the good. Nothing I have said, then, should be a threat to the notion that a plurality of ways of life can count as free. But some preferences will be rejected in light of good reasons and must on that account be regarded as products of irrelevant causal influences. This determination is not one that can be made from an objective perspective, however, but must be a product of the individual's own conviction.[29] But in contrast to Frankfurt, it is not merely subjective but includes intersubjective and rationality components.

Preferences and Paternalism: Sunstein

Like Elster, Sunstein is interested in endogenous preference formation. His intervention arises from a concern to defend government regulation and economic redistribution. It also is part of an argument for deliberative democracy, but this aim is not well integrated with the first aim, or so I argue. A main aim of *The Partial Constitution* is to argue against what Sunstein calls status quo neutrality, that is, the idea that there is some justice to things as they are, and that any change in distribution is a form of partiality.[30] In terms of preferences, this idea means that for the state to act neutrally it must take preferences as given and satisfy them equally. But preferences themselves can be shaped by legal rules, Sunstein argues, and hence cannot be used to justify them without circularity.[31] In other words, if preferences are a product of the system, then how can they be used to justify it? This is a strong point, but from the standpoint of the normative commitment to deliberative freedom, we see that Sunstein is going too far in disregarding and disrespecting existing preferences. Particularly, it is a weakness of his account that it is unclear from which perspective he is speaking and also who the agent of change should be. Both of these questions need to be answered by a theory with critical-transformative intent.

   Sunstein argues that democratic governments should not always respect private preferences, because these preferences are "adaptive to a wide range of factors—including the context in which the preference is expressed, the existing legal rules, past consumption choices, and culture in general."[32] This leads him to reject the notion of autonomy as preference satisfaction. "The notion of autonomy should refer instead to decisions reached with a *full and vivid* awareness of available opportunities, with reference to *all* relevant information, and without illegitimate or excessive constraints on the process of preference formation. When these conditions are not met, decisions should be described as unfree or non-autonomous; for this reason it is most difficult to identify autonomy with preference satisfaction."[33] Given these commitments, Sunstein concludes, "a democratic government should sometimes take private preferences as an object of regulation and control ... and precisely in the interest of welfare and autonomy."[34]

With this one-dimensional take on freedom and autonomy, Sunstein opens himself up to the charge of paternalism, for who is to decide when a preference is free if not a paternalistic state? Sunstein's requirements for autonomy are so demanding that it is clear that no one will ever be autonomous, and the state hence always is justified in overruling our—the citizens'—preferences. There are two problems here. First, there is a danger in seeing autonomy as a matter of either/or instead of as a matter of degree. It means that one who is not fully autonomous is not autonomous at all, and hence others cannot violate her autonomy. In Sunstein's analysis, preferences that are not fully autonomous lose all worth.

Second, even if it is true that our preferences are not autonomous, this does not mean that they can be made so by the action of an external authority, such as Sunstein describes the state. According to Sunstein, "Respect for preferences that have resulted from unjust background conditions and that will lead to human deprivation or misery hardly appears the proper course for a liberal democracy."[35] Thus he goes directly from the problem of adaptive preference formation to a justification of state intervention. But this is too quick. It is one thing to say that adaptive preference formation is damaging to freedom and quite another to say that adaptive preferences should not be respected. We might try to solve the problem of adaptive preference formation while simultaneously respecting the preferences people actually have. This requires that we bring in the process of public deliberation. Public deliberation should aim at making people reflect on their own political preferences. By emphasizing that the aim of deliberation in the first instance should be to foster *self*-reflection, it is made clear that it is the person herself who has to reflect on the status of her preferences.

Sunstein says, "Social outcomes should not be based on existing preferences."[36] But that is an unfortunate way to put what deliberative democracy is about. Political decisions *should* be based on existing preferences; the ideal of public autonomy requires that. The issue deliberative democrats should raise is *how* existing political preferences have been shaped. And the perspective we should take is as critics in the public sphere who attempt to provoke reflection and contribute to processes of common deliberation.[37] As critical theorists, we can analyze how certain conditions and processes are detrimental to the free formation of preferences. But we should never from an external perspective take some preferences as not worthy of respect, and we should not see the state as an instrument to changing these preferences from without. That would violate both the negative freedom and the public autonomy of citizens. The normative commitment to deliberative freedom entails that we try only to change others' preferences by attempting to convince them or make them reflect about their own situation and opinions. We cannot implement new conditions before we have convinced each other of their justifiability.

To avoid misunderstanding of the idea that even adaptive preferences must be respected, we have to be clear on which perspective we are speaking from and which dimension of freedom we are invoking. From the perspective of the dimension of freedom that says that everyone should have the opportunity to be a participant in collective self-legislation, we have to let people's actual preferences count as their real preferences. What we respect in the democratic process is each person's equal right to express and vote on his or her preferences no matter their source. But from the perspective of internal autonomy, it is the aim that people become emancipated from their adaptive preferences. When we are committed to both of these dimensions of freedom, adaptive preferences must be attempted to be changed through processes of public deliberation rather than directly through state interference. I am assuming here that criticizing others' political preferences in public deliberation is not disrespectful (because we treat each other as responsive to reasons and as capable of giving their own), while direct state action aimed at making people autonomous is disrespectful (because such an action wil bypass their rational capabilities).[38]

Sunstein does in fact address the issues of deliberation and public autonomy, but he separates them from the issue of preferences. According to Sunstein, citizens should not decide, "what they 'want', but instead who they are, what their values are, and what those values require."[39] Hereby he excludes the possibility of changing one's preferences about what one wants in the process of deliberation and makes it the concern solely of the output side of the state. It seems to me that Sunstein makes a too-sharp distinction between wants and values. Even if we in politics cannot be concerned with our own interests and wants *alone*, it does not mean we cannot be concerned with them *also*. Political decisions should not transcend what we want individually but include it. Sunstein seems to want some preferences to be excluded before the process of deliberation gets started. I, in contrast, argue that it must be in the process of deliberation that it is decided what are and are not "relevant preferences." People should be allowed (but not required) to bring their private desires and interests to the process of deliberation; whether they should be satisfied must depend on whether there are good arguments for their satisfaction. And whether the preferences are autonomous must depend on whether people still hold them after they have seen them in light of the reasons given in and the information imparted by public deliberation.

Sunstein makes the interesting observation that there often is a difference between people's wants as consumers in the market and their political values.[40] This is a very important point to raise against those who say, "Hey, see people really don't want that" (those opera houses, speed limits, or whatever) and then point to their private consumption choices as proof. Sunstein is right to point out that the same people might have social aspirations and collective judgments that go against their private behavior. But he is not precise enough in relating this to the public process of deliberation and to the idea of public autonomy. The problem with his perspective is that he, exactly as those he criticizes, speaks on others' behalf. Sunstein's response to the objector to regulation is, "Yes, that is what *they* really want—as citizens." But it is exactly such an observer's perspective that the ideal of public deliberation and respect for the multiple dimensions of freedom of citizens demand that we abandon. A basic normative commitment of deliberative democracy should be that everyone must speak for herself; this ideal also is presupposed by the idea of public deliberation. It is crucial to emphasize that it is *in* public deliberation that we form our legitimate collective judgments and justify laws that might overrule our private desires. And, hence, it is only as participants in public deliberation that we can *know* what each other's political values are. This cannot be determined by observing theorists or judges, and not by opinion polls either. Consequently, there would be no question of the state's not respecting people's preferences and attempting to control them. The citizens *themselves* would formulate their collective aspirations and how they should relate to their own private desires.

The objections I have raised against Sunstein have their root in a tension between a substantial commitment to state regulation and an argument for solving political problems through processes of public deliberation. Sunstein represents the tendency to weigh substantial commitments higher than respect for the democratic genesis of law through public deliberation. It is an implication of the ideal of deliberative freedom, in contrast, that we should not only be concerned with the effects of the output of the state but also focus on the input. It makes a difference whether we see adaptive preference formation as an issue that should be solved by a state that takes an objective attitude (in P. F. Strawson's sense) toward its citizens, that is, as "subject . . . [to] treatment . . . to be managed or handled or cured,"[41] or whether we see it as an issue to be dealt with in public deliberation generating legitimate law. In the democratic genesis of law, citizens take a participant attitude toward each other and, therefore, have to show respect for each other's preferences, even if they are the result of adaptation to unjust background conditions. This is crucial, not the least because we never will arrive at the situation of perfect justice and full autonomy. Instead of seeing the possibility of adaptive preferences as a direct justification for not respecting preferences, the thematization of the problem should be seen as a contribution to public deliberation. As critics in the public sphere, theorists of deliberative democracy should provoke processes of self-reflection about possible adaptive preferences, but they do not have the final word on the issue. When engaging in deliberation with each other and when seeing each other as coauthors of law and public policy, we must show respect for each other and let people speak for themselves.

Sunstein might object that he is not arguing for imposing anything on anybody. The social justice measures he proposes should, of course, be subject to debate and democratic voting. But this response misses the point. My argument is primarily directed at a too-simplistic account of autonomy. Sunstein might say that he wants to combine this with a theory of deliberation and public autonomy; my point is that he has not done so. But the argument also has institutional implications. Sunstein's account of autonomy will be less critical of forms of policy making that are isolated from popular participation and common deliberation than a theory that wants to combine the ideal of autonomous preference formation with a concern for public autonomy and the respect for each and everyone as an authority on matters of common concern.[42]

We should not see autonomous preferences as preferences that are not adaptive at all. All preferences are adaptive to some degree—and they *should* be adaptive, both to circumstances and to who we are if they are to be preferences of real people and not of noumenal selves. And deliberation needs to be based on the preferences of real people in order to be an actual intersubjective enterprise, which aims at agreements that are equally good for all—and not merely right for a disembedded self. What we need is an account of when preferences are adaptive in the wrong way as distinguished from when they are adaptive in the right way. Whether preferences are adaptive in the right or wrong way is, as mentioned, not only a matter of *how* they are adapted but also what they are adapted *to*. In connection to the latter issue, Sunstein is right to emphasize the adaptation to unjust circumstances as the problematic form of adaptation. But this leaves open the question of what circumstances are just and unjust. This is an issue that must itself be determined by public deliberation. We should not separate process and conditions too sharply. Since we are always influenced by our circumstances, freedom requires that these circumstances be subject to questioning, alteration, and justification in processes of public deliberation.

In a couple of recent articles, Sunstein has made an argument in favor of what he and his coauthor, Richard Thaler, call "libertarian paternalism." Like the work discussed previously, this argument relies heavily on the premise of endogenous preference formation. The argument differs from Sunstein's argument concerning deliberative democracy by not being concerned with the effects of preference formation on the political process but by being concerned with welfare alone.[43] But it is instructive to see again what the empirical data that show that preferences often lack rationality and autonomy are believed to justify.

Libertarian paternalism is "an approach that preserves freedom of choice but that encourages both private and public institutions to steer people in directions that will promote their own welfare."[44] Sunstein and Thaler's argument is based on two main premises: first, there are no viable alternatives to paternalism; second, paternalism does not always involve coercion. To illustrate the argument that there are no viable alternatives to paternalism, they give the following example:

> Consider the problem facing the director of a company cafeteria who
> discovers that the order in which food is arranged influences the choices
> people make. To simplify, consider three alternative strategies: (1) she
> could make choices that she thinks would make the customers best

off; (2) she could make choices at random; or (3) she could maliciously choose those items that she thinks would make the customers as obese as possible. Option 1 appears to be paternalistic, which it is, but would anyone advocate option 2 or 3?[45]

That the arrangement of the food influences the choices the customers make is an example of a number of ways in which behavioral economics and cognitive psychology research have shown that context shapes choices.[46] I do not have a quarrel with this research but with what is done with it. Paternalism is inevitable, according to Sunstein and Thaler, because (a) the director has to make a choice about the arrangement of the food, and (b) options 2 and 3 are not viable. It is undeniable that a choice has to be made (though it is less clear why it is the director who has to make it). But is it really true that 2 is such a far-fetched option? Would it not be preferable in terms of freedom that the food be arranged randomly than that the director place the food in an order that makes the customers buy what she believes is best for them? Sunstein and Thaler propose that institutional planners ("anyone who must design plans for others, from human resource directors, to bureaucrats, to kings"[47]) study what behavioral economics and cognitive psychology can tell them about how people choose as a result of different institutional designs, default options, starting points, and so on, and on this basis steer people in a direction that will promote the latter's welfare. Then, to meet the concerns of the libertarian, they note that this form of paternalism is not coercive because it leaves people free to choose. The cafeteria director puts the unhealthy food in the back but does not make it unavailable; the employer makes her preferred pension savings plan the default option but makes it possible for the employees to opt out. However, only a very crude notion of coercion would see this as being coercion-free. Coercion is a matter not merely of making options unavailable but also of raising the costs of certain options.

What we witness is an argument for making people feel free by giving them the choice between a number of options while the institutional planners design the context so they achieve the desired outcome. The main objection to this way of thinking is the objectivating attitude it takes toward the subjects. The customers in the cafeteria and the employees choosing pension plans are treated as not being responsive to reasons but as mere objects that react in calculable and predictable ways to default rules, framing effects, starting points, and so on.[48] Then there is more respect in randomness.

This discussion gives us even more reason to emphasize the public dimension of deliberative freedom. In cases where some decision needs to be made by "planners," the notion of negative freedom does not help us very much, and the decision cannot be made in anticipation of what choices people would make if the choices they make depend on the options they have: there would be no clear preferences to track.[49] The fact that institutional rules affect the choices made gives us a good reason to make these institutional rules the object of reflection and collective decision making. So does the fact that steering choices, even if less oppressive than making certain choices unavailable, hardly can be seen as noncoercive. This does not mean that all areas of life should be democratized and no tasks could be delegated, for example, to bureaucratic agencies. But it does mean that the only way we can avoid paternalism is by making institutional rules subject to democratic legitimation.

Paternalism

In the Introduction to this book I mentioned the classical problem that in attempting to remove one form of oppression, we impose another. Sunstein fails on this account, because in his argument for state intervention for the sake of the autonomy of the subjects, he accepts paternalism. I am making this criticism from the perspective of an understanding of deliberative democracy as committed to multiple dimensions of freedom, that is, from the perspective of deliberative freedom. To elaborate on this perspective and show why it must be critical of paternalism, I spell out exactly what paternalism is, when it is at play, and why it is objectionable.[50] I also consider if there is anything that can be done about non-autonomous preferences without turning to paternalism.

Gerald Dworkin helpfully defines an act as paternalistic if it "constitutes an attempt to substitute one person's judgment for another's, to promote the latter's benefit."[51] Any form of paternalism involves a person or a group of persons believing that she or it knows better what is in the best interest of another or others and attempts to impose her or its view on others. It is a case of legal paternalism when the judgment of the first party is backed by law, which in the last instance means that it is backed by force. A political system is paternalistic if it gives some the authority to judge on others' behalf what they believe promote the latter's benefit.

Acting paternalistically entails that the subject does not know what is in her interest or what is good for her. But there is an ambiguity in saying that the subject does not know what is in her interest or what is good for her. It could mean that the person is mistaken about what her interests are, or that she is mistaken about what best *serves* her interests; that is, she may be seen as mistaken about either her ends or means, or both. Regarding ends, note that the subject of a paternalistic act does not necessarily object because she does not share the end or good promoted but because she does not see it as the *highest* good.[52] Thus a smoker who is against paternalistic smoking regulation may not be so because she does not agree that health is a good, but because she does not agree that it is the highest good. She might think it is a higher good to live well than to live for a long time. The judgment that the paternalist wants to substitute for that of the subject is, thus, a composite of not only what is good but also of what is best and of how best to achieve this end. This leads to three different forms of justification for paternalistic legislation: (1) People do not know what is good for themselves; (2) People do not know what is best for themselves (they do not have the right priorities); and (3) People do not know how to achieve what is good for themselves.

These forms leave out another candidate for justifications of paternalism, namely, weakness of will. If we accept—against Socrates, but with Aristotle[53]—that it is possible for a person to know what is good for her, to have the right priorities, and to know how to achieve her ends and nevertheless fail to act accordingly, then there seems to be a prima facie justification for intervention. Among proponents of deliberative democracy, Amy Gutmann and Dennis Thompson, for example, see protecting against weakness of will as an act of paternalism and as justified.[54] But I do not think it is a case of paternalism at all. When another person or the law helps me do what I judge it best to do, or refrain from doing what I judge it detrimental to do, then it is reinforcing my own judgment rather than putting another's judgment in its place. So according to the definition I have appropriated from Dworkin, acts that adjust for weakness of will are not paternalistic—which is not to say that they are always justified.

The focus on judgment in this definition is important. If we instead defined a paternalist act as one that goes contrary to the subject's operative preference,[55] then acts and laws adjusting for weakness of will would be paternalistic. But it is important to be able to distinguish between acts or laws that go against the subject's own judgment and those that reinforce her judgment against her weakness of will or some (ephemeral) operative preference. It is unhelpful to class them together in the same category. We see an important difference between the two in the ways in which they address their subjects. In the case of paternalistic acts, the subject is treated as being incapable of judgment; in the second case, she is seen as being incapable of following through on her own judgments. But the most important difference is that the latter type can be self-imposed, while paternalistic acts cannot. Gutmann and Thompson's idea of "self-imposed paternalism" seems to me an oxymoron.[56] Paternalism implies that someone else thinks she knows better than I do what is good for me and attempts to impose it on me, against my own judgment, for my own good. Self-imposition requires that I know what is good for me, but that is exactly what the paternalist denies. But it is possible for me to impose on myself or ask others to impose on me constraints that help me overcome my weakness of will.

Of course, legislation aimed at adjusting for weakness of will might, when accepted by a majority only, follow the judgment of some, while being paternalistic toward others. But then we are back to the case of some judging on behalf of others what are in the latter's best interest. And it is for this reason—that it sets the judgment of some over the judgment of others—that the legislation should be seen as paternalistic, and not because it sets judgment over operative preference. To be sure, the practical need for decision making according to the majority principle leads to further difficulties, because the deciding self is not coterminous with the affected self.[57]

Can antipaternalism be paternalistic? From Gutmann and Thompson's perspective, it seems it cannot. For them, legal paternalism is defined as "the restriction by law of an individual's liberty for his or her own good."[58] Now consider a situation in which a population has lived for centuries without any individual rights and its enlightened despot wants to introduce individual liberties out of a concern for his subjects. He wants them to be free and no longer be subject to his paternalistic legislation. If the people resist and do not want to be free, then is the imposition not a form of paternalism? After all, the despot is here substituting his own judgment for that of his subjects for their own good. The despot does not cease to be a paternalist (supposing he has always been one) because he has changed from thinking it best for his subjects that he should decide everything and now give them the right to make individual choices about what they want to do, for he imposes on them a law that requires that they have to decide for themselves. But for Gutmann and Thompson, this cannot be a case of paternalism, for the imposition of individual rights does not take away a negative freedom the subjects formerly had. Furthermore, for Gutmann and Thompson, it is irrelevant to the issue of paternalism who imposes the law. This might be because they do not realize that equal rights to decide for oneself require laws to be imposed by someone and to be justified by someone; their definition of paternalism entails a conception of negative freedom as something neutral and naturally given.[59] In contrast to Gutmann and Thompson, I would argue that the despot who imposes laws establishing equal liberty is a paternalist, because he judges what is good or right on others' behalf. And the same is true of the liberal theorist who sets up standards that are independent of actual processes of collective self-legislation, even if these standards justify protection of individual liberty and antipaternalism. Despotism is a paternalist political system even when used to increase the subjects' negative liberty; the absence of freedom as collective self-legislation makes it so. Paternalism should not be understood only from the perspective of negative freedom but also from that of collective self-legislation. Without public autonomy, every law imposed on the subjects for their own good is paternalistic.

To avoid misunderstanding, the argument is not that a freedom, which one has not acquired for oneself, is not a freedom at all and is not worth having. Negative freedoms given by a despot are freedoms and they are worth having, but they are nevertheless paternalistically imposed. In this sense antipaternalism can operate in a paternalistic way; others can judge on your behalf that it would be better for you to judge by yourself. It also might be argued that no one is forced to use the newly won negative liberties but can refrain from using them. But clearly the subjects' situation has changed by having acquired new liberties. They have been placed in a new situation where they are bound to make choices—whether to use their new liberties or not—where no choices formerly were required.

Can Deliberation be Paternalistic?

The idea of public deliberation presupposes and deliberative freedom entails, in contrast to the position Sunstein is representative of, that citizens' preferences must be respected and changed only as part of a process of public deliberation itself. I now elaborate and defend this position more fully in light of what I have said about the concept of paternalism. I do so by way of a response to Dworkin's claim, "It is not as if rational argument cannot be paternalistic while brute force must be. Some people may want to make their decisions impulsively, without rational deliberation; insisting that they hear rational argument (for their own good) is paternalism."[60]

The following analysis concerns *argument* rather than all forms of public deliberation. The processes of political opinion and will formation could never be restricted to rational argumentation—that would overburden citizens and no decisions would be made—but must include also bargaining and voting.[61] The aspiration for deliberative democrats should be that when bargaining and voting are necessary, the conditions and procedures are fair and have been justified and accepted as such in rational argumentation.[62] Thus deliberative processes cannot be reduced to argumentation, but the latter is the fundamental form of deliberation. Since the idea of rational argumentation as the justificatory basis for other forms of communication is what differentiates deliberative democracy from other models of democracy, it is what has to be analyzed.

Let us consider, then, in what sense, if at all, rational argument might be considered a case of substituting the judgment of one for another's, for the sake of the latter. First we must distinguish between imposing a substantial judgment on another and imposing a judgment about which decision procedure to follow. Dworkin seems to be concerned with the latter, but I begin by arguing why deliberation cannot be seen as a matter of imposing substantial judgments on others, and then I return to the issue of procedure.

The argument for public deliberation as presupposing a multidimensional conception of freedom does rely on the assumption that people do not always know what is in their own best interest or what means best serves their interest. Public deliberation should aim not only at coordinating action and determining collective goals but also at gaining greater insights into what is in our best interest individually as well as collectively and how best to satisfy those interests. This description can lead some to suppose that deliberation is inherently paternalistic. But it is not paternalistic to point out that people might be mistaken about their own interests; it only becomes so if one thinks one knows better and attempts to substitute one's own judgment for another's. Deliberation does not work by imposing one person's judgment on others. It should rather be thought of as a *joint activity of mutual learning*. As I see it, one of the basic premises of deliberative democracy is that no one has privileged access to and uncriticizable beliefs about what the true interests of anyone are. In deliberation, it is true, there is a substitution of one judgment for another, but it is not of mine for yours, rather of what results from deliberation for both of them.

It could be argued that usually a person goes into an argument to substitute her own judgment for her listener's. To be sure, this can be the *motivation* for entering into an argument, but this in itself clearly does not constitute a process of argumentation. While the reason for entering into an argument may be paternalistic, there is something about the process of argumentation that makes it defy being so. This is because the addressee of an argument will be able to accept or reject the argument in light of her own judgment, if nothing but argument is involved. If the initiator of the argument is able to avoid that the addressee considers the argument on its merits, then it will be not by means of argument but rather by means of something external to it, such as superior power or manipulation.[63] In that case, what makes the act paternalistic is not the argument but the first person's ability to avoid a real argument from taking place, using forces external to argument itself. Thus as speech acts, arguments do not fit the definition of paternalistic acts. That also is the case because they are directed at a person's conscious and reflective capacities and hence may be either accepted or rejected by the recipient on the basis of her own judgment. This is the reason arguments cannot be said to be irrelevant causal influences in the sense that they limit our freedom. Irrelevant causal influences can be characterized by their *bypassing* our reflective capacities.[64] It makes a difference whether, on the one side, another's judgment has been substituted for mine without my knowing it (as in the case of manipulation) or by means of overt force, or, on the other side, I have come to rationally accept this judgment as my own.

The preceding arguments, however, require that people participate in argument in the first place. They apply only to persons who have already accepted participating in argumentation. So let us return to Dworkin's point, that "insisting that [impulsive people] hear rational argument (for their own good) is paternalism." The situation here is not one of the substitution of another's substantive judgment for one's own but one of the substitution of another's preferred decision procedure for one's own. That is, it is not a case of *A* insisting that *B* do *x* rather than *y* for her own sake, but of *A* insisting that *B* follow a certain procedure before she decides whether to do x or y, for her own sake. And it is clearly the *insisting* that Dworkin calls paternalistic and not rational argument itself. But what is meant by "insisting"? Let us consider two examples regarding legal paternalism, one that relates to the output side of the state and one that relates to the democratic genesis of law.

Consider a law that requires a woman who wants to have an abortion to go to counseling before she gains the right to have it.[65] Suppose this law is made for the sake of the autonomy of the woman in the sense that her choice will only reflect what she really wants if it is made after having considered the pros and cons of the case.[66] This is a case of insisting that someone hear rational arguments before she makes up her mind. Note that the complaint against such a law would most likely not be against rational arguments as such but be against being forced to listen to them. The complaint would be against the legal rule not the argument. If one were against arguments as such, one would have to be in favor of prohibiting from the public sphere arguments that make pregnant women reflect on whether to have an abortion. A law forcing people to listen to arguments for their own good before they make personal choices would be paternalistic, I contend, but a law that allows in the public sphere arguments meant to make people reflect on their choices is not. The difference is that in the first case people are forced to do something independently of their own judgment, while in the latter case they will only listen to the arguments if they so choose. I draw this distinction not merely to affirm the importance of freedom of speech but to argue that *an increase* in public deliberation should not be seen as a threat to freedom. As long as citizens have the right not to participate in public deliberation, the negative dimension of freedom has been respected. The problem with obligatory abortion counseling is the lack of a right to say no; it is paternalistic when it is justified with reference to one's own good.

The second example, relevant to the democratic genesis of law and public autonomy, is the idea that people would be given the right to vote only if they took part in public deliberation.[67] Suppose that such a law was justified with reference to the fact that many individuals vote contrary to their own best interests. Justified in this way, the law is paternalistic vis-à-vis those who would prefer to make up their mind about what to vote without participating in public deliberation. But again the objection would be not that arguments are paternalistic per se but that being forced to participate in giving and listening to them is. The problem for deliberative democracy in this connection is not that deliberation is paternalistic but that it is impotent by itself in the face of those who do not want to listen and participate. It is when deliberation becomes dependent on auxiliaries (that is, on forces beyond that of argument, such as rewards or punishments) that it runs the risk of becoming paternalistic in the sense of imposing a procedure on people against their will. Deliberative freedom does not by its very idea prohibit using the law in order to promote participation in deliberation.[68] But the justification for such laws should not be a paternalistic one. Rather than being justified by reference to the good of the person herself, it should be justified by reference to the fact that when we act politically, we make choices that not only affect us but everyone else.[69] So any argument for institutions and laws that make people take part in deliberation before they vote—or encourage them to do so—should not be justified with reference to their own good but with reference to the idea that they are not merely exercising power over themselves but rather also over others.

In these two examples, the negative dimension of freedom, the freedom from coercive interference, also shows its importance. But I argue that we should be careful not to confuse this dimension of freedom with the idea that public deliberation in itself encroaches upon freedom, or at least we should distinguish coercive interference from the unavoidable and unobjectionable "interference" posed by the existence in one's society of arguments that contradict one's own convictions (see the fourth section in Chapter 6).

Collective Self-Legislation and Freedom as Status

Some arguments against paternalism are inherent to the idea of public deliberation. These arguments become clearer when we explicate the dimensions of freedom that this idea presupposes. They show why one cannot at one and the same time be a paternalist and a deliberative democrat. What distinguishes the paternalist and the deliberative democratic point of view is not that one holds that people do not know what is good for themselves, while the other thinks they do. Both perspectives agree that people may not know what is good or best for themselves. Rather, the difference is that the paternalist believes she knows what is good for others and feels herself justified in imposing her judgment on others, while the deliberative democrat believes that what is right must be justified and accepted in public deliberation. As already mentioned, a basic assumption underlying deliberative democracy, as I see it, is that no one has privileged access to truth or to the true interests of others. The only way to arrive at judgments that have the presumption of being right on their side is through public processes of deliberation where everyone is free and able to participate.[70]

From the standpoint of deliberative freedom, we can see why it is unsatisfactory to limit freedom to the idea that preferences be formed consciously and under just circumstances. Elster and Sunstein neglect two dimensions of freedom, both presupposed by the idea of public deliberation: freedom as collective self-legislation and freedom as status.

What is objectionable about paternalism from the perspective of the normative commitment to deliberative freedom is that the paternalist does not want to go into an argument about her own view but wants to impose it on the subject from without. This goes against the very idea of deliberation. Deliberation is about convincing, and when a speaker is successful in convincing the listener about her proposal, the implementation of this proposal will not be a case of imposing the judgment of the former on the latter but of the two having come to share judgment. This leads us to the idea of collective self-legislation. Paternalism is a matter of some attempting to judge and legislate on behalf of others for the latter's own good, while self-legislation is a matter of giving a law to oneself on the basis of one's own best judgment. On this understanding, laws given to oneself can never be paternalistic, since they are reinforcing rather than going against one's own best judgment. The deliberative genesis of law, however, refers not to a direct individual giving a law to oneself. The dimension of freedom involved in collective self-legislation is seen as expressed less in the vote than in the intersubjective processes in which citizens form opinions about how to vote. To be sure, it is the final decision that makes law, but citizens exercise their political freedom as colegislators just as much in the fact that they try to influence how each other votes. The public opinion to which democratic decisions ought to be responsive should be the product of a common process among all citizens. In any democracy, citizens influence how others vote; the deliberative ideal is that this influence should be based not on unequally distributed economic or social power but on good reasons to which everyone has equal access.

The paternalist's attitude not only goes against freedom as collective self-legislation but also against freedom as a form of status. Status can be seen as a dimension of freedom, as we saw in the preceding chapter, that it is in the republican tradition. Deliberative democracy implies a specific view of what it is to be a citizen, and it involves a particular conception of freedom as status. This conception of status is derived from what is involved in being an active participant in public deliberation. The paternalist does not recognize the discursive status we must give each other in order for common deliberation to succeed. In deliberation, we must respect the status of each other as free persons, in the sense of persons worth arguing with and as persons who can contribute with and respond appropriately to reasons. Everyone must be given the status of an authority on matters taken up in public deliberation.[71] This status is violated when others over-rule our judgments and implement what they deem good for us, even if it is something they believe will increase our autonomy.

In light of the realities of politics, the argument for collective self-legislation will naturally be met by the majority-minority objection. We need to distinguish more clearly than I have done hitherto between "my judgment" and "our judgment." Without consensus, my judgment and the collective judgment that determines political decisions do not necessarily coincide. Consensus is rarely, if ever, forthcoming regarding matters of legislation, the objection goes, and the majority who make the decision will thus judge on behalf of the rest. It is undeniable that consensus rarely occurs in legislative politics, but it is true only up to a point that this means that the majority has to impose its judgment on the minority. If there has been an inclusive and a free process of deliberation up to the point of decision making, then the freedom of even the minority has been respected in two ways.

First, the results of deliberation also are products of the contributions made by those who ended up in the minority. As Bernard Manin puts it, "Although the result does not conform to all points of view, it is the result of the confrontation between them."[72] The deliberative process constitutes for everyone *freedom as being a participant in collective self-legislation.* I distinguish being a participant in collective self-legislation from being a self-legislator. The latter requires that one be in agreement with the final decision made, while being a participant in collective self-legislation is possible even if one disagrees with the final result, as long as the final decision is also affected by one's contribution and as long as it is seen as fallible and reversible and therefore subject to further debate by the demos as a whole. It is only when we see democracy as a deliberative democracy that we see this possibility, that is, when we see that there is more to democracy than the counting of votes. It might be objected that this argument requires that the results of democratic decision making be different because of the contributions made by the outvoted minority, and that that condition is not always fulfilled. But if we look not at isolated instances of decision making but at the long-term effects of a more deliberative society, then the condition that all participants actually do affect the decisions is harder to refute. Decision making will be embedded in a different environment, which will affect the opinion and will formation of everyone and hence will lead to different results. Moreover, the deliberative ideal that everyone should enjoy the freedom of being a participant in collective self-legislation should make us seek out institutional arrangement that will give the minority an influence on decisions. The counting of votes after an election gives a voice only to the majority, but what is just as important is the influence that can be exerted between elections. An aspect of the public autonomy enjoyed in a deliberative democracy lies in that civil society actors have equal chances to influence decision makers also between elections.[73]

Second, under these conditions even if one ends up in the minority one's status is respected. The fact that the majority does not end up agreeing with the individual does not mean it has not listened to the individual's arguments and given theirs; and they have to respect it if the individual ex post facto criticizes its judgment and attempts to change the decision that was made. It is important in this connection not to see the decision made by a majority as an expression of the will of the people. "As long as one considers the will of the majority the expression of the general will, the minority has no status at all."[74] Using the majority principle is most often a necessity when decisions have to be made, but that does not mean that majority decisions should be viewed as expressing the voice of the people. The voice of the people can be heard only in its plurality as expressed in public deliberation. This voice does not have to be silenced by the need for decision making. If the voice of the minority is listened to and argued with in a process in which "the decision reached by the majority only represents a caesura in an ongoing discussion,"[75] then the discursive status of everyone is upheld.

Thus the fact that decisions in the end have to be made following the majority principle does not mean that the argument for the anti-paternalism of deliberative self-legislation fails. A decision reached after public deliberation is not merely a case of the judgment of the majority substituting for that of the minority but one of judgments clashing and resulting in something new. And even if the outvoted minority must obey the decision made by the majority until it can win the majority, it is not required to accept the judgment behind the decision made as its own. Most importantly, deliberative democracy directs one's attention to the process of opinion formation as a part of the exercise of public autonomy. In this process, the influence one can have is not necessarily determined by numbers; under good conditions one's influence is determined by the force of the arguments one makes. Of course, at least since Tocqueville and Mill, we have known that the majority also can dominate public opinion. But that is a case of a distorted opinion forming process, a problem the deliberative democratic ideal is particularly apt to elucidate and criticize.

Conclusion

If we do not see the issue of nonautonomous preferences in the context of a complex theory of deliberative freedom, then we too easily end up in the paradoxical situation of seeking to increase autonomy in ways that simultaneously undermine it. Sunstein ends up in this predicament because he wants to make people's preferences autonomous in a way that disrespects their freedom as reason-responsive beings and undermines the freedom of being participants in collective self-legislation. Or, we end up in a too-narrow focus on the self at the cost of the political and external dimensions of freedom, as there is a tendency to in Elster. The analysis of Elster and Sunstein also shows that one-dimensional views of freedom and autonomy fail to give us standards in light of which social criticism can be made. Elster's idea of character planning moves the focus away from social conditions to psychological ones, while Sunstein fails to clarify the perspective from which criticism should be made and who the agent of change should be.

Juxtaposing the idea of a normative commitment to deliberative freedom to Elster and Sunstein matters particularly in terms of what we think the possibility of adaptive preferences can justify. My argument is that the existence of adaptive preference formation cannot be used as a direct or an unmediated justification for state intervention. If we begin to set up external standards for when people's preferences are autonomous, then we have betrayed the promise of deliberative democracy as a truly democratic model committed to multiple dimensions of freedom, a model where standards must be the product of processes that give each one of us the ability to contribute and learn and that treats each one of us as responsive to reasons rather than to authority and force. The issue of adaptive preferences is something that should be taken up for discussion in the public sphere. Critical theorists of deliberative democracy can raise the issue of adaptive preferences but not solve it, for people cannot be made autonomous from without. For preferences to be autonomously formed, citizens need to have formed them by their own lights and under conditions that they have been able to participate in the justification of. If there is a problem of adaptive preference formation in society, then this is not an individual problem with an individual solution or a problem that some can solve for others through state action. Rather, it is a problem with the communication structure in which *all of us* form our preferences and something that can be solved only on the basis of intersubjective processes of deliberation.

To integrate the arguments about autonomous preferences, paternalism, and deliberation requires a complex theory of freedom. The issue of autonomous preference formation should be seen in relation to and as balanced by two other dimensions of freedom, namely, freedom as discursive status and freedom as having the opportunity of being a participant in collective self-legislation. The focus on multiple dimensions of freedom entails an argument for seeing deliberative democracy as situated between models of democracy that claim democracy requires that we hold that people are never wrong about their own interests, or even if they are, that there is nothing we can do about it (that is, negative freedom models of democracy, as discussed in Chapter 1) and paternalistic models that set up independent standards of what is good for people. It is possible to raise the issue of nonautonomous preferences without substituting one's own judgment for others'. Public deliberation is a means of dealing with nonautonomous preferences without becoming paternalistic. It works through the participants' own critical faculties and is undermined by mechanisms that bypass these. Because of its procedural and dialogical character, deliberation cannot impose anything on anybody. The strength of deliberative democracy is exactly that it can challenge uncritically accepted forms of oppression without being paternalistic and setting up external standards of true and false interests. (This is a theme I will return to in Chapter 5.)

CHAPTER FOUR

Freedom as Accommodation

The Limits of Rawlsian Deliberative Democracy

"Deliberative democracy is the American version of German theories of communicative action and ideal speech," Michael Walzer recently wrote.[1] The German theories to which he refers are most prominently (if not only) those of Jürgen Habermas. Walzer goes on to claim that the main difference between American deliberative democrats and Habermas is that the former more readily turn to issues of public policy and institutional design, while the latter is more concerned with philosophical foundations. This description ignores the role played by the work of John Rawls in the development of deliberative democratic theory. Rawls is a principal source of inspiration for the most influential American deliberative democrats, such as Joshua Cohen and Amy Gutmann and Dennis Thompson.[2] However, even though it is wrong to see deliberative democracy as an American *version* of Habermas's theories, it *is* a theory upon which Rawlsian political liberals and Habermasian critical theorists have converged. Followers of Rawls and Habermas are all deliberative democrats now,[3] as are the two philosophers themselves.[4] In this and the following chapter, I shall argue that this convergence is unfortunate, because it obscures some fundamental differences between the two traditions.[5]

Although Rawlsians and Habermasians discuss some disagreements, these are seen as remaining "within the bounds of a family quarrel."[6] I believe that the disagreements are actually rooted in a more fundamental difference between the two traditions, a difference that lies in their distinct normative commitments and emphases with regard to dimensions of freedom. Generally speaking, Rawls's view of freedom is indebted to a liberal tradition of toleration or accommodation (going back to the Reformation and Locke), while Habermas's stems from a critical tradition, in the lineage of Kant and Marx,[7] that views freedom as a matter of enlightenment and emancipation from all forms of oppression, including those that originate from false consciousness.[8] These different conceptions of freedom inform two very different understandings of the role and aim of deliberation: one of accommodating people with irreconcilable views and another of deliberation as a matter of learning and emancipation.

In their 1995 discussion, Habermas and Rawls identified freedom as an issue upon which they disagree.[9] However, this discussion focused on modern versus ancient liberties, or negative freedom versus public autonomy.[10] Habermas criticizes Rawls for overemphasizing the negative liberties at the expense of public autonomy, while Rawls criticizes Habermas for doing the opposite.[11] This discussion misses an important third dimension of freedom that concerns the free formation of individual opinions, or *internal autonomy*. I argue that it is this dimension of freedom that distinguishes Habermas from Rawls, and that it implicitly informs their discussion of negative freedom and public autonomy. This third dimension of freedom needs to be thematized and integrated with discussions of the other two.

Indeed, in his later writings, Rawls moves closer to the idea of freedom as merely a matter of living in accordance with one's individually determined comprehensive doctrine, while Habermas has distanced himself from the radically emancipatory view of freedom, and especially from his roots in the critical theory tradition of ideology critique (*Ideologiekritik*). Insofar as others have followed the two, deliberative democratic theory has converged around a less critical and more accommodationist view of freedom. I shall show that, appearances notwithstanding, there remain some crucial divergences between Rawls and Habermas. I further argue that theories of deliberative democracy should resist moving too close to the accommodationist pole.

The divergences between the two traditions also reveal an unresolved tension in theories of deliberative democracy. There is a tension between the heritage of ideology critique, with its concern for emancipation from false consciousness, and the heritage of toleration liberalism, with its concern for letting people decide for themselves what constitutes the good life and the sources of morality. I see this as a tension between two dimensions of freedom, between the free and rational formation of individual beliefs (or internal autonomy) and negative freedom. Resolution of this tension requires a systematic exploration of the multiple dimensions of freedom that public deliberation presupposes and to which deliberative democracy should be normatively committed. The challenge is to develop a more complex and comprehensive theory of freedom that, where possible, integrates the different dimensions and, where integration is not possible, elucidates the conflicts.

In this chapter and the next two, I clarify the fundamental difference between the two traditions' views of freedom and autonomy and discuss whether or not, or to what extent, they should be combined. The first section here makes explicit the dimension of freedom that is prioritized by the Rawlsian diagnosis of contemporary society as characterized by "the fact of reasonable pluralism." The second section elucidates how the Rawlsian idea of public reason relates to the role and strengths of deliberation and how this, in turn, ties in to the view of freedom. The third section discusses the relationship between moral and political autonomy, as well as the issue of perfectionism. In Chapter 5, I turn to Habermasian versions of deliberative democracy, particularly to argue that deliberative democrats should not sever their roots in critical theory and ideology critique. Chapter 6 considers whether and how this commitment can be combined with a commitment to the dimension of freedom stressed by political liberalism.

The Accommodation of Reasonable Doctrines and Negative Freedom

The focus on accommodation of irreconcilable comprehensive doctrines is a relatively recent development related to the Rawlsians' discovery of "the fact of reasonable pluralism." Rawls himself characterizes the main difference between his 1971 *A Theory of Justice* and his 1993 *Political Liberalism* as an adjustment for this fact.[12] The idea of reasonable pluralism also plays a central role in Joshua Cohen's deliberative democracy articles from the 1990s,[13] but it is absent from his influential 1989 "Deliberation and Democratic Legitimacy." A society characterized by reasonable pluralism is one in which the citizens hold irreconcilable but reasonable comprehensive doctrines; that is, they hold irreconcilable views about metaphysics, the meaning of life, the sources of morality, and the like.[14] Reasonable pluralism is central to the Rawlsian view not only because of the fact that citizens hold different views of the good life. The aim is not merely to take us beyond a classical, perfectionist political philosophy of the good life to a Kantian, neutralist one that recognizes that people

have different ideas about what constitutes human happiness or fulfillment. Reasonable pluralism refers to a more fundamental disagreement,
one that concerns both issues of the good life and the reasons behind
the norms that guide citizens' common life. Note that the disagreement is
about the reasons behind the norms guiding our common life, not about
the norms themselves. Regarding the latter, Rawls believes there can be
an "overlapping consensus" among reasonable comprehensive doctrines.[15]
This fundamental disagreement is not seen as a regrettable fact, which
citizens can overcome through enlightenment or learning. Rather, "It is
a permanent feature of the public culture of democracy" (PL, 36).

The Rawlsians see the fundamental challenge of contemporary society
as one of accommodating citizens who hold different worldviews. "[T]he
problem of political liberalism is: How is it possible that there might exist
over time a stable and just society of free and equal citizens profoundly
divided by reasonable though incompatible religious, philosophical, and
moral doctrines?" (PL, xviii). Political liberalism takes citizens' doctrines
as being beyond challenge; it "does not attack or criticize any reasonable
view" (PL, xix).[16] Note that political liberalism does not criticize in its
role *as a theory*; it is not a critical theory in relation to comprehensive
doctrines. Insofar as the function of political philosophy is concerned,
Rawls's premise is the idea of applying "the principles of toleration to
philosophy itself," which entails leaving it "to citizens themselves to settle
the questions of religion, philosophy, and morals in accordance with views
they freely affirm" (PL, 154). This idea seems to exclude the idea that it
is an aim of political philosophy to provoke self-reflection regarding one's
fundamental commitments and beliefs. These commitments and beliefs are
seen as protected by a principle of toleration, which applies not merely
to the coercive powers of the state but to philosophy too. Citizens should
be free from a political philosophy that questions their comprehensive
doctrines. Political liberalism, thus, cannot be a critical theory, as I argue
in Chapter 5 that deliberative democracy should be.

This places political liberals squarely on the terrain of toleration
or Reformation liberalism.[17] By toleration liberalism, I mean a liberalism whose main concern is to accommodate citizens who hold different and irreconcilable views. Its primary normative commitment is the
protection of the negative liberty to live according to one's own ideas.
This liberalism has been contrasted with a liberalism whose central ideal
is autonomy and is connected to the Enlightenment project.[18] Rawls
explicitly denies that political liberalism belongs to the latter project

(PL, xviii).[19] According to political liberalism, people should be left to themselves with their comprehensive views even (apparently) if they hold them nonautonomously.

Autonomy or Enlightenment liberalism is sometimes seen as requiring that citizens live according to views that they have rationally scrutinized and reflectively endorsed themselves, that is, as being committed to an ideal of comprehensive autonomy.[20] Although I return to the question of autonomy later, I emphasize here that adhering to autonomy as opposed to toleration does not necessarily imply a commitment to perfectionism or to the idea that autonomy is a constituent of the good life.

Neither Rawls nor Joshua Cohen believes reasonable pluralism is defective, that it is something citizens should attempt to overcome. It should not, for example, be seen as a result of oppression and therefore "remediable" by emancipation. Rather, it is a product of what Rawls calls the "burdens of judgment" (PL, 54 ff.).[21] Judgment of both theoretical and practical issues is so complex that even reasonable people are unlikely to reach the same conclusions. For Rawls, negative liberty is grounded in the fact that even perfectly reasonable and rational citizens will disagree on many fundamental issues. Thus he says, "Reasonable persons see that the burdens of judgment set limits on what can be reasonably justified to others, and *so* they endorse some form of liberty of conscience and freedom of thought" (PL, 61, emphasis added). There is no expectation that the divisions resulting from the burdens of judgment will be overcome; the aim is to answer how justice is possible for citizens "who *remain* profoundly divided" (PL, 4, emphasis added). There is a clear Madisonian strand here. According to Rawls, reasonable pluralism is "the inevitable long-run result of the powers of human reason at work within the background of enduring free institutions" (PL, 4, cf. 37). Like Madison's factions, the price of defeating comprehensive doctrines is the violation of negative freedom, a cure worse than the disease.[22] Rawls's focus, though, unlike Madison's, is not on interest groups but on ideological-cultural groups, paradigmatically religious groups.[23]

Rawls argues that the fact of reasonable pluralism should result in our acceptance not only of the idea that people decide on issues concerning their private lives individually, but also that "citizens individually decide for themselves in what way the public political conception [of justice] all affirm is related to their own more comprehensive views" (PL, 38). The political conception is based on the public political culture of a democratic society and is supported for *different* reasons by people who hold different comprehensive views. In Rawls's terms, there is an "overlapping consensus" of reasonable comprehensive doctrines about the political conception of justice (PL, 13 ff., 90, 94, 133 ff.). Such an overlapping consensus is all we can and should hope for in a society characterized by reasonable pluralism. The idea of an overlapping consensus entails a very limited role for the practice of public deliberation. There is no aim of finding *common* reasons for supporting the conception of justice that should guide the choice of the basic structure of society. There is also, therefore, no room for the idea that deliberation is a matter of *learning* from each other what are good reasons for supporting or rejecting certain principles of justice. There is, finally, no possibility of deliberatively *changing* the public political culture on which the political conception of justice is based. How can there be public learning and change of the public culture if each relates in different ways to the political conception of justice?

In terms of the relationship between the different dimensions of freedom, there are two remarkable features of Rawls's view. First, the negative dimension of freedom is clearly given pride of place. Second, reasonable citizens are seen as willing to submit their comprehensive views and life plans to the overarching idea of respect for the equal negative liberty of everyone else. I take it that Rawls believes that this equal respect "is implicit in the public political culture of a democratic society," as fundamental ideas of a political conception of justice should be (PL, 13). What is unclear is why respect should have *priority*. The idea that respect should be given priority over imposing one's comprehensive views on others cannot be learned from insights gained from public deliberation, for in Rawls's view reasonable pluralism means that citizens *already* agree on certain fundamentals (such as respect), that they are reasonable from the start, and only refer to presently held beliefs. A person who observes the disagreement that results from the burdens of judgment is given no reason this should lead her to accept the norm of equal negative liberty rather than force everyone else to live according to her preferred comprehensive view. Furthermore, she would have no way of *knowing* the exact boundaries of negative liberty.[24] For a norm such as respect for the equal negative liberty of everyone to have precedence over our other commitments and aims, the overriding epistemic authority of that norm needs to be identified. But the focus on reasonable pluralism does not allow for such an epistemic authority that can trump the other aspects of reasonable comprehensive doctrines.[25]

In political liberalism, negative freedom is disconnected from other dimensions of freedom. It is detached from freedom as the gaining of insights regarding the norms that regulate our common interaction. The acceptance of negative freedom and the determination of its bounds are not seen as products of learning but as given premises, as part of the public political culture of a democratic society. Moreover, negative liberty is disconnected from freedom as public autonomy, since negative liberty is seen as a constraint on, rather than a product of, the common process of deliberation that should be the basis of political decision making. But we may ask if the public political culture of a democratic society, and the norms embedded in it, is not better seen as a *product* of the exercise of deliberative freedom rather than as a given. If we see it in that way, then negative freedom cannot be seen as independent from or prior to the other dimensions of deliberative freedom but rather as coconstitutive with them. That is, of course, the way in which I suggest we should see it. Because Rawls *begins* from a public political culture where equal negative freedom is already a part, he fails to see how such a culture is generated, maintained, and, when necessary, changed. In other words, he ignores the importance of learning and political participation, of internal and public autonomy, for the creation and sustenance of a political culture that respects the equal freedom of people to live in accordance with their own views of the good life.

Rawls's view of the challenges facing modern society entails a conception of freedom that excludes the possibility that freedom could be augmented if fundamental ideas were discussed and criticized. From the perspective of a political conception of justice, freedom cannot refer to the process of the free formation of comprehensive views. On the contrary, the Rawlsian conception of freedom prevents the thematization of this dimension of freedom. Internal autonomy is outside the field of political philosophy (and beyond the idea of public reason, as we shall see). This reveals the clear link between the Rawlsian view and the tradition of negative freedom I discussed in Chapter 1.[26] According to political liberalism, citizens' comprehensive views are off-limits to politics. Since they are the products of freedom, it would be a violation of freedom to criticize them. So peoples' views of truth and morality are a nonpublic matter protected by a principle of toleration or negative freedom. The dimension of freedom that is off-limits as a result of this point of departure common to Rawlsian deliberative democrats concerns the free formation of fundamental views. The focus on reasonable pluralism leads to a priority for negative freedom over free opinion formation or internal autonomy. In short, it provides for a one-dimensional conception of freedom.

The conception of freedom underlying political liberalism implicitly assumes that all interaction, and especially interaction in the political sphere, is a threat to freedom. It thereby obscures the distinction between free and noncoercive interaction, on the one hand, and violent and manipulative interference, on the other. It is therefore unsuitable as a conception on the basis of which we can see public deliberation as an exercise of freedom. To understand public deliberation and deliberative freedom properly, we must make the distinction obscured by negative liberty theorists. When we deliberate, there is a sense in which we interfere with one other, but we do not force one another to do anything. The freedom of the deliberative process cannot be understood in purely negative terms, since it requires the presence of and interaction with others. It does, however, include a negative element, since it must be free *from* force and manipulation.[27] (I discuss this issue more fully in the fourth section of Chapter 6).

Public Reason and Reasonableness

Public reason is the idea that (ostensibly) connects Rawls's political liberalism to the theory of deliberative democracy. I shall discuss the idea of public reason in relation to the concomitant idea of reasonableness. We saw earlier that Rawlsian deliberative democrats begin with *reasonable* pluralism, not merely pluralism. Let us now analyze more closely what reasonable means. There is no short answer to this question. Indeed, I think the discussions around this idea have been somewhat confused, and that clearer distinctions should be drawn between the different uses of reasonableness.[28] Before discussing whether a norm of "reasonableness" should constrain public deliberation, I next make three distinctions and propose five definitions regarding how this norm might be understood. I then argue that some uses of the norm are appropriate, while others are not. Finally, I discuss the issue of when and where this constraint should apply.

Three Distinctions and Five Definitions Regarding the Use of Reasonableness

First, willingness to contribute to or participate in deliberation must be distinguished from the reasonableness of the *content* of one's contributions.

Let us call these two ideas "participation reasonableness" and "content reasonableness," respectively. To explain the first in negative terms, we might say that the most extreme form of participation unreasonableness is to be unwilling to give any type of reason for one's political views and to be unwilling to listen to and accommodate the contributions made by others. This type of reasonableness forms part of Rawls's idea of civility: "[T]he ideal of citizenship imposes a moral, not a legal duty—the duty of civility—to be able to explain to one another on those fundamental questions [regarding constitutional essentials and basic justice] how the principles and policies they advocate and vote for can be supported by the political values of public reason" (PL, 217). The duty of civility, as Rawls defines it, does not separate the idea of being willing to justify one's position and to listen to others from the *content* of the reasons one gives. For Rawlsians, in order to be reasonable, the content of contributions to public deliberation must be political. "The point of the ideal of public reason," Rawls says, "is that citizens are to conduct their fundamental discussions within the framework of what each regards as a political conception of justice based on values that the others can reasonably be expected to endorse and each is, in good faith, prepared to defend that conception so understood" (PL, 226). "Thus the content of public reason is given by a family of political conceptions of justice."[29] So the Rawlsian view implies a constraint on what is an admissible *content* of contributions to public deliberation. Now it is possible to agree with the necessity of the reasonableness constraint of the first kind—regarding the willingness to join deliberation—while disagreeing with the necessity of constraining the content of contributions to deliberation (though we do need *some* form of constraint in order to be able to distinguish participating in deliberation from participating in other forms of communication). Thus there can be participation reasonableness without content reasonableness—though of course not the reverse. Indeed, it would be difficult for anyone to argue that deliberative democracy does not require willingness to participate in deliberation, to argue and listen. But this does not mean accepting the constraints on content such as the one suggested by the Rawlsian idea of public reason.

Second, we should distinguish between reasonableness as a constraint applying to any and all contributions citizens make to deliberation and the reasonableness of their final justifications for decisions, mainly, justifications for coercive laws. Let us call these "contributions to deliberation reasonableness" and "decision justification reasonableness," respectively.

Consider here two quotes from Joshua Cohen regarding reasonableness: (1) "Let us say that people are reasonable, politically speaking, only if they are concerned to live with others on terms that others, as free and equal, also find acceptable."[30] (2) Citizens "are *reasonable* in that they aim to defend and criticize institutions and programs in terms of considerations that others, as free and equal, have *reason to accept*."[31] Cohen is not quite clear here, but it seems to me that two different ideas are being expressed. On the one hand, we might say that to be reasonable, citizens must be concerned that the terms under which they live—the institutions, laws, and policies that regulate interaction—be acceptable to all.[32] On the other hand, we might say that reasonableness requires that any and all points raised in public for or against these institutions, laws, or policies should be acceptable to all. I think that the first of these ideas is one all deliberative democrats would have to accept. The very idea of deliberation, as I see it, entails an attempt to reach agreement on common institutions and laws, and this requires one to seek arguments convincing to all. This is not to say that consensus will be reached, only that the process aims at it; to be concerned to live on mutually acceptable terms is not the same as actually reaching consensus. But the first idea does not commit us to the idea expressed by the second quote, that *all contributions* to deliberation should be acceptable to all. One can be concerned to live on mutually acceptable terms, without restricting oneself to raising points that one believes are (already) acceptable to others. This distinction is obscured in both Joshua Cohen and Rawls, because public reason is not seen as a process.[33] But when we relate public reason to the idea of deliberative democracy, we must see it as such, as I argue later.

Clearly there must be a difference between the contributions we initially bring to a process of public deliberation and the justifications we settle on when we make decisions. During the process of public deliberation, citizens will raise many points and probe many arguments that are not acceptable to others, but citizens present them to provoke deliberation and/or to see how they fare, to see what others might have to say about them, and also to consider more fully whether they might themselves accept them when they have heard the perspectives of their fellow citizens. There is a difference between raising points others have *reason to consider* and raising points others have *reason to accept*. In the deliberative process we might raise points we want others to consider without having any intention that they should or could be accepted as presented, but because we want them to be further developed and refined—or rejected. Accepting openness to all kinds of contributions during the process of deliberation, however, does not entail rejection of the idea that when the decision is to be made or the vote taken, we must adhere to the constraint of reasonableness in the sense of deciding on the basis of a justification we believe is acceptable to all as free, equal, and reasonable. Sometimes it seems as if Rawls means to apply the idea of public reason and reasonableness only to the act of voting or authorizing coercion,[34] but as we saw earlier he also believes it should guide "fundamental discussions" among citizens.[35] To sum up, we can reject contributions to deliberation reasonableness while accepting decision justification reasonableness—there is no logical impossibility in the reverse either, but this is hardly a view anyone would favor.[36]

A third distinction is between reasonableness of content and of form. This is a distinction between *what* is said and *how* it is said. As an example of reasonableness as a constraint on content, I have mentioned the Rawlsian idea of the political. As examples of constraints on the form of deliberation, we might say that it is unreasonable to use manipulation, deception, and threats. Of course, threats also concern both what is said as well as how it is said. But excluding threats from deliberation does not mean excluding certain kinds of reasons, but avoiding what are not properly reasons. The Rawlsians are concerned with "the *kind* of reasons that should be given" in deliberation[37] and not merely with the idea that reasons, as opposed to threats, for example, should be given. By reasonableness of form, then, I am thinking about what it means to distinguish, for instance, between arguing and bargaining. In argumentation, the participants are allowed only to seek to rationally motivate each other, that is, to make the other agree on the basis of the merits of the case and nothing external to it. The only force that is supposed to count in argument is, in Habermas's famous phrase, "the peculiarly constraint-free force of the better argument."[38] Arguing becomes bargaining when the participants start threatening one another or offering one another rewards external to the case at hand. When A bargains with B, A tries to influence B by means of positive or negative sanctions. A is here trying to influence B by controlling her situation. In contrast, when A argues with B, A tries to come to an understanding with B. A is here trying to rationally motivate B, not by controlling her situation but by attempting to affect her intentions.[39] In this case, a reasonableness constraint would be one that required the participants to offer only reasons rather than threats or rewards.[40] I am not saying that a deliberative democracy can only accept strict argument as opposed to, for example, bargaining or rhetoric, but I am stressing how discussions of this issue differ from discussions of constraints on content of reasons *within* argument.[41] And restrictions of content and form can be seen as manifesting emphases on different dimensions of freedom, as we shall see later.

In these three distinctions, reasonableness does not have any epistemic connotations but refers to the civic-mindedness of citizens. It seems that this is the sense in which Rawls and Joshua Cohen use the term.[42] For Rawls, "being reasonable is not an epistemological idea. . . . Rather, it is part of a political ideal of democratic citizenship that includes the idea of public reason" (PL, 62). When presenting the idea, Rawls says, "I specify its basic aspects as virtues of persons" (PL, 48). There are two aspects to the Rawlsian view: (1) a willingness to propose fair terms of cooperation and abide by them; (2) recognizing and accepting the consequences of the burdens of judgment (PL, 48 ff.).[43]

The three distinctions give us five different uses of reasonableness. I do not claim that this list is exhaustive, but I do believe it covers and clarifies some important debates about deliberative democracy. Some short definitions follow for use in the upcoming discussion.[44]

1. *Participation reasonableness*: Citizens are reasonable if they are willing to participate in public deliberation by contributing their own perspectives and listening to those of others.

2. *Content reasonableness*: Citizens are reasonable if they restrict the content of their contributions to deliberation to reasons they can reasonably expect others to endorse.

3. *Contributions to deliberation reasonableness*: Citizens are reasonable if any and all contributions to deliberation they make are reasonable.

4. *Decision justification reasonableness*: Citizens are reasonable if the justifications for their political decisions are reasonable.

5. *Form reasonableness*: Citizens are reasonable if they give their contributions to deliberation a reasonable form.

Discussion of Reasonableness Constraints

Reasonableness in any of its forms should be seen as a virtue and not as a legal obligation. Deliberative democrats do not, to my knowledge, disagree on this; no one suggests *forcing* people to deliberate or to do so in any specific way.[45] Nor does this imply a discussion of the legal limits of free speech. The question is which forms of reasonableness are conducive to deliberation, and to what dimensions of freedom do they relate? That is, reasonableness will be discussed as a possible form of civic virtue, as a quality of citizens that may or may not contribute to the aims of deliberative democracy. This does not mean that we are only interested in civic virtues as independent variables; there are ways to facilitate and encourage their development that do not amount to legal enforcement. To what extent the latter is permissible and desirable depends largely on our conception of freedom.

Participation Reasonableness. All deliberative democrats must accept participation reasonableness, at least in that it is desirable or conducive to deliberation. Clearly, a well-functioning deliberative democracy does require that people be willing to participate in public deliberation. It might be questioned whether this idea can be separated from any idea of reasonableness of content and/or form of contributions to deliberation. It could be said that to participate in deliberation is to contribute with certain kinds of reasons (content constraint) or to contribute only with reasons (form constraint). But I think it makes better sense to separate these ideas. This becomes especially clear when we see deliberation as a process, in particular as a process of learning. In such a process all contributions need not be constrained from the beginning, as I argue later. What matters for the success of deliberation is in the first phase that people are willing to show up and communicate with each other, to speak their minds, and to listen to each other. To be sure, there is a kind of constraint here on both content and form, since reasonableness demands that citizens be willing to speak and listen when they want to change laws and institutions rather than to merely fight or vote. The idea of being willing to deliberate is not freestanding; it must be accompanied by at least a minimal description of what it means to deliberate.

Content reasonableness. Content reasonableness is more controversial and divides Rawlsians from Habermasians. In general, Rawlsians favor such a constraint, while Habermasians reject it.[46] There are two parts to Rawls's own understanding of content reasonableness. First he says that the reasons we offer for political actions must be such that we "reasonably think that other citizens might also reasonably accept those reasons."[47] Then he suggests that such reasons are those that refer to "a family of political conceptions of justice."[48] Comprehensive views, which include any reference to the whole truth, are excluded from public reason. Moreover, anything controversial also is excluded. In public deliberation, "we are to appeal only to presently accepted beliefs" (PL, 224). Reasonable pluralism and the burdens of judgment constitute the background and justification for this requirement (PL, 58 ff.). Because people cannot agree on issues of truth, they should stick to political values, values implicit in the public political culture of a democratic society, and tolerate different views. By not appealing to the whole truth, citizens recognize one another's comprehensive views as reasonable, if mistaken (PL, 127). This is important: Rawls implies that we treat each other respectfully, as free and equal, by *not* engaging each others' comprehensive views.

I have several objections to content reasonableness as a constraint on deliberation. At the most general level, content reasonableness undermines *the very point* of common deliberation, because it sets reasonableness as a predeliberative constraint and not as a product of deliberation. In many ways I think it is difficult to see Rawls's idea of public reason as an ideal for a process of public deliberation at all. Rawls's notion of public reason does not rely on the resources intrinsic to public deliberation as a dialogical process of reaching reasonable outcomes. There is no taking into account that citizens need to hear what others have to say before they can know what is reasonable. The assumption is that citizens already know what might count as reasonable arguments and outcomes. But then there is no need for any actual processes of exchanging information and reasons.[49] All that is required of citizens is that they make arguments that they *believe* others can accept as reasonable persons. This might involve private or internal deliberation, but it does not require a public process of forming one's opinions in light of what others have to say.

There is an interesting parallel to Jean-Jacques Rousseau in the requirements of public reason, a parallel that Rawls himself acknowledges (PL, 219 ff.). In *On the Social Contract*, Rousseau asks citizens to vote not in accordance with what they want but in accordance with what they think the general will is.[50] The general will is formed not by learning what others want but by asking the right question to oneself. It is formed by each person voting what he or she thinks is in the common interest.[51] Similarly, in Rawls, public reason is a matter of answering the right question when one votes; it is a regulative ideal for how one ought to vote. Public reason is about voting for what one thinks others also would find reasonable. Thus all we get from the voting according to public reason is an aggregation of what various citizens believe might be acceptable to each other.

A primary problem with the content reasonableness constraint is that it does not consider deliberation as a process, a process that when stylized can be seen as involving stages of (1) presentation of information, claims, ideas, and opinions, (2) arguments pro and con, and (3) agreement or decision making. It is not necessary that claims and new ideas be reasonable in the presentation stage—we often cannot know whether claims and new ideas are reasonable until we have heard what others have to say. What matters is that the final decisions are reasonable and acceptable to all.[52] When deliberation is not seen as a process, then its value as a form of learning also falls out of sight. And in order to see the full significance of public deliberation for freedom, we should see it as a learning process. Before I enter the deliberative process, I do not know what others think and want, or what I exactly think and want. And, essentially, we do not know what we would want to do together. When we first enter the deliberative process, we cannot know what others would find reasonable and justifiable. All these are things we learn in the process of deliberation, by speaking and listening to others, by presenting our needs, interests, and opinions, by finding reasons that we learn whether others can accept, by raising objections to reasons we cannot accept, and so on. Those reasons that survive a nondistorted deliberative process are reasonable and acceptable.

The lack of concern for deliberation as a learning process can fruitfully be connected to a lack of normative commitment to freedom as internal autonomy or freedom as the opportunity to form one's political opinions on the basis of the best available information and reasons. The former also can be seen as neglect of a certain aspect of public autonomy, namely, that if citizens are to rule themselves, they must first ascertain what they really want, both individually and collectively.

There are some further implications regarding freedom that can be drawn from the way Rawls construes content reasonableness. These can be seen from two different angles—one regards which view of freedom is taken as the point of departure, the other regards what citizens hope to achieve from deliberation in terms of freedom. In the first section of this chapter I dealt with the starting point of freedom as a matter of respecting people's irreconcilable comprehensive doctrines. Regarding the second aspect, deliberation is not seen as a way for citizens to overcome their reasonable differences, or to emancipate themselves from their mis-conceptions. Rather, it is regarded as a means for coming to some kind of agreement despite enduring differences. A conservative bias can be detected in Rawls's insistence that citizens must refer only to presently accepted beliefs. Rawlsian public reason is not a means of overcoming prejudices, entrenched meanings, ideologies, or any of the other issues that concern critical theorists. As we saw, Rawls claims that excluding comprehensive views or the whole truth from public reason is a way of respecting each other as reasonable. But this also excludes the possibility of helping one another to overcome our prejudices, misconceptions, or ideological delusions. Reasonableness as a content constraint favors the protection of the negative freedom to determine one's own views over the autonomous, intersubjective formation of those views. Whether there is a conflict between these two dimensions of freedom is an issue that I return to in Chapter 6. It seems Rawls believes there is a conflict, since he wants to shield citizens from the discussion of their comprehensive views in the public forum.

Contributions and justifications. The distinction between contribution to deliberation reasonableness and decision justification reasonableness also becomes clearer when we see deliberation as a process. Rawls's failure to draw this distinction is, moreover, related to his tendency to reduce politics to coercion. He says, "Political power is always coercive power backed by the government's use of sanctions" (PL, 136). And, "It would be unreasonable to use state power to enforce our own comprehensive view" (PL, 138). But even if Rawls is right, that it would be unreasonable to enforce one's comprehensive view using force, this is not the same as saying that it is unreasonable to discuss at the comprehensive as opposed to the political level. Political discussion is not coercion.[53]

For Rawls, the use of public reason is largely related to the moment of decision-making. When, for instance, he is explaining how the ideal of public reason applies to citizens who do not hold public office, he says: "Ideally citizens are to think of themselves *as if* they were legisla-tors and ask themselves what statutes, supported by what reasons . . . they would think it most reasonable to enact."[54] Thus Rawls's view of public reason applies to the final stage of deliberation. This might be intentional, although, as I mentioned earlier, he sometimes says it should guide our fundamental *discussions* and not merely our decisions. But if that is the case, then public reason is not a criterion for public deliberation, but only a regulative ideal for decision making.[55] Understood as the latter, I could accept it with certain modifications. *After* processes of deliberation in which citizens have learned from one another, they ought to vote in accordance with what they believe the different contributions have taught them is most reasonable for all. Clearly it would be unreasonable and contrary to the aims of deliberative democracy if citizens first deliberated with one other and then went on to vote contrary to the insights they had gained in the process. This does not mean, however, that citizens are obligated to go along with the mood of the majority. If they have not been convinced by the arguments given, then it would not be unreasonable to vote against what others believe most reasonable. Thus I do think it makes sense to see decision justification reasonableness as a virtue conducive to deliberative democracy. But the requirement that all contributions made in deliberation should be reasonable in the sense of being acceptable to others undermines the very idea of public deliberation. To sum up, the point is that before we can know what is reasonable, we have to try out different ideas in the back and forth of deliberation, and sometimes it is acceptable to provoke deliberation with means that are not themselves strictly deliberative.

Regarding the last point, the criterion for using nondeliberative forms of communication should be whether the contribution furthers or obstructs the chances for deliberation in the future.[56] Many forms of political action are not deliberative in themselves but are nevertheless perfectly legitimate in a deliberative democracy because they contribute to the deliberative agenda and spark deliberation of neglected issues. Mass demonstrations, for example, are a show of power rather than a form of deliberation, but if they lead to more inclusive deliberations—inclusive in terms both of topics and participants—then there is nothing unreasonable about them. But, of course, mass demonstrations should not by themselves determine political outcomes—that would undermine the idea that decisions have to be justified by reasons and not enforced by superior strength or threats.[57]

One further remark is necessary in order to avoid misunderstanding regarding calling decision justification reasonableness "a virtue." This virtue entails that when I as a citizen make a political decision, I should be able to justify it both to myself and to others. For example, I am unreasonable if I vote for my original choice after I have learned in deliberation that others regard my position as outrageous and that its implementation cannot be justified. But speaking of virtues in this context should not be seen as a matter of purity of motive. It is not a requirement that I vote for something *because* there is a mutually acceptable justification for it. As long as there is such a justification for the decision, my deeper motivations can be as they may. I also stress this point because I do not think that such a virtuous disposition is one of the requirements (or dimensions) of the freedom to which deliberative democracy is or should be committed. The conception of deliberative freedom I propose has no such perfectionist implications.

Form reasonableness. Although Habermas has carefully distinguished between different forms of communication,[58] he has not articulated the requirements of only using arguments as a matter of reasonableness or as a virtue. Nevertheless, in the Habermasian framework, it would clearly be an advantage if citizens limited themselves to using only arguments rather than threats or other resources external to the issue under discussion. Still, it is important to see—also to understand his view of freedom—that Habermas's project never has been to tell people that they ought to argue. Such a moralistic outlook lies far from the idea of a critical theory. His theories of communicative action, discourse ethics, and deliberative politics have been more concerned with the *conditions and procedures* of deliberation than with the virtues of the participants.[59] Some have thought that Habermas has thereby neglected the need for a democratic ethos.[60] I shall not go into that discussion here.[61] What I am interested in at this point is how, in terms of dimensions of freedom, the concern with form differs from the concern with content of deliberation. I believe this perspective shows an essential and a significant difference between Rawlsians and Habermasians.[62]

A core idea in Habermas is that people interpret their needs and form their identities, desires, and opinions in communication, or intersubjectively. When this communication is distorted, the processes of identity and opinion formation do not take place rationally and autonomously. So the concern for the form of communication is a concern that the formation of identities, need interpretations, interest articulation, and opinion and will formation all happen rationally and autonomously. The dimension of freedom that comes to the fore here is not the right to form one's comprehensive views individually or nonpublicly, as in Rawlsian content reasonableness, but the ideal of forming one's views in communication free from all forces other than that of the better argument. Both of these dimensions of freedom can be seen as negative dimensions, since they both protect citizens *from* something. The constraint on content protects citizens against discussion of their comprehensive views. The constraint on form protects citizens against all forces other than the better argument. But the Habermasian view cannot be *purely* negative, since we need others to be free. "Because persons are individuated only by way of socialization, the freedom of one individual cannot be tied to the freedom of everybody else in a purely negative way, through reciprocal restrictions."[63] The two dimensions also can both be positively formulated. The constraint on content is concerned with the freedom *to* determine one's own comprehensive views. The constraint on form is concerned with the freedom *to* rationally and intersubjectively form one's opinion and will; in other words, its positive aim is internal autonomy.

Thus the Habermasian view shifts the focus away from reasonableness as a virtue of citizens to a concern for the social conditions under which people form their views. We move from restricting the admissible content of reasons as a screening mechanism to a critique of social conditions and procedures of deliberation. I believe this point relates to Habermas's roots in critical theory, in particular ideology critique, and therefore I turn to that issue in the following chapter.

Public Forum and Background Culture

The proceeding discussion has been critical of the constraints on deliberation that the Rawlsian idea of public reason entails. It might be objected that I have ignored that Rawls's view of public reason applies only to what he calls the public forum and not to deliberation in the public sphere of civil society. Criticisms of Rawls for wanting to constrain civil society discussions are misdirected, it could be said, since public reason does not apply to what he calls the background culture: Rawls's public forum should not be confused with Habermas's public sphere.[64] In "The Idea of Public Reason Revisited," Rawls explicitly notes that the idea of public reason applies only to the public political forum. He sees this forum as divided into three parts: (1) "the judges in their decisions"; (2) "the discourse of government officials, especially chief executives and legislators"; and (3) "the discourse of candidates for public office and their campaign managers."[65] In contrast, the idea of public reason does not apply to the background culture, that is, "the culture of civil society."[66]

It is certainly important to recognize that Rawls limits the application of the idea of public reason to a certain forum and does not believe it should guide all political discussions in society. My criticism, however, has been directed at the very idea of restricting what can be said in public deliberation, no matter which institutional forum it applies to. Furthermore, the institutional separation that Rawls makes is not as clear-cut as he claims. First, public reason does not merely apply to the three groups of people listed in the previous paragraph but also to citizens who, as mentioned, are to think of themselves *as if* they were legislators when they elect representatives and hold them accountable. Second, public reason does not seem to be an ideal that should merely regulate decision making; that is, it is not merely an ideal that requires what I have called "decision justification reasonableness" but also an ideal that requires "contributions to deliberation reasonableness." This is clearly the case for government officials whose discourse Rawls says it should regulate. But it seems to apply also to citizens' discussions and not merely to their vote: "When citizens deliberate, they exchange views and debate their supporting reasons concerning public political questions. . . . It is at this point that public reason is crucial, for it characterizes such citizens' reasoning concerning constitutional essentials and matters of basic justice."[67] Thus Rawls's ideal of public reason constrains not only government officials but also ordinary citizens, and it applies not only to the justifications of decisions but also regulates and restricts contributions to deliberation.

I think Rawls draws the wrong distinctions here, even for his own purposes. I suppose public reason should apply only to the public political forum because this forum is directly connected to the making, execution, and adjudication of coercive law. Civil society actors can discuss without constraints because their deliberations do not directly relate to the coercive powers of the state. As we have seen, the constraint imposed by public reason is that there must be no reference to controversial issues of truth and morality; citizens should be free to determine these individually. Thus the purpose of public reason seems to be this: State coercion should have a justification, which does not require any reasonable person to question his or her fundamental beliefs. There can be discussion of issues of truth and ultimate foundations in civil society, as long as they are not directed at or concerned with the making or application of law. But to achieve these aims, Rawls would need to see public reason as imposing a "decision justification reasonableness" constraint, not a "contributions to deliberation reasonableness" constraint. There is no need to constrain the discourses of legislators and political candidates; what matters is that the final decisions they make are justified in a way that is accessible and acceptable to all.[68] If Rawls's concern is with the justification of coercion, then why should we restrict the debate that *precedes* the final justifications? The public political forum is not merely a forum of decision making but of debate; it is not merely the site of the closure of society-wide deliberations but itself a forum of deliberation. Parliamentary debates may lead to coercion, but they are not themselves coercive.

I am especially troubled by the idea of restricting the deliberations of legislators. In a deliberative democracy the legislature should be a prime forum of public deliberation, and its members should not be restricted in terms of which types of arguments they may use. This is the case because the legislature is the arena that ideally brings together all the information and reasons generated in the multiple deliberations that take place in all corners of society. The legislature is a central forum to which citizens can direct their ideas and reasons and from which all citizens can learn about the types of reasons that are given and found convincing in other parts of society, to which they are otherwise not exposed. And the legislature is the place that ideally turns the myriad of civil society deliberations into law and makes the citizens who are their source authors of the laws. If the deliberations of the legislature are conducted in a different language, the language of political conceptions of justice, then there is an unfortunate disconnect between civil society deliberations, which in Rawls are unrestricted, and the deliberations of legislators.

Rawls acknowledges that there can be rigorous discussions of comprehensive issues among civil associations in the background culture, indeed, that this is part of a society that "has vitality and spirit." But he insists that such discussion exhibits "the culture of the social, not of the publicly political."[69] From the point of view of learning and internal autonomy, restricting rigorous discussion of comprehensive issues of truth and morality to the background culture in Rawls's sense has detrimental consequences. The nonpublic discussions of the background culture are not society-wide but take place *within* civil society associations such as "churches and universities, scientific societies and professional groups"; they are "public with respect to their members, but nonpublic with respect to political society and to citizens generally" (PL, 220). The problem in terms of learning is that the members of these associations, even if they have internal discussions about the validity of their views, do not have such discussions with people who fundamentally disagree with them. They are discussions among the like-minded, which do not tend to have the salutary effects in terms of self-reflection and reaching agreement that we should hope for from the perspective of a deliberative democratic theory committed to the ideal of internal autonomy. These effects depend on institutional arrangements and social settings that bring people with different views and perspectives together in comprehensive deliberations.[70]

Political and Moral Autonomy

I claimed in the first section of this chapter that arguing for autonomy rather than toleration does not necessarily commit one to perfectionism, that is, to the idea that autonomy is a constituent of the good life, which the state should promote. The following argument supports that claim. Rawls distinguishes political liberalism from "the comprehensive liberalisms of Kant and Mill" on more than one occasion, and he sees both theorists as espousing ideals of both political and ethical autonomy, which applies to the whole of life (PL, 78; see also 37, 145). But this pairing of Mill and Kant obscures the important distinction between autonomy as an ethical value, that is, as constituting the good life, and autonomy as a source of our moral obligations. Mill uses autonomy (or liberty) in the first, perfectionist sense when he speaks of the values of spontaneity and individuality in Chapter 3 of *On Liberty*.[71] Autonomy plays a quite different role in Kant's moral philosophy. Kant's understanding of autonomy is complex and even obscure and refers to a number of different ideas.[72] The usage I am emphasizing is what Christine Korsgaard calls the appeal to autonomy as a "source of normativity."[73] As a source of normativity, autonomy is not a matter of the good life but of the source of the authority of our moral obligations. To say that autonomy is the source of our moral obligations is to say that their authority comes from the fact that their genesis is our own (rational) will. Now Rawls also would see this as being too comprehensive. A commitment to autonomy as the source of morality is incompatible with religious views that hold that God is the source of our moral obligations, for example.[74] Kantian autonomy involves a commitment to rational standards of choice that cannot be accepted by all comprehensive doctrines. Still, it is important to distinguish this form of comprehensiveness from an ethical one, that is, one regarding what constitutes a good and happy life.

The question that must be raised is whether Rawls and Joshua Cohen are ultimately relying on some unthematized version of Kantian autonomy[75]—and whether deliberative democracy must necessarily do so as well. Reasonable pluralism, Cohen says, includes "persistent disagreement about . . . the values of choice and self-determination."[76] And it is not the role of deliberation to overcome this disagreement; it is (somewhat paradoxically) protected by the citizens' negative liberty. But public autonomy is seen as something reasonable citizens agree on and as a substantive value of Rawlsian deliberative democracy. According to Cohen, "Deliberative democracy provides for a form of political autonomy: that all those who are governed by collective decisions—who are expected to govern their own conduct by those decisions—must find the bases of those decisions acceptable."[77] Full autonomy, in Rawls's terminology, is a political and not an ethical value; it is achieved in citizens' "public recognition and *informed* application of the principles of justice in their political life," and "it is also realized by *participating* in society's public affairs and sharing in its collective self-determination over time" (PL, 77 ff., emphasis added).

Now I do not disagree with Rawls and Joshua Cohen on the idea that public autonomy is an integral part of deliberative democracy, while a commitment to autonomy as an ethical value is not. But some of what they say here seems to contradict some of the other normative commitments of political liberalism. Note that citizens are required to participate in politics and to make informed decisions regarding the application of the principles of justice. It is only if they do so that they are fully autonomous as citizens. We must assume that this is also what makes coercive law legitimate. But if that is the case, then the source of the authority of law is based on the fact that it is given by citizens themselves on the basis of their reason. This is a basically Kantian notion of autonomy, which clashes, for example, with political obligation based on an appeal to the authority of tradition or God, and hence with the way Rawls and Joshua Cohen believe we should respect comprehensive doctrines. I think deliberative democrats should accept that their ideal implies a commitment to a notion of public autonomy that is basically Kantian and a part of the Enlightenment project. This, of course, contradicts Rawls's insistence that political liberalism is not committed to the latter project. It also is difficult to reconcile with Cohen's insistence that there need not be any agreement on the value of choice and self-determination. Deliberative democracy *does* require agreement on the value of freedom and autonomy as the source of our political obligations, but this does not imply agreement on autonomy being constitutive of the good life.

Conclusion

Because of their starting point in the fact of reasonable pluralism and the consequences they draw from it, Rawlsian deliberative democrats undermine the enlightenment and emancipatory potentials of processes of public deliberation. The Rawlsians take deliberative democracy in an unfortunate uncritical direction and confuse the potentials of public deliberation. The one-dimensional concern for accommodation of citizens with different and incompatible comprehensive doctrines excludes the possibility and even the thematization of the fact that freedom might be enhanced by critical discussion of fundamental differences in worldviews. From the perspective of political liberalism, the importance of the free formation of political opinions, of internal autonomy, is invisible. The content reasonableness required by Rawlsians in the exercise of public reason shows a concern not with the free and enlightened formation of political opinions but with protecting citizens from discussion of their fundamental ideas.

When it comes to defining political autonomy, however, Rawls and Cohen do see the importance of informed participation but fail to explain how this relates to respect for each citizen's individual decision about how to connect her or his comprehensive views to justification of the laws. And, in particular, they fail to explain how their basically Kantian notion of autonomy, even if it applies to us only as citizens, can be combined with mere accommodation of those citizens who see political obligation as based on the appeal to the authority of tradition or God rather than to the fact that we have given the laws to ourselves on the basis of our reason.

I have suggested that Kantian autonomy—seen as the source of our moral and political obligations rather than as an ethical value—is a valuable and an essential aspect of deliberative democracy. (I will make this argument more fully in Chapters 5 and 6.) I have also indicated that a one-dimensional focus on negative liberty at the expense of any concern for the free formation of political opinions, or internal autonomy, is problematic. I should emphasize that despite my criticisms of negative freedom theorists, I do see negative freedom as a *dimension* of freedom; my argument is against seeing it as the *only* dimension of freedom. I will flesh out the arguments on the meaning and requirements of internal autonomy, as well as how it can be combined with respect for some degree of negative freedom, in the following two chapters. In Chapter 5, I consider a view that focuses on the relation between internal and public autonomy.

CHAPTER FIVE

Freedom as Emancipation

Deliberative Democracy as Critical Theory

*I*n his early *The Structural Transformation of the Public Sphere*, Jürgen Habermas reproaches John Stuart Mill for demanding "not criticism but tolerance."[1] What Mill lacks, according to Habermas, is an idea of a universal interest to which criticism can refer as criterion. It is exactly the search for a way to solve the problem of how a plurality of competing interests could converge in a general interest that has animated Habermas's writings since 1962.[2] The theories of communicative action and discourse ethics are aimed at discovering a normative potential and a criterion to which we can refer despite our differences (of interests as well as values). We do not need to go into the complicated details of these theoretical developments here. What matters for our discussion is to make explicit Habermas's normative commitments, especially in terms of his view of freedom, and to show how they contrast with those of Rawlsian models of deliberative democracy discussed in the previous chapter.

A main difference between Habermas and the Rawlsians is that Habermas's theory does not stand back from criticizing citizens' metaphysical doctrines. Habermas is still interested not merely in tolerance but in criticism: "Philosophy should not merely accept established convictions but must also be able to *judge* them by the standards of a rational conception of justice."[3] This conception of justice, however, is not a substantial one determined by the philosopher who then imposes it from without on the citizens as subjects.[4] Rather, the criticism is aimed at convictions only indirectly; it is primarily focused on procedures and conditions, the procedure of which the convictions are the product and the conditions under which they were formed. But, it is true, it is a conception that must be the product of reason, albeit a procedural reason. This is a central

Kantian element in Habermas. Thus in the Preface to *Between Facts and Norms*, Habermas says that modernity "depends on a procedural reason, that is, on a reason that puts itself on trial."[5] According to Habermas, such a procedural reason should be distinguished from and substitute for essentialist Platonic reason and Natural Law—as well as from unreason and relativism. Rawls takes exception to such a view. It is too comprehensive, he thinks, because it criticizes comprehensive views and asks citizens to replace their comprehensive views with procedural reason.[6] The question is whether deliberative democracy can do without a commitment to procedural reason. It is a thesis of this book that it cannot and should not, because of the internal relationship between procedural reason and deliberative freedom. The chapter on Rawlsian deliberative democracy gave part of the argument for this thesis; this chapter and the next two supply further arguments.

Let me begin by briefly noting two important dimensions of freedom involved in Habermas's view of the 1990s when he returns to democratic theory in a comprehensive manner.[7] First, the reason for criticizing established convictions can be seen as grounded in a concern that these convictions, even if citizens see them as their own, are not reflectively and freely endorsed. Such convictions are not freely endorsed when they are not the product of insights gained in free and public deliberation. Second, Habermas always connects the idea of criticism to an idea of public autonomy. For criticism to avoid becoming paternalistic or authoritarian, it must be part of and speak to the common exercise of public autonomy in processes of public deliberation. Both of these dimensions of freedom are combined in what Habermas admits to be the "dogmatic core" of his theory: "the idea of autonomy according to which human beings act as free subjects only insofar as [1] they obey just those laws they give themselves [2] in accordance with insights they have acquired intersubjectively."[8] In order to be autonomous, citizens must not only give laws to themselves but must do so on the basis of the best available reasons. Rawls's notion of full autonomy, which is a specifically political value, includes the first, but it excludes the second because of his reluctance to criticize comprehensive doctrines.[9] Thus we do find an idea of public autonomy in Rawls, but it differs from Habermas's view in not being concerned with *how* citizens come to hold the views that make them support some legal norms over others. I see this "how" as a matter of internal autonomy, or lack thereof.

Habermas's theory attempts to be comprehensive only in the sense in which Kant's is it, and not in the fuller sense of giving answers to what constitutes a good and fulfilling life.[10] Habermas's view is more comprehensive than Rawls's purports to be, because it requires that the laws we give to ourselves must be based on insights that are the product of what we might call comprehensive deliberation, that is, deliberation that *may* include all issues. In terms of freedom and autonomy, it is more comprehensive because it requires that when citizens assent to a law they do so on the basis of insights gained in public deliberation and not merely on the basis of their in-public, noncriticizable, comprehensive views. But in Habermas, only the reasons for supporting laws are publicly discussed and scrutinized, not citizens' private life projects.

I share Habermas's general commitments and aims as briefly outlined above but also want to hold onto some of the earlier concerns of critical theory, especially as expressed in the theory of ideology. In this chapter and the next I analyze what the earlier concern with ideology implies in terms of dimensions of freedom, and I discuss whether they can—or to what extent they can—be combined with other dimensions of freedom, in particular with the concern for the negative freedom to determine one's own conception of the good. My approach differs from Habermas's by being based on a theory of freedom rather than on a theory of argumentation, and it departs from Habermas's current writings by explicitly incorporating the freedom commitment entailed by the theory of ideology.

In the previous chapter I argued that the focus on ancient versus modern liberties or public autonomy versus negative freedom obscures the existence of a third dimension of freedom: internal autonomy. In order to explicate this dimension of freedom and understand how it found its way into models of deliberative democracy with roots in the critical theory tradition of the Frankfurt School, I suggest we look more closely at the idea of ideology. The concern for internal autonomy might, however, come into conflict with the equally important commitment to ethical pluralism, that is, pluralism of conceptions of the good. I discuss to what extent this fear is justified and relate this discussion to an argument about the dependence of deliberative freedom on a democratic ethos in Chapter 6.

The Critique of Ideology and Internal Autonomy

Recent writings on deliberative democracy have not been particularly concerned with the critique of ideology.[11] The critique of ideology does not sit well with political liberalism,[12] and it also is not part of Habermas's writings on deliberative democracy. There are, however, still some strands in later Habermasian writings that reveal their roots in the tradition of ideology critique, though they need to demarcate themselves more strongly from Rawlsian political liberalism than they do. I argue that there are some elements of ideology critique that deliberative democratic theory could only abandon at the cost of blunting its critical edge. And, in particular, the critique of ideology thematizes an important dimension of freedom that has a tendency to fall out of view in liberal theories, namely, the free formation of political opinions or, for short, internal autonomy. To make explicit the idea of internal autonomy I return to the earlier Habermas as well as to other writings on ideology. It is crucial in light of my concern for multiple dimensions of freedom, however, not to base ideology critique on perfectionism or a conception of the good; rather, it should be based on reasons of justification. The acceptance of ideology critique, moreover, means we must give a stronger weight to public autonomy, because we otherwise fall into paternalism. Before we go into these issues, however, we have to clarify what ideology critique is.

It is not possible or necessary to go into a full account of the theory of ideology here.[13] What I shall do instead is take the perspective of ideology critique as expressing a specific dimension of freedom.[14] Thus my question is: Which understanding of freedom does the theory of ideology entail?

When we are concerned with the oppressive effects of ideology, we are not concerned with external but *internal* obstacles to emancipation, at least in the first instance. Our lack of freedom when we are ideologically delusioned has not so much to do with the external world (that we cannot do something because others prevent us from doing it) as with our own beliefs and desires. The theory of ideology thus rests on a concern for *internal* autonomy.

We should draw a distinction here regarding two ways in which ideology can block emancipation. First, ideology might have the effect that we do not believe things *should* be different than they are. Second, ideology has the effect that we do not think things *could* be different than they are. In the latter case, ideological delusion means "that the agents' form of consciousness is artificially limited, i.e. that they suffer from restrictions on what they can perceive as real possibilities for themselves."[15] The first form of ideology makes certain relations and conditions appear legitimate. This might be the most obvious form of ideology. It is the form that Marxists speak of when they say that bourgeois ideology makes capitalist relations of production appear legitimate. Marx's labor theory of value and exploitation has a critical intent insofar as it shows that the relationship between the bourgeoisie and the proletariat was not a free and an equal form of exchange, as it was claimed to be in bourgeois ideology.[16] Marx saw the political economists that preceded him as "ideologists of capital," because their theories obscured "the workings of power, either by ignoring them or by couching them in technical terms, such as 'value' or 'rent.'"[17]

Ideologies do not only function by legitimizing certain relationships and institutions but also by reifying them, that is, making them seem "'natural' and thus, ineradicable, unavoidable, and unalterable."[18] When Habermas in the late 1960s described science and technology as (a new form of) ideology, he saw them as having this second function. He saw science and technology not as explicit forms of legitimation, not as what we might call moral ideologies. They do not—as bourgeois ideology does—include norms and values that can legitimize certain developments. Rather, they are precisely characterized by a professed value-freedom, promoted by the epistemological theory of positivism. It is exactly the bracketing of moral questions that makes science an ideology.[19] This "new ideology," as Habermas calls it, "is distinguished from its predecessor in that it severs the criteria for justifying the organization of social life from any normative regulation of interaction, thus depoliticizing them."[20] This form of ideology still has legitimating power, albeit an implicit one.[21] No one objects to or questions the natural and inevitable.

In terms of freedom, an important "point of a theory of ideology is that agents are sometimes suffering from a coercion of which they are not immediately aware."[22] As such, it relies on a dimension of freedom hidden to the liberal theorist, what I call internal autonomy. Liberalism can be the basis of one form of critique based on its understanding of freedom, namely, critique of institutions that rely on direct interference with our actions and choices beyond those that harm others. But this is too limited. Ideology critique, with its implied idea of internal autonomy, gets at two closely related issues that we cannot get at from the perspective of a social criticism based on the concept of negative freedom alone. First, the fact that there are no external constraints on an action is not sufficient for me being free to do it, for I may be prevented from choosing to do it by my form of consciousness, that is, by my constellation of beliefs and desires.[23] To be free to do what I want does not cover all dimensions of freedom. If I am not also free to want what I want, or if my very wants are shaped unfreely, then I still lack freedom in the sense of internal autonomy. The person who is ideologically constrained cannot be said to be unfree from the perspective of Hobbes's or Berlin's notion of freedom, since she finds no obstacles to doing what she wants. The point of ideology critique is that there is more to be said about freedom, more questions that need to be asked. We want not to ask merely whether there were any external obstacles to an omitted action, such as legal restrictions, but also whether the individual came to her conclusions whether to perform the action or not freely. So if a certain group or class of people, for example, does not run for office, we do not merely ask whether there, for example, is legal discrimination that prevents them from doing so but also whether their own self-understanding is freely formed, whether they based their decision (or nondecision) on good reasons. The theory of ideology rejects the answer that if someone does not do something to which there are no external obstacles, then there are no objections in terms of freedom. Another dimension of freedom with which we should be concerned is internal autonomy.[24]

There is an analogy here between the criticism I make of negative freedom from the perspective of ideology critique and Steven Lukes's critique of the behaviorist conception of power, as Robert Dahl famously defined it: "*A* has power over *B* to the extent that he can get *B* to do something *B* would not otherwise do."[25] According to Lukes, this definition fails to capture all dimensions of power: "*A* may exercise power over *B* by getting him to do what he does not want to do, but he also exercises power over him by influencing, shaping, or determining his very wants."[26] Lukes's analysis of power shows an important point, namely, that *A*, when successfully shaping *B's* desires, does not need to exercise power in the sense of making *B* do something contrary to his (*B's*) desires. If *A* can prevent conflicts of interest "from arising in the first place," that is, if *A* can suppress *B's* grievances, then *A* does not need to use power to win an explicit conflict.[27] Similarly, if *A* wants *B* to do something (or avoid that she does something), *A* does not need to limit *B's* negative freedom, in the sense of freedom from external obstacles to doing what she wants to do, if he can make *B* want what he wants her to want. This shows that a person can be free to do what she wants to do and still not be free. These formulations illustrate that not only external "physical" obstacles—chains, imprisonment, enslavement[28]—limit freedom but also such phenomena as manipulation, propaganda, and hegemonic domination that do not directly interfere with action but with desires and opinions.

The second issue made clear by the theory of ideology, while neglected by the negative freedom perspective, is that freedom is not only limited by the interference of *others* but might be *self*-imposed. "The agents in a society impose coercive institutions on themselves by participating in them, accepting them without protest, etc. Simply by acting in an apparently 'free' way according to the dictates of their world-picture, the agents reproduce relations of coercion."[29] The notion of negative freedom cannot address such situations, because people, in a sense, are not prevented from doing what they want. They consent to their situation and hence must be free from a liberal perspective. Negative freedom, thus, is not a sufficiently complex conception of freedom for a critical theory; it is only a conception of one *dimension* of freedom.

The Rawlsian adherence to the negative freedom tradition and its commitment to not criticizing comprehensive doctrines makes political liberalism incapable of approaching this third dimension of freedom (internal autonomy) manifest in the theory of ideology. Indeed, Rawls explicitly rejects the critique of ideology: "We should not readily accuse one another of self- or group-interest, prejudice or bias, and of such deeply entrenched errors as ideological blindness and delusion. Such accusations arouse resentment and hostility, and block the way to reasonable agreement. The disposition to make such accusations without compelling grounds is plainly unreasonable, and often a declaration of intellectual war."[30] By taking this stance, Rawls excludes the possibility of investigating whether even reasonable comprehensive doctrines and the overlapping consensus between them could not be such worldviews that inadvertently reproduce relations of coercion. If there is no probing of citizens' comprehensive views in deliberation, then there is no nonviolent way in which it can be checked whether the policies and institutions they support are defensible. Moreover, Rawls's concern with stability leads in effect to a *strategy of depoliticization*.

We should not disregard Rawls's point that charges of ideological delusion might create resentment, however. Jack Knight and James Johnson are too quick in dismissing Rawls on this point when they object, "It very plausibly is among the desirable features of democratic deliberation that it allows participants to raise [the possibility that some are deluded by ideology], to challenge those to whom they believe the charge applies, to do so publicly and, thereby, to afford those so challenged to respond."[31]

Knight and Johnson here reduce ideology to other forms of error and self-interest. In the Marxist and critical theory tradition, however, ideology is something more systemic. Not all cases of persons being wrong about what they can get and what they want are cases of ideological delusion. There are many other sorts of mistakes than those caused by ideology.[32] The critique of ideology is only concerned with beliefs and desires that are *systematically* distorted by the circumstances under which they are formed.[33] In the Habermasian version, the concern is "systematically distorted communication," since he maintains that communication is the process by which we form our beliefs and desires.[34] Moreover, and as I shall argue more fully later, ideology critique is not directed immediately at certain people's beliefs but rather at the conditions under which these beliefs are formed and at the general structure of communication. Ideology critique does not need to challenge specific people with being deluded—something Rawls probably is right to say would create resentment and undermine rather than promote deliberation—but intends to suggest that the conditions under which *all of us* form our beliefs are distorting. That is, it aims to show that there is a problem with the general structure of communication in our society. The connection between ideology critique and deliberation, then, is not that we in deliberation can charge each other with being ideologically deluded (as Knight and Johnson hold) but that we need nondistorted deliberation in order to overcome our ideological one-sidedness.

Furthermore, ideology critique rejects the idealistic notion that we can overcome ideology merely through critically discussing it.[35] Ideologies do not disappear until the power structures that uphold them are dissolved. However, from the perspective of deliberative democracy that I am advancing—as committed to multiple dimensions of freedom—the critique of ideology must *begin* with critical discussion, but as I argue later in this chapter this is a discussion aimed at changing the structures that uphold ideology.

The problem with ideological domination is that it excludes certain issues from being publicly discussed at all. The call for a more deliberative democracy on this basis is a call for politicization, politicization in the sense of opening up for reflection the practical-moral sides of our relationships and the conditions under which we live. Increased deliberation in order to overcome ideology does not require that we question each other's deepest motives. What matters is that the validity of the beliefs is being probed in a free and nondistorted manner. Thus we can accept Rawls's statement that it is unreasonable in public deliberation to charge others with being ideologically deluded—unreasonable because it is unnecessary for the free formation of beliefs. My disagreement with Rawls is that he excludes certain basic questions from reflection and deliberation. If certain issues are not discussed at all, then we have no way of knowing if they are valid or whether or not they are freely held.

I have said something about what ideology does, how it limits our freedom, and what dimension of freedom it emphasizes. Now we need to consider what ideology *critique* is directed at. What is it that is being criticized by the theorist engaged in ideology critique? In very general terms, it is directed at that which prevents people from forming their politically relevant beliefs and desires in a free manner.

From the perspective of deliberative democracy as committed to multiple dimensions of freedom, that is, to deliberative freedom, we should limit the aim of deliberation to what matters for justification of public policies and law, which is not the same as limiting topics that can be discussed. We are concerned only with the free formation of beliefs regarding issues of common concern. We are not concerned here with how people form their views of the good life, at least not insofar as these can be separated from processes of justification.[36] In Rainer Forst's words, "Critical theory . . . is a critique of existing 'relations of justification' as the presupposition for establishing and developing a justified basic structure of society."[37] To Forst's formulation it should be added that here is included hidden relations of justification of ideological character. The critique is not perfectionist in the sense of being concerned with whether people live examined lives and critically scrutinize their private life projects. It is concerned with people's internal autonomy only insofar as it affects how public policies and laws are justified and legitimized. Of course, there might be (and most likely is) a causal relationship between free formation of opinions in processes of justification of political-moral norms and citizens' views of their own good, but the normative commitment to internal autonomy is independent of such an effect. This is why I speak of internal autonomy rather than personal autonomy (see the first section in Chapter 8).

Deliberation and Politicization

In advanced liberal democracies, reification is not merely a product of the capitalist relations of production (the aspect emphasized by Marx) but just as importantly of welfare-state bureaucratization. The critique of reification, therefore, is not only directed at market relationships but also at the functioning of the welfare state. Habermas has discussed this issue in the second volume of *The Theory of Communicative Action* under the idea of the "colonization" of the lifeworld by subsystems, such as the state and the economy.[38] The lifeworld is integrated by communicative action, that is, by action aimed at reaching mutual understanding. Subsystems, in contrast, are integrated by nonlinguistic media, money in the market, and power in the state. The colonization thesis states that system media threatens the process of reaching mutual understanding in the lifeworld.[39] In the terms used in this book, processes of common deliberation are threatened by the nondeliberative means that are used in the market and by the state. Colonization happens when nondeliberative means intrude upon or substitute for common deliberation, not by the fact that not all social integration happens by common deliberation. Colonization is a form of reification because it turns moral and political issues either into issues of economic efficiency and profit or into technical issues that have to be dealt with administratively by technocrats; as such, colonization leaves less room for deliberation by ordinary citizens. I cannot here explain and much less justify the social theory underlying Habermas's colonization thesis, but I want to include in our discussion the idea that the welfare state, if it is not embedded in a deliberative democracy, can threaten freedom because it preempts public deliberation.

The reification that happens as a result of bureaucratization gives critical theorists a unique critical reason for promoting a more deliberative democracy.[40] As Habermas puts it, "The bureaucratic disempowering and desiccation of spontaneous processes of opinion and will formation expands the scope for engineering mass loyalty and makes it easier to uncouple political decision-making from concrete, identity-forming contexts of life."[41] The welfare state makes citizens into clients, and "the client role is a companion piece that makes political participation that has been evaporated into an abstraction and robbed of its effectiveness acceptable."[42] Thus even if the aim of welfare-state provisions is to promote freedom by giving citizens the means (material and symbolic, economic and educational) to use their formal liberties, it also might disempower citizens by substituting bureaucratic regulation for communicative networks and common deliberation.

Habermas's discussion of colonization is not made in terms of a critique of ideology, but this diagnosis shares the concern for what I call internal autonomy, and there is still a concern for nondistorted consciousness formation. "In place of 'false consciousness' we today have a 'fragmented consciousness' that blocks enlightenment by the mechanism of reification."[43] The protection of the lifeworld against colonization is not merely a concern for negative freedom but a concern for free identity and opinion formation, a concern for internal and public autonomy.

The problem that Habermas points out in *The Theory of Communicative Action* is the uncoupling of lifeworld and system, that is, the disconnection between processes of reaching mutual understanding and strategic action. The aim of a critical theory that he outlines in the "Concluding Reflections" of that work is "to examine the conditions for recoupling" processes of mutual understanding and the system.[44] I suggest that we see deliberative democracy as an answer to this question. The reason we need more public deliberation is to counteract the reifications of the market and the state, to make object of reflection the moral-practical questions they reify. Habermas himself does not explicitly present his own theory of deliberative democracy in this way in *Between Facts and Norms*. Both the idea of ideology and the colonization thesis are largely absent from that work.

There are some crucial elements of Habermas's model of deliberative democracy—elements that are not present in Rawlsian models—that can be seen as having their roots in the earlier concerns of critical theory. The earlier concern with reification gives both a unique perspective on why public deliberation matters and helps identify new dimensions of freedom. At this point let me mention two issues, the theme of depoliticization and welfare state colonization.

When we contrast the earlier Habermas with Rawls, the former's critique of depoliticization stands out. Habermas's critique of the ideology of science and technology owes much to earlier critical theory, in particular, Herbert Marcuse.[45] The critique of depoliticization is a critique of the way in which moral and political questions are turned into technical ones and of the concomitant idea of decisionism—the belief that moral questions are incapable of truth and hence "cannot be discussed cogently [but] in the final instance must be decided upon, one way or another."[46] Decisionist politics stands, of course, in the sharpest contrast to deliberative politics. Decisionism denies what the idea of public deliberation confirms, that normative questions can be rationally discussed, and that some solutions are better than others. A main contrast between Habermas's and Rawlsian models of deliberative democracy today concerns whether public deliberation should be concerned with truth claims. Habermas's insistence on seeing deliberation as being about truth and not merely about the politically reasonable could be seen as having its roots in his critique of the depoliticizing tendencies of technocracy and positivism. From the perspective of the early Habermas, the importance of deliberation is exactly that it politicizes or makes the object of reflection what is seen as natural or what is otherwise excluded from questioning. Rawlsian deliberative democracy clearly does not share the ethical decisionism of positivism. Nevertheless, by excluding fundamental issues from deliberation, it might have the same depoliticizing effect.

A second important lesson from earlier critical theory is the critique of the welfare state. Habermasians agree with liberal egalitarians that redistribution is necessary for guaranteeing the worth of formal liberties. But Habermas's critical theory has shown that welfare state provisions are ambivalent, because while guaranteeing freedom they may simultaneously take it away. This he notes both in *The Theory of Communicative Action II* and in *Between Facts and Norms*.[47] It is important to note here a difference between the old and the new type of ideology. The new ideology oppresses not one class but everyone, because it undermines communicative action for the sake of purposive rationality[48]; that is, it undermines processes of reaching reciprocal agreements among the affected parties for the sake of finding the most efficient administrative means to ends given by bureaucratic experts. The solution, therefore, cannot merely be economic redistribution—not that Marxists ever thought it was, but liberal egalitarians and social democrats often do so. Habermas is critical of the welfare state as a technocratic entity that relies on expertise. The welfare state may give us equal ability to exercise freedom, but this is insufficient if it does so in a way that undermines communication and neutralizes participation.[49] It is, therefore, crucial that welfare state provisions be justified in public deliberation or, in other words, that the concern for the economic conditions of freedom be combined with the concern for the freedom that depends on an intact lifeworld, that is, a lifeworld that has not been colonized by the imperatives of the economy or of the state as a system. This latter point is neglected not only by critics of deliberative democracy, who argue for firm action from above, in a decisionistic vein,[50] or in arguments regarding adaptive preference formation, but also in Rawlsian models of deliberative democracy. These approaches share a focus on economic redistribution to the neglect of the ambivalence of welfare state regulation.[51]

A third issue comes to light in Habermas's earlier writings. We should not merely be concerned that redistribution takes place, and that it is something that is agreed upon as justified, but also that this agreement is rooted in a lifeworld that gives meaning to our lives. In the absence of the latter, something is missing. What is missing could be seen as what Habermas used to thematize under Max Weber's notion of the "loss of meaning."[52] This theme, however, seems to have disappeared from his later writings, including those on deliberative democracy. The reason for this, it has been suggested, is his acceptance of the liberal idea of the priority of the right over the good.[53] However, Habermas is still concerned with the protection of an intact lifeworld and with the right balance between the system and the lifeworld.

We should ask in this connection whether a concern for the loss of meaning necessarily violates negative freedom, and hence whether an acceptance of the priority of the right over the good requires that we give up the concern for meaning. I do not see why that should be the case. Indeed, it could be seen as the opposite insofar as the possibility of a meaningful life requires the protection of the lifeworld from the intrusion of system imperatives from the state and the market. The loss of meaning is not counteracted and symbolic interaction is not protected, however, merely by negative freedom. We do need a welfare state that secures the equal opportunity to exercise deliberative freedom. In order for this welfare state not to undermine the meaning generated in communicative action, it is crucial that its provisions are themselves justified in processes of public deliberation with roots in lifeworld contexts. To those (some liberals and libertarians) who think that this argument relies on an untenable perfectionism or notion of the good life, we should remind them that both a strong welfare state and a laissez-faire economy also lead to the promotion of certain forms of life. Moreover, even if a political system should not advance one view of human flourishing, it should make human flourishing possible. The problem with both a strong, paternalist state and a laissez-faire economy is that they exclude certain forms of life and even reflection on what the good life is.

Social Critics, Triggering Self-Reflection, and Public Autonomy

A main objection to ideology critique is that it can be paternalistic. In light of my criticism of paternalist versions of deliberative democracy in

Chapter 3, this is a concern I take very seriously. However, I think it is possible to see ideology critique as *part of* processes of public deliberation and thereby as *part of the exercise of public autonomy*, and not a threat to the latter.

One way in which we can see that the type of ideology critique that I am advocating is not contrary to public autonomy has to do with its epistemological assumptions. We should distinguish between critique being directed at what the ideology says (its content) and how it came into being, that is, between the epistemic properties of its composite beliefs and its genetic properties.[54] If the critical theorist wants to make a criticism based on the epistemic properties of the ideology alone, then she needs an independent standard, a correct answer, toward which she can hold the constituent beliefs of the ideology. Such an approach would violate an important dimension of freedom, the freedom of the agents to think for themselves—a dimension of freedom the meaning of which is elaborated on in Chapter 6. If, on the other hand, the criticism were directed at the genesis of the ideology alone, then it might be asked why it matters how an ideology came into being if its constituent beliefs are correct and do not support oppressive institutions (the so-called genetic fallacy).[55]

In Habermas we find an approach that combines a criticism directed at genesis with one directed at epistemic properties.[56] It is exactly by—*and only by*—analyzing how a specific form of legitimation or justification came into being that we can *know* whether it can be presumed to be right or not. If processes of legitimation are systematically distorted, then their results are ideological and epistemically dubious. "Ideology on this definition is ... the result of asymmetric communication, where asymmetries can include ones that result from information, power, status and role, and cultural differences."[57] The critique of ideology is therefore aimed at that which distorts communication. The content or epistemic properties of the beliefs of the addressees, therefore, are not the direct aim of ideology critique.

The *proceduralism* of this approach entails that we cannot have any presumptions about what are true or false beliefs except as results of processes of deliberation free from domination. The advantage of this approach is that the theorist does not and cannot take the paternalistic role of the philosopher expert who comes down from Mount Olympus to tell people what is right or wrong. Rather, what has the presumption of being right and wrong must be determined through practices of common deliberation. The weakness of this approach is that we might never get to deliberation free from domination, or at least it is not a reality now. Thus a possibility is to speak of hypothetical deliberation. This is Habermas's approach in *Legitimation Crisis*, in which he says that a social theory critical of ideology "compares normative structures existing at a given time with the hypothetical state of a system of norms formed, *ceteris paribus*, discursively."[58] But this solution cancels the advantages in terms of freedom of the proceduralist approach. If the theorist could know what would result from free deliberation, then there would be no need for actual and common deliberation.[59] If ideology critique is to be compatible with the normative commitments of deliberative democracy (that is, with deliberative freedom) and be able to contribute to their realization, then it should avoid preempting actual processes of deliberation. Instead, it should play the role of *provoking* such processes of deliberation by *initiating* processes of self-reflection. In this way, ideology critique can be seen as part of public autonomy rather than as undermining it.

To be true to the normative commitments of deliberative democracy as I see them in general and in order to avoid paternalism in particular, it is crucial, then, to distinguish between the theory of ideology as a way of showing people what their real interests are and as a means of triggering *self*-reflection.[60] The first view requires the theorist to know what real interests are from some external point of view and hence incompatible with the proceduralism that I think should be the core of deliberative democracy and the only way to protect the dimension of freedom involved in the right to think for oneself (see the fourth section in Chapter 6). The second view is compatible with proceduralism and with a conception of freedom that sees freedom as a matter of individuals coming to insights by their own efforts as participants in processes of public deliberation. As James Bohman has argued, critical theorists should participate as critics in the public sphere. The claims they make "are successful not insofar as they bring agents to particular true insights, but rather insofar as they initiate processes of self-reflection, the outcome of which agents determine for themselves."[61] Critical theory should not say *that* people are deluded but make them consider *whether* they are so. This is done by provoking them to participate in processes of public deliberation.

Thus the aim of ideology critique is emancipation from a specific form of oppression, achieved via processes of self-reflection.[62] An important point in this connection is that the first step is not to remove coercion and oppression, for example, an oppressive state and an exploitative market economy. The first step is for people themselves to realize that the present institutions are not in fact in the common interest.[63] It is only if people themselves realize that their present situation is unjust and then overturn it that this change can happen democratically and in accordance with the commitment to deliberative freedom.

A theory of ideology along the lines briefly sketched here should be intimately related to a concern for public autonomy; first, because ideology is related to legitimation and, second, because the critique of ideology to avoid paternalism cannot rely on negative freedom alone but also must focus on the common exercise of public autonomy. The critique of ideology shows how we uphold certain institutions with our active support or with mere compliance. One point of the theory of ideology is that political institutions and social relations are upheld by constellations of beliefs and desires—or by certain structures of communication, and not merely by violence. Indeed, successful ideological domination means that there is no need to use violence at all, because the subjects "freely" accept the structures. As such, it is in a sense self-imposed or at least reproduced by the subjects. Here there is no possible criticism from the perspective of negative freedom and the concomitant consent theory; we need to go deeper or to another dimension of freedom. The question raised from the perspective of the critique of ideology is how political authority legitimizes itself. The critique of ideology is of certain forms of legitimation. In the Habermasian version, it is specifically a critique of forms of legitimation that takes place by limiting communication, that is, by excluding some validity claims from being discussed.[64] Processes of legitimation in order to be nonideological need to be free from domination, and this is exactly how we should define the aim of deliberative democracy. As Bohman puts it, "*democracy* is also a particular structure of communication."[65] This structure of communication should be one that promotes deliberative freedom.

As noted in Chapter 1, it is a crucial point—and one sometimes overlooked by its critics—that deliberative democracy is not merely a call for more communication but a call for a particular structure of communication—namely, one free from distortion and domination, in my formulation, a structure of communication that enhances deliberative freedom. We can now see that when the roots in the theory of ideology are forgotten or abandoned this important point tends to fall out of view. A common misunderstanding of deliberative democracy is that it sees any agreement reached on the basis of talk as good.[66] But clearly language is not only a medium of reaching free agreements; it also can be used as a means of domination, exclusion, and social power. And proponents of deliberative democracy, at least those coming out of the tradition of critical theory, are or should be well aware of this. The way to understand language as a medium of domination is exactly via the critique of ideology.[67] Part of the misunderstanding—which deliberative democrats themselves are not without fault in—is that the aim of deliberation is always to go from disagreement to agreement, and that if there is agreement, there is nothing to be worried about from the perspective of democratic legitimacy. But if agreement is the product of ideological domination, then the aim of deliberation is to show that the agreement is only apparent, or that it is not the product of free deliberation.[68] To see this, deliberative democrats should not forget their roots in critical theory and the importance of the critique of ideology. I believe that including the notion of internal autonomy in the conception of freedom that deliberative democracy should be committed to clarifies as well as justifies the idea that the aim is neither increasing communication as such nor promoting consensus under all circumstances.

The critique of ideology should be related to public autonomy also in order to avoid paternalism. In a discussion with Rawls, Habermas writes that philosophy "must avoid equally the uncritical affirmation of the status quo and the assumption of a paternalistic role."[69] The traditional liberal critical standard and solution to the danger of paternalism is negative freedom. We avoid a paternalistic state and paternalistic cocitizens, according to this view, by giving citizens equal rights to determine and live according to their own ideas. But negative freedom is not sufficient when we have become aware of the problem of ideology. In this respect, Habermasian critical theory is more ambitious than Rawlsian political liberalism.[70] It is so because it does not leave people's comprehensive views outside politics or outside political philosophy. It criticizes them. Here we see that Habermas has not left the critique of ideology entirely behind. But for this reason Habermas also might be regarded as being in greater danger of succumbing to paternalism than Rawls.

To clarify, the difference between critical theory and Rawls is not that the first sees the importance of social circumstances while the other does not. Rawls, of course, is not a libertarian who thinks formal liberties are sufficient. He is aware that social conditions affect our preferences,[71] and he advocates giving fair value to political liberties.[72] But there is an important difference between Rawls's worth of freedom argument and my argument regarding internal autonomy. The first is concerned with giving people objectively fair conditions in order to make their formal freedoms worth their nominal value. The second is concerned with self-reflection on the basis of which citizens *themselves* can overturn oppressive institutions and unjust social conditions. Rawls's perspective is purely external, while critical theory takes the perspective of a participant and makes the change of circumstances dependent on it being accepted in the exercise of public autonomy, that is, in processes of public deliberation. This latter route is closed to Rawls, because he sees it as a violation of the principle of toleration to discuss people's comprehensive views. He is therefore forced to go directly to implementing social justice. Thus it seems that opposite to what one might expect, it is Rawls who turns out to be the paternalist and not the critical theorist with his or her basis in ideology critique.

This argument is supported by a recent article by Simone Chambers in which she argues that there is a tension in Rawls between his radical egalitarianism and his political liberalism. The problem is that the form of egalitarianism that Rawls defends is *not* part of U.S. political culture. As Chambers puts it: "To bring our system more in line with a Rawlsian vision [i.e., with his egalitarianism] would involve actually *creating* the public political culture that Rawls simply *assumed* was present within contemporary liberalism. . . . Transformation, however, was never on Rawls's agenda."[73] Including internal autonomy as a dimension of freedom is to put transformation on the agenda of deliberative democrats.

Paternalism is not only wrong because it violates negative freedom, but also because it violates public autonomy. Moreover, the legitimate scope of negative freedom cannot be freely determined and known by the participants independently of processes of public autonomy. Finally, as argued more fully later (see the fourth section in Chapter 6), dependence is not always a threat to freedom. In some cases we can help each other become more free not by leaving each other alone but by engaging in dialogue.

Habermas's answer to the problem of paternalism is proceduralism and an emphasis on public autonomy.[74] But he does not thematize the third dimension of freedom, the free formation of one's beliefs and desires that I have stressed. It is possible that he sees this dimension included in his notion of "public autonomy"; indeed, it must be. But we need to highlight this dimension of freedom in order to make explicit the difference with Rawls. When Habermas and Rawls discuss who best accommodates both ancient and modern liberties, the internal autonomy dimension falls out of view. Now if Habermas would wish to see internal autonomy as part and parcel of public autonomy, then he should have seen that what distinguishes him and Rawls is not the weight they give to negative freedom and public autonomy, respectively, but that they view public autonomy in different ways. And Rawls should have seen the same. The crucial difference from a Rawlsian perspective is not that Habermas gives too much weight to public autonomy (as Rawls claims, see Chapter 4 in this book), but that Habermas sees the free formation of one's comprehensive views (insofar as they affect political legitimation) as part of what the exercise of public autonomy entails. I have separated the third dimension of freedom in order to make this clear. But I would agree that internal autonomy only matters insofar as it affects processes of legitimation—and not when it bears only on issues of the good life. Whether this separation can be upheld is discussed in Chapter 6. Internal autonomy should be part of public autonomy—and of deliberative freedom more generally—also in the way that it is only people themselves in the process of deliberation who can determine whether or not something really is in their interest.

Conclusion

If we want to understand deliberative democracy as a critical theory of contemporary society—as I have argued we should—then we should resist the synthesis between Rawlsian and Habermasian deliberative democracy. The Rawlsians draw deliberative democracy in an unfortunate uncritical direction and confuse the potentials of public deliberation. The strength of deliberation is not merely to accommodate and uphold existing differences but to initiate processes of reflection about policies and institutions that are uncritically accepted by most people. Hence, the starting point for deliberative democracy should not be "the fact of reasonable pluralism" but rather "the fact of unreflective acquiescence." The aim of public deliberation should not merely be accommodation but emancipation. Rawlsian deliberative democrats are so focused on the negative freedom to live according to one's own conception of the good that they close off the potential of comprehensive deliberation to achieve its emancipatory aims. People's comprehensive doctrines are sometimes intrinsically linked to their acceptance of injustices in society. The Habermasians, on their side, have followed the liberals too far and have forgotten their roots in the critique of ideology and what I have emphasized as a third dimension of freedom, internal autonomy.

CHAPTER SIX

Democratic Ethos and Procedural Independence

I argued in Chapter 5 that we should be concerned with the free formation of beliefs only insofar as these beliefs affect processes of justification of issues of common concern. The aim of public deliberation is to establish a justified basic structure of society and not perfectionistically securing that all members of society live self-examined, Socratic lives. A perfectionistic political theory is concerned with the promotion of a certain way of life that it regards as constituting human perfection or excellence.[1] Now it might not be as easy to separate free formation of political views from the free formation of ethical convictions (that is, beliefs concerning what constitutes the good or perfect life) as these formulations require—or at least seem to require. This chapter begins by considering whether or not it is possible—or to what extent it is possible—to separate free political opinion and will formation from free formation of ethical views, and if it is not possible, then whether or not that is a problem for a model of deliberative democracy committed to multiple dimensions of freedom. The issue involved here is whether or not the requirements of public deliberation undermine the right to determine one's own conception of the good as one wants to. This question is relevant from the perspective of deliberative freedom, because the aim is to incorporate not merely internal and public autonomy and discursive status but also the negative freedom to form one's own conception of the good.

The second section discusses the related problem of whether the requirements of successful deliberation violate the privacy right not to disclose one's innermost motives and feelings (another aspect of negative freedom). The issue there is not whether one should be legally forced to self-disclosure—no one argues for such a view—but to what extent

153

the strong model of deliberation for which I have argued *can succeed* if people do not disclose their motives and needs and make them subject to public scrutiny.

The third section argues that deliberative freedom is compatible with privacy only in a country with a democratic ethos, that is, when citizens have strong deliberative dispositions. A democratic ethos often is seen as an Aristotelian and a perfectionist idea, but I argue that its promotion is justified not because it contributes to the good life but because it is required for the practice and enjoyment of deliberative freedom (which itself is not justified for perfectionist reasons). The idea of a democratic ethos, furthermore, is invoked to argue that the different dimensions of freedom come together empirically only under certain political-cultural conditions. The ideology critique discussed in Chapter 5 is supposed to help create those conditions.

The fourth section develops the idea that deliberative freedom must include the freedom to think for oneself. The right to think for oneself, however, is not merely a negative right to be left alone; one cannot think by oneself by being left entirely alone but is dependent on others as partners in the common deliberation that makes it possible for one to think and decide for oneself. Hence, I argue for the idea that deliberative freedom entails procedural but not substantive independence. There is a connection between procedural independence and the epistemic proce-duralism of the ideology critique discussed in Chapter 5, because ideology critique works by making people think for themselves, which makes them substantively dependent but recognizes their procedural independence. Distinguishing procedural and substantive independence, moreover, is itself a part of the critique of contemporary ideology, because it promotes the idea that being substantively independent cannot be seen as the core of freedom, not even of the negative dimension of freedom.

The Interdependence of the Ethical and the Moral

The discussion in this section is concerned with the relationship between the ethical and the moral, the good and the right; it is not concerned with legal rights. The issue I want to analyze is whether or not citizens can exercise their deliberative freedom in the way described earlier (in particular, as including internal autonomy) without—at least sometimes or to an extent—justifying their ethical differences to each other. By ethical differences I mean differences regarding what constitutes a good, happy, and fulfilling life. The question is when and to what extent citizens are required to justify their ethical differences to each other in order to enjoy deliberative freedom. The concern, in other words, is whether citizens can form their political opinions freely and rationally, if they form their views of the good, their ethical views, in an unfree and irrational manner. Can my agreement with political decisions be rationally motivated if my motivation to agree builds on an understanding of what is good for me that is not rationally motivated? This question is relevant because in deliberative democracy, as it is understood in this book, agreement is found neither by abstracting from difference nor by looking only for an overlapping consensus. Rather, deliberation happens between real and embodied persons and allows for the expression of all sorts of differences.[2] And the aim of public deliberation is to find agreements that, *taking these differences into account,* are acceptable to everyone.

It seems to me inevitable that the ethical convictions of citizens will influence deliberation and its results. Ethical discourses in which citizens get clearer about their needs and interests are part of political deliberation.[3] Only on the basis of ethical discourses can citizens determine the justice issue that Habermas identifies as "what is equally good for all."[4] Thomas McCarthy makes a similar point in arguing that moral and ethical discourses, even if analytically distinguishable *in practice*, are dialectically interdependent.[5] In a critique of Habermas, he argues that questions of justice are not independent of the ethical and therefore not immune to ethical disagreements.[6] My concern, however, is different from McCarthy's. Namely, how can agreements about what is equally good for all be free and rational, if the parties come to their respective views of what is good for them separately unfreely and irrationally? In other words, my concern is the relationship between different dimensions of freedom: on the one hand, internal and public autonomy and, on the other hand, the negative freedom to determine one's own conception of the good. Can these dimensions of freedom be reconciled?

In his response to McCarthy, Habermas argues that what matters in deliberation is the perspective taken by participants: "Each participant must turn away from the *ethical* question of which regulation is respectively 'best for us' from 'our' point of view. They must, instead, take the *moral* point of view and examine which regulation is 'equally good for all' in view of the prior claim to an equal right to coexist."[7] But clearly, before participants can take the moral point of view, they must first have

Deliberative Freedom

articulated what they find good for them individually from their own point of view. What is equally good for all *includes* what is good for each. And deliberation about what is equally good for all includes individual understandings of what is good for each separately.

Habermas seems to admit this in an accommodation of feminist criticisms: "The individual rights that are supposed to guarantee women the autonomy to shape their private lives cannot even be appropriately formulated unless those affected articulate and justify in public discussion what is relevant to equal and unequal treatment in typical cases. Safeguarding private autonomy of citizens with equal rights must go hand in hand with activating their autonomy as citizens of the nation."[8] This quote suggests both that (1) citizens must form their ethical views before they can know what is equally good for all, and (2) safeguarding negative freedom requires the exercise of public autonomy. It seems, therefore, that public autonomy requires that the needs, desires, and interests that should be dealt with equally should be formed freely. It is clear that in Habermas to form or interpret one's needs and interest freely means to form them in undistorted communication.[9] Hence, to bracket out ethical questions of discourse would be, in Habermas's own words, to "forfeit its power to rationally change prepolitical attitudes, need interpretations, and value orientations."[10]

Our problem thus arises from the fact that people's ethical convictions influence their political opinions. Deliberative freedom (in particular, the dimensions of internal and public autonomy) requires that political opinions be formed freely, in free deliberation. But must they not be freely formed all the way down, as it were? The problem from the perspective of deliberative freedom is that many convictions that relate to the way people define their conceptions of the good may reflect self-understandings that are formed in unfree ways. An alleged advantage of public deliberation is that it can deal with unfreely formed convictions by subjecting them to critical, intersubjective scrutiny. Issues such as self-deception, adaptive preference formation, manipulation, ideological domination, and the like may all be contributing factors to the way in which people understand what is good for them. Manipulation and hegemonic domination not only affect people's explicitly political opinions but also their ethical-existential self-understanding. If people's reasons for how they interpret their interests, needs, and desires are not probed in public deliberation, then there is no nonviolent way to address these freedom-undermining factors. And if people are deceived or are deceiving themselves about who they are and what they want then this creates not just a problem for their personal autonomy but also for their public autonomy, for the latter is influenced by the former.[11]

Nancy Fraser has argued that distributive justice cannot merely be seen as a matter of satisfying given needs but also must and in the first instance be a matter of *interpreting needs*. What we perceive our needs to be depends on the society in which we form them, on structures of domination and communication. And, importantly, "members of subordinate groups commonly internalize need interpretations that work to their own disadvantage."[12] Clearly, if disadvantaged people adopt an identity or a conception of the good that suits or is uncritical of the situation in which they find themselves as a consequence of adaptive preference formation, manipulation, or ideological domination, then this has immense political consequences; it sustains the status quo. This is problematic from the point of view of deliberative freedom. If these satisfied, disadvantaged people did participate in public deliberation at all—though it is hard to see why they should—all they would ask for would be to uphold the status quo. If people find the status quo good for them, then there is no reason to think they would object to it as not being just in the sense of equally good for all. Why would they ask for changes if they were satisfied with what they have and if no one is allowed to criticize their ethical convictions?

It might be argued that what is required for free ethical-existential self-understanding is a certain external condition such as the protection of the lifeworld from the state and economic forces.[13] But to impose from without a certain understanding of social justice and personal autonomy (as distinguished from internal autonomy, see Chapter 8) goes against the core of the idea of deliberative democracy as committed to multiple dimensions of freedom. The very act of imposing solutions from a point outside and independently of the deliberative process undermines the very processes we wish to protect. We cannot secure free opinion formation by bypassing processes of deliberative justification (see Chapter 3). The deliberative conception of freedom requires that norms of economic distribution and individual rights be justified in deliberation. Deliberative freedom requires that citizens submit only to decisions that are the product of a deliberative process in which they have been able to take part in giving and responding to reasons. It might be said that people *would* accept certain norms in deliberation *if* they were free and equal. But then we have turned from actual to hypothetical deliberation, and thereby we have abandoned the idea that participation in deliberation itself is the core of deliberative freedom. Deliberation presupposes the different dimensions of freedom not merely as an idea; the only way to understand, express, and develop the different dimensions of freedom is through the actual practice of common deliberation (cf. Introduction).[14]

It often has been pointed out that the conditions of delibera-tion—social justice and rights—also are some it must justify. My point is different. It concerns how much deliberation can accomplish in the absence of ideal conditions, and how the answer to this question affects how we see the relationship between different dimensions of freedom. Under less-than-ideal conditions, people will form their conceptions of the good in unfree ways, ways that are affected by their conditions and not just by good reasons. The role of public deliberation should be both to scrutinize the claims people make, including those that are the product of their ethical convictions, and to criticize social conditions that affect opinion formation in adverse ways. In deliberation we cannot see the opinions of others as mere products of their conditions and impose new—allegedly better—conditions on them so they can form more free and rational opinions (cf. Chapter 3). Deliberative freedom entails that we regard each other as being capable of giving reasons for our opinions and as being capable of revising them in light of good reasons, that is, that we respect everyone's discursive status (cf. Chapter 2). Hence, we must give reasons for changes and convince others of the justifiability of them. We cannot just impose what we regard as freedom-enhancing conditions on others if they have not become convinced that these conditions are just and good. But if we are to convince someone who is satisfied with her life of changes, which are basically meant to give her an opportunity to change the way she lives her life, then public deliberation must include discussion of the ethical-existential convictions that make her satisfied with her life.

Deliberation and Privacy

The interdependence of free political opinion and will formation, on the one hand, and discussion of conceptions of the good and need interpreta-tions, on the other hand, raise worries regarding the respect for privacy. Borrowing a formulation from Jean Cohen, I see the right to privacy as entailing being free "from the obligation to justify one's actions in a discursive process by giving reasons that everyone together could accept as their own.... [The right to privacy] means that one has the liberty to withdraw certain concerns, motives, and aspects of the self from the public scrutiny and control."[15] This, indeed, is an important dimension of freedom (it is an aspect of negative freedom). What we need to consider now is whether, keeping in mind the argument concerning the interdependence between ethical and moral views, the ideal of internal autonomy does lead to a violation of privacy.

J. Donald Moon argues that models of deliberative democracy in which interests and needs are made the object of discourse entail a "bias against privacy."[16] Unconstrained dialogue, he argues, "is at least potentially coercive, denying values or ideals that may be important to at least some participants in discourse. Viewed as a form of public discourse, unconstrained discourse rests upon the unacknowledged assumption that there is no limit to the claims others can make upon one to render one's needs transparent—not only to oneself but to them as well. Indeed, this assumption could be said to *constitute* moral-transformative discourse."[17]

Habermas has responded to Moon's worry by distinguishing between regulating and talking about something. "Making something that so far has been considered a private matter a topic for public discussion does not yet imply any *infringement* of individual rights.... To talk about something is not necessarily the same as meddling in another's affairs."[18] This is indeed an important distinction—and one I return to in the fourth section of this chapter—but it does not dispel Moon's concern. Moon's point, as I read him, is that self-disclosure *constitutes* moral-transformative discourse—that is, discourse concerned with scrutinizing and, if need be, changing interest and need interpretations—and hence citizens are required to disclose their motives and needs to each other *in order for public deliberation to succeed.*

One also might think of Moon's concern in terms of Alexis de Tocqueville's and John Stuart Mill's fear of the tyranny of public opinion and its pressure to conform to a specific form of life. Tocqueville describes how the tyranny of democratic republics "leaves the body alone and goes straight for the soul."[19] This "social tyranny," according to Mill, is "more formidable" than government control, because it "enslav[es] the soul itself."[20] But note that at least Mill's concern with public opinion as a form of coercion is not an argument against public deliberation and not even against arguments concerning the good life. Mill argues most strongly for the "liberty of tastes and pursuits," the freedom to do as we like, "without impediments from our fellow-creatures . . . even though they should think our conduct foolish, perverse or wrong."[21] Yet he thinks, "Human beings owe to each other help to distinguish the better from the worse."[22] What matters is that the individual "himself is the final judge."[23] According to Mill, we are allowed to advise and warn others about their private lives but not to constrain them with legal or social punishment. I return later in this chapter to how the individual can remain the final judge in the argument about procedural independence.

Of course, there is no problem if citizens freely disclose their needs, interests, and desires to each other; to have a right *not* to do something entails the converse right to do it. I return to this issue shortly, when I discuss the dependence of deliberative democracy on a democratic ethos. First, however, I want to question that what I have argued concerning internal autonomy and the interdependence of the ethical and the moral really does require the form of self-disclosure that Moon talks about. My arguments do support the idea of unconstrained dialogue; that is, no topic can a priori be excluded from public scrutiny and deliberation. But they do not entail the form of *personalization* of deliberation that Moon's argument assumes. Even if we in public deliberation discuss, for example, whether the heterosexual patriarchal family is the best and only form of family, this does not mean that each of us has to disclose and justify in public her or his innermost needs and desires in these most intimate matters. The important thing for learning processes is that the issue is "out there" to be reflected upon, not that we make ourselves transparent to each other. What matters is that new and different possibilities are being discussed out in the open for everyone to hear and learn from. It is a distortion of public deliberation when certain issues that could matter for justice are blocked from being discussed because they are regarded as private and a matter of the good life. As especially feminist writers have pointed out, excluding some topics from political deliberation tends to uphold existing or traditional power structures and may hide oppression in the private sphere. This may be bad for negative freedom.[24]

This does not mean that our views of the good life have to be publicly and intersubjectively justified. It is one thing to say that formerly private issues may be discussed and quite another to say that citizens are required to justify their needs and desires to each other. We can have discussions of whether certain forms of life violate important principles of justice and of whether there are alternative forms of life, without having to justify our needs and desires on these issues. Some might learn from these discussions that what they formerly regarded as the good life, the only possible form of life, or the natural form of life is not actually so and hence might change their conception of the good. Such a change is sometimes necessary for the acceptance of the new principles of justice; only when it takes place can everyone see the new norms as being equally good for everyone. But even if forms of life are being discussed in public and people change their minds about them, it is not their private needs and desires that must be justified but the norms that guide interaction.

As an aside, it also might be noted that the pressure for self-disclosure and the bias against privacy might be much stronger from market forces and mass communication than from an idea of unconstrained dialogue. The most unbearable forms of self-disclosure today are seen on TV talk and reality shows.[25] Even though it is likely that it now and then leads to new need and interest interpretations, this form of disclosure exists for no purpose other than entertainment. Herbert Marcuse noted forty years ago how mass production and the mass media "claim the *entire* individual," and how they have "invaded the inner space of privacy and practically eliminated the possibility of that isolation in which the individual, thrown back on himself alone, can think and question and find."[26] "In this process, the 'inner' dimension of the mind in which opposition to the status quo can take root is whittled down."[27]

Democratic Ethos

If the preceding argument is right, then there is no reason for demanding self-disclosure; the aims of public deliberation can succeed without it. But there is another understanding of privacy that might be more damaging to the aims of deliberative democracy in general and to my formulation in particular. This understanding of privacy was expressed by the focus groups in an empirical study done recently in the United States and Great Britain by Pamela Johnston Conover, Donald D. Searing, and Ivor M. Crewe. Most respondents in the study said that they avoided participating in public discussion because they dislike making their political opinions known to others. They said they neither like to have their own views challenged nor to challenge the views of others: "We have a right to our own opinions whatever they are, they say, and therefore, we ought 'to allow a person to believe what they want to believe.' To try

to persuade people to change their minds is an invasion of their privacy
and 'a violation of their rights'—a kind of 'verbal force.' "[28] This view
indicates a lack of a democratic ethos or deliberative dispositions among
citizens of the United States and Great Britain.

Richard Bernstein has characterized the democratic ethos necessary
for a deliberative democracy thus: "[D]emocratic debate, ideally, requires
a *willingness* to listen to and *evaluate* the opinions of one's opponents,
respecting the views of minorities, advancing arguments *in good faith* to
support one's convictions, and having the *courage* to change one's mind
when confronted with new evidence or better arguments. There is an
ethos involved in the *practice* of democratic debate."[29]

Bernstein argues that Habermas's theory of deliberative democracy
presupposes such a democratic ethos and certain virtues. In a response,
Habermas accepts Bernstein's argument if "read in its weaker sense. . . . A
political system based on the system of the rule of law is not self-
contained but *also* depends on 'a liberal political culture' and a population
accustomed to freedom."[30] Habermas strongly emphasizes the "also" and
thinks it is what separates his own weaker, less demanding position from
Bernstein's classical republican position. Habermas seems to be using two
different versions of "also." I agree with the first, namely, that citizens
should not be required always to take a deliberative attitude but *also* can
use their individual rights to take a strategic attitude and withdraw from
the obligations involved in deliberation. This follows from the commitment
to the dimension of freedom that entails a right to drop out of deliberation (an aspect of negative freedom), and from the idea that it would not
contribute to deliberative freedom to force people to deliberate.

Regarding the other, related "also" Habermas says, "the success of
deliberative politics depends not on a collectively acting citizenry but on
the institutionalization of the corresponding procedures and conditions of
communication, as well as on the interplay of institutionalized deliberative
processes with informally developed public opinions."[31] Habermas believes
that this "structural argument . . . relieves citizens of the Rousseauian
expectation of virtue . . . insofar as practical reason withdraws from the
hearts and heads of collective actors into the procedures and forms of
communication of political opinion and will formation."[32] This account,
Habermas holds, "replaces the expectation of virtue with a supposition
of rationality."[33] Habermas's proceduralization of popular sovereignty is
an important step, but it seems he thinks it can achieve more than it
in fact can.

It appears to me that Habermas confounds the need for democratic virtues with an Aristotelian argument about the good life. He criticizes republicanism for being "too idealistic in that it makes the democratic process dependent on the virtues of citizens devoted to the public weal. *For* politics is not concerned in the first place with ethical self-understanding."[34] What is this "for"? I do not see why there should be a necessary connection between the requirement for democratic virtues, such as Bernstein's virtues of deliberation, on the one hand, and the allegiance to the idea of politics as a matter either of defining a common identity or seeing political participation as a matter of the good life, on the other hand. But Habermas seems to think that *any* talk of the need for virtues leads to communitarianism and perfectionism. This represents a failure of drawing an important distinction. Virtues need not be related to a shared conception of the good life or to a common identity but can be seen as a requirement of the practice of democracy and freedom. The communicative freedom that Habermas sees as the basis of legitimate democratic decision making clearly is an exercise concept of freedom—it is a freedom that one can enjoy only by exercising it[35]—and thus it requires certain dispositions on the parts of the participants. In Habermas's own words, "Communicative freedom exists *only* between actors who, *adopting* a performative attitude, *want* to reach an understanding with one another about something and *expect* one another to take positions on reciprocally raised validity claims."[36]

Habermas underestimates how demanding his own theory of deliberative democracy is.[37] Some of the formulations given earlier, such as the idea that practical reason is moved from the individual to the procedures, seem to me a bit of a cop-out. For even though it is crucial, and in line with my own argument, that practical reason is seen as dialogical, it still has to find its way into the heads of individuals, otherwise it cannot matter for our freedom and autonomy. Habermas sometimes speaks as if by making rationality procedural we can almost suspend the need for individual rationality. But clearly, deliberative procedures are nothing without participants in deliberation; citizens must not only be able to participate, they also must be willing to do so. Replacing virtue with rationality will not do either, for the issue is not so much having rationality as being willing to use it. Even Kant saw that Enlightenment requires courage, a classical virtue: "Have courage to use your own understanding."[38] Hannah Arendt emphasizes that courage is indispensable for the willingness to enter the public realm at all; "courage or even boldness are already present in leaving one's private hiding place and showing who one is, in disclosing and exposing one's self."[39] This form of courage—political courage—seems to be neither widespread nor highly valued today.

To be sure, Habermas does admit that deliberative democracy depends on a rationalized lifeworld and a population accustomed to freedom, but he speaks as if these are small and fulfilled requirements. But if we can trust the findings of Conover, Searing, and Crewe, not even the citizens of the world's oldest democracies have been accustomed to freedom *in the way that is required for deliberation to succeed*. Being accustomed to one dimension of freedom also might not contribute to the desire for other dimensions of freedom. Tocqueville noted that in the America he visited (in 1830), "People enjoying [freedom of the press] become attached to their opinions as much from pride as from conviction. They love them because they think them correct, but also because they have *chosen* them; and they stick to them, not only as something true but also as something *of their very own*."[40] And later on, he notes, "I know no country in which, speaking generally, there is less independence of mind and true freedom of discussion than in America."[41] A certain understanding of freedom where opinions are seen as a matter of choice and belonging to oneself can thus inhibit freedom of discussion.

Interestingly, the empirical study referred to earlier indicates that today Americans and the British also regard having whatever opinions one wants as a right and part of one's identity.[42] This does by no means secure that one has adopted the opinions freely in the sense of having critically evaluated them in light of the best available information and the strongest reasons. They might be the product of conformity in the way talked about by Tocqueville and Mill, or of ideology, as discussed in Chapter 5. This indicates that we live in a political culture in which opinions are seen in a decisionistic vein, as something freely chosen and therefore right, which relates to seeing freedom as only negative and rejecting the other dimensions of freedom that are incorporated in deliberative freedom. It is this influential conception of freedom that needs to be challenged if deliberative democracy is to have a chance of succeeding. And it is for this reason that deliberative democracy must be seen as critical theory and as committed to the critique of ideology.

Habermas speaks as if his presuppositions of deliberation do not create special problems for certain groups in society. But the fact is, certain comprehensive doctrines are not readily compatible with "post-metaphysical" ways of justification, do not care much about freedom, and reject political participation.[43] When we share a political system with such groups, Habermas's argument for the co-originality of and internal relationship between negative freedom and public autonomy loses some of its force. The intuition expressed by this idea is that "citizens can make adequate use of their public autonomy" only if their private autonomy is secured, and, "on the other hand, they can arrive at consensual regulation of their private autonomy only if they make adequate use of their political autonomy as enfranchised citizens."[44] This argument presupposes that people do not only use their negative liberties as a protection of their own way of life but also for participation in common processes of deliberation. The problem with Habermas's argument is that he takes the existence of a population accustomed to freedom as a given, while empirically this seems to be a doubtful assumption. All he says is "Unlike morality, law cannot *obligate* its addressees to use individual rights in ways oriented to reaching understanding, even if political rights *call for* precisely this kind of use."[45] Hence, "Law must draw on sources of legitimation that are not at its disposal."[46] Habermas forgets to mention that *without* a population accustomed to freedom, negative liberties and public autonomy will be in tension. Citizens will "see argumentation and persuasion . . . as an inappropriate invasion of their privacy," as many citizens in the United States and Great Britain apparently do.[47]

I agree with Habermas that we should not enforce participation, because this would violate an important dimension of freedom. But this is not all there is to be said about the issue. Even if it is true that law cannot obligate citizens to use individual rights for participation in deliberation, and that "law must draw on sources of legitimation that are not at its disposal," this does not mean that there is nothing that can be done through law in terms of creating a political culture favorable to deliberative democracy. Law not only works by direct enforcement but also by facilitating and encouraging. Most evidently, the educational system can, and in many places does, encourage critical thinking and autonomy and has as its aim educating children to become good citizens.[48]

Education, however, is not sufficient; the current political culture also needs to be challenged by social critics engaged in the kind of critique of ideology discussed in Chapter 5. Under current political-cultural conditions, however, the exercise of critique will be seen as a violation of negative freedom and privacy. That is why we first need a theory that shows that critique exercised as part of the process of public deliberation is not a threat to freedom but a precondition for a fuller freedom. Social criticism needs both to clarify and justify its own normative standards, the different dimensions of freedom, and to contribute to their realization. It is only when we have created the right political-cultural conditions that the different dimensions of freedom will reinforce rather than counteract each other. That is why deliberative freedom presupposes a certain democratic ethos.

Thinking for Oneself

Much of the preceding discussion relates to the issue of sectarianism. The underlying concern is that by endorsing deliberative democracy, we might be forced to accept a certain, sectarian view of the good life. Why should we be concerned with sectarianism? The standard liberal reason for worrying about sectarianism is that it violates the individual right to live according to one's own conception of the good. Sectarianism, hence, is seen as a violation of the freedom to choose for oneself. I argue that deliberative democracy does imply a respect for the individual right to think and decide for oneself, and that the conditions for this go beyond negative freedom to the multiple dimensions of freedom that this book is elucidating. The aim of enhancing deliberative freedom requires that we secure the conditions and processes necessary for the individual not only to choose for herself but also for making up her mind about what to choose for herself. The standard construal of negative freedom is not sufficient to secure the ability of the individual to make up her own mind, for the threat of sectarianism comes not only from the state but also from private actors and impersonal forces. Pressure for living a certain form of life comes not only from the state but also from mass culture, one's parents, one's religion, one's partner, and also from one's socioeconomic condition. Ideological mechanisms such as those discussed in Chapter 5 can be the source of sectarianism. Freedom should be seen in this light too.

The negative freedom tradition entails the idea that other people are a threat to one's own liberty. This idea also is strong in contemporary political culture and in the dominant ideology (see the third section in this chapter). Deliberative democrats committed to multiple dimensions of freedom cannot accept this view. Rather than seeing dependence per se as limiting freedom, we must distinguish forms of dependence and interaction that limit the individual's ability to make up her own mind and forms that enhance or are neutral with regard to that ability. Deliberative freedom does not require that we leave individuals to themselves, but it does require that we leave individuals to make up their minds for themselves. This has to do with the distinction between speaking and regulating mentioned in the second section of this chapter. Negative freedom, as I see it, requires that we do not coerce others, but it does not require that we do not try to convince them. What is required as a protection against sectarianism is not negative freedom as commonly understood but procedural independence, or the ability to think and decide for oneself.

The Freedom to Say No

When we discuss the deliberative process, we are concerned with the democratic genesis of law, not its enforcement. The very core of my deliberative view of the democratic process is that it must exclude any form of force, not only government force but also force exercised by private actors, and not only force directed at limiting freedom of action, but also force that works on the very formation of preferences and opinions. In argumentation—which is the fundamental though not only form of deliberation[49]—the only force that is supposed to count is, to repeat Habermas's famous phrase, "the peculiarly constraint-free force of the better argument."[50]

In argumentation we seek to rationally motivate each other; that is, we aim to come to an understanding using reasons. This aim excludes the use of positive and negative sanctions, which do not concern the merits of the claim but seek to make the recipient agree from other causes than reasons.[51] Threats and rewards can only lead to heteronomy, since they do not make the recipient agree because she is convinced of the claim but because of something external to it. A speaker, furthermore, does not rationally motivate a listener by saying what from some independent standard can be regarded as true or rational, but by offering to give reasons for the validity claim her speech act has raised.[52] This presupposes that we as listeners must have the freedom to say "no" to any claim whatever and ask for reasons. It is only when everyone has this freedom and the effective ability to use it that we can be sure that her acceptance of any claim is an expression of insight and not a product of external forces.

Deliberation entails both independence and dependence. On the one hand, the rationality of deliberation presupposes the Kantian maxim that one must "think for oneself" (*Selbstdenken*).[53] If people do not think for themselves—that is, if they submit to force, are led by authority, conform to the view of the majority, and the like—the deliberation cannot achieve its purpose. Deliberation requires that people, when they take yes and no positions on claims and proposals, do so out of insights, not because of fear, manipulation, and the like. It requires independence. But, on the other hand, as an intersubjective process in which we depend on each other as partners, it also creates dependence. I turn now to an argument that tries to solve this apparent tension.

Procedural Independence

Freedom often is seen as requiring independence. Independence may refer both to freedom of action and to freedom of forming opinions and preferences. In the first case I lack independence when my options are diminished by others. In the second case I lack independence when I, in forming my opinions or preferences, am influenced by others.[54] I concentrate on the second case here, because it is the one that is relevant to my discussion of ideology and internal autonomy. In this case, a person is said to be free only if others are not influencing her in the formation of her beliefs, desires, and opinions. A person lacks independence in this view when she is influenced by others in the sense that she holds beliefs and desires that she would otherwise not hold because of the effects of what someone else did or said.[55] Clearly, independence in opinion formation, as it is formulated here, cannot be a necessary condition for a conception of freedom suitable for deliberative democracy; it is not a dimension of freedom presupposed by deliberation. Citizens exercise their deliberative freedom exactly by trying to influence the opinion and will formation of each other.[56]

Deliberative freedom, however, requires that persons have some form of independence. Proponents of deliberative democracy would not regard, for example, persons who adapt their views unconsciously to their social or cultural situation as free, nor would they regard persons who come to hold their opinions as the result of manipulation as free. We need to be able, then, to distinguish forms of dependence that limit freedom from forms that are either neutral with regard to freedom or enhance freedom. Here I bring into my argument a distinction made by several philosophers between substantive and procedural (in)dependence.[57] "Spelling out the conditions of procedural independence involves distinguishing ways of influencing people's reflective and critical faculties which subvert them from those which promote and improve them."[58] I am substantively dependent, for example, when I look to others for advice and guidance. I am procedurally dependent when I am under the influence of "hypnotic suggestion, manipulation, coercive persuasion, subliminal influence, and so forth."[59] For the philosophers who have made this distinction, what matters for autonomy is procedural independence, not substantive independence. A person who enjoys procedural independence is able to critically reflect on the advice she gets and hence free to either accept it or reject it. My freedom is not limited by being dependent on others for advice, but it would be limited if I were not independent to critically scrutinize this advice.

Deliberative democracy, of course, entails being substantively dependent on each other; deliberative democrats accept mutual interdependence as a basic premise. Deliberation is essentially a "joint, cooperative activity"[60] in which we depend on the opinions and criticisms of others. In forming my political opinions I am substantively dependent on all of the sources of information and reasons I come into contact with: the media, public authorities, politicians, social movements, interest organizations, and so on, as well as those with whom I discuss political issues. I could not possibly form *any* political opinions without the information and advice I get from others, and I could not form any *enlightened* opinions without being challenged by others.

But it also is crucial to emphasize the idea of procedural independence. That I am procedurally independent means that when I agree in some proposal it is because *I* have been convinced of it being right or good, not because I was forced or manipulated into agreeing. Seeing procedural independence as a condition for deliberative freedom means that each individual must think and decide for herself or himself. In other words, procedural independence means that the individual is the final judge, a requirement for which I cited Mill earlier. The idea of the individual as the final judge connects to the importance of fallibilism and reversibility in the exercise of public autonomy, which I stressed in Chapter 3. My procedural independence would be violated if any political decision were claimed to be final and infallible, for if that were the case, my right to make up my mind for myself and judge for myself would not be respected; I would have to surrender my own judgment to that of others.

The idea of procedural independence is crucial, furthermore, to see that deliberative freedom is a freedom of individuals and not of a macro-subject or a collective freedom.[61] Each individual must be free to critically scrutinize the political system. "Failure to submit the system to continuing scrutiny . . . invalidates the claim to *self*-governance, for the individual thereby remains indistinct from the group."[62] Procedural independence lies at the heart of what successful deliberation presupposes: the possibility of saying "no" to the claims made by others and of asking them for reasons.[63] It is only when we are procedurally independent and free to say "no" that we can regard the results of the deliberative process as our own achievement, and that we can see public autonomy as an expression of our *individual* freedom.[64]

The distinction between substantive and procedural (in)dependence also can elucidate the relationship between being subject to laws and being authors of laws. According to the negative conception of freedom (Hobbes, Bentham, Berlin), law is a form of interference and therefore limits freedom.[65] Law clearly creates a form of substantive dependence. As subjects of law, we cannot transgress certain rules, but if we are free to criticize and try to change the law, then we are still procedurally independent. Of course, deliberative democrats would have to agree with Berlin, that law does limit freedom in a sense, that as subjects of law we cannot do whatever we wish. Law does limit a dimension of freedom. But in contrast to Berlin, on the deliberative view it matters who gives the law. There is a difference between being limited in one's negative freedom by a law that has been imposed on one and being limited in one's negative freedom by a law one has been able to influence and make in a public process of deliberation. Insofar as laws are discursively justified and insofar as they can be challenged and changed after a public process of deliberation, they do not take away our procedural independence. This is because discursively justified and revisable laws do not subvert our reflective and critical faculties. When laws, in contrast, are imposed on us, we lose our procedural independence. Laws then are not only something we cannot transgress but also an alien force that we cannot criticize or change. To clarify, I do not want to say that laws given by ourselves do not violate freedom (as, for example, Philip Pettit does, see Chapter 2); they do limit a dimension of freedom. My argument is that the negative freedom that is most important for overall freedom, for deliberative freedom, is procedural independence, and that the latter is not violated by law that is a product of our public autonomy.

Procedural independence involves both a capacity and a right. It involves the capacities necessary to critically reflect on and accept and reject the influences to which we are subject. Whether or not we enjoy procedural independence, thus, depends on socioeconomic and educational conditions and on power structures. Hence, procedural independence might sometimes be enhanced by state action. If state interference helps remove conditions that limit my procedural independence, that is, my ability to make up my mind consciously and in free, uncoerced exchange with others, then it cannot be said to diminish my overall deliberative freedom. Procedural independence as a right is intimately connected to procedural independence as a capacity. When my right to procedural independence is violated, I am treated as someone who lacks the capacity to think for myself; my capacity for procedural independence is not respected.[66] Capacity relates to the respect intrinsic to being regarded as an equal participant in deliberation. Procedural independence combines the need for the right to say no for learning and the respect for the capacity of each individual to think for herself or himself; that is, procedural independence is intimately related to internal and public autonomy as well as to the status dimension of freedom.

Heteronomy as Bypassing Critical Reflection

According to the theory of deliberative freedom that I am developing, what matters the most is not *what* people think but *how* they come to hold the preferences and opinions they hold, and how they come to agree with political proposals. Freedom has a historical dimension; the degree of freedom cannot be evaluated synchronically. Citizens come only to their opinions freely if they have acquired them critically and reflectively in light of good reasons. From this we also can understand what constitutes heteronomy. Heteronymous opinions and agreements are those that are the product of processes that *bypass* the conditions of deliberation. A person comes to hold heteronymous opinions if she is caused to hold these opinions by forms of influence or forces that bypass her critical faculties or her ability to control her mental life.[67] A person is not free if the opinions she holds (or expresses) are not some she has critically and consciously adopted but some that have been "implanted" in her without her knowledge or are products of forces or structures that influence her situation rather than motivate her rationally.

Bypassing happens, for example, when money and power influence the opinion-forming process and replace arguments with rewards and punishments.[68] The success of utterances backed by power "depends upon asymmetries in communication produced by social relations of power between speakers and hearers. In bypassing communicative constraints, their success can only be maintained by restrictions and barriers on communication."[69] Manipulation is another form of bypassing deliberation. For deliberative democrats, manipulation is a paradigmatic type of distorted communication and is seen as a form of coercion.[70] The problem with manipulation is that it is "directed toward the reactive rather than the conscious person and designed to restrict rather than to enlarge conscious deliberation."[71]

In cases of manipulation there is an agent who limits the freedom of another agent by intentionally changing her values and beliefs. But bypassing of deliberation also might be the product of impersonal forces. For Habermasian theorists of deliberative democracy, the absence of freedom is not only a consequence of the (intentional) interference of one person (or group) in the activities of others, as it is in a liberal conception of negative freedom. Impersonal social forces, institutionalized routines, entrenched meanings, and the like can also limit our freedom.[72] In order to understand what is required for deliberative freedom, we must analyze the political, administrative, social, and economic power structures that bypass critical reflection and distort deliberation.[73]

The reason the force of the better argument does not limit freedom is that it is directed toward the person's conscious and reflective capacities rather than being aimed at bypassing these.[74] This is an important distinction. To interfere with others in ways that bypass their critical capacities is intolerant and wrong, but to engage in argument with them is not.

Now, some people might feel arguments are a form of "verbal force" (as I mentioned earlier in this chapter that many in fact do), and see the respect for the freedom of others involving *not* challenging their views. But this view involves a bizarre understanding of respect and of what it means to be a human being and a citizen. It implies that the greatest respect we can show for others is to leave them alone and not engage in discussion with them. It implies that any form of advice or suggestion we give each other is a violation of freedom. This view cannot be made compatible with deliberative democracy, as I see it.[75] It is an important motivation behind the present book to show that this view of respect is unfounded and confused; it is based on an untenable or incomplete understanding of freedom—and *in this* it blocks the acceptance of a more deliberative democracy. Contemporary culture is imbued with the dangerous idea that political discussion is a threat to freedom, while it is blind to the freedom-undermining aspects of the ideological forces that bypass our critical faculties.

A difficulty for my argument is how to deal with factors that influence both our options and our preferences and opinions but that fit neither side of the distinction made: they are neither arguments that feed into our critical faculties, nor are they manipulative, oppressive, or dominating in themselves. I am thinking both of our socioeconomic situation and of socialization broadly construed. The theory of freedom that I am developing has to be empirically feasible, which a conception of freedom that requires us to be independent of influences from our society is not.[76] I also contend that since we always are influenced by our surroundings, freedom must be defined by these having been democratically justified through, or at least not rejected by, a public process of deliberation.[77]

The argument in this section shows that a dimension of deliberative freedom can be construed as a negative conception. The forms of influence and the forces described here are some that citizens must be free *from* in order to be free. But deliberative democrats must distinguish forms of dependence that limit freedom and those that do not. The freedom-limiting forms of interference identified here make citizens procedurally dependent by bypassing their critical capacities and distorting deliberation. This is not true of the interference of laws justified in a process of deliberation in which arguments have been directed at the critical capacities of citizens. Furthermore, even though this dimension of the deliberative conception of freedom can be seen as a form of negative freedom, it also is a freedom that is required for and is part of the positive dimensions of citizens' deliberative freedom. This does not mean that procedural independence automatically or necessarily reinforces the *exercise* of freedom. Procedural independence is by its nature an opportunity concept, "where being free is a matter of what we can do ... whether or not we do anything to exercise these options."[78] But in contrast to negative freedom as noninterference, and in contrast also to Habermas's co-originality argument, my argument concerning procedural independence takes it seriously that even to enjoy opportunities not only for acting freely but also for forming preferences freely some positive state action may be necessary, *and* that without such encouragement and facilitation of the creation of a democratic ethos, negative freedom will not necessarily reinforce democracy or the full exercise of deliberative freedom.

Conclusion

This chapter has mainly been concerned with the negative dimension of freedom. On the one hand, I have argued that deliberation does not require that we make ourselves transparent to each other, and hence it is not a threat to the aspect of negative freedom that we call privacy. On the other hand, I have argued that even though deliberation presupposes the legal right to not participate in deliberation, the widespread use of this right would undermine the deliberative project. But not only that, the use of negative freedom to privatistic retreat would undermine equal negative liberty, because we can only *know* what it means for everyone to enjoy equal negative freedom if they use their public autonomy (this is part of the epistemological argument that I have been making throughout this book). Only a population that understands this and act accordingly, that is, only a population with a democratic ethos, indeed a deliberative democratic ethos, can enjoy all of the different dimensions of freedom to their fullest extent. A society with a deliberative democratic ethos is one in which the citizens understand that they are dependent on each other for their freedom and use their deliberative freedom in order to protect and promote it. The greatest ideological threat to this understanding is the idea that freedom is defined by complete independence from others, and that even arguing with others is a threat to one's negative freedom and a violation of one's rights.

The connection between the argument about privacy, procedural independence, and democratic ethos, on the one hand, and the argument in Chapter 5, on the other hand, is that the current ideology makes many people see deliberation as a threat to privacy. If we see any form of interaction as a threat to privacy and negative freedom, then we cannot see the emancipatory power of common deliberation. Ideology critique should help us see that freedom is more than absence of interference; it should contribute to creating the prerequisite democratic ethos. The deliberative perspective cannot see all forms of dependence as limiting freedom but has to be able to distinguish between forms of dependence that limit freedom and forms of dependence that enhance freedom. The notion of procedural independence has been invoked to distinguish forms of dependence that limit freedom (such as ideological domination) and forms of dependence that enhance freedom (common deliberation).

CHAPTER SEVEN

Freedom, Reason, and Participation

The argument that deliberation presupposes multiple dimensions of freedom and that these dimensions presuppose each other is to a large extent an epistemic one. In this chapter I elaborate on the procedural and intersubjective epistemology that informs my view of public deliberation and how it relates to deliberative freedom. In particular I argue that deliberative freedom is what I call a *procedural epistemic conception of freedom:* it is realized by living under political procedures that have the epistemic quality of giving all the opportunity to gain insights into what is true and right in politics and to participate in giving the law to all on that basis. Only a procedural epistemic conception of freedom can incorporate all four dimensions of freedom I have been discussing.

It might be thought that deliberative democracy does *not* require the opportunity for everyone to participate in the political process, but that the commitment to reason giving and knowledge would in fact favor rule by an enlightened elite who enjoys engaging in public deliberation. This chapter, therefore, attempts also to counter two objections that arise from the epistemic dimension of deliberative democracy. Both objections claim, but from opposite points of view, that the focus on reason leads deliberative democracy toward elitism and hence is a threat to the political freedom of the masses. The first objection (see the second section in this chapter) holds that deliberative democracy, because of its emphasis on reason, does not require participation by everyone and hence could lead to a justification that political participation be limited to an elite few.[1] In response to this objection, I argue that deliberative democracy can achieve its epistemic aims only through widespread political participation. It is in the course of making this argument that I develop the idea that deliberative freedom is a procedural epistemic conception of freedom. It is not the correctness of outcomes per se that makes people free, I argue, but the epistemic value of the deliberative procedure presupposes and contributes to the deliberative freedom of citizens. Part of this argument requires defending and elaborating on the Kantian aspects of my version of deliberative democracy. But I also will indicate how my theory of deliberative freedom departs from Kant and is less susceptible to Isaiah Berlin's objection to conceptions of freedom based on a commitment to reason such as Kant's.

The argument that the epistemic aim of deliberative democracy contributes to making it radically democratic leads to a very different objection. The second objection, which I consider (see the third section in this chapter), holds that the defect of deliberative democracy exactly is that it requires everyone to participate in public reason giving. This is held as being elitist, because it appeals to "a rare taste" for political participation in the form of reason giving.[2] Deliberative democracy, I argue in response, is neutral with regard to conceptions of the good but, it is true, it is not neutral with regard to its own normative content: freedom based on insights gained in common deliberation. Deliberative democrats have failed to stress the obligations in terms of participation that this normative commitment entails. Before answering the objections regarding elitism, I next specify what I mean by the epistemic dimension of deliberative democracy.

The Epistemic Dimension of Deliberative Democracy

First I make clear that the epistemic dimension of deliberation is an instrumental concern. I therefore have to distinguish the latter concern from the form of instrumentalism criticized in Chapter 1. Then I give a sketch of what participants learn in public deliberation.

The Instrumental Dimension of Deliberative Freedom

Chapter 1 argued that in the negative liberty tradition, freedom comes to signify the freedom to act on one's individual desires or personal preferences. On the aggregative model of democracy, this idea translates into the idea of freedom as a matter of having one's preferences counted in the political process. These views involve what I called an individual-instrumental conception of freedom. The aggregative model of democracy entails an instrumental view of the political process in the *narrow sense* of a process where citizens pursue their private and selfish interests. The individualistic and instrumental understanding of individual liberty and the democratic process is related to the idea that the individual knows her own interests and desires best and can know and express them best by being left alone.

The version of the theory of deliberative democracy developed in this book rejects that overall political freedom can be patterned on an individual-instrumental view of freedom. This, however, does not mean that we should not see deliberative freedom as instrumental in some sense. Deliberative democrats sometimes move too far away from an instrumental view of political freedom, or at least formulate the issue in ways that open up for obvious objections. James Bohman, for example, argues, "The achievement of individual goals is not even a proper measure for failure or success in the political domain."[3] Rather, "The success in communication in the context of deliberation is the uptake by others of one's reasons for acting."[4] Bohman is of course right to emphasize that politics is a cooperative and an intersubjective activity where individuals should *not only* think of the success of their own goals. But there is a tendency here to move to another extreme where there is no concern for one's own needs and desires.[5]

Deliberative democracy—not the least for the purposes of formulating a theory of political freedom—needs something between the narrow instrumental concern for private interests and the selfless search for the right or truth. Amy Gutmann and Dennis Thompson's notion of reciprocity can be seen as an attempt to formulate such an idea. They place reciprocity between prudence, which is concerned only with self-interest, and impartiality, which relies on altruism.[6] Reciprocity regards what is mutually acceptable and relies on the motivation on behalf of citizens to justify their claims to each other.[7] This understanding of reciprocity brings out something important, but I argue that the motivation to justify one's claims is not sufficient for understanding the desire for deliberative freedom. The notion of reciprocity also makes clear that deliberation does *not* happen among intelligible beings without needs, interests, and desires, (a point the importance of which I shall return to). Deliberation happens between citizens with different needs, interests, and desires, and political decisions must be acceptable from the standpoints of these differently situated individuals, or as Gutmann and Thompson say, political decisions must be "mutually acceptable." But this means that citizens are not only motivated by the desire to justify their claims to each other, they are motivated also by their different desires, needs, and interests.

Thus there are two aspects of the deliberative conception of freedom, where one is communicative and the other is instrumental. The communicative aspect of deliberative freedom concerns the requirement to justify claims to each other.[8] The instrumental aspect concerns the substance of political decisions. Citizens are occupied with political decisions because they affect their lives; they are concerned that political decisions help and do not hinder them in achieving their goals.

There need not be a conflict between the communicative and the instrumental aspect of deliberative freedom. In fact, I believe the two are merged in Habermas's test for the validity of a norm, namely, that it must be "equally good for all" or "in the equal interest of all."[9] What is equally good for all involves both the dimension of what citizens can justify to each other and the concern for what is good for them as individuals. As Jack Knight and James Johnson rightly point out, insofar as deliberation is concerned with fairness, self-interested claims cannot be excluded from deliberation. "Members of previously excluded groups, for example, typically demand entry into the relevant decision-making arenas precisely because, so long as they remain excluded, their *interests* are not adequately considered."[10] Citizens must have the opportunity to express their interests so they can learn what will be in the equal interest of all, that is, what is just, under particular circumstances. To exclude instrumental concerns from deliberation would be to empty it of the very stuff deliberation is about. Moreover, it would go against the aim that citizens clarify their needs and interests in light of the insights they gain from participating in the deliberative process.[11]

According to Habermas, "The question having *priority* in legislative politics concerns how a matter can be regulated in the equal interest of all," which is a question of justice.[12] What is just cannot be known by abstracting from what different individuals actually want. Rather, we need to know the interests of everybody to determine what is in the equal interest of all. This knowledge can be created only through actual deliberation, where we learn what people with different needs and interests actually (have learned they) want.[13] This does not mean that justice in this view is to give people equally what they want. Clearly some might have desires that are immoral or oppressive. And, as Brian Barry puts it, "Those who start by making the most oppressive demands must naturally expect to have them cut back the most."[14] In a deliberative democracy it is required that we can justify to others that we should have what we want. In deliberation we learn whether what we want can be justified to others. And we might also learn that we did not really want what we thought we wanted. Insofar as deliberation is aimed at justice, its focus "is on ways of advancing the aims of each party to it."[15] In this sense, deliberative democracy sees politics as instrumental to private interests.[16]

To clarify, we should not see the political process as instrumental in the *narrow sense* of being a matter of satisfying prepolitical private and egoistic preferences. The aim of the self-reflection, which deliberative democratic theory attempts to trigger with its critique, is that political opinions become as freely formed as possible, that is, that citizens gain internal autonomy. The participants' free formation of political opinions, however, is not sufficient to determine which opinions should win out in democratic decision making. The individual wills must be united in a "general will" that can be the basis of democratic decision making. Assume—optimistically—that all participants have formed their individual opinions and wills in a process of deliberation that is free from all those factors that limit free opinion and will formation: ideological domination, social and economic inequalities, unequal power structures, and so on. These participants might then be said to want what they want and believe what they believe without delusion; they have interpreted their needs and formed their wants and beliefs on the basis of insights gained in deliberation; in short, they are internally autonomous. It might be thought that citizens in that case also would already agree on what is to be done, that they have already formed a general will. But I do not see why that should be the case. After citizens have become clearer on what they really want and need individually, they have to figure out which of the freely held needs and desires can be justified to others and should be satisfied politically. There are two analytically distinguishable, but not in practice separable, steps in the deliberative exercise of political freedom. First, citizens become clearer on what they really want and need individually; they become internally autonomous. These more reflective, freely formed interpretations of needs and desires are relevant for democratic decision making. Second, citizens must *justify* to each other which of these freely held need and interest interpretations should be accommodated by political decisions.

Learning and the Epistemic Dimension of Public Deliberation

It is not sufficient for democratic legitimacy that political decisions ensue from a process in which only the better argument counts; they also must be based on the relevant information and knowledge. The issue of the better argument and the issue of relevant information and knowledge are not separate, of course. What the better argument is can only be determined in light of the relevant information and knowledge.

One of the problems with the aggregative model of democracy, which was pointed out in Chapter 1, is that it makes purely private and self-regarding preferences the basis of democratic legitimacy and public autonomy. On the aggregative model, citizens do not need to consider what the opinions, interests, and needs of others are except in a strategic manner. Deliberative democrats have tried to overcome this limitation in the aggregative model in two ways. The Rawlsian deliberative democrats have argued that citizens should give only reasons they think others would accept (see Chapter 4). This solution fails to see that the problem with the aggregative model is not just that people express egoistic or sectarian preferences, but also that they lack information about the opinions, interests, and needs of others, and about the possible justifications for accommodating them. Instead of overcoming the aggregative model by imposing external constraints on which kinds of reasons are allowable, I have argued, we should see deliberation as a learning process that screens out unjustifiably egoistic and sectarian preferences.

Most proponents of deliberative democracy see it as an epistemic conception of democracy.[17] An epistemic conception of democracy is one that not only praises the virtues of the procedures of democracy but also believes them to have a tendency[18] to lead to good and rational outcomes.[19] If we see deliberative democracy in terms of public autonomy, then the point of deliberation must be to reach a better understanding of the will of the people, than the mere aggregation of private preferences.[20] Jane Mansbridge argues that we need a full deliberative system "if citizens are, in any sense, to rule themselves." Her reason is that in a full deliberative system "people come to understand better what they want and need, individually as well as collectively."[21] I have argued that the Rawlsian understanding of deliberative democracy is not much help here, because it does not say anything about what we learn in deliberation. But what then is it we learn in deliberation?

According to the version of deliberative democracy developed in this book, only the opinions and will that result from free and open public deliberation can be the basis of democratic decision making. My concern in this section is what goes on in the process of public deliberation, what kind of knowledge and information may make persons change their minds and hence show what they "really want" or what their democratic will "really is."

First we have to disaggregate the idea of "what we want." What "we want" might mean either what we want individually or what we want collectively, as a people. It should be emphasized that I am speaking here only about what we want from political decisions or what we want there to be no political decisions about, that is, what should be left to private choice. As an individual I might want, say, good schools for my children, and I might want to be left alone in matters I consider private. But I also might think that *everybody* should have good schools for their kids, and that *everybody* should be protected from intrusion into their private lives. The latter concerns what we should will as a people.

It is sometimes thought that deliberative democracy requires that we take a universal or transcendental standpoint that disregards our differences in needs, interest, culture, and so on. Feminist critics especially have made this accusation against deliberative democracy.[22] But as feminist writers, such as Anne Phillips and Iris Young, themselves realize, "Deliberation matters only because there *is* difference."[23] If what we are looking for could be ascertained by monological reflection, then there would be no need for public deliberation. So the feminist critique does not apply to what should be essential to the idea of public deliberation. It is only because people have different needs, interests, and points of view that we have a reason to speak and listen to each other. So one thing we learn in deliberation is what people who are different from ourselves need, want, and think. What we gain here might be called "social knowledge"[24] or "intersubjective knowledge." And it is crucial to emphasize, we cannot gain this knowledge any other way than by having people speak for themselves.[25] Social knowledge is a form of knowledge that can only be generated by the participation of all in deliberation. By its very nature, it is a form of knowledge to which no one could possibly have privileged access.

In deliberation, I also might learn something that affects my interpretation of my needs, interests, and desires. Here it seems my learning is of two kinds. First, I might learn that what I thought I wanted for myself is not really a valuable object of desire. My learning is purely self-regarding; it concerns the desires I have about my own, private life. Does this not make deliberation perfectionist? To avoid misunderstanding, I am still speaking about what we want from political decisions, not about our private desires. But some of what we want from political decisions is self-regarding. I might want, say, a new road for purely egoistic reasons;

it brings me to work faster. In deliberation, I might learn that I do not want this road anyway. I might learn that the road does not bring me to work faster, or I might learn that the road destroys something that I value more highly, say, a clean environment. These aspects of learning concern facts. What is gained here is "objective knowledge," or knowledge about the objective world. It is not a matter of learning what the good life is. Deliberative freedom does not involve a politics of the good life, as I have repeatedly stressed.

Second, I might learn that what I wanted for myself has harmful effects on others, which I was not aware of before deliberating with them. This learning regards my relations with others. In this case, I might actually still want what I wanted, but in deliberation I have learned that I cannot justify the fulfillment of this desire to others.[26] Actually I am learning two things here: how the fulfillment of my desire affects others, how it looks from their perspective; and, whether the fulfillment of my desire can be justified to others—and to myself when I have learned how it affects others.[27] This is a case of social knowledge, but here we see how social knowledge can affect what I want for myself or what I find it possible to justify to claim for myself.

Apart from learning something about the social world and the objective world, it also might be thought that we can learn something in deliberation about our own "subjective world," about our own self.[28] This aspect of knowledge I call "self-knowledge." Self-knowledge requires that we have true beliefs about our mental states, that we know what they are and why we have them.[29] An interesting form of lack of self-knowledge is self-deception. If I, for example, have a wish to do x and think I have this desire because of reasons R_1 and R_2, but in fact I have this desire because of Z, then I deceive myself.[30] Z might be such phenomena as manipulation, fear, or the like. Can deliberation help us overcome a lack of self-knowledge? It would, of course, be hubristic to claim that it can do so entirely. Self-knowledge is something we can only approximate.

It might be objected that deliberation aimed at self-knowledge requires that we disclose our innermost needs and desires for public scrutiny and critique; in other words, the privacy objection discussed earlier could be invoked here. It was argued in Chapter 6 that we do not need to make ourselves transparent to each other in order for public deliberation to succeed. Such personalization also is not required for public deliberation to contribute to self-knowledge. What is important for gaining self-knowledge is that the forces that might undermine it are openly discussed and as far as possible eradicated. That is, social criticism, which I have argued should be part of public deliberation, should make us aware of cultural, social, and economic factors that make us deceive ourselves about the true causes of our interest interpretations and beliefs, and the political opinions that result. The deliberative epistemic argument is that problems of self-knowledge cannot be solved by leaving people to their own devices but can be mitigated by participating in a deliberative process in which people openly discuss factors that make them deceive themselves about the true causes of their political opinions. The aim here is not transparency but self-reflection.

In order to understand how citizens form their opinions and will in deliberation, we need to consider how the different forms of knowledge relate to each other. It should be noted here that when I speak of knowledge it should be understood as fallibilistic knowledge, that is, what we have come to believe in deliberation might be proven wrong in further deliberation. The insights we gain about ourselves and others could be said to result in something I call "normative knowledge." This knowledge constitutes what we have come to believe is the ideally right or good thing for us to aim for—without yet having considered the means. In politics, normative knowledge must be connected to knowledge about the objective world, knowledge about facts and about causal relationships, mainly about relationships between policies and their outcomes. From our normative knowledge combined with objective knowledge we derive knowledge about what to do, about what course of action to take.[31] I am not entirely satisfied with this way of describing the process by which citizens come to decisions about what to do or what political decisions to make. Surely the actual process is much more dialectical. Nevertheless, the analytic distinctions I have drawn show that deliberation is a complicated process that concern issues about (1) what the right values or principles are to pursue (normative knowledge), (2) what is true about the objective world (factual knowledge), and (3) what the best means are to the ends. Actually the last concerns both normative and factual knowledge, for citizens must consider both whether certain means (policies) will achieve their ends and whether they in themselves are normatively justifiable means.

Discussed in this section were some of the insights we gain in public deliberation: (1) knowledge about the interests, needs, and opinions of others; (2) knowledge about our own needs, interests, and opinions; (3) knowledge about what can be justified to others; (4) knowledge about what we want together as a people; and (5) knowledge about causal relationships. The aim of deliberation is, in general terms, to arrive at political decisions that take into account the needs, interests, opinions, interpretations, and knowledge of participants. And political decisions must take this information and knowledge into account in a way that is justifiable to all.

Reason, Freedom, and Radical Democracy

In *Considerations on Representative Government*, John Stuart Mill takes it upon himself to counter the "common saying, that if a good despot could be ensured, despotic monarchy would be the best form of government."[32] One of Mill's responses to this claim is that such a monarch need "not merely [be] a good monarch, but an all-seeing one."[33] And that clearly is an impossible demand: no one person is capable of seeing a case from all perspectives and considering all interests. Mill is concerned not only with interests being overlooked, for even if an interest is looked at, but "in the absence of its natural defender," it "is seen with very different eyes from those of the persons whom it directly concerns."[34] Even when the included want to do good to the excluded, this might have bad consequences when it is based on inadequate knowledge of the needs, interests, and opinions of the excluded. Mill is here articulating some important points that also lie behind the rationale for deliberative democracy.[35] Mill and contemporary deliberative democrats share the view that the best and most just decisions are reached if the interests of all affected are heard and taken into account. In other words, they share an epistemological argument for inclusive public discussion and democracy.

Deliberative democrats might be met with a different question than the one Mill tried to answer, namely, why *every single person* should have the opportunity to be heard, and why it would not be sufficient that *all interests or perspectives* be spoken for.[36] Why would the ideal form of deliberative government be democratic and participatory rather than some form of aristocracy of expert deliberators? This urges me to answer not what is wrong with the good despot but what is wrong with rule by a deliberative assembly that includes spokespersons or advocates for all interests or, as I shall say for short, a Perfectly Representative Deliberative Assembly. It is not that I reject representative government, but I would object to a view of deliberative democracy that saw parliament as the *only* forum for deliberation. My version of deliberative democracy is a participatory one (cf. Chapter 2). The aim here is, moreover, to argue what would be wrong with something like Burkean virtual representation from the perspective of deliberative freedom. Virtual representation means in Burke's words that "there is a communion of interest and sympathy in feelings and desires between those who act in the name of any description of people and the people in whose name they act, though the trustees are not actually chosen by them."[37] We need to be able to counter the Burkean view of what is required for deliberation both in order to argue why deliberative democrats should emphasize extraparliamentary forms of deliberation and why it would be wrong for some people to be merely virtually represented. I also make this argument in order to counter Lynn M. Sanders's charge that deliberative democracy has an affinity for conservatism and that it shares some key ideas with Edmund Burke,[38] as well as to counter Jon Elster's assertion that Burke, in his speech to the electors of Bristol in 1774, made "the most famous statement of the case for deliberative democracy."[39]

I next group my arguments concerning why deliberative democrats should reject rule by an assembly of virtual representatives or a Perfectly Representative Deliberative Assembly under two headings. First I give some epistemic reasons. Then I give reasons that go beyond the epistemic and instrumental concern to the intrinsic values of participating in deliberation. I emphasize the epistemic reasons, since they seem to be the hardest to make, and also because it is here that the objection has its roots, not because they can be sharply separated from intrinsic reasons.

Epistemic Reasons for Participation

This section argues on the basis of the epistemic dimension of deliberative democracy why it would *not* lead to the acceptance of rule by a Perfectly Representative Deliberative Assembly. The aim is to show that the epistemic dimension of deliberative democracy *contributes* to its respect for the political freedom of everyone, rather than being detrimental to it, as some critics fear. It is inherent to the concern for individual learning, for internal and public autonomy, that everyone should have an opportunity to participate, and that everyone should have the right to reject what they have not been convinced is right or true.

Institutional issues. The Burkean view requires that we know what interests or "description" to represent, but it is far from self-evident what group interests or "identities" should be represented, and it is unclear who would have the necessary "communion of interest." This is not the place to go into a discussion of group representation, so I note only that the danger of exclusion of certain interests is especially urgent in the case of sovereign rule by a (an alleged) Perfectly Representative Deliberative Assembly, because some people are effectively silenced and disenfranchised. In all cases, the danger of exclusion of some views gives us a reason not to confine political deliberation to a formal assembly. Furthermore, although deliberation should not exclude interests as a legitimate object of deliberation, it is concerned also with other forms of information and knowledge, and with finding arguments. Information might be possessed by anyone, and the best argument might come from anywhere.[40]

It might be thought that the aim should be to compose a deliberative assembly of the best arguers, but this idea is in conflict with the intersubjective epistemology that the ideal of democratic deliberation entails. Deliberation is not only a matter of arguing but also of gathering information and learning how the world looks from perspectives different from one's own. It is inconceivable how any model of virtual representation could include all interests, all possible arguments, and all pieces of information. It is exactly the advantage of a deliberative model that relies on widespread participation that it can do this, or at least that it can do this better than any alternative model.

Another reason for rejecting the Perfectly Representative Deliberative Assembly as the natural consequence of the deliberative model concerns not the composition of the assembly but its institutionalization, or precisely *that* it will have to be formally institutionalized. If the assembly is to be sovereign, then we must assume that it has to be formally institutionalized as a legislative body, with procedures of deliberation and decision making. This will put certain constraints and limitations on its deliberations, which we do not find in the deliberations of the public sphere of civil society. I argue that any assembly deliberating only internally must fall short of attaining the necessary insights for making wise and just decisions, and that there are good epistemic reasons a deliberative democracy cannot do without the deliberations of the informal public sphere.[41]

The kind of deliberations that take place in the formally institutionalized assembly is, unlike the deliberations of informal public spheres, "decision-oriented deliberations."[42] This means that the formal publics are under some constraints, especially time constraints, which the informal publics are not.[43] The pressure to decide in formal publics also entails that many issues of discussion are excluded. Both time pressure and the inevitable routinized character of formal publics tend to make them less sensitive to new issues and conflicts than the informal publics.[44] By necessity, formal publics are regulated by procedures that limit the openness and extent of deliberation. In contrast, deliberation in informal publics is under no formal constraints. Any issue can be discussed, time is unlimited, and needs can be articulated without limits.[45] And, crucially, in the informal publics, everybody can participate; there is, in principle, open access to participation and to participating in the way one chooses.[46] For this reason the informal publics are more sensitive to new problems and issues than are the formal public spheres. Informal publics constitute a "*context of discovery*"[47] and have "sensors that . . . are sensitive throughout society"[48]; that is, the networks of communication that constitute the public sphere are present in all corners of society. But the public sphere not only detects problems, it also generates opinions. Associations are an important part of the public sphere of civil society.[49] "Such associations *specialize* in the generation of practical convictions. They specialize, that is, in discovering issues relevant for all of society, contributing possible solutions to problems, interpreting values, producing good reasons, and invalidating others."[50] Formalized deliberations, even in a perfectly representative and rational assembly, will inevitably be less open to innovation and creativity and will likely be less sensitive to new issues that arise in the periphery of society.

The argument made here is meant to indicate why a deliberative democracy cannot achieve its epistemic aims if only deliberations taking place in a formally institutionalized assembly are allowed to be efficacious. But my argument also suggests that deliberation cannot be limited to civil society either. The respective advantages of formal and informal publics depend on their being kept institutionally separate. This means that I do not see deliberative democracy as a criticism of representative government, with its separation of formal and informal publics, as such. Critics of this separation contend that it is not democratic enough.[51] What they neglect is that the advantages of informal publics depend on a separation of informal and formal publics, of decision-free deliberation and decision-oriented deliberation. The potential openness, inclusiveness, sensitivity, and so on of the civil publics depend on their being relieved of the burden of decision making.[52] It is partly because they are free from routines of decision making that informal publics are sensitive to the new issues and conflicts, to which formal publics are blind. The fact that civil publics do not decide is not only a limit, it also is enabling and liberating.

Of course, for the deliberations in the informal public spheres to be democratically relevant and effective, they must be able to influence decision making. How this works is a complicated issue, which we cannot go into here. The aim has been to argue that deliberative democracy cannot achieve its epistemic aims by deliberation in a formal assembly alone—and that we therefore have to consider how deliberations in the informal publics can be connected to those in legislative bodies. Admittedly, this is no minor difficulty. Indeed, this is one of the institutional issues most gravely neglected in the literature on deliberative democracy hitherto, and one of the main challenges for the development of the theory. The preceding argument should encourage us to think hard about which institutional mechanisms best mediate between informal opinion formation and formal decision making rather than to devise institutions that undermine the separation (see further the third section in Chapter 8).

Procedural epistemic freedom. Until now I have dealt with the issue of what is institutionally required for deliberation to achieve its epistemic aims and have argued in favor of the opportunity for participation in public deliberation by everyone. Now I focus on freedom and outline a conception of freedom I call *procedural epistemic freedom.* Deliberative freedom, I suggest, is a procedural epistemic conception of freedom. I shall argue that the deliberative freedom of citizens is not achieved by the correctness of political outcomes but rather is related to the epistemic value of democratic procedures. This does not mean that I go beyond the epistemic dimension of deliberation, but that I see it as a property of the procedure rather than of outcomes.

Recall David Estlund's distinction (introduced in Chapter 2) between *correctness theory,* according to which outcomes are legitimate if they are correct, and *epistemic proceduralism,* according to which outcomes do not have to be correct to be legitimate as long as the procedure is the epistemically best possible. I have argued that the epistemic value of deliberation increases if everyone is able to participate and if deliberation can take different institutional forms. Taking the cue from Estlund's distinction, I make some further distinctions regarding the ways in which freedom and rationality can be related. First we must distinguish between substantive and procedural freedom. Substantive conceptions of freedom take the following form:

F_S: P is free if and only if she believes, values, and chooses x, where P is a person or a collective and where x may stand for anything that can be believed, valued, or chosen (a maxim, a norm, an action, a policy, etc.).

Procedural conceptions of freedom take the following form:

F_P: P is free if and only if her beliefs, values, and choices are the result of a certain procedure,

where "procedure" includes institutions and conditions under which beliefs and values are formed and choices are made.

Two aspects of substantive conceptions of freedom should be highlighted. First, x is seen as a given and constant; it is believing, valuing, or choosing x that matters for freedom, not the origins of the authority of x. Second, it is regarded as irrelevant how the person has come to believe, value, or choose x. Procedural conceptions, in contrast, are concerned with origins in both cases, that is, both regarding how x has achieved its authority, or how it has been justified and how individuals have come to believe, value, or choose x.

Neither substantive nor procedural conceptions of freedom needs to be epistemic, but both types can be so. Substantive conceptions become epistemic when the x is seen as having cognitive content. Hence, substantive epistemic conceptions of freedom take the following form:

F_{SE}: P is free if and only if she believes, values, and chooses what is true and right.

Procedural conceptions of freedom are epistemic when the procedure is one that is believed to have epistemic value, that is, to have a tendency to produce results with cognitive content. Hence, procedural epistemic conceptions of freedom take the following form:

F_{PE}: P is free if and only if her beliefs, values, and choices are the result of a procedure with epistemic value.

According to substantive epistemic conceptions, the very fact of *holding* true beliefs and true values makes one free. When this view of personal autonomy is seen in terms of public autonomy, it is translated into the idea that one is free when one lives under just laws. In this view rightness is constitutive of freedom. Call this view *freedom as being right*. According to the procedural epistemic view, rightness as such is not constitutive of freedom, but a procedure that tends to produce valid results is.

I think those who criticize the idea of relating freedom and reason mainly aim their salvos at the notion of freedom as being right, while they neglect the possibility of a procedural epistemic conception of freedom. I am arguing in favor of a version of this latter possibility. In doing so I hope to counter the Berlinian claim that relating freedom to reason necessarily leads to oppression.[53] Thus I suggest that deliberative freedom is a form of procedural epistemic freedom. According to the deliberative conception of freedom, only under procedures and conditions that make it possible for one to come to hold rational beliefs and values by oneself (internal autonomy and procedural independence) and that respect one as a free being (discursive status) can rightness contribute to the individual's freedom. This is not freedom as being right but freedom as gaining insights by oneself in the company of others. The problem with substantive epistemic conceptions of freedom is that they cannot include all the different dimensions of freedom; they do not include procedural independence and the right to think for oneself, nor do they include the idea of being a participant in self-legislation. As long as the norms are right, it does not matter who gives them, according to substantive conceptions of freedom. Procedural epistemic conceptions of freedom, such as deliberative freedom, in contrast, have the advantage of being able to incorporate several dimensions of freedom.

My argument requires that we draw a further distinction, namely, between *reaching* the right decision and *knowing* that we have done so or, more precisely, knowing that we have reached a decision with the presumption of being right on its side. Here it also matters *who* knows it. The epistemic dimension of deliberative democracy only contributes to freedom—or only does so to its full extent—when it is seen that it is not sufficient that political decisions have a tendency to be right, but that everyone must have the opportunity to gain insight into this fact. And this insight can only be attained as a participant in public deliberation (see Chapter 2). The epistemic value of deliberation does not lie only in its tendency to produce the best collective outcomes but also in the *individual* learning of each citizen. The epistemic dimension of deliberative democracy, thus, is not merely a matter of the polity getting it right but also of individuals having the opportunity to achieve insights. Deliberative freedom is a freedom of individuals, not a collective freedom.

We can now return to our discussion of the Perfectly Representative Deliberative Assembly. The insights gained by this Assembly have to be made into law in order to be implemented. For the citizens who have been excluded from the process of deliberation and who have therefore not had the opportunity to gain the insights that these laws embody, these laws will present themselves *only* as a coercive force. But outward force, as John Locke noted, cannot create "inward perswasion of the Mind."[54] And it is exactly inward persuasion of the mind that is necessary before we can see a law as an expression of our *own* freedom. To be free is not just a matter of doing what is right or living under just laws but of having the opportunity of learning and knowing by one's own lights what is right and participating in giving the laws on that basis. The fact that a political decision is just and wise is not sufficient to make us free. The content as well as the genesis of law matter for deliberative freedom. A decision that is just would not be an expression of *my* deliberative freedom if I did not have the opportunity to give and be given reasons for it. My submission to it would be a submission to an external authority (see Chapter 2, the section "Common Knowledge"). This would violate the (Kantian) "freedom from the authority of anything but our own reason to determine our wills."[55] If I am unable to participate in the deliberations that lead to the making of the decision, then I will have no way of gaining the insights necessary to understand its validity. And the law cannot make me free *after* it has been implemented, because it will merely be an external force imposed on my will from the outside.

Ideally, I have to be convinced personally and to have accepted the law by my own lights. But in actual politics, where consensus is a rare occurrence, my deliberative freedom is respected if others sincerely have attempted to convince me and listened to my arguments. In this way, even if I end up in the minority, I will still have gained knowledge of why the decision was made. A law is not merely an external imposition on my will when reasons have been given for it and my own reasons have been responded to. However, we must still hold up consensus as the regulative ideal because it is what requires us to find reasons that are convincing not merely to the majority but to everyone. The ideal of deliberative freedom requires that everyone involved in influencing and making law must seek to find reasons that are convincing to everyone else in light of what they learn others want and believe.

Kant, Berlin, and deliberative freedom. My argument is largely a Kantian one, but the idea of deliberative freedom goes beyond Kant.[56] Principally, deliberative freedom is less susceptible to the Berlinian objection against positive conceptions of freedom related to rationality. According to Isaiah Berlin, if the subjects of a rational ruler "disapprove, they must, *pro tanto*, be irrational; then they will need to be repressed by reason: whether their own or mine cannot matter, for the pronouncements of reason must be the same in all minds."[57] This objection works only against monological theories and fails to apply to a dialogical theory of reason and an intersubjective epistemology as the one that underlies the conception of deliberative freedom presented in this book. What deliberative democrats should deny is exactly that what is right or true can be justified by the reasoning of a single individual. The pronouncements of reason are results of intersubjective processes of deliberation; they do not exist prediscursively in our minds or in anybody's mind. That is why common deliberation is necessary. And this is one of the reasons deliberative democracy cannot build on a substantive epistemic conception of freedom: standards are not given and hence cannot be imposed from outside common deliberation.

If we follow Habermas, the right or just outcome is defined by being able to be accepted in a practical discourse in which all affected take part. "Just those action norms are valid to which all possibly affected persons could agree as participants in rational discourses."[58] So the very definition of validity includes a commitment to participation by all. Habermas's understanding of reason is a communicative one. To say that something is rational is to say that there is a preponderance of good reasons for it. Which reasons are good and which are bad will depend on what citizens would accept in a free process of deliberation in which all other forces than that of reasons are excluded. There is no point outside deliberation from which what the better argument is could be determined. In deliberation there is no other authority than the positions taken by participants.[59] It is only when citizens have been able to participate in the reason-giving process that they can be confident that the outcome is based on no other force than that of the better argument. Furthermore, in order to gain insights in deliberation, any claim must be open to contestation. Any claim to authority, superior reason, or infallibility is the same as terminating deliberation. For deliberation to be a process of gaining insights, speakers must back their claims with reasons, and all individuals must have the right to reject them if they have not been convinced, that is, they must enjoy procedural independence.

Berlin's objection fails to apply to Kant also—and to the Kantian aspects of my version of deliberative democracy. Berlin does not make the necessary distinction between law (*Recht*) and morality in his criticism of

Kant,[60] but in fact his objection fails to apply to both Kant's philosophy of law and his moral philosophy. Regarding Kant's view of juridical law, he is in fact defending a negative conception of freedom, which rejects using the law for any paternalistic purposes. Kant is unequivocal about this in *The Metaphysics of Morals*.[61] Regarding morality, it is very clear that Kant's view is incompatible with the enforcement of virtue. What gives an action moral worth is that it is done "from duty," that I do it *because* it is right. And, crucially, I can act only because it is right if *I am convinced* it is right. We can be forced to act *in accordance with* duty, but we cannot be forced to act *from* duty.[62] Clearly, if I do something because I have been forced to do it, then I do it because I have been forced to do it and not from duty. My will is heteronymous because it is given by an external object and not by my own reason. We might say that a law, the justice of which I am not convinced, presents itself to me as a hypothetical imperative. Kant says of a hypothetical imperative that it takes the form "I ought to do something because I will something else."[63] A law that is imposed on me from the outside similarly means that I ought to obey even if what I will is not the commanded action but avoiding the penalty for disobeying. For example, I ought to accept military conscription because I do not will the penalty for deserting. To accept the conscription is not an expression of my freedom because that is not what I will do or what I have been convinced is right to do. This basic Kantian idea I agree with; I can never become autonomous by external force but only by being personally convinced. This idea also shows that deliberative freedom is a procedural epistemic conception of freedom rather than a substantive epistemic conception of freedom. It is not acting in accordance with given standards per se that makes me free (F_{SE}—substantive epistemic freedom) but having been personally convinced of their validity following a certain procedure that does so (F_{PE}—procedural epistemic freedom). What distinguishes the deliberative democratic view from Kant is how the convincing takes place, that insights are gained intersubjectively.

The deliberative conception of freedom should be distinguished from Kant in a second way too. Deliberation happens between embodied persons with real and different needs, interests, desires, and opinions. The parties to deliberation are, in Seyla Benhabib's words, "finite, embodied, and fragile creatures, and not disembodied cogitos or abstract unities of transcendental apperception."[64] It is only because people have different needs, interests, and points of view that we have a reason to speak and listen to each other. As we have seen, to obtain the information and knowledge required by the epistemic dimension of deliberative democracy, what Kant wants to suppress and exclude in moral reasoning cannot be excluded in public deliberation. That is the case, first, because it would exclude the possibility of changing or reinterpreting one's needs, interest, desires, and opinions in light of the insights gained in the deliberative process and, second, because the agreement, which deliberation aims at, concerns and includes how and which needs, interests, and desires should be dealt with politically. The answers that participants in deliberation seek are not some that exist over and above their own needs and interests, but some that include these. We need deliberation between real, embodied, and embedded people exactly in order for the participants to get a clearer understanding of what they want and need. Democratic deliberation should not be seen primarily as a matter of developing abstract principles of justice but of learning what is wanted and needed and on that background determining what just and good decisions would be in particular cases.[65] Thus the kind of knowledge related to epistemic legislation is not one that transcends our differences or is to be found in pure reason alone. The insights that we gain in common deliberation include the (interpretations of) needs, wants, and interests of the participants. My point is not only that it includes knowledge of these but also that it includes *our own* knowledge of these, and that both aspects are required for political decisions to be an expression of our freedom to the fullest possible extent. We rule ourselves not only by having our interests accommodated but also by coming to a clearer understanding of what they are and by knowing that they are (or to what extent they are) accommodated in political decisions.[66]

It could be argued that I have not satisfactorily answered the Berlinian objection. It might be said that even if the person who comes out in the minority has some understanding of the reasons behind the decision made, she might still feel she is being repressed in the name of reason. The Berlinian might here change her objection and say, "Aha, it is those who do not agree after deliberation who are irrational and need to be repressed by reason." But there is no "after" deliberation. The search for the best possible decisions never ends; no decision is the expression of the Truth or the Rational. The Berlinian objection may apply to substantive epistemic freedom or freedom as being right, but it fails as a criticism of deliberative freedom as a procedural epistemic conception of freedom, because the latter form of freedom can, by its very nature, never be imposed on anyone, since it has no final content. And deliberative freedom as a form of procedural epistemic freedom is a complex conception of freedom, which includes dimensions of freedom that preclude imposing someone's notion of rationality on others. Imposing someone's view of rationality on others not only violates their procedural independence, public autonomy, and discursive status, but it also undermines the epistemic quality of the deliberative procedure, which depends on these dimensions of freedom being respected.

To avoid the Rousseauian conclusion that because you are in the minority you are mistaken, it is important to stress another aspect of the distinction between epistemic proceduralism and correctness theory. Rousseau's theory is (on one interpretation) an example of a correctness theory. As is well known, Rousseau believed that "the general will is always right,"[67] and when "the opinion contrary to mine prevails, this proves merely that I was in error, and that what I took to be the general will was not so."[68] Estlund argues that this view requires not only that those in the minority obey but also that they surrender their moral judgment to others. Epistemic proceduralism only requires that the minority obey, not that they surrender their judgment.[69] This is because the deliberative procedure, even if seen as having epistemic value, is seen as imperfect. In other words, the outcomes of the deliberative procedure should be seen as fallible. And I contend that the acknowledgment of fallibilism contributes to the epistemic value of the deliberative procedure. The adherence to fallibilism is by no means in contradiction to the epistemic dimension of deliberative democracy. On the contrary, it would be the presumption of infallibility that would undermine the epistemic aims of deliberative democracy, since it is a presumption against the possibility of further learning and improvement.

"Deliberation is an ongoing process, producing results that in a deep sense are always provisional," say Gutmann and Thompson.[70] This means that no political decision with confidence can be said to be the will of the people or express their deliberative freedom. Who the people are and what the general will is should always and continually be under discussion. No one can speak for the rest as representing "the People." No one can force the rest to be free in the name of the general will. Institutionally, this connects to the argument concerning the importance of complementing formal deliberations with informal ones. The purpose of having a decision-free public sphere also is to have a check on any presumption on behalf of the decisional public of being "the People." It is crucial that the people can "manifest itself as a political entity having a (usually incomplete) unity independent of the representatives," that is, "a system in which the representatives can never say with complete confidence and certainty 'We the People.' "[71]

The significance of the insistence on the fallibility of any decision is, furthermore, that criticism is always legitimate. Decisions made after a process of deliberation do not represent the last word on a matter. Citizens "remain free to approve or refuse the conclusions developed from the argument."[72] Fallibilism gives everyone the right not to accept any decision as the final truth, but of course this does not mean that those who disagree are not obliged to obey. They must obey the decisions because a majority of their fellow citizens were convinced, but they retain the freedom to criticize the outcome and to try to change it.

Intrinsic Reasons for Participation

I have given some reasons a concern with the epistemic value of deliberation would not lead to exclusion or be a threat to the political freedom of the masses. Even though I describe this as a matter of procedure rather than outcome, it is a concern for the procedure in terms of the outcomes that it has a tendency to produce. There is, however, a danger in deliberative democracy becoming too outcome oriented. Procedures should not merely be evaluated in terms of their epistemic properties but also for their intrinsic merits. Being free is not only a matter of living under epistemic procedures, it also is a matter of being *respected* as an equal participant in deliberation. There are not only epistemic reasons for rejecting the Perfectly Representative Deliberative Assembly but also intrinsic ones. By intrinsic reasons I mean factors that are *part of* rather than results of being a participant in the deliberative process. If we focus on the instrumental-epistemic dimension alone, then we might end up with a procedure that by itself undermines the very freedom it was supposed to secure. Decision-making procedures should be judged not only in terms of which results they produce or in terms of whether they give us the opportunity to participate in giving laws to ourselves but also in terms of their intrinsic properties. The value of the epistemic end of securing justice and equal freedom for all would be undermined if the process followed to reach that end itself violated the discursive status of citizens, a dimension of freedom.

Earlier I argued that the plight of being in the minority is mitigated when decisions are seen as fallible, and hence to disagree is not seen as an expression of irrationality. There is a reason intrinsic to having the opportunity of being a participant in public deliberation that works in a similar way. By being recognized as a participant, the individual is given a certain status. Status can be seen as a dimension of freedom, as argued in Chapter 2. Freedom as status "identifies freedom as a position occupied by a person within a particular political and social structure."[73] Deliberative democracy implies a specific view of what it is to be a citizen and involves a particular conception of freedom as status, namely, discursive status. We must respect the status of each other as free persons in the sense of persons worth arguing with, as persons who can contribute with and respond appropriately to reasons. Everyone is given the status of an authority on matters taken up in public deliberation. This form of status is not constituted by one's legal status alone. It is a status that presupposes and lies in the *activity* of participating in common deliberation. In contrast, to exclude people either from voting, as is the case with a scheme of virtual representation, or to exclude them from participating in deliberation is a form of disrespect. What matters for our freedom is not merely that our interests are spoken for and protected, but we also want to be treated as free beings with a will and reason of our own, as active participators.

As mentioned, one of the problems with rule by a Perfectly Representative Deliberative Assembly is that the subjects would lack the understanding necessary to appreciate the insights embodied in the laws to which they are subject as addressees. Suppose now that it was possible to overcome this difficulty. The Perfectly Representative Deliberative Assembly wants the best for its people; it wants them not only to live under just laws but also to have the insights necessary to appreciate that they live under just and good laws. Hence, it invents a way of implanting the necessary insights into the minds of its subjects. I am supposing here that the Assembly knows what is right and that it has only good intentions but still does not want the people to engage in public deliberation or criticisms of its policies (it might believe that public deliberation, as distinguished from its own official deliberations, would lead people away from the truth). The implantation of right beliefs engaged in by the Assembly would be a form of benevolent manipulation. Manipulation is a type of influence where the influenced person does not know she is being influenced.[74] A person who is successfully manipulated comes to hold certain beliefs and desires without being aware of their origin.

Why would benevolent manipulation be objectionable? From a purely epistemic point of view, it would be hard to see why it would. The manipulated subject would have an understanding that the laws are just, and she would even be able to see them as given by her own reason (or at least she could not find any way of reasonably rejecting them). But does history not matter for our freedom? John Christman has argued for the importance of history for autonomy: "The notion of autonomy is essentially *historical*, in that the conditions of desires and values that must be met for them to be autonomous are properties of the *formation* of those desires."[75] Deliberative democracy must incorporate such a historical understanding of freedom, because the process of forming opinions plays center stage. Thus it is because the *origins* of our beliefs, values, and opinions matter that benevolent manipulation becomes a problem. We cannot look only at how things are with us now and conclude from that whether or not we are free.[76] It matters how we have become as we are, even if we have become insightful and rational.[77]

I place this argument under the rubric of intrinsic values of deliberation, because being a participant in deliberation is the opposite of being subject to manipulation.[78] Deliberation is a process of making explicit and public; manipulation works by hiding and covering its true intentions.[79] Deliberation is aimed at conscious opinion and will formation; manipulation bypasses its subject's conscious faculties in order to create opinions that she cannot knowingly have adopted and to form a will that she could not have willed to will. The problem with benevolent manipulation is not epistemic but that it shows disrespect for the person to whom it is directed. The subject of manipulation is not respected as a free person who is capable of responding to reasons and thinking for herself. And she is, of course, not regarded as someone who might have ideas of her own to contribute. She is not regarded as an actor, a participator, or a contributor.

This discussion shows the inadequacy of substantive epistemic conceptions of freedom, which would have nothing to object to manipulation. The focus on origins and history fits my argument for deliberative freedom as a procedural conception of freedom. The epistemic argument in the preceding section does not take us far enough, however. It is not sufficient to argue that we should focus on procedures with epistemic value. Procedures can be objected to for other than epistemic reasons.

It is necessary, therefore, to draw on arguments concerning the intrinsic values of the procedure in addition to the epistemic ones. I see this as a question of there being more dimensions to freedom; deliberative freedom is a matter of having the opportunity for gaining insights, but it also is a matter of being respected as a free being who is able to respond reflectively with and to reasons, of being an actor in and a contributor to our common world.

The manipulative implantation of true beliefs, then, violates an important dimension of freedom. Freedom is not only a matter of knowing the right but also of reaching this stage by oneself. To stress the historical dimension of freedom also is to point to the idea that deliberative freedom should be seen as a form of achievement. Having gained knowledge must be *my own achievement* in order to contribute to *my* freedom. This requires that I have the opportunity to reflect on and reject what influences me. Obviously, manipulation does not give us that opportunity, no matter how benevolent it is.

The argument for the intrinsic values of participation is not just an addition to the epistemic reasons. It is not merely one we can use against those who are not convinced by the epistemic arguments. The intrinsic reasons for participation are closely interwoven with the epistemic ones. What united the epistemic arguments for the idea that deliberative democracy presupposes a commitment to the participation of everyone was that it is not merely the only way in which the collective can gain insights into what justice and freedom means and implies, but also the only way in which each citizen can gain those insights. The argument concerning the importance of the intrinsic merits of the process that leads us to those insights partakes in the same concern for freedom of individuals severally understood. If the process itself violates a dimension of freedom, then it undermines its own purpose. Even though I, for analytical purposes, distinguish between different dimensions of freedom, I believe that they are united in the same normative commitment.

Participation, Freedom, and Neutrality

I have argued that the theory of deliberative democracy cannot be used to justify elitism; on the contrary, it depends on the opportunity for widespread participation and participation of different forms, both to achieve its epistemic aims and to show respect for the discursive status of everyone.

This response might, however, lead to another objection against deliberative democracy, an objection that also focuses on reason and freedom but that comes from another corner. Whereas the first objection could be said to be concerned with *exclusion* from deliberation, the objection that I turn to now concerns a fear of (over) *inclusion* in deliberation.

Radical democratic multiculturalists (such as Iris Young, who wants to make deliberative democracy more inclusive by opening up more forms of communication, such as rhetoric, storytelling, and greetings) fail to see that the issue oftentimes is that some groups do not want to participate at all, and this rejection of political participation is an integral part of their cultural or religious identification.[80] The Old Order Amish sect in the United States, for instance, rejects any participation in and responsibility for the wider society of which it is a part.[81] The issue, it seems, is not only the form of participation but also the call for participation as such. The rejection of democratic participation by some parts of society is, in particular, something that radical democrats ought to discuss.

The concern articulated by the second objection, then, is not, as with the first, that deliberative democracy differentiates between people, but that it makes them all the same, that it builds on a certain view of the good life as one devoted to public deliberation, autonomy, and rationality. The fear is that the focus on autonomy and rationality does not allow for a plurality of ways of life. Liberals discuss whether autonomy or diversity is the fundamental value.[82] Will Kymlicka, for example, defends autonomy as the main value of liberalism[83]; William Galston argues for giving "diversity" pride of place.[84] To borrow Galston's definitions, autonomy is "linked with the commitment to sustained rational examination of self, other, and social practices"; diversity means "legitimate differences among individuals and groups over such matters as the nature of the good life, sources of moral authority, reason versus faith, and the like."[85] My concern in this section is whether deliberative democracy, when involving a commitment to deliberative freedom, is susceptible to the objection raised by those who criticize autonomy or Enlightenment liberalism.[86] Thus I return to the issue of sectarianism, but now from the perspective of the commitment to widespread political participation or active citizenship. The reason it is important to do this is that the aim of this book is to show that the different dimensions of deliberative freedom do not contradict each other; part of this aim is to argue that we can be committed to the freedom to choose our own conception of the good (nonsectarianism) at the same time we are committed to a participatory understanding of public autonomy."

Diversity and Tolerance

In his *Liberal Pluralism*, William Galston criticizes deliberative democracy for not taking tolerance seriously enough. He picks up on a passage in Gutmann and Thompson in which they speak of the insufficiency of "mere toleration" (for moral progress) and counters, "In the real world, there is nothing 'mere' about toleration."[87]

Galston sees deliberative democracy as violating the right not to give reasons for or justifying being different.[88] In other words, he sees a conflict between the deliberative view of public autonomy and negative freedom. However, it is unclear why we should fear that deliberation—or the deliberative exercise of public autonomy—would entail scrutinizing people's ethical-existential convictions and require them to justify them to each other. It is surely important that citizens are allowed to claim a right to privacy protection of their ethical convictions (cf. the second section in Chapter 6). And when citizens argue for this privacy right, there is no need to argue for the goodness, rationality, or truthfulness of their conceptions of the good in public deliberation. Deliberative freedom does not imply that people cannot claim anything without giving justifications for their ethical convictions, that is, for their conception of the good.

Consider the right to free exercise of religion. When citizens argue for this right, they need not do so by giving arguments for the *content* of their religion. Rather, they first need to argue that the free exercise of their religion is important to them. When a negative liberty comes into conflict with other values, it must be argued that its exercise is significant.[89] It is not sufficient, however, that one states the fact of one's religious beliefs, as Galston thinks,[90] for how can such statements of the *fact* of religious beliefs ever lead to any agreements? Clearly someone has to evaluate such claims and accept or reject them for some reason. My point is that if we do accept that the fact of holding a religious belief gives a prima facie good reason for accepting the person's claim, then this relies on the acceptance of the significance of free exercise of religion and on the right to free exercise or on toleration. But then the question is really determined with reference to this prior norm. The deliberation, then, need not concern the content of religious beliefs, as

Galston fears, but only whether we should tolerate all or only some, and which, exercises of religion. This does not mean that people cannot offer as *a* reason in public, "I object because of my religious beliefs"; nor do I mean to say that such a statement should not have any influence on our deliberations. But it cannot be a *sufficient* reason for accepting the claim; it must be accompanied by reasons we should see the fact of holding a religious belief as important.[91] The difference between deliberative democracy and Galston's liberalism here is that the first believes the extent of privacy rights must be determined by public deliberation, while Galston thinks it can be determined by the liberal philosopher (him) prepolitically. This difference is based on divergent epistemological assumptions (intersubjective versus monological) and divergent freedom commitments (deliberative freedom versus negative freedom).

A problem with Galston's argument concerning toleration is that it is unclear whether he is speaking of enforcing law or making law, the content of law or how to make law, about addressees of law or authors of law. He is oscillating between the participant perspective of what we should decide *in* deliberation, which is concerned with what should be backed by force, and the observer's perspective about *how* we should deliberate. It is one thing to say that we should decide on a policy of toleration, but it is another to say that toleration should constrain deliberation. Deliberative democracy has nothing against tolerance and privacy rights but their extent is seen as product of learning and is never a settled issue, as it seems to be for Galston.[92] Regarding tolerance as a way *how* to deliberate, I agree with Gutmann and Thompson, that it can be detrimental to deliberation as a learning process. For "mere toleration . . . locks into place the moral divisions in society and makes collective moral progress far more difficult."[93] That is, if we accept that the opinion of the other party is part of his religion or culture and therefore cannot be subjected to discussion, then we preclude the possibility of learning from each other. In other words, when we see the opposing beliefs of others as a threat to our own negative freedom, we preclude developing internal autonomy.

Actually I find the use of "toleration" as requiring us not to question or discuss the fundamental views of others misplaced. I argued earlier that an intrinsic value of deliberation is that we are treated as persons capable of responding to and giving reasons. To respect someone is not to accept his views but rather to discuss them. *Not* to discuss the views of someone is to treat her as if she is incapable of responding to reasons, as irrational, and to disregard her status as a fellow citizen. As Peter Jones notes, "On almost any view of what constitutes respecting a person, it is hard to take seriously the complaint that conducting a sober examination of the truth of another's beliefs amounts to not treating him, or his beliefs, with respect. Arguably, it is more insulting to have one's beliefs treated as though their truth or falsity were of no consequence; for that is to have one's beliefs not taken seriously as *beliefs*."[94]

Also, when we go into a discussion with someone, it is not only to correct her but also to learn from her. Hence, if I do not go into a discussion with someone, I am not only acting as if she is incapable of responding to my arguments, I also am assuming that I have nothing to learn from her. Moreover, it is not really possible to authentically affirm one's own views without rejecting the validity of others' views. As Jeremy Waldron puts it in relation to religion, "It is not possible for me to avoid criticizing the tenets of your faith without stifling my own. So mutual respect cannot require us to refrain from criticism, if only because criticism of other sects is implicit already in the affirmation of any creed."[95]

Arguing with someone cannot be regarded as limiting her freedom but on the contrary is a necessary condition of free opinion formation and mutual respect for her status as a free being, for internal autonomy and discursive status. It would be disingenuous of deliberative democrats to run away from their commitment to freedom as combined with criticism and learning. Indeed, it would be to abandon the very basis of the theory, as I see it.

Exercising Freedom

Joshua Cohen attempts to avoid the complaint that deliberative democracy is sectarian by making a distinction between two ways in which conceptions of the good figure in political conceptions. First, conceptions of the good may enter as part of the *justification* of deliberative democracy, as if it was argued that participating in deliberation was part of the good life. Second, the *stability* of deliberative democracy may require widespread allegiance to the good of participation. "A political conception," according to Cohen, "is objectionable only if its *justification* depends on a particular view of the human good, and not simply because its stability is contingent on widespread agreement on the value of certain activities and aspirations."[96] Deliberative democracy is not sectarian, he argues, since the good does not figure in its justification, though "it is plausible that the stability of a deliberative democracy depends on encouraging the ideal of active citizenship."[97] This indeed is an important distinction. But even if some philosophical disputes concern the form of justification, and these are important to keep apart, the charge of sectarianism can apply *also* to social preconditions of a political conception. Clearly some objections from "diversity" rely on exactly the fear that deliberative democracy "depends on encouraging the ideal of active citizenship."

A recent criticism of deliberative democracy that articulates this fear is made by Andrew Sabl: "The demand that ordinary people justify their public opinions, aims, and aspirations through moral reasoning is therefore elitist in a special sense . . . it appeals to a rare taste. . . . [Deliberative democracy is] asking [ordinary people] to do more than they want to, feel they have to, or expect others to do."[98]

Cohen's assurance that deliberative democracy does not include active citizenship in the justification does not put to rest the fear that a deliberative democracy *in practice* would need to encourage the ideal of active citizenship. In defending a model of democracy, we should not simply be able to defend it in theory but also to defend its practical consequences. Still, Cohen is right to separate the types of arguments that would be needed.

We have to look more closely at the mode of justification, however. In the response to the first objection, I argued that deliberative democracy entails a commitment to participation by everyone. Now Cohen says participation is not part of the justification of deliberative democracy, and I agree in the sense that we do not need to see it as *constituent of the good life*. But it is important to remember that deliberative democracy does depend on widespread participation in order for justification and legitimation to take place at all. I would even say that this is a radical dependency, and that it is what makes deliberative democracy radically democratic.

I already argued in the second section of this chapter why deliberative democracy presupposes widespread participation. I sometimes said there that it depends on the "opportunity" for participation by everyone, and the idea of opportunity *is* crucial in order to make participation voluntary. But what happens if people do not use their opportunity for participation in public deliberation? We should recognize here that what gives deliberative democracy its advantages over rationalistic and elitist models and what distinguishes it from Kant also will get it into new difficulties. Deliberative democracy, as I see it, entails there being no answer to what is right without *actual* deliberation between real people, and no deliberative freedom unless citizens have been convinced of the justifiability of political decisions in public processes of deliberation. This makes deliberative democracy radically dependent on participation, for without participation we cannot have any rational assumptions about what is just. It is not only for its stability that deliberative democracy depends on participation but also for its *mode of justification*. The intersubjective epistemology that is a main reason for promoting deliberative democracy depends on widespread participation in common deliberation.

The reason the opportunity for participation is not sufficient also is that deliberative freedom entails an exercise concept of freedom, not merely an opportunity concept, to use Charles Taylor's terms.[99] Of course, exercising freedom requires the opportunity to do so. The free formation of opinions in deliberation requires the absence of external forces and is thus a "freedom from," and this "freedom from" supplies the opportunity. But in order for an opinion to be freely formed, it is not sufficient that it is negatively free from force; it also must be formed consciously and on the basis of the insights that can be gained only by participating in public deliberation. And not only that, deliberation itself may free the participants *from* certain inhibitions such as self-deception.[100] Furthermore, deliberation is clearly an activity; it does not exist as an opportunity alone.[101] It also is crucial to note here that others can give you opportunities, while exercising freedom is something you can do only by yourself.

The Obligation to Participate

In the discussion of Habermas in Chapter 6, I argued that even if it would violate an important dimension of freedom to legally enforce political participation, law could and should be used to encourage and facilitate participation in public deliberation. Let me elaborate on this point and relate it to the issue of diversity and the rare taste for participation. We cannot say a priori that because some groups in society are adverse to rationality, freedom, and democratic participation, it would be wrong to use the law to encourage free opinion formation and participation.[102] On the contrary, the latter would be required by the deliberative conception of freedom, though its exact form, of course, would have to be justified in public deliberation.

As a Kantian conception, deliberative democracy aims at being neutral with regard to conceptions of the good. But this does not entail that it is neutral with regard to its own normative content. Habermas correctly writes that the procedure of discursive justification "is by no means free of normative implications . . . for it is intertwined with a concept of autonomy that integrates 'reason' and 'free will'; *to that extent* it cannot be normatively neutral. An autonomous will is one that is guided by practical reason."[103] It follows from my intersubjective epistemology and its relation to deliberative freedom that we cannot be guided by practical reason except as participants in public deliberation. Deliberative democracy should, as noted, be distinguished from the Kantian view that the precepts of practical reason are directly available to the individual: rather, they become available only as (fallible) results of public deliberation. There is no other way we can be guided by practical reason than by participating in public deliberation. And there is no other way for us to be so as free beings. It is only as participants in deliberation that we can freely gain the necessary insights into which decisions are just, and hence it is only as participants in deliberation that we can be free as subject to those decisions. Thus since deliberative democracy cannot and should not be neutral with regard to its own normative content, deliberative freedom, it is required that we facilitate and encourage participation in deliberation.

To clarify the epistemological point and its relationship to deliberative freedom let me note that it is possible for a decision to be just without having been arrived at through public deliberation. What is just may happen to be discovered by an individual who does not participate in deliberation. My point is that there is no alternative way that a law can be *justified and rationally believed* to be just than via actual and common deliberation. And, crucially, it is only as participants in deliberation that we can be said to give those laws to ourselves by gaining insights into and by being convinced of their validity (public autonomy). Only as participants in deliberation are we spoken to as free beings who are responsive to reasons rather than force (discursive status). To avoid misunderstanding, it should be emphasized also that the focus on being guided by practical reason does not mean that we have moved from a procedural epistemic to a substantive epistemic conception of freedom. It is not acting according to practical reason as such that makes one free but rather following a procedure that tends to produce results that have the presumption of practical reason on their side and that gives one the possibility of contributing to determining what is right that does so.

A theory of deliberative democracy that accepts this view of freedom and practical reason must, furthermore, involve an obligation to participate in deliberation. It cannot be true that we have an obligation to do what is right but not one of learning what is right. And if there is no way of knowing the demands of practical reason without widespread participation, and if we have an obligation to gain insights into the demands of practical reason, then it follows that there is an obligation to participate in deliberation. This cannot be a legal obligation for reasons already given, but it must be a moral obligation. The deliberative democratic view of practical reason and freedom, as I see it, has as its basic premise a *mutual interdependence* between people. It is this interdependence in acquiring the necessary insights to live in freedom—for knowing oneself and others better and for finding out what are just collective decisions—that imposes on us an obligation to participate in common deliberation with our fellow citizens.

That some people do not have a taste for participating in public deliberation is not a reason for not seeing it as an obligation. Moral obligations do not depend on whether we like to fulfill them or not. We might not all like to do what is required by the fact of our mutual dependence, but clearly that cannot have any bearing on what we ought to do.

Conclusion

The argument in this chapter might make deliberative democracy more demanding than some of its proponents would like. But from the normative basis of deliberative democracy in deliberative freedom, some obligations follow. Deliberative democrats should acknowledge their commitment to freedom, reason, and participation. Any tenable understanding of deliberative democracy must see it as committed to the Enlightenment project. Deliberative freedom entails the ideal that we submit to no political decisions except the results of a procedure that has epistemic value, that gives us the opportunity to gain insights and to become participants in self-legislation, where we recognize each other as reason givers and reason responsive. This involves the freedom from any authority except ourselves. Deliberative democracy does not rely on a specific view of the good life, but it must accept a certain view of practical reason and freedom to which it cannot be neutral, and this is one that does depend on the fulfillment of certain obligations.

CHAPTER EIGHT

Conclusion

Toward a Theory of Deliberative Freedom

Does deliberative democracy entail a distinctive conception of freedom? Is it related to freedom in a new and distinct way? Does deliberative democracy make people more free than other models of democracy? I answer all of these questions in the affirmative, and in this chapter I summarize and elaborate why. The chapter is organized into three sections. The first shows how the four traditional conceptions of freedom (and democracy's relation to them) have been reinterpreted and gained a more compelling meaning within deliberative democratic theory. The second provides an argument for why deliberative democracy calls for and why we need a multidimensional and complex conception of freedom. The third addresses some possible practical consequences of applying a conception of deliberative democracy committed to multiple dimensions of freedom. In particular, it points to the value of institutional experimentation and a dispersed public arena with multiple and diverse deliberative forums.

Four Conceptions of Freedom Reinterpreted

This book began by quoting Aristotle's insight that all democracies have liberty for their aim. For most people, I suspect, this idea is rather unremarkable. However, it is noteworthy that different people have understood this general idea in so many different ways at different times. In the Introduction, I listed four ways democracy has been seen as aiming at freedom in the history of Western political thought. These different ways of connecting democracy and freedom encompassed four different

209

conceptions of freedom. Instead of seeing these four different models as competing *conceptions* of the relationship between democracy and freedom and four different *conceptions* of freedom, I have argued for the possibility of a model of democracy that incorporates all four *dimensions* of freedom. The discussions in the intervening chapters have shown that deliberative democracy can be seen as both incorporating and reinterpreting the four ways of connecting democracy to freedom and the four different conceptions of freedom. Many different conceptions and dimensions of freedom have been discussed, however, and a clarification of how they relate to the four traditional conceptions is in order. I shall discuss most extensively the two dimensions of freedom that have been ignored by other theorists of deliberative democracy, namely, internal autonomy and discursive status, and I shall be relatively brief on the liberties of the ancients and moderns and how deliberative democracy relates to these.

1. *Democracy as popular sovereignty*: The only way in which we can be free in society is to be authors of the laws to which we are subject. Democracy aims at *converting* an inevitable dependence into freedom (Rousseau).

We are not merely free in the silence of the laws, as Hobbes would have it; it also matters for our freedom who gives the laws. The tradition of negative freedom with its concern for noncoercion should itself be concerned with this dimension of freedom, freedom as public autonomy, insofar as the latter is an attempt to determine the boundaries of freedom in a noncoercive manner. So far deliberative democracy falls within the tradition that Rousseau initiated. The deliberative democratic perspective developed here, however, differs from that of Rousseau in seeing public autonomy as less a collective exercise of will than as general participation in effective deliberation. One can enjoy public autonomy without agreeing with every decision reached and without seeing results with which one disagrees as mistakes on one's own part. To make this clear, I have distinguished between being a self-legislator and being a participant in self-legislation (see the third section in Chapter 3). It is only the latter we can and should hope for in a deliberative democracy. The theory of deliberative democracy is unique in seeing this third possibility between Rousseauian collective self-legislation and the liberal reduction of the political process to a matter of protecting negative freedom.

As participants in self-legislation, we see public autonomy as embedded in the *procedures* of deliberative opinion and will formation, and we see decisions as fallible and reversible interim results of an ongoing practice. The idea of public autonomy and legitimacy as embedded in the procedures of public deliberation, rather than in the correctness of the results, has a further significance that I attempted to clarify, in Chapter 7, with the argument that deliberative freedom is a procedural epistemic conception of freedom. The idea is that public autonomy depends on each one of us having the opportunity to gain insights into what would be the most just and pragmatically wise laws to implement. We are participants in self-legislation not merely by participating in procedures that have epistemic value in terms of the polity getting it right but also in terms of *each single citizen's* ability to judge whether or not the polity is getting it right. In this respect, the theory of democracy and freedom developed in this book is an *individualist* one. The freedom of which I am speaking is always the freedom of individuals and not of a collective subject.

2. *Democracy as instrumental to negative freedom*: Democracy is required in order to protect a form of freedom that in itself is prepolitical or outside political activity. Democracy aims at *protecting* an already understood and demarcated freedom (the liberal view).

First, the theory of deliberative democracy that I am proposing does accept that democracy is aiming at protecting individual and nonpolitical freedoms. But it sees the instrumental value of democracy for freedom not in its ability to protect something pregiven but in its epistemic value in terms of developing, determining, and justifying which individual freedoms we should grant each other. Second, the individual freedom that we should expect from living in a deliberative democracy committed to multiple dimensions of freedom is not one of independence. Deliberative democracy shares the focus on *interdependence* with republicanism but, as argued in Chapter 2, republicanism in Pettit's recent reconstruction does not give an adequate definition of freedom and its relationship to democracy. Only when we properly understand the centrality of procedures of public deliberation can we show that individual freedom is parasitic upon intersubjective, discursive practices of justification and recognition. While we cannot expect to be free of obligations to participate with others in processes of public deliberation, we can and should expect to have the procedural independence to say "no" and to make up our minds for ourselves.

3. *Democracy as instrumental to personal autonomy*: Participation in democratic politics creates citizens with autonomous characters. Democracy aims to *transform* individuals into autonomous persons (Rousseau, Mill).

The theory of deliberative democracy, as developed and defended in this book, does see democracy as aiming to transform citizens in a specific way. However, this aim of transformation should not be seen in contrast to the possibility of nontransformative democracy but rather in contrast to models that *because of their conception of freedom* ignore or disregard that social conditions and political institutions inevitably shape individuals (see Chapter 1). A dimension of deliberative freedom concerns which social conditions and political institutions best promote the free formation of political opinions.

I have argued for understanding the democratic process of deliberative opinion and will formation as a learning process and as such as aiming at developing internal autonomy. Internal autonomy, however, has not been defended as an end in itself but as a necessary condition for being a free participant in self-legislation and, thereby, as an aspect of overall freedom. There are two ways in which internal autonomy is required for the exercise of public autonomy. First, the processes in which the laws are generated must be based not only on free and voluntary consent but also on prior free opinion formation. Second, the preferences and needs and interest interpretations on the basis of which we decide what is in the equal interest of everyone must themselves be freely formed. To clarify, I do not mean to say that internal autonomy has only instrumental value, since it as a dimension of freedom is a part of deliberative freedom, which *is* an end in itself. My point is that internal autonomy only has intrinsic value as a part of deliberative freedom and not by itself alone, and it becomes part of deliberative freedom because it is required by the deliberative exercise of public autonomy.

The difficult question, of course, is what it means or what is required for opinions to be freely formed. A necessary but not sufficient condition is that they be subject to rigorous debate. Deliberative democrats do not hold the idealistic belief that discussion alone can create autonomous preferences, as is clear both in theories of adaptive preference formation and in the theory of ideology. Conditions external to the practice of deliberation also affect how we interpret our needs and interests and which beliefs and desires we form. In this respect, deliberative democracy is less optimistic about the prospects of what discussion on its own can achieve and more critical of societal factors than earlier liberal models of democracy (see the first section in Chapter 5). But I have warned that an exclusive focus on external conditions can lead to paternalism (Chapter 3). Neither a change of circumstances or deliberation under less than ideal circumstances can alone secure internal autonomy. We must use the abilities we have now to deliberate as well as we can and attempt to gradually change the circumstances that inhibit free opinion formation. I have described it as the role of the deliberative democrat as a critical theorist to provoke processes of self-reflection about the opinions we hold and the conditions under which we live.

It might be thought that the idea of internal autonomy could be reduced to either the notion of personal autonomy or the notion of moral autonomy. Let me therefore clarify how my conception of internal autonomy differs from these two notions. I take personal autonomy to refer to a character ideal.[1] It might, for example, refer to an ideal of being reflective regarding one's commitments, of not merely conforming to the standards of the society and culture in which one lives, or of choosing one's own life project. John Stuart Mill clearly espouses such an ideal of autonomy, and he believes participation in public discussion and politics can contribute to it.[2] Personal autonomy is a more comprehensive ideal than internal autonomy. Internal autonomy does require some degree of self-reflection regarding one's commitments, like personal autonomy does, but it does so only to the extent that these commitments matter for what I, following Rainer Forst, call "relations of justification" (see the first section in Chapter 5). The ideals of self-reflection and internal autonomy come into play only insofar as our relationship to our commitments affects our ability to participate in processes of public deliberation. The justification for internal autonomy is not a perfectionistic ideal of human flourishing but rather an ideal of what is required for public deliberation to succeed. To be sure, internal autonomy is only one dimension of freedom among others, so we cannot implement the conditions necessary for internal autonomy if that means violating other dimensions of freedom; the different freedom concerns must be balanced against each other.

Many contemporary discussions of personal autonomy focus on individual failures of achieving personal autonomy, while the relationship I draw between ideology critique and internal autonomy involves seeing failures of internal autonomy in more structural and social terms. Whether or not citizens are capable of achieving internal autonomy depends on the communication structure of their society. If this communication structure is distorted because of power inequalities and unequal access to participation in public deliberation, then *everyone* lacks internal autonomy (see Chapters 3 and 5).

How does internal autonomy differ from moral autonomy? Moral autonomy involves two aspects: (1) that I am guided by moral principles rather than nonmoral ones, or at least that the latter will trump or constrain the former[3]; and (2) that the moral principles by which I am guided are in some sense my own or given by myself.[4] The ideal of moral autonomy can be seen as having both an individual and a collective application. I am morally autonomous as an individual if the moral principles by which I live are my own, those I have given myself. The theory of deliberative democracy and freedom developed in this book is not concerned with moral autonomy in this sense per se. In its collective sense, moral autonomy refers to the ideal that the moral norms enshrined in positive law are those we collectively have given ourselves. This ideal is part of my theory but of the dimension of freedom concerning being a participant in self-legislation rather than of the dimension concerning internal autonomy. The ideal of being participants in self-legislation is that the norms backed by law are those that we have given ourselves. Processes of public deliberation aim at establishing what is true and right, and it is a dimension of freedom that we are guided by the insights gained in deliberation. Insofar as part of what public deliberation establishes is the dictates of practical reason,[5] and insofar as we should be guided by the results of deliberation, a dimension of our freedom is to be guided by practical reason. In this way my argument does involve a commitment to moral autonomy in its collective sense.

It may be asked whether the collective and the individual senses of moral autonomy are not internally connected in deliberative democratic theory.[6] They are in the sense that I have argued that my theory is individualist in that the insights gained in deliberation must be insights of individuals and not of a collective subject. But I have limited the deliberative conception of freedom to a concern with individuals having and using the opportunity to gain insights into the moral norms that are backed by the coercive force of positive law. I see it as lying outside of the concern of a theory of deliberative democracy to consider whether or not individuals in their private lives are morally autonomous. This response raises the question of whether or not internal autonomy requires individual moral autonomy. In other words, can we form our political opinions freely, in particular, can we form our views of which moral norms should be backed by law, if we do not live individually morally autonomous lives? First, moral autonomy requires that one actually live according to one's moral principles, while internal autonomy requires only that one autonomously forms one's views of which laws should be backed by law. Second, internal autonomy is concerned with only a subset of moral norms, namely, those that should be put into law. Thus internal autonomy is less demanding than moral autonomy. Internal autonomy requires us to reflect on and understand what practical reason demands of us. This requirement relates to the democratic genesis of the law. But as subjects of law, we are not required to obey the law because it is right; we are free to obey for heteronomous reasons. Of course, I have argued that citizens should be able to see the laws they are forced to obey as legitimate and just, but internal autonomy does not extend to the demand that we always obey the laws because of their rightness. Internal autonomy refers (primarily) to the perspective of making law and is not undermined if we as subjects of law obey for strategic rather than moral reasons. Thus internal autonomy fits better than moral autonomy into a multidimensional conception of freedom, where we regard ourselves as taking different perspectives on ourselves as authors of law and as subjects to law, as explained in the next section.

4. *Democracy as intrinsic to freedom as praxis*: Participation in democratic politics is a form of freedom. Democracy aims at *creating a new experience* of being free (one republican view).

My version of deliberative democracy does *not* entail the idea that *because* it is what constitutes the good life, the aim of democracy should be to create the possibility of experiencing freedom in participation. Such a view violates the dimension of freedom that relates to determining one's own conception of the good. However, deliberative democracy, as understood in this book, does require processes of democratic politics to not merely protect but also to be expressions of freedom. Since democratic participation is necessary both for defining and justifying which freedoms to protect and in order to make the limitations of negative freedom that we inevitably experience products of self-legislative procedures, the political process must itself at least be capable of being seen as an experience and expression of freedom.

Deliberative processes can be seen as expressions of freedom because of the way in which participants regard each other. In deliberation, each person is given the status of one who can freely give and respond to reasons. I have, following Philip Pettit, called this discursive status (Chapter 2). Discursive status works as a dimension of freedom that can, for example, check the dangers of paternalism and elitism, as argued in Chapters 3 and 7, respectively. Thus the use of freedom as a form of status is from the perspective of deliberative freedom transformed from being a matter of a uniform idea of the good life to being a matter of recognizing individuals as equal authorities in deliberation, individuals who cannot be talked down to, ignored, or excluded on paternalistic or elitist grounds.

Is status a dimension of freedom at all, or is it another value altogether? Isaiah Berlin famously argues the latter. While he sees dangers in a positive conception of freedom, he accepts that it is a conception of freedom, because it, like negative freedom, is a matter of "holding off of something or someone." The desire for status and recognition "is a desire for something different" than liberty, according to Berlin.[7] I argue for discursive status not as a conception of freedom in itself but as a dimension of freedom within a complex conception of freedom. But is it even a dimension of freedom? Discursive status is as much a matter of "holding off of something" as is positive freedom in its collective sense.[8] There is an important similarity between these two dimensions; both are concerned with how to be free *in society*, among other human beings. Collective self-legislation can be seen as a matter of "holding off of something" only under the condition that human beings are interdependent and need positive laws to live by. If human beings could live by themselves, if they were self-sufficient, then giving a law to oneself as part of a collectivity would not be "holding off of something or someone" but accepting an unnecessary constraint. But when we have become dependent on others, and when we need coercive measures to live together, we can be free only by being authors of the laws to which we are subject. What collectively self-legislating citizens hold off are nonfree forms of association, where a few have a right to coerce the rest, where I am ruled by others rather than by myself in cooperation with others. This I take to be the basic Rousseauian insight. Similarly, discursive status should be seen as holding off of other, nonfree forms of relating to each other in society. In society, human beings inevitably influence each other, and citizens whose discursive status is respected are free from forms of interference that do not recognize their ability to give and respond with reasons. Discursive status differs from the dimension of freedom relating to the question "Who governs me?" by focusing on the *processes* of self-government, on how we treat each other while collectively governing each other. But not only that, discursive status is concerned not merely with the processes of creating and justifying law but also with the other side, with how we are treated as subjects of law. This dimension of freedom puts limits on how the state can treat its subjects; it cannot turn them into clients, treat them as children, or in any other way undermine their discursive abilities.

It should be emphasized that discursive status does not require all forms of social interaction to be discursive. Not all relations in society can be based on common deliberation; clearly there is a need for a market economy where we are not required to justify our actions to each other, and it is inevitable that certain relationships be based on hierarchies, for example, within bureaucratic organizations.[9] But these other forms of relationships should (1) be justified in discursive processes of deliberation, and (2) not undermine our ability to participate in deliberation. The first of these points relates discursive status to the freedom of being a participant in self-legislation. When nondiscursive relationships have been justified in public deliberation, they do not entail that someone is not respected as capable of giving and responding to reasons but are rather based on the common knowledge and acceptance that we all need to turn our attention to other issues to make the market work and get other things done.

The second of these points relates discursive status to a more negative dimension of freedom. Discursive status requires not only that we be able to participate in deliberative processes that influence lawmaking but also that citizens be *protected* from something. Discursive status might be harmed by what Habermas used to call the colonization of the lifeworld, an issue that I argued in Chapter 5 is crucial for discussions of deliberative democracy and freedom. Colonization is the intrusion in the lifeworld of imperatives from the market or the state that undermines citizens' ability to interact on the basis of communication aimed at reaching understanding. Clearly discursive status requires that we hold off colonization of that sort, since it treats people as incapable of giving and responding to reasons. The conclusion that not all forms of interaction need to be discursive is based not only on the inevitable complexity of modern society, however, but also can be made with reference to my theory of deliberative freedom. For participation in deliberation to be free, everyone needs to be free *not* to participate in deliberation (see the third section in Chapter 3 and the fourth section in Chapter 6). Moreover, citizens should have the freedom to withhold certain concerns from the requirement of justification (see the second section in Chapter 6).

When I argue for discursive status as a dimension of freedom, it is because we should not see only the results of deliberation as normatively significant but also the process that leads to these results as being so.[10] Deliberative processes are not merely instrumentally important for justifying which freedoms we should grant each, nor are they only aiming at making us authors of the laws under which we live; the process itself expresses a dimension of freedom. Alternative processes of self-legislation can be found, but if these processes do not respect our ability to speak for ourselves, then they would undermine an important dimension of what it means to be a free citizen.

A Multidimensional Theory of Deliberation and Freedom

Deliberative democracy does entail a distinctive conception of freedom. This conception, deliberative freedom, I have argued, includes several dimensions of freedom. Recall the distinction between conceptions and dimensions of freedom made in the Introduction. Conceptions are rivals attempting to outdo each other in giving the best formulation of a common concept, and a conception is seen as belonging to one moral or political perspective. One cannot endorse several conceptions at once but must take sides. The overall theory of deliberative democracy and freedom presented in this book entails a conception in this sense. My version of deliberative democracy is a specific conception of the concept of deliberative democracy. Similarly, the overall theory of freedom presented here, deliberative freedom, constitutes a conception of freedom that will compete with other theories of freedom. But *within* my conception of deliberative freedom, I have suggested the possibility of simultaneously adhering to four different dimensions of freedom. These (or similar ones) often are seen as competing conceptions. My suggestion is to see them as not necessarily in competition but as complementary. And I have argued that my version of deliberative democracy incorporates all four. Of course, the formulations of the different dimensions of freedom are fallible and open for improvement, as is the overall conception.

It might be asked why it matters beyond a merely terminological dispute to insist on seeing the four notions of freedom as dimensions rather than conceptions or, more precisely, as dimensions within a more complex conception of freedom. I think the implications are wide-ranging. Adherents of different conceptions will hold that we can and should aim at enjoying only freedom as they see it, and that accepting one conception of freedom entails accepting one moral or political theory. I suggest that we can adhere to different dimensions of freedom at one and the same time without contradiction. If the theory of deliberative freedom I have developed is coherent, then deliberative democracy should afford us the ability to enjoy the different dimensions of freedom, and therefore it promises more than earlier models of democracy in terms of freedom. This is what makes deliberative democracy unique and a superior model of democracy, in my view.

Earlier versions of the theory of deliberative democracy have been concerned with only some of the dimensions of freedom. My argument about the shortcomings of these earlier versions has been twofold. First, lack of concern for all of the dimensions of freedom makes deliberative democracy complacent and uncritical. Without concern for all four dimensions of freedom, we are not aiming at all of the kinds of freedom that we should expect to experience from living in a deliberative democracy. My focus in this connection has been on internal autonomy. Theories of deliberative democracy unconcerned with or uncommitted to this dimension of freedom are complacent with the status quo. This is the case with Rawlsian deliberative democracy, because of its emphasis on freedom as accommodation and its exclusion of fundamental beliefs from the purview of public deliberation.

Second, versions of deliberative democracy that emphasize only some dimensions of freedom lack the needed "checks and balances" of the other dimensions. This has been made quite clear in terms of theories of adaptive preference formation, which I have argued run the risk of turning into justifications of paternalism if they are not checked by freedom as status and freedom as being a participant in self-legislation. The same is true of deliberative democratic theory seen as aiming at overcoming ideological delusion. In the discussion of the latter, I have focused on the fears that ideology critique is based on an unwarranted perfectionism, and that making all beliefs potential objects of deliberation is a threat to privacy. I countered the first fear by arguing that deliberative democracy should be committed to the promotion of internal autonomy only so far as the latter matters for relations of justification. Regarding privacy, I argued that deliberation in order to succeed does not in fact require that we disclose our innermost feelings and desires. It is sufficient that all *issues* are politicized and made objects of reflection. This, admittedly, does not constitute a security against demands for self-disclosure in deliberative settings. It is therefore crucial that such demands be checked by citizens' procedural independence from being forced by means that bypass their reflective capabilities to say no as well as the negative freedom to withdraw from deliberation.

Taking the perspective of a normative commitment to multiple dimensions of freedom allows us, then, on the one hand, to see and theorize the problems with the uncritical direction that discussions of deliberative democracy have taken over the last decade, because of lack of concern for emancipation from self-imposed forms of oppression (that is, forms of oppression that citizens consent to because of lack of internal autonomy). Indeed, the diagnosis of contemporary society should not be one of moral disagreement but rather of unreflective complacency and acquiescence. The greatest strength of deliberative democracy is not to solve deep moral disagreements, such as those over abortion and gene technology, but to politicize and initiate reflection about beliefs, policies, and institutions that are uncritically accepted by most people, and hence not discussed at all.

On the other hand, the commitment to multiple dimensions of freedom clarifies why and how the concern of critical theory for emancipation must be coupled both with some idea of negative freedom and with a commitment to seeing everyone as free and equal participants in self-legislation (the latter commitment combines freedom as public autonomy and freedom as discursive status). Deliberation, I have argued, has the great advantage in that it can challenge uncritically accepted forms of oppression and inequality without being paternalistic or setting up external standards of true and false interests. Because of its requirement of nondomination and its procedural nature, public deliberation cannot impose anything on anyone but can only aim at emancipation by encouraging and provoking processes of self-reflection.

Deliberative Freedom and Complex Citizenship

What is it about deliberative democracy that calls for a conception of freedom with several dimensions? I would like here to say something more systematic than I have been able to say hitherto about this question.

The reason a conception of freedom related to deliberative democracy must be multidimensional is that we as members of political society occupy multiple roles, that is, we can as citizens look at ourselves and our freedom from a number of different perspectives. Each of these perspectives supplies us with a different point of view from which we can evaluate political arrangements and social conditions. First we can take the perspective of a subject to law; we can see ourselves in the role of the passive "matter" of political society. Here we can ask either about the quantity or reach of law (Hobbes and Berlin, see Chapter 1), or about the quality of law (Pettit, see Chapter 2). Both of these are legitimate concerns regarding the extent of our freedom, but they concern only a *dimension* of freedom; they see us only in our passive role as subjects of law. Then we shift perspective and ask the question, "Who makes the law?" Now we see ourselves not merely as the passive matter of political society but also in the role of its active makers.[11] From the latter perspective, we are free if we can participate in the making of the law by which we are bound. Here we have the dimension of freedom that we call public autonomy or popular sovereignty.

These two dimensions of freedom, passive and active, are the only ones that come into view if we reduce politics to a matter of decision making and being subject to decisions, or when politics is based on will alone (as in both Hobbes and Rousseau). If politics is seen as nothing but a matter of the coercive use of force, then we can see freedom either in terms of the extent to which we are subject to coercion or the extent to which we are the source of that coercion (this also is the basis for Berlin's two concepts of liberty). These two perspectives on politics and freedom are certainly important, and I argue for incorporating corresponding dimensions of freedom. But when we see politics and democracy as not only matters of making decisions and being subject to coercive law, but also as involving the processes that precede and follow collective decision making, when politics is regarded as a matter not only of willing but also of reasoning and influencing, when, in other words, we see democracy as deliberative, then two other dimensions of freedom present themselves to us.

A dimension of citizenship that the deliberative democratic perspective makes clearer is the one constituted by the horizontal relationship between citizens. As citizens, we are not merely subject to and authors of laws, we also form a web of horizontal relationships.[12] In society, such relationships are inevitable, but they also are essential for both material and symbolic reproduction. Societal relationships beyond those mediated directly by law are both necessary to freedom and can turn into a threat to freedom, depending on the form they take. The role citizens see themselves in here goes beyond being either passive objects of law or its active makers to being members of a number of social relationships. In terms of freedom, the question we ask from this perspective is whether or not the social relationships of which we are part allow us to uphold and participate in forms of interaction where no force except that of the better argument is at play. For social relationships to do this, they must respect our ability to give and respond to reasons, that is, they must honor our discursive status. Discursive status involves both a negative and a positive dimension, since it requires both the absence of interaction that undermines our discursive abilities and the presence of social relationships based on communicative action and public deliberation (see the first section in Chapter 5). Discursive status is itself a complex notion insofar as it relates not only to the horizontal relationships stressed here but also to the making of law and to being subject to law (see the first section in this chapter). Moreover, discursive status must be part of a complex theory of freedom. Because the social complexity of modern society entails not all social relationships being communicative or discursive, we should be free to interact in other ways as well.[13]

The final dimension of citizenship that becomes visible when we go beyond politics as a matter of decision making and coercive force relates to the intricate processes of opinion and preference formation. The role citizens take in this connection is reflective and critical. It requires us to distance ourselves from our environment and from our commitments and critically reflect on them. In this reflective role, we do not ask to what extent the law interferes with us or whether or not we are authors of the law but rather how we came to evaluate the law the way we do. We regard ourselves as citizens who hold certain opinions, who have values and beliefs, and who form judgments. In this role, we reflect on the external and internal conditions that made us arrive at the opinions we hold. This perspective can be taken by the critical theorist when she asks whether social and political institutions afford citizens the opportunity to form opinions autonomously, that is, in communication free from distorting factors. However, the perspective taken in this fourth dimension is concerned not only with opportunity but also with exercise. Citizens must not only have the opportunity to exercise but also must actually exercise their ability to critically reflect on their commitments and opinions.[14] Internal autonomy entails its own complexity. It has social as well as individual preconditions, and it has negative as well as positive preconditions. Socially it depends on the absence of relationships under-mining our critical faculties, on procedural independence (see the fourth section in Chapter 6), and on the presence of deliberative forums where one can achieve the necessary insights.[15] Of the individual, it requires that she actually participate in public deliberation and that she exercise her capacities for critically reflecting on and revising her opinions according to the insights that she has gained from public deliberation.

Thus we can take four different perspectives when we want to judge whether actually existing democracies secure and promote delib-erative freedom. We can ask four different types of questions in terms of freedom regarding our social conditions and political institutions. However, I do not see these four perspectives as being unconnected or independent of each other. The four dimensions of deliberative freedom are each incomplete without the others; we cannot fully understand or enjoy any of the dimensions without the others. This, however, does not mean that we a priori can say that the four dimensions exist in harmony with each other. On the contrary, I have argued that they must often be used to balance each other.

There is further reason for stressing the need for a complex and multidimensional conception of freedom. This reason can be formulated best in response to both liberal egalitarian theories and social democratic or welfare state practices. The latter have emphasized that the formal lib-erties of classical liberalism are insufficient for enjoying "real freedom" or for enjoying "the worth of freedom."[16] In order to make formal freedoms substantive, economic redistribution is necessary. I agree with this, but more needs to be said; other dimensions of freedom need to be brought into the picture. Securing greater economic equality cannot be done in a neutral or nonintrusive way. The danger is that in attempting to enhance the value of freedom by creating the necessary economic conditions, we may at the same time threaten other dimensions of freedom by turn-ing citizens into clients (see the second section in Chapter 5). Here we need both to make sure that welfare state policies have been justified in processes of self-legislation and that citizens as objects of welfare state provisions are respected as discursive subjects. The complexity needed in our conception of freedom in this connection relates to the complexities created by the fact that the freedom we enjoy is not external to the means securing this freedom. In other words, substantive freedom must be seen in relation to the state apparatus needed to create it.

The Coconstitutionality of Deliberation and Freedom

The four dimensions of freedom are not imposed on or external to deliberative democracy and its epistemic aims. On the contrary, they are presupposed or required by these aims. This is true if we regard deliberative democracy as based on epistemic proceduralism, as I have argued we should (see the third section in Chapter 2 and the second section in Chapter 7). Epistemic proceduralism has some important consequences for freedom. In the description and use of procedures with epistemic value, all four dimensions of freedom are incorporated. The description of the procedure includes one required for internal autonomy. In the processes of participating in deliberative procedures, citizens attain internal autonomy and recognize each other as worth arguing with, since rational results are seen as capable of resulting only when all citizens have a chance to contribute their views and these views are freely formed. Procedures of public deliberation, moreover, give one the status of a free person who responds only to reasons and hence gives one the opportunity to experience a praxis that is free from any constraints beyond reasons. The deliberative procedure also must include respect for the procedural independence of all citizens, for unless citizens try to affect each other only with arguments and not with means that bypass others' critical faculties, deliberation cannot achieve its epistemic aims. Finally, epistemic proceduralism means that nothing but the results of deliberation will have any authority over the participants, so citizens will be bound only by the results of processes in which they were free to participate as free beings.

Because the epistemic aims of deliberative democracy cannot be achieved unless all citizens have the opportunity to participate in public deliberation, the four dimensions of freedom must be given to everyone by everyone if they are to be given to anyone.

The four dimensions of freedom, then, are required for deliberation to take place and succeed. However, the fundamental value is not deliberation as such, and the dimensions of freedom are not merely functionally justified as prerequisites of public deliberation. I have developed my conception of deliberative democracy also on the basis of which dimensions of freedom it protects and enhances. As a matter of justifying the theory of democracy and freedom developed in this book, the relationship between the proper conception of public deliberation and the dimensions of freedom that should be included is dialectical. Public deliberation has been taken as a prima facie normatively attractive idea, and the dimensions of freedom have been formulated in relation to this idea. But in order to characterize public deliberation and deliberative democracy in the most defensible way possible, I have been guided by different normative concerns that relate to freedom and autonomy. Thus public deliberation and deliberative freedom mutually constitute, reinforce, and justify each other. It has not been my aim to give a foundationalist justification of deliberative democracy and freedom. I have attempted to clarify and refine the theory of deliberative democracy in terms of how it relates to different dimensions of freedom. It is my hope that this makes the theory and practice more appealing.

I began this book by noting the connection commonly drawn between democracy and freedom in the normative self-understanding of both governments and social movements. I think this popular view is basically correct but also very vague. It is important to make explicit what drawing this connection means. My analyses and discussions have shown complex and multidimensional connections between democracy and freedom. My argument matters in particular as a basis for judging whether or not the societies in which we live meet aspirations for enjoying the different dimensions of freedom a democracy could and should afford. Do the social, economic, and political conditions under which we live make it possible for us to fully experience the different dimensions of freedom? Since the answer to this question clearly is no, even for citizens of the most fortunate nations of the world, the more pressing question is what can be done to approximate the ideal. But in order to criticize the status quo and approximate an ideal, we must first have an ideal and justify it.

There is a further reason for formulating deliberative democracy in terms of a theory of freedom and for clarifying the dimensions of freedom to which it should be committed. This reason is that a certain narrow-mindedness in the understanding of what freedom means and requires often blocks the acceptance of a more participatory and deliberative democracy, on the level of ideas and norms. Even though it is commonly accepted that democracy is connected to freedom, there often is also a fear that too much democracy might be a threat to freedom.[17] My argument is an attempt to counter the view that a more participatory democracy necessarily is a threat to individual freedom. To be sure, some forms of participatory democracy do constitute a threat to individual freedom, especially to the liberties of unpopular minorities. I have for that reason attempted to develop a specific model of participatory democracy, a model that is not merely participatory but also deliberative and committed to multiple dimensions of freedom. Now my version of deliberative democracy might be a threat to what some people regard as their inviolable liberties, but that is the case only if they are unable to give convincing arguments for these liberties to their fellow citizens. If they are not able to do so, for example, if the rich are unable to give convincing reasons to the poor for the absolute right to their property, then it is justified that these rights be curbed.[18] It might be argued that it is not ideas or norms but self-interest that impedes the development of a more participatory democracy and economic reform. That might be true to some extent, but the remarkable thing is that many of those who have no interest in upholding the status quo accept the ideals that hinder both deliberative democracy and social justice. Furthermore, if the marginalized and oppressed not only lack social power but also coherent ideals to appeal to, then there is absolutely no hope for change.

On the Need for Institutional Reform and Economic Redistribution

The discussions of deliberation and freedom in this book should make clear that we can and should expect more of democracy in terms of freedom than we do presently. Thus I have aimed at developing the normative basis for a critical theory of contemporary society. The different dimensions of freedom and the ideal of deliberation have been explicated as a contribution to the judgments we make of the social conditions and political institutions under which we live.[19] If our society does not approximate the ideal requirements, we should consider if or to what extent it can be changed to do so. Thus it is my hope that the normative theory that I have developed can inspire social and political reform as well as experimentation with new forms of participatory deliberation.

This book, however, has not developed a blueprint for how a deliberative democratic society would look economically and institutionally. This is certainly not because my normative argument has no implications for economic redistribution or institutional design. On the contrary, I do believe that a society committed to the value of public deliberation and deliberative freedom would have to be radically changed in terms of economic and political structures and institutions. The ideal clearly calls for a more egalitarian distribution of resources and for more participatory political institutions. However, I want to caution against moving too quickly here, for two different reasons. First, we should be careful when we translate normative ideals into institutional practice and prescriptions for social and economic restructuring. There is no *direct* inference from normative ideals to institutional design and public policy.[20] When we want to apply an ideal, we have to consider a large number of empirical factors, the realities of human nature, economic efficiency, and so on. This is a complex task that cannot be carried out here. Second, deliberative freedom demands that we leave the exact form of institutional design and economic redistribution up to citizens themselves. If all aspects of institutional design and policy are specified as prerequisites of public deliberation, then nothing is left to actual deliberation, and the freedom of citizens to decide for themselves is violated. However, I am not implying that political theorists (or other academics) cannot contribute with substantive proposals regarding which political institutions are most conducive to public deliberation or which forms of educational, economic, cultural, and other policies are the best. However, it should be made clear that political theorists contribute to public deliberation with everyone else as equal participants.[21]

Some critics of deliberative democracy believe that what we need—or what we more urgently need—is not more deliberation but rather social justice and a more egalitarian distribution of resources (see the first section in Chapter 1). Others—libertarians—believe that any form of economic redistribution is a threat to individual freedom, more precisely to freedom as noninterference (see the second section in Chapter 1). My argument is that social justice and a more egalitarian distribution of resources are urgently needed in, for example, the United States. And I agree with liberal egalitarians that economic redistribution should be seen as required by freedom rather than as a threat to freedom, but my argument for this differs from theirs. To the libertarian, I would reply that any regime of rights, also one limited to protecting the functioning of the so-called free market, already implies a certain interpretation and demarcation of freedom and hence must be justified to the affected parties in a way that respects their freedom. And in this process of justification, the other dimensions of freedom are inevitably brought into play, so there is no way to remain with a purely negative conception of freedom.[22] However, my theory calls for more modesty than is displayed by liberal egalitarians who independently of public deliberation have decided in favor of a specific theory of social justice and determined which public policies will promote it. The implication of being guided by the commitment to deliberative freedom for economic reform is that well-meaning elites cannot impose certain policies from without, even if they can show that these policies promote a certain dimension of freedom, for example, a specific conception of personal autonomy (see Chapter 3). Rather, economic reforms must be justified to and by the affected in order to respect their individual freedom to say no, to respect their status as discursive beings, and to make them participants in self-legislation.

It might be objected that deliberation could not take place at all under present conditions of inequalities of resources, power, and status. It is certainly true that public deliberation in its ideal form has very demanding preconditions, and that these are missing in most, if not all, contemporary societies.[23] However, we should not a priori rule out the possibility that there can be valuable forms of public deliberation under less than ideal conditions. It is an empirical question to what extent economic and other inequalities undermine the equality of opportunity of influence required within deliberative processes. Indeed, empirical research of some experiments with deliberative forums has suggested that, for example, income inequalities do not translate directly into unequal ability to participate effectively in deliberation.[24] My argument against the idea that economic redistribution is a problem that must be solved prior to public deliberation's becoming a relevant form of political participation does not require that present processes of public deliberation be ideal, for example, that everyone must have the exact equal ability to make an argument that others will find convincing.[25] What my argument requires is that experiments with actual deliberation result not only in participants gaining greater understanding of their own interest and of the general interest but also supporting measures that will make future deliberation approximate the ideal more closely, that is, that the participants will agree to the necessary social and institutional reforms. If experiments with public deliberation entrench existing inequalities and uphold a status quo that is hostile to deliberation, then we will of course have to consider other methods of change than public deliberation.[26] To determine whether public deliberation under present conditions will be self-improving or merely uphold existing inequalities and institutions requires that we experiment with new institutional forms based on the ideal of deliberation and that we analyze their outcomes. Experiments with new forms of public deliberation already take place, and academics as well as practitioners are closely monitoring their results.[27]

The normative basis in deliberative freedom entails an argument for a *participatory* conception of deliberative democracy, a conception that stresses the importance of all citizens having the opportunity to participate in and learn from processes of public deliberation (see especially Chapters 2 and 7). The ideal of participation is not that "every citizen deliberates every issue," but that "everyone seriously deliberates something."[28] But where can citizens participate in public deliberation? Where do we have the opportunity "of *being* republicans and of *acting* as citizens," as Hannah Arendt puts it?[29] Theorists and practitioners of deliberative democracy have focused on many different venues of deliberation. Some have focused on existing representative institutions such as legislatures, which they argue should rely less on bargaining and aggregation and more on reason giving.[30] This is an important but a one-sided application of the deliberative ideal. In Joseph Bessette's ideal of deliberative democracy, for example, "the citizenry would reason, or deliberate, *through* their representatives," and "the deliberative sense of the community would emerge not so much through debate and persuasion among the citizens themselves as through the functioning of their governing institutions."[31] My discussion, in contrast, has emphasized the importance of the inclusion of ordinary citizens in processes of public deliberation. Therefore, models of deliberative democracy that stress widespread participation in informal public spheres and civil society associations, which can coexist with representative institutions, are more promising.[32] In addition to the formal public sphere of a legislature and the disorganized public sphere of civil society (Chapter 7), a number of innovative experiments exist in the United States and around the world that organize public deliberation in more formal ways than the "wild" civil society but also do not have legislative power, for example, Deliberative Polling, Citizens Juries, and 21st Century Town Meetings.[33] What is encouraging about these experiments is that they show that public deliberation that engages ordinary citizens is not merely a dream of the normative political theorist; the ideal connects with actual experience.

New forums of public deliberation are emerging under many different circumstances and under less than ideal conditions, from deliberation about planning in the Kerala province in India, to the Participatory Budget in Porto Alegre in Brazil, to deliberation about policing in Chicago in the United States.[34] We can typologize and evaluate these experiments in public deliberation in many ways. From the perspective of deliberative freedom, three questions are of particular importance. The first concerns how closely these deliberative forums are integrated into the state. Are they sponsored by a public institution, for example, or by a nonprofit organization? Second, are these forums connected to the making of the law or to the implementation of law? Institutionally, they might be connected either to the legislature or to administrative agencies. Third, who participates? Here we should ask the basic quantitative question, how many people are involved? But we should in addition ask if they are randomly selected, self-selected, or stakeholders, that is, made up of representatives from affected groups.[35]

I cannot possibly comment on all of these different forms of promoting and organizing deliberation. That would require another book. On the most abstract level, however, my multidimensional conception of freedom fits well with an organizationally dispersed public arena that enables citizens to participate in many different types of deliberative forums. The public arena must be "organizationally dispersed, because public opinion crystallises not only in reference to national legislatures, but also in the work of the local school governance committee, the community policing beat organization, and their analogies in areas such as the provision of services to firms or to distressed families."[36]

Apart from the aim of making already existing representative institutions themselves more deliberative, the great challenge is to connect processes of public deliberation in forums without legislative or administrative power to actual decision making. This issue often is theorized as a problem of *influence*. Influence might be understood broadly as a matter of public deliberation's effect on decision making, its ability to make decision makers change their minds and be responsive to the results of public deliberation. Influence also might be given a more specialized meaning, as Talcott Parsons and Habermas do, namely, as an effect on others that happens not through positive or negative sanctions, not by money or power, but only by persuasion and building normative consensus.[37] Influence in the narrower meaning is not merely a matter of decision makers changing their minds in response to deliberative forums, but that they do so *because they have been convinced* by the arguments given in public deliberation. In the first case (the broader meaning of influence), decision makers could change their minds and be responsive, for example, because many people participated in deliberation and the decision makers needed their vote, not because they were convinced by the arguments as such.

Public deliberation generates information and arguments, but how does it influence actual law and policy making? This is a problem both for the deliberation that happens in the public sphere of civil society emphasized by, for example, Jean Cohen and Andrew Arato as well as Habermas, and for the more organized experiments of public deliberation described in the recent *Handbook of Deliberative Democracy*. In Chapter 7, I discussed some of the dangers of collapsing the informal public spheres of civil society and the formal public spheres where binding decisions are made. I discussed this in terms of the epistemic aims of deliberative democracy, but it clearly matters for freedom as well. It is important for freedom in all of its dimensions that there be forums for participation and influence that are independent of the constraining logic of formalized decision making and the coercive power of the state. However, civil society associations that are entirely independent of the state might have difficulty attaining any influence on decision making.[38] Some of the more organized forms of deliberation, such as 21st Century Town Meetings, often are sponsored by public institutions. The advantage is that they are more likely to have actual influence on policy making.[39] The danger is that they might become co-opted by the state. Citizen deliberations might need a critical distance to "the powers that be" in order to be able to challenge them.[40] Ideally, we would have both civil society action that is independent of state power and more organized forms of deliberation with more direct connections to state institutions.

Citizens meet the state both as makers and matter, as I said earlier. However, a multidimensional conception of freedom points to the idea that as the "matter" of the state we should not merely regard our freedom from the quantitative perspective of the extent to which we are interfered with. The form of the interference—its quality and its justification—matters for our freedom as well. From the perspective of deliberative freedom, therefore, it is interesting that contemporary deliberative experiments connect not merely to the making of law but also to its implementation, or to what

is often called governance. The opportunity for participation in "deliberative governance" could be a way of avoiding the state's turning citizens
into clients (see the second section in Chapter 5).[41] However, deliberative
governance as a way of satisfying a dimension of freedom must be balanced against the freedom involved in making the law. The participation
involved in the implementation stage might be seen as undermining the
prerogatives of citizens seen in the role of makers of law. This is a matter of balancing different dimensions against each other.[42] There is no a
priori answer to which balance is best; it is not something that can be
determined from the level of abstraction of my argument. Citizens must
make their own judgments, but they could do so with a view to the different dimensions of freedom explicated and defended here.

Even though a number of different forums of deliberation exist in
many societies today, they still engage only a fragment of the citizenry
as a whole. One of the great challenges is therefore for public deliberation initiatives to "scale out" and include many more people.[43] The aim
of deliberative freedom is not merely to get a truer picture of the will
of the people. Even if it were possible for a representative sample of
the population to gather and through their common deliberation reach
conclusions that the people as a whole would also have reached if they
had had the same opportunity, this would not be sufficient for the conception of deliberation and freedom that I have advanced. The rest of
the people who did not have access to the same information or did not
hear the same arguments would clearly lack an understanding of why
the representative sample reached the conclusions or decisions they did.
Theorists who argue for the virtue of representative sampling, such as
James Fishkin, are well aware of the need to spread the arguments and
information of their deliberative experiments.[44] The more fundamental
problem, however, is that a representative sample engaged in a few days
of deliberation will not reach the same conclusions as a whole population in a radically more deliberative and democratic society would. The
long-term aim of deliberative democrats should not merely be to find
better methods for discovering what people in societies as we know them
would vote for if they were better informed and had more chances to
discuss their views with others but to transform society in radical ways so
everyone would be able to participate in public deliberation. Only with
radically reformed social circumstances and political institutions that allow
for the equal participation of everyone in processes of effective public
deliberation can we expect to experience the full range of the kinds of
freedom that democracy should have as its aim.

Notes

Introduction

Aristotle, *The Politics*, trans. T. A. Sinclair, rev. T. J. Saunders (Harmondsworth, UK: Penguin, 1992), 362–63; see also 332, 369.

1. In a recent book, Fareed Zakaria also notes this fact, but he deplores and rejects the tight connection between democracy and freedom in public discourse. He argues that too much democracy is a threat to freedom. See *The Future of Freedom: Illiberal Democracy at Home and Abroad* (New York: Norton, 2003).

2. "Freedom" seems to have been substituted for "liberty" as the preferred term in popular usage in the United States. See Geoffrey Nunberg, "More Than Just Another Word for Nothing Left to Lose," *New York Times,* March 23, 2003, who notes that in connection to the contemporary American wars, Operation Enduring Freedom in Afghanistan and Operation Iraqi Freedom, the term most commonly used is "freedom," while during World War I "liberty" was more often used. Most political theorists use "freedom" and "liberty" interchangeably; Hannah Arendt is one of the few exceptions; see *The Human Condition*, 2nd ed. (Chicago: University of Chicago Press, 1998); "What Is Freedom?" in her *Between Past and Future: Eight Exercises in Political Thought*, 143–72 (Harmondsworth, UK: Penguin Books, 1993); *On Revolution* (Harmondsworth, UK: Penguin Books, 1990). For an exploration of whether there is a difference in the use of "freedom" and "liberty," see Hanna F. Pitkin, "Are Freedom and Liberty Twins?" *Political Theory* 16:4 (1988): 523–52.

3. "President Discusses Iraq in State of the Union Address—January 20, 2004," http://www.whitehouse.gov/news/releases/2004/01/20040120-12.html, accessed September 12, 2006, emphases added.

4. David Miller also refers to this example; see "Introduction," in *Liberty*, ed. D. Miller, 1–2 (Oxford: Oxford University Press, 1991).

5. For Plato, democracy is characterized by the freedom to do as one likes without restraints and without concern for the true and right; see Rep. 557bff. (*Republic*, trans. G. M. A. Grube [Indianapolis, IN: Hackett, 1992]). For Aristotle, liberty is the basic principle of democracy in a twofold and contradictory manner: (1) ruling and being ruled in turn, and (2) living as one likes, that is, not

being ruled; see Pol. 1317a40ff. (*The Politics*, trans. T. A. Sinclair [Harmondsworth, UK: Penguin, 1992], 362–63, see also 332, 369).

6. Main contributions to the theory of deliberative democracy are James Bohman, *Public Deliberation: Pluralism, Complexity, and Democracy* (Cambridge, MA: MIT Press, 1996); Jean Cohen and Andrew Arato, *Civil Society and Political Theory* (Cambridge, MA: MIT Press, 1992); Joshua Cohen, "Deliberation and Democratic Legitimacy," in *Deliberative Democracy: Essays on Reason and Politics*, ed. J. Bohman and W. Rehg, 67–92 (Cambridge, MA: MIT Press, 1997); John S. Dryzek, *Deliberative Democracy and Beyond: Liberals, Critics, Contestations* (Oxford: Oxford University Press, 2000); Jon Elster, "The Market and the Forum: Three Varieties of Political Theory," in *Deliberative Democracy: Essays on Reason and Politics*, ed. J. Bohman and W. Rehg, 3–33; James S. Fishkin, *Democracy and Deliberation: New Directions for Democratic Reform* (New Haven, CT: Yale University Press, 1991); Amy Gutmann and Dennis Thompson, *Democracy and Disagreement* (Cambridge, MA: Belknap Press of Harvard University Press, 1996); Jürgen Habermas, *Between Facts and Norms*, trans. William Rehg (Cambridge, UK: Polity Press, 1996); Bernard Manin, "On Legitimacy and Political Deliberation," *Political Theory* 15:3 (August 1987): 338–68; Cass Sunstein, *The Partial Constitution* (Cambridge, MA: Harvard University Press, 1993); Iris Young, *Inclusion and Democracy* (Oxford: Oxford University Press, 2000). Useful collections are *Democracy and Difference: Contesting the Boundaries of the Political*, ed. S. Benhabib (Princeton, NJ: Princeton University Press, 1996); *Deliberative Democracy: Essays on Reason and Politics*, ed. J. Bohman and W. Rehg (Cambridge, MA: MIT Press, 1996); *Deliberative Democracy*, ed. J. Elster (Cambridge: Cambridge University Press, 1998); *Debating Deliberative Democracy* [*Philosophy, Politics, and Society* 7] ed. J. Fishkin and P. Laslett (Malden, MA: Blackwell, 2003); *Deliberative Politics: Essays on* Democracy and Disagreement, ed. S. Macedo (New York: Oxford University Press, 1999). For reviews of the literature on deliberative democracy, see Christian F. Rostbøll, "On Deliberative Democracy," *Sats: Nordic Journal of Philosophy* 2:2 (2001): 166–181; Simone Chambers, "Deliberative Democratic Theory," *Annual Review of Political Science* 6 (2003): 307–26.

7. Of course, whether an ideal is worth striving for is not merely a matter of whether it is normatively justifiable as an ideal but also whether striving for it brings us some of the promised benefits. But under all circumstances and in the first instance, the ideal itself should be defensible.

8. On different "models of democracy," see C. B. Macpherson, *The Life and Times of Liberal Democracy* (Oxford: Oxford University Press, 1977); David Held, *Models of Democracy*, 2d ed. (Cambridge, UK: Polity Press, 1996).

9. I am grateful to Pablo Gilabert for numerous discussions of this issue. In his work, Gilabert argues for an "expressive-elaboration model," according to which "the basic moral ideas of solidarity, equality, and freedom are expressed and elaborated in the practice of deliberation." See "The Substantive Dimension of

Deliberative Practical Rationality," *Philosophy & Social Criticism* 31:2 (2005): 191. See also "A Substantivist Construal of Discourse Ethics," *International Journal of Philosophical Studies* 13:3 (2005): 405–37. For our collaborative work, see Pablo Gilabert and Christian F. Rostbøll, "Beyond Libertarianism and Republicanism: The Deliberative Conception of Political Freedom," paper presented at the 11th Annual Critical Theory Roundtable, Stony Brook University, October 24–26, 2003.

10. But deliberation is not a regulative ideal in the sense that people ought to deliberate no matter the circumstances; see my "Dissent, Criticism, and Transformative Political Action in Deliberate Democracy," *CRISPP*, forthcoming.

11. The latter distinction was suggested by Benjamin Constant, "The Liberty of the Ancients Compared to That of the Moderns," in *Political Writings*, ed. B. Fontana, 307–28 (Cambridge: Cambridge University Press, 1988).

12. The most ambitious attempt at reconciliation is Jürgen Habermas, *Between Facts and Norms*. It also is an aspiration for John Rawls; see *Political Liberalism* (New York: Columbia University Press, 1993), 4–5; and for Joshua Cohen, who makes two quite different arguments for it in "Deliberation and Democratic Legitimacy" and in "Procedure and Substance in Deliberative Democracy," both in *Deliberative Democracy: Essays on Reason and Politics*.

13. For some important contributions to the latter debate, see *Constitutionalism and Democracy: Studies in Rationality and Social Change*, ed. J. Elster and R. Slagstad (Cambridge: Cambridge University Press, 1988). I discuss the issue in *Human Rights, Popular Sovereignty and Freedom* (Copenhagen: Copenhagen Political Studies Press, 1998), chap. 11.

14. Arendt describes the ancient Greek understanding of freedom as follows. "To be free meant both not to be subject to the necessity of life or to the command of another *and* not to be in command oneself. It meant neither to rule nor to be ruled." See *The Human Condition*, 32. Arendt directly rejects identifying freedom with sovereignty (ibid., 234). Clearly, Arendt is not advocating a Rousseauian or a positive conception of freedom in the sense of Isaiah Berlin's "Who governs me?" See his "Two Concepts of Liberty," in his *Four Essays on Liberty*, 130 (Oxford: Oxford University Press, 1969). Margaret Canovan also points out that Arendt is not advocating positive liberty. See *Hannah Arendt: A Reinterpretation of Her Political Thought* (Cambridge: Cambridge University Press, 1992), 212, 214. The notion of positive freedom is as much a part of the philosophical tradition that Arendt wants to circumvent as negative freedom is. Both ideas rely basically on a view of politics as a matter of ruling and of power as violence. This tradition has resulted in a definition of freedom as either freedom from the coercion of politics or freedom as being the author of that coercion, even if one is also subject to it, that is, to the dichotomy between negative and positive freedom. See my "Hannah Arendt: Magt som handling i fællesskab," in

Magtens tænkere: Politisk teori fra Machiavelli to Honneth ["Hannah Arendt: Power as Acting in Concert," in *The Theoreticians of Power: Political Theory from Machiavelli to Honneth,*] ed. C. B. Laustsen and J. Myrup, 293–314 (Frederiksberg: Roskilde University Press, 2006).

15. The dependence that modern society inevitably creates was a main concern for Rousseau. While the *Discourse on the Origin of Inequality* to a large extent laments this dependence, *On the Social Contract* attempts to show how the inevitable bonds of society could be made voluntary (both in *The Basic Political Writings,* trans. D. A. Cress [Indianapolis, IN: Hackett, 1987]). Benjamin Barber explains the Rousseauian view as follows: "If the human essence is social, then men and women have to choose not between independence or dependence but between citizenship and slavery"; see *Strong Democracy: Participatory Politics for a New Age* (Berkeley: University of California Press, 1984), 216.

16. See the second section in Chapter 1.

17. This aspect of Rousseau and Mill is emphasized by Carole Pateman, *Participation and Democratic Theory* (Cambridge: Cambridge University Press, 1970), chap. 2.

18. Not all republicans subscribe to this view of the connection between democracy and freedom. See Iseult Honohan, *Civic Republicanism* (London: Routledge, 2002), 181. According to Quentin Skinner's influential interpretation, the republican tradition rather sees democracy or political participation as a *means* to secure freedom. See "Machiavelli on the Maintenance of Liberty," *Politics* 18 (1983): 3–15. This interpretation is accepted by Philip Pettit, whose work I discuss in Chapter 2; see *Republicanism: A Theory of Freedom and Government* (Oxford: Oxford University Press, 1997), 27ff. The idea I am defining is often associated with Hannah Arendt. See especially "What Is Freedom?" and *The Human Condition,* chaps. 2 and 5.

19. On the point that critical theory is intrinsically linked to a theory of freedom, see Albrecht Wellmer, *Critical Theory of Society,* trans. J. Cumming (New York: Herder and Herder, 1971), 48–49; Raymond Geuss, *The Idea of a Critical Theory: Habermas and the Frankfurt School* (Cambridge: Cambridge University Press, 1981), 78. For the point that a critical theory must clarify its normative standards, see Seyla Benhabib, *Situating the Self: Gender, Community, and Postmodernism in Contemporary Ethics* (New York: Routledge, 1992), 33; Bohman, *Public Deliberation,* 11.

20. See Dryzek, *Deliberative Democracy and Beyond,* 2–3, 20ff.; William E. Scheuerman, "Between Radicalism and Resignation: Democratic Theory in Habermas's *Between Facts and Norms,*" in *Habermas: A Critical Reader,* ed. P. Dews, 153–77 (Oxford: Blackwell, 1999); Iris Young, *Inclusion and Democracy,* 10–11, and "Activist Challenges to Deliberative Democracy," *Political Theory* 29 (2001): 670–90.

21. An article that does consider something similar to the dimension of freedom that I call internal autonomy is Maeve Cook, "Habermas, Feminism, and the Question of Autonomy," in *Habermas: A Critical Reader*, ed. P. Dews, 178–210 (Oxford: Blackwell, 1999). But Cook is concerned only with the dimension of autonomy and not with its relationship to a broader theory of freedom and deliberative democracy.

22. I am grateful to Jeremy Waldron for his suggestions for this section.

23. See Christine Swanton, "On the 'Essential Contestedness' of Political Concepts," *Ethics* 95:4 (July 1985): 811; Jeremy Waldron, "Is the Rule of Law an Essentially Contested Concept (in Florida)?" *Law and Philosophy* 21 (2002): 150. For a critique of the distinction, see Swanton, esp. 818.

24. John Rawls, *A Theory of Justice*, rev. ed. (Cambridge, MA: Belknap Press of Harvard University Press, 1999), 5.

25. W. B. Gallie, "Essentially Contested Concepts," *Proceedings of the Aristotelian Society* 56 (1955–1956): 186.

26. Gallie, "Essentially Contested Concepts," 175ff.; John N. Gray, "On the Contestability of Social and Political Concepts," *Political Theory* 5:3 (August, 1977): 341–42; Swanton, "On the 'Essential Contestedness' of Political Concepts," 811.

27. For a discussion of freedom that relies on the latter distinction, see Tim Gray, *Freedom* (Houndmills, UK: Macmillan, 1991), 17–18. In contrast, Nancy J. Hirschmann argues that external and internal barriers to freedom cannot be seen separately but are interdependent; see *The Subject of Liberty: Toward a Feminist Theory of Freedom* (Princeton, NJ: Princeton University Press, 2003), 10, 14.

28. Gallie, "Essentially Contested Concepts," 172.

29. Waldron, "Is the Rule of Law an Essentially Contested Concept (in Florida)?" 150–51, first emphasis added.

30. Steven Lukes, *Power: A Radical View* (Houndmills, UK: Macmillan, 1974), 26. See also William E. Connolly, *The Terms of Political Discourse*, 3rd ed. (Oxford: Blackwell, 1993), 21–22.

31. Gray, "On the Contestability of Social and Political Concepts," 332–33.

32. Gallie, "Essentially Contested Concepts," 170–71.

33. Essentially contested concepts are "concepts the proper use of which inevitably involves endless disputes about their proper uses on the part of their users." See Gallie, "Essentially Contested Concepts," 169.

34. Gallie, "Essentially Contested Concepts," 179.

35. Kristján Kristjánsson, *Social Freedom: The Responsibility View* (Cambridge: Cambridge University Press, 1996), 181.

36. Waldron, "Is the Rule of Law an Essentially Contested Concept (in Florida)?," 160, emphasis in original. Waldron himself, however, does not agree

that it is a necessary condition that the parties know or agree that the concept is essentially contested for it to be so (162–63).

37. In this I differ from Felix E. Oppenheim, who thinks it is possible to construe a neutral concept of freedom in descriptive terms; see "Social Freedom and Its Parameters," *Journal of Theoretical Politics* 7:4 (1995): 403. Such attempts are criticized by Connolly, *The Terms of Political Discourse*, 30, 40, 140ff.

Chapter 1

1. See, e.g., Joshua Cohen, "Democracy and Liberty," in *Deliberative Democracy*, ed. J. Elster, 185ff. (Cambridge: Cambridge University Press, 1998); and Iris Young, *Inclusion and Democracy* (Oxford: Oxford University Press, 2000), 18ff.

2. Elster, for example, identifies deliberative democracy as "the idea that democracy revolves around the transformation of preferences rather than simply the aggregation of preferences." See "Introduction," in *Deliberative Democracy*, ed. Elster, 1. Similarly, Ian Shapiro says the deliberative view is concerned with "transforming preferences rather than aggregating them." See *The State of Democratic Theory* (Princeton, NJ: Princeton University Press, 2003), 21.

3. Adam Przeworski defines deliberation as "a form of discussion intended to change the preferences on the basis of which people decide how to act." See "Deliberation and Ideological Domination," in *Deliberative Democracy*, ed. Elster, 140. Cf. Susan Stokes "Pathologies of Deliberation," in *Deliberative Democracy*, ed. Elster, 123.

4. See also my "On Deliberative Democracy," *Sats: Nordic Journal of Philosophy* 2:2 (2001): 171–72.

5. See Jürgen Habermas, *The Structural Transformation of the Public Sphere* (Cambridge, MA: MIT Press, 1989), which was first published in 1962. It is concerned with the decline of public communication, an issue that has animated much of Habermas's later work. In *Legitimation Crisis* (trans. T. McCarthy [Boston: Beacon Press, 1975], 112–13), Habermas contrasted discursive justification and the ideological form of justification. The ideological form of justification is a form of justification that limits and distorts deliberation and obstructs the free formation of opinions by excluding thematization of some validity claims.

6. See also John S. Dryzek, *Deliberative Democracy and Beyond: Liberals, Critics, Contestations* (Oxford: Oxford University Press, 2000), 38.

7. Stokes, "Pathologies of Deliberation," 123.

8. See also Iris Young, "Activist Challenges to Deliberative Democracy," *Political Theory* 29:5 (October 2001): 688.

9. Joseph A. Schumpeter, *Capitalism, Socialism and Democracy* (New York: Harper Torchbooks, 1976), 263.

10. For an argument about this in response to William Riker's critique of populist democracy, see Joshua Cohen, "Deliberation and Democratic Legitimacy," in *Deliberative Democracy: Essays on Reason and Politics,* ed. J. Bohman and W. Rehg, 81–82 (Cambridge, MA: MIT Press, 1997).

11. In the fourth section in Chapter 6, I suggest which forms of independence are and are not required to be free.

12. For such criticisms, see Adam Przeworski, *Democracy and the Market: Political and Economic Reform in Eastern Europe and Latin America* (New York: Cambridge University Press, 1991), 18; Ian Shapiro, "Enough of Deliberation: Politics Is about Interests and Power," in *Deliberative Politics: Essays on* Democracy and Disagreement, ed. S. Macedo, 30–32 (New York: Oxford University Press, 1999); Ian Shapiro, "Optimal Deliberation," in *Debating Deliberative Democracy,* ed. J. S. Fishkin and P. Laslett, 123–24 (Malden, MA: Blackwell, 2003).

13. *Democracy and Disagreement* (Cambridge, MA: Belknap Press of Harvard University Press, 1996); Jon Elster, *Sour Grapes: Studies in the Subversion of Rationality* (Cambridge: Cambridge University Press, 1983), 40.

14. Przeworski, *Democracy and the Market,* 18; Shapiro, "Enough of Deliberation," 30–32. See also Young, *Inclusion and Democracy,* 40ff., 82ff., 107ff., 116ff.

15. Thomas Christiano is an exception; see "The Significance of Public Deliberation," in *Deliberative Democracy: Essays on Reason and Politics,* ed. J. Bohman and W. Rehg, 249–50 (Cambridge, MA: MIT Press, 1997). Actually the proponents of deliberative democracy who come out of the tradition of critical theory should be aware of this. "A critical theory of society is a normative social theory: it distinguishes real from false consensus, true communication from pseudo-communication, and so the appearance of freedom from real liberty." See Jay Bernstein, "Habermas," in *Conceptions of Liberty in Political Philosophy,* ed. Z. Pelczynski and J. Gray, 411 (New York: St. Martin's Press, 1984).

16. Both Przeworski and Shapiro use the example of workers realizing that their interests are in conflict with the bourgeoisie as a way of criticizing the focus on agreement in deliberative democracy. See Przeworski, *Democracy and the Market,* 18; Shapiro, "Enough of Deliberation," 31–32, *The State of Democratic Theory,* 26–27, and "Optimal Deliberation," 123–24.

17. Iris M. Young, *Justice and the Politics of Difference* (Princeton, NJ: Princeton University Press, 1990), 59.

18. Catharine A. MacKinnon, *Toward a Feminist Theory of the State* (Cambridge, MA: Harvard University Press, 1989), 229.

19. This is most prevalent in the early Habermas; see, for example, *Legitimation Crisis,* 112–13.

20. Young, *Justice and the Politics of Difference,* 116, and *Inclusion and Democracy,* 108. See also my critique of Young in "On Deliberative Democracy," 175–76.

21. Peter Jones, "Political Theory and Cultural Diversity," *CRISPP* 1:1 (Spring 1998): 39.

22. Young, *Justice and the Politics of Difference*, 112.

23. Adam Przeworski, "Minimalist Conception of Democracy: A Defense," in *Democracy's Value*, ed. I. Shapiro and C. Hacker-Cordón, 44 (Cambridge: Cambridge University Press, 1999).

24. Shapiro, "Enough of Deliberation," 34.

25. Lynn M. Sanders, "Against Deliberation," *Political Theory* 25:3 (June 1997): 369.

26. See Chapter 3 for a more detailed discussion of paternalism.

27. To be sure, there can be conflicts between religious preferences and religious tolerance. But to some extent we can separate what we ourselves prefer to do and what we believe others should have a right to do.

28. See Jon Elster on the difference between behavior appropriate in the market and in the forum. "The Market and the Forum: Three Varieties of Political Theory," in *Deliberative Democracy: Essays on Reason and Politics*, ed. J. Bohman and W. Rehg, 10 (Cambridge, MA: MIT Press, 1997).

29. Jack Knight and James Johnson make a similar argument in "Aggregation and Deliberation: On the Possibility of Democratic Legitimacy," *Political Theory* 22:2, (May 1994): 285. See also Cohen, "Democracy and Liberty," 199.

30. As I shall discuss in Chapter 6, this distinction might not be so clear-cut and easy to uphold. The point at this juncture is merely that the concern of deliberation is not how we form all of our preferences but how we reach political agreements.

31. See Jon Elster, "Deliberation and Constitution Making" in *Deliberative Democracy*, ed. J. Elster, 100–101.

32. This is an issue on which I expand in Chapter 7.

33. Formulations that see deliberation as a matter of transforming egoistic preferences into "other-regarding" or "impartial" ones can be found in Elster, "The Market and the Forum," 11, and Carlos S. Nino, *The Constitution of Deliberative Democracy* (New Haven, CT: Yale University Press, 1996), 144. Elster, however, does make it clear that aggregation is not necessarily of egoistic preferences.

34. Jane Mansbridge, "Practice-Thought-Practice," in *Deepening Democracy: Institutional Innovations in Empowered Participatory Governance*, ed. A. Fung and E. O. Wright, 183 (London: Verso, 2003).

35. Shapiro, "Enough of Deliberation," 30–32.

36. Cf. Elster, "The Market and the Forum," 14.

37. This does not mean they do not think they are mistaken—Schumpeter (as mentioned) thinks they are—but they do not think there is anything to do about it.

38. Isaiah Berlin, "Two Concepts of Liberty," in his *Four Essays on Liberty*, 130 (Oxford: Oxford University Press, 1969). Thomas Hobbes: "Whether a commonwealth be monarchical, or popular, the freedom is still the same." See *Leviathan* (Oxford: Oxford University Press, 1996), chap. 21, p. 143. This passage

in Hobbes is discussed in Philip Pettit, *Republicanism: A Theory of Freedom and Government* (Oxford: Oxford University Press, 1997), 38ff.; Quentin Skinner, *Liberty before Liberalism* (Cambridge: Cambridge University Press, 1998), 85ff.

39. Habermas argues that liberals see political rights as having the same structure and meaning as private rights. See *Between Facts and Norms,* trans. W. Rehg (Cambridge, UK: Polity Press, 1996), 270, and "Three Normative Models of Democracy," in *The Inclusion of the Other,* ed. C. Cronin and P. De Greiff, 2 (Cambridge, MA: MIT Press, 1998). See also Jane Mansbridge, *Beyond Adversary Democracy* (Chicago: University of Chicago Press, 1983), 16ff.

40. I thank Jon Elster for pressing this point.

41. C. B. Macpherson discusses protective democracy in Chapter 2 of *The Life and Times of Liberal Democracy* (Oxford: Oxford University Press, 1977). This model of democracy, he says, took "man as he had been shaped by market society, and assumed that he was unalterable" (ibid., 43). David Held says negative freedom "was the perfect complement to the growing market economy." See *Models of Democracy,* 2d ed. (Cambridge, UK: Polity Press, 1996), 98. He summarizes the protective model of democracy on pp. 88–89, 99.

42. "Liberty, or freedom, signifieth (properly) the absence of opposition; (by opposition, I mean external impediments of motion;)." See Hobbes, *Leviathan,* chap. 21, p. 139.

43. Berlin, "Two Concepts," 122.

44. Hobbes, *Leviathan,* chap. 21, pp. 139, 140, emphasis deleted.

45. Berlin, "Two Concepts," 122.

46. Ibid., 123.

47. Ibid., 128. But in the "Introduction" to *Four Essays on Liberty,* written some ten years later, Berlin admits that this is a wrong way of putting the issue, since this would mean that freedom could be increased by eliminating desires just as well as by satisfying them (xxxviii). But he does not have a real alternative. The alternative he does suggest takes him even farther away from his starting point. First he suggests "absence of obstacles to possible choices and activities," but then, as if he realizes this might be too broad, he says, "freedom ultimately depends not on whether I wish to walk at all, or how far, but on how many doors are open, how open they are, upon *their relative importance in my life*" (p. xxxix, emphasis added). In a footnote on p. 130, which he refers to in the Introduction (n1, p. xl), Berlin adds, "the value not merely the agent, but the general sentiment of the society in which he lives, puts on the various possibilities." These qualifications clearly take him far beyond how he defined negative liberty and into the realm of positive liberty. See also William L. McBride (" 'Two Concepts of Liberty' Thirty Years Later: A Sartre-Inspired Critique," *Social Theory and Practice* 16:3 [Fall 1990]: 305), who argues that Berlin here makes a "rank-ordering of the values of individuals' various ends," which is incompatible with his defense of negative liberty as well as with his pluralism.

48. Hobbes rejects this. For him, every act I do I do because I have a desire to do it. He rejects the issue of free will as absurd; we can only speak of free or unfree actions. See *Leviathan*, 29, 40, 88.

49. On the difference between concept and conception, see the Introduction.

50. Samuel Fleischacker, *A Third Concept of Liberty: Judgment and Freedom in Kant and Adam Smith* (Princeton, NJ: Princeton University Press, 1999), 251–52.

51. For an argument that Berlin's notion of "negative liberty presupposes a certain notion of positive liberty," see Rainer Forst, "Political Liberty" (typescript, University of Frankfurt, n.d.), 4. See also Gerald C. MacCallum, "Negative and Positive Freedom" (in *Liberty*, ed. D. Miller, 100–22 [Oxford: Oxford University Press, 1991]), who argues that there is only one concept of liberty, and it includes both the elements of freedom from what and freedom to what. See also Tim Gray, *Freedom* (Houndmills, UK: Macmillan, 1991), 30, who argues that "the absence of impediments conception of freedom is a parasitic conception: it cannot stand convincingly on its own, since for its elucidation we must have recourse to some other conception."

52. Dworkin, "Do Liberal Values Conflict?," in *The Legacy of Isaiah Berlin*, ed. M. Lilla, R. Dworkin, and R. B. Silvers, 88, 89 (New York: New York Review Books, 2001).

53. On the idea of an incomplete moral notion, see William E. Connolly, *The Terms of Political Discourse*, 3rd ed. (Oxford: Blackwell, 1993), 26–27.

54. Benjamin Constant, "The Liberty of the Ancients Compared to that of the Moderns," in *Political Writings*, ed. B. Fontana, 317 (Cambridge: Cambridge University Press, 1988), emphasis added. On the focus on private pleasures in Hobbes, Bentham, Constant, and Berlin, see also Fleischacker, *A Third Concept of Liberty*, 252, who describes this as "the dominant modern view."

55. Miller, "Introduction," in *Liberty*, ed. D. Miller, 3 (Oxford: Oxford University Press, 1991).

56. Hannah Arendt, "What Is Freedom?," in *Between Past and Future: Eight Exercises in Political Thought* (Harmondsworth, UK: Penguin Books, 1993), 155.

57. Here I draw on Pablo Gilabert and Christian F. Rostbøll, "Beyond Libertarianism and Republicanism: The Deliberative Conception of Political Freedom," paper presented at the 11th Annual Critical Theory Roundtable, Stony Brook University, October 24–26, 2003.

58. Benjamin Barber similarly remarks, "What we *want* the terms *freedom* and *equality* and *justice* and *right* to stand for is what politics is about. Freedom, justice, equality, and autonomy are all products of common living; democracy creates them." See *Strong Democracy: Participatory Politics for a New Age* (Berkeley: University of California Press, 1984), 157, xxiii.

59. Karl Marx, "On the Jewish Question," in *The Marx-Engels Reader*, 2d ed., ed. R. Tucker, 43 (New York: Norton, 1978).

60. Claude Lefort, "Politics and Human Rights," in *The Political Forms of Modern Society* (Cambridge, MA: MIT Press), 250. See also Kenneth Baynes, "Rights as Critique and the Critique of Rights," in *Political Theory* 28:4 (August 2000): 458; Jean L. Cohen, *Regulating Intimacy: A New Legal Paradigm* (Princeton, NJ: Princeton University Press, 2002), 46–47.

61. See Seyla Benhabib, "Models of the Public Sphere: Hannah Arendt, the Liberal Tradition, and Jürgen Habermas," in *Habermas and the Public Sphere,* ed. C. Calhoun, 84 (Cambridge, MA: MIT Press, 1992); Nancy Fraser, "Rethinking the Public Sphere: A Contribution to the Critique of Actually Existing Democracy," in *Habermas and the Public Sphere,* 128ff., 131ff.; Nancy Fraser, "Talking about Needs: Interpretive Contests as Political Conflicts in Welfare-State Societies," *Ethics* 99 (January 1989): 298ff.

62. According to Charles Taylor, negative freedom springs from a reductive-empiricist tradition. "On this view, our feelings are brute facts about us; that is, it is a fact about us that we are affected in such and such a way, but our feelings cannot themselves be understood as involving some perception or sense of what they relate to, and hence as potentially veridical or illusory, authentic or inauthentic." See "What's Wrong with Negative Liberty," in *Philosophy and The Human Sciences: Philosophical Papers 2* (Cambridge: Cambridge University Press, 1985), 223.

63. On the development of the idea of interest as something that is seen as more and more subjective from Madison to utilitarianism, see Hanna F. Pitkin, *The Concept of Representation* (Berkeley: University of California Press, 1967), chap. 9.

64. Cf. Schumpeter's view of democracy as a competition among the elites for the people's vote. Here the main function of the citizens is to choose a government; see *Capitalism, Socialism and Democracy*, 269ff.

65. David Held notes, "The liberal conception of negative freedom is linked to . . . the idea of choosing among alternatives." See *Models of Democracy*, 98.

66. Cf. Mansbridge, *Beyond Adversary Democracy*, 17.

67. I emphasize the distinction because practical or moral questions often are turned into theoretical ones. For a good critique of this category mistake in communitarianism, see Jean Cohen's discussion of Michael Sandel in *Regulating Intimacy*, 46–47.

68. James Mill, "Essay on Government," in *Utilitarian Logic and Politics,* ed. J. Lively and J. Rees, 53–95 (Oxford: Clarendon Press, 1978). See also the very helpful article on James Mill by Alan Ryan, "Two Concepts of Politics and Democracy: James and John Stuart Mill," in *Machiavelli and the Nature of Political Thought*, ed. M. Flischer, 76–113 (London: Croom Helm, 1972). Macpherson, *The Life and Times of Liberal Democracy*, 37; Held, *Models of Democracy*, 94ff.

69. J. S. Mill, "Considerations on Representative Government," in *Utilitarianism: On Liberty and Considerations on Representative Government*, ed. G. Williams, 224 (London: Everyman, 1993).

70. William Riker, *Liberalism against Populism* (Prospect Heights, IL: Waveland Press, 1982), 14.

71. Ibid., 244.

72. Ibid., 245. Riker says he does not want to take sides regarding negative and positive freedom but then goes on to say that negative freedom is necessary for freedom and to show that it is what democracy protects—but this of course does not show negative freedom to be sufficient.

73. I write "narrowly instrumental" because I later argue that deliberative democracy also entails a partly instrumental view of politics but in a broader sense than the tradition I am discussing here. See Chapter 7, the section "The Instrumental Dimension of Deliberative Freedom."

74. Nancy Fraser convincingly argues that the politics of needs is not just a matter of the distribution of satisfaction of given needs but of *interpreting* needs; see Nancy Fraser, "Talking about Needs."

75. Cf. Steven Lukes's discussion of power in *Power: A Radical View* (Houndmills, UK: Macmillan, 1974).

76. James Mill, "Essay on Government," 55.

77. Cf. G. A. Cohen, "Capitalism, Freedom, and the Proletariat," in *Liberty*, ed. D. Miller, 169–70 (Oxford: Oxford University Press, 1991).

78. We find this view in Anthony Downs, *An Economic Theory of Democracy* (New York: Harper Collins, 1957); Ryan traces it back to James Mill in "Two Concepts of Politics and Democracy," 90.

79. Constant, "The Liberty of the Ancients Compared to That of the Moderns," 315.

80. James Mill thought for this reason that women did not need the right to participate/vote. See "Essay on Government," 79–80; see also Ryan, "Two Concepts of Politics and Democracy," 90ff.

81. Ryan, "Two Concepts of Politics and Democracy," 110. It should be noted that Constant saw political liberty as the guarantee of individual liberty. See "The Liberty of the Ancients Compared to that of the Moderns," 323.

82. Arendt was very afraid of this and saw it as a source of totalitarianism that people were concerned only with their private lives and lacked understanding of public principles. See Christian F. Rostbøll, *Human Rights, Popular Sovereignty and Freedom* (Copenhagen: Copenhagen Political Studies Press, 1998), and "Humanitet, pluralitet og ret—Arendts svar på erfaringerne med totalitarismen," in *Ondskabens banalitet—Om Hannah Arendts "Eichmann i Jerusalem"* ["Humanity, Plurality, and Law—Arendt's Response to the Experience with Totalitarianism," in *The Banality of Evil—On Hannah Arendt's* Eichmann in Jerusalem], ed. C. B. Laustsen og J. Rendtorff, 61–90 (Copenhagen: Museum Tusculanum, 2002).

83. James Mill, "Essay on Government," 79–80.

84. I agree with Nadia Urbinati, who describes infantilization as a form of subjection. See *Mill on Democracy: From the Athenian Polis to Representative Government* (Chicago: University of Chicago Press, 2002), 172ff.

Chapter 2

1. Philip Pettit connects his republican theory to deliberative democracy in numerous places. See, e.g., *Republicanism: A Theory of Freedom and Government* (Oxford: Oxford University Press, 1997), 187ff. [hereafter cited in the text as R]; *A Theory of Freedom: From the Psychology to the Politics of Agency* (New York: Oxford University Press, 2001), 168 [hereafter cited in the text as TF]; "Deliberative Democracy, the Discursive Dilemma, and Republican Theory," in *Debating Deliberative Democracy*, ed. J. S. Fishkin and P. Laslett, 138–62 (Malden, MA: Blackwell, 2003); "Discourse Theory and Republican Freedom," in *Republicanism: History, Theory, and Practice*, ed. D. Weinstock and C. Nadeau, 72–95 (London: Frank Cass, 2004); "Depoliticizing Democracy," *Ratio Juris* 17:1 (March 2004): 52–65. Iris Young appropriates Pettit's conception of freedom as part of her version of deliberative democracy. See *Inclusion and Democracy* (Oxford: Oxford University Press, 2000), 32–33. Henry Richardson gives an even more prominent place to freedom as nondomination; see *Democratic Autonomy: Public Reasoning about the Ends of Policy* (New York: Oxford University Press, 2002), esp. 28–36.

2. For the extent of Pettit's influence on republican theory, see Daniel M. Weinstock, "Introduction," in *Republicanism: History, Theory and Practice*, ed. D. Weinstock and C. Nadeau, 1–4 (London: Frank Cass, 2004).

3. See also Christopher McMahon, "The Indeterminacy of Republican Policy," *Philosophy & Public Affairs* 33 (2005): 68.

4. For some critical comments on the accuracy of Pettit's historical account, see Roger Boesche, "Thinking about Freedom," *Political Theory* 26 (December 1998): 861–66. For an argument that Pettit's notion of freedom is not really republican but falls within the liberal tradition, see Charles Larmore, "A Critique of Philip Pettit's Republicanism," *Philosophical Issues* 11 (2001): 229–43.

5. Philip Pettit, "Republican Freedom and Contestatory Democratization," in *Democracy's Value*, ed. I. Shapiro and C. Hacker-Cordón, 164, 167 (Cambridge: Cambridge University Press, 1999). For a critical discussion of the distinction between compromising and conditioning freedom, see Richard Dagger, "Autonomy, Domination, and the Republican Challenge to Liberalism," in *Autonomy and the Challenges to Liberalism*, ed. J. Christman and J. Anderson, 189ff., 198 (Cambridge: Cambridge University Press, 2005). Dagger argues that the distinction can be defended with a conception of autonomy but not with reference to nondomination alone.

6. In *Republicanism*, 37, Pettit holds that Hobbes was of the same view as Bentham and Berlin, but in a recent article he argues that Hobbes does not see the threat of punishment by the law as compromising freedom. See "Liberty and Leviathan," *Politics, Philosophy & Economics* 4 (2005): 139–40, 145ff.

7. R, 17, 37; TF, 132.

8. Pettit sees his conception of freedom as congenial to both feminists and socialists (R, 138–43). Gerald F. Gaus has described his theory as "profoundly

antimarket." See "Backwards into the Future: Neorepublicanism as a Postsocialist Critique of Market Society," *Social Philosophy & Policy* 20 (2003): 68. However, Pettit does not show the same understanding of the effect of economic structures on freedom as Marxists do.

9. See *Democratic Autonomy*, 34.

10. See also Gaus, "Backwards into the Future," 72, and Charles Larmore, "Liberal and Republican Conceptions of Freedom," in *Republicanism: History, Theory and Practice*, ed. D. Weinstock and C. Nadeau, 113–14 (London: Frank Cass, 2004).

11. W. E. B. DuBois, *The Souls of Black Folk* (New York: Dover, 1994), 107.

12. Virginia Woolf, *Three Guineas* (San Diego: Harcourt, 1966), 135.

13. I do not mean to say that domination exists only when the right to interfere is expressively backed by law, that is, by the state's monopoly on the means of violence. The accepted right can also be a matter of convention, but then it at least has to be permitted by the state.

14. Marx and Engels saw this when they noted, "To be a capitalist is to have not only a purely personal but a social *status* in production." See Marx and Engels, "Manifesto of the Communist Party," in *The Marx-Engels Reader*, 2nd ed., ed. R. Tucker, 485, emphasis in original (New York: Norton, 1978).

15. Parts of Pettit's discussion indicate that he is aware of and agrees with what I am saying here. My criticism is directed at his specific formulations and definitions more than at the broader idea.

16. In *A Theory of Freedom*, 140–41, Pettit claims that one of the attractions of freedom as nondomination is that it is a "sociologically rich ideal." I think he is right that the idea of domination is sociologically richer than interference is, but he still does not present a sociologically rich theory.

17. See Bernstein, "Habermas"; Raymond Geuss, *The Idea of a Critical Theory: Habermas and the Frankfurt School* (Cambridge: Cambridge University Press, 1981), 26ff.

18. See Pettit, "Discourse Theory and Republican Freedom," 74ff.

19. The exceptions to this statement are manipulation and ideological domination. As I argue later, Pettit does not adequately address those possibilities either.

20. On freedom as status, see Tim Gray, *Freedom* (Houndmills, UK: Macmillan, 1991), 46ff.

21. Quentin Skinner, "The Paradoxes of Political Liberty," in *Liberty*, ed. D. Miller, 202 (New York: Oxford University Press, 1991).

22. See Benjamin Constant, "The Liberty of the Ancients Compared to That of the Moderns," in *Political Writings*, ed. B. Fontana, 307–28 (Cambridge: Cambridge University Press, 1988).

23. Larmore also laments Pettit's attempt to establish a unitary conception of freedom, but for different reasons than mine; see "Liberal and Republican Conceptions of Freedom," 103ff.

24. Pettit, "Republican Freedom and Contestatory Democratization," 165.

25. On the difference between "dimensions" and "conceptions" of freedom, see Introduction.

26. Such a contrast between liberalism and republicanism is drawn, for example, by Charles Taylor, "Cross-Purposes: The Liberal-Communitarian Debate," in *Philosophical Arguments* (Cambridge, MA.: Harvard University Press, 1995), 192, and Jürgen Habermas, "Equal Treatment of Cultures and the Limits of Postmodern Liberalism," *The Journal of Political Philosophy* 13 (2005): 1ff.

27. Quentin Skinner, "Machiavelli on the Maintenance of Liberty," *Politics* 18 (1983): 3–15; "The Paradoxes of Political Liberty"; *Liberty before Liberalism* (Cambridge: Cambridge University Press, 1998); "A Third Concept of Liberty," *Proceedings of the British Academy* 117 (2002): 247ff.

28. Arendt, *The Human Condition*, 2nd ed. (Chicago: University of Chicago Press, 1998), esp. 30ff., 175ff.

29. "[O]bedience to the law one has prescribed for oneself is liberty." See Jean-Jacques Rousseau, "On the Social Contract," in *The Basic Political Writings*, trans. D. A Cress (Indianapolis, IN: Hackett, 1987), 141–227, bk. I, chap. 8, p. 151.

30. Pettit, "Reworking Sandel's Republicanism," *The Journal of Philosophy* 95 (February 1998): 79, 82–83.

31. In some respects my argument is similar to Charles Taylor's in "What's Wrong with Negative Liberty," in *Philosophy and The Human Sciences: Philosophical Papers 2* (Cambridge: Cambridge University Press, 1985), 211–29. Taylor argues that holding on to the Maginot Line of negative liberty and rejecting all forms of positive freedom lead to an impoverished notion of freedom.

32. Pettit distances himself from Rousseau and Arendt, as already mentioned, but also from contemporary republicans such as Michael Sandel and Charles Taylor. See Sandel, *Democracy's Discontent: America in Search of a Public Philosophy* (Cambridge, MA: Harvard University Press, 1996). Taylor contrasts his view of the republican tradition to Skinner's in "Cross-Purposes: The Liberal-Communitarian Debate," 192–94, n.15, 302.

33. For Pettit's argument regarding the relationship of freedom as non-domination to democracy, see especially "Republican Freedom and Contestatory Democratization."

34. John McCormick criticizes this line in Pettit: "Given the secure position of the wealthy in liberal democratic regimes . . . Pettit's anxiety about a tyranny of the majority—or at least over what is relevant here, the majority

against the rich—seems less appropriate than the opposite anxiety: that politics conducted primarily through elections decisively favors the autonomous elites." See McCormick, "Machiavelli against Republicanism: On the Cambridge School's 'Guicciardinian Moments,'" *Political Theory* 31 (2003): 635. It is anxiety over the tyranny of the majority that makes Pettit accentuate contestation over participation, as McCormick notes, ibid., 634.

35. See TF, 160ff., and "Depoliticizing Democracy," 60–61.

36. The following discussion is indebted to Jürgen Habermas's criticism of moral realism, a position that Pettit holds but does not defend in the works under consideration here. It is outside the scope of this book to go into that issue. See Habermas, "Richtigkeit versus Wahrheit: Zum Sinn der Sollgeltung moralischer Urteile und Normen," in *Wahrheit und Rechtfertigung* (Frankfurt a.M.: Suhrkamp, 1999), 307ff.

37. Ibid., 309.

38. I cannot go into what institutional mechanisms would be required for actual participation by the people, but Pettit's endorsement of judicial politics clearly excludes it, and it would go beyond Schumpeterian elite democracy. I discuss some venues of popular participation in the third section in Chapter 8.

39. Jürgen Habermas, *Legitimation Crisis*, trans. T. McCarthy (Boston: Beacon Press, 1975), 112–13; Franz Neumann, "The Concept of Political Freedom," in *The Democratic and Authoritarian State: Essays in Political and Legal Theory,* ed. H. Marcuse, 161 (Glencoe, IL: The Free Press, 1957).

40. Pettit, "Republican Freedom and Contestatory Democratization," 173.

41. In "Republicanism: Once More with Hindsight," 291, Pettit describes republicanism as antipaternalistic.

42. "Deliberative Democracy, the Discursive Dilemma, and Republican Theory," 138.

43. As John Christman similarly argues, nondomination is "not fully *defined* until the institutional requirements of the proper procedures of the state are spelled out (those that properly track a person's interest). For until then, it is unclear . . . what counts as freedom" (emphasis in original). See John Christman's review of Philip Pettit, *Republicanism: A Theory of Freedom and Government*, in *Ethics* 109 (October 1998): 205.

44. Philip Pettit, "Democracy, Electoral and Contestatory," in *Designing Democratic Institutions*, ed. I. Shapiro and S. Macedo, *Nomos* XLII, 139 (New York: New York University Press, 2000).

45. Pettit, "Democracy, Electoral, and Contestatory," 140.

46. As David Miller notes, Berlin confusingly uses "positive freedom" to refer to a number of different ideas: (1) "Freedom as the power or capacity to act in certain ways"; (2) "Freedom as rational self-direction"; (3) "Freedom as collective self-determination"; see "Introduction," in *Liberty*, ed. D. Miller, 10 (New York: Oxford University Press, 1991).

47. For an insightful argument that Pettit is not advancing an alternative conception of freedom, but the composite value of noninterference and security, see Ian Carter, *A Measure of Freedom* (New York: Oxford University Press, 1999), 237ff.

48. And further on, "Non-domination *in the sense that concerns us*, then, is the position that someone enjoys when they live in the presence of others" (R, 67, emphasis added).

49. Milton Friedman, *Capitalism and Freedom* (Chicago: University of Chicago Press, 2002), 12.

50. Pettit does not see Arendt as belonging to the republican tradition that he is reconstructing. He only has contempt for her and (wrongly, I think) describes her in one place as a communitarian and a populist and in another as a nostalgic. See R, 8, 19.

51. I discuss Arendt's view of freedom more fully in "Hannah Arendt: Magt som handling i fællesskab," in *Magtens tænkere: Politisk teori fra Machiavelli til Honneth* ["Hannah Arendt: Power as Acting in Concert," in *The Theoreticians of Power: Political Theory from Machiavelli to Honneth*], ed. Carsten Bagge Laustsen and Jesper Myrup, 293–314 (Frederiksberg: Roskilde University Press, 2006).

52. Hannah Arendt, "What Is Freedom?," in *Between Past and Future: Eight Exercises in Political Thought* (Harmondsworth, UK: Penguin Books, 1993), 148.

53. Hannah Arendt, *The Origins of Totalitarianism* (New York: Harcourt Brace, 1979), 296.

54. Pettit, "Discourse Theory and Republican Freedom," 84.

55. Ibid., 91ff.

56. Ibid., 93.

57. This idea is prominent in Rousseau, a republican to whom Pettit pays only scant attention. Rousseau distinguishes natural liberty, which is limited only by force, and civil liberty, which is limited by the general will. Natural liberty connects with "a stupid, limited animal," while civil liberty is appropriate for "an intelligent being." To enjoy civil liberty, we must be transformed and understand the validity of the limits set by the general will. See "On the Social Contract," bk. I, chap. 8.

58. There is sometimes a tendency among civic republicans to neglect the intersubjective and discursive elements of private life; that is often true of Arendt. And such republicans might see liberalism as more atomistic or individualistic than it in fact is. On this point, see Will Kymlicka, *Contemporary Political Philosophy: An Introduction* (New York: Oxford University Press, 2002), 295–96. However, the rich associational life that some liberals praise is dependent on the public dimensions of freedom.

59. For the general idea and some arguments in its favor, see Charles Taylor, "Atomism," in *Philosophy and the Human Sciences: Philosophical Papers 2* (Cambridge: Cambridge University Press, 1985), 187–210.

60. See Jürgen Habermas, *Between Facts and Norms: Contributions to a Discourse Theory of Law and Democracy*, trans. W. Rehg (Cambridge: Polity Press, 1996), 305–306.

61. David Estlund, "Beyond Fairness and Deliberation: The Epistemic Dimension of Democratic Authority," in *Deliberative Democracy: Essays on Reason and Politics*, ed. J. Bohman and W. Rehg, 185 (Cambridge, MA: MIT Press, 1997).

62. Estlund, "Beyond Fairness and Deliberation," 174.

63. My arguments about seeing law both as a coercive force and as embodying validity draw upon Habermas's discussion of law as involving both facticity and validity. See *Between Facts and Norms*.

64. "Only an intersubjective process of reaching understanding can produce an agreement that is reflexive in nature; only it can give the participants the knowledge that they have collectively become convinced of something." See Jürgen Habermas, "Discourse Ethics: Notes on a Program of Philosophical Justification," in *Moral Consciousness and Communicative Action*, trans C. Lenhardt and S. W. Nicholson (Cambridge: Polity Press, 1992), 67.

65. "Democracy, Electoral and Contestatory," 129.

66. See also Pettit, "Deliberative Democracy and the Discursive Dilemma," *Philosophical Issues* 11 (2001): 280–83.

67. John Rawls, *Political Liberalism* (New York: Columbia University Press, 1993), 218.

68. See also Christian F. Rostbøll, "On Deliberative Democracy," *Sats: Nordic Journal of Philosophy* 2:2 (2001): 172–73.

Chapter 3

1. Cf. Iris Young, *Inclusion and Democracy* (Oxford: Oxford University Press, 2000), 20.

2. While this chapter for the sake of simplicity focuses on autonomous preferences independently of their justifiability, it is important to keep in mind that the two issues cannot be disentangled when we are concerned with democracy as a theory of what is right rather than a theory of the good life. In deliberative democracy, as I see it, the value of autonomy is relevant only insofar as it affects the process of mutual justification of issues of common concern. See Chapters 5 and 6.

3. The dimension of freedom that I call internal autonomy is most fully discussed in Chapter 5.

4. See, e.g., Joshua Cohen, "Democracy and Liberty," in *Deliberative Democracy*, ed. J. Elster, 185ff. (Cambridge: Cambridge University Press, 1998); Iris Young, *Inclusion and Democracy* (Oxford: Oxford University Press, 2000), 18ff.

5. I use public autonomy and freedom as being a participant in collective self-legislation synonymously.

6. Jon Elster, *Sour Grapes: Studies in the Subversion of Rationality* (Cambridge: Cambridge University Press, 1983), esp. chap. 3; Cass Sunstein, "Preferences and Politics," *Philosophy and Public Affairs* 20 (1991): 3–34; Sunstein, *The Partial Constitution* (Cambridge, MA: Harvard University Press, 1993), chap. 6.

7. Elster admits he "can offer no satisfactory definition of autonomy"; see *Sour Grapes*, 21. Instead he delineates autonomy negatively, ibid., 22; see also Jon Elster "The Market and the Forum: Three Varieties of Political Theory," in *Deliberative Democracy: Essays on Reason and Politics*, ed. J. Bohman and W. Rehg, 9 (Cambridge, MA: MIT Press, 1997).

8. Elster, *Sour Grapes*, 109.

9. Ibid., 25, emphasis in original.

10. Ibid., 110, 117.

11. Ibid., 110.

12. Ibid., 128.

13. Ibid., 118.

14. Ibid., 21, 127–28, 138. It does seem, however, that Elster is committed to the idea of character planning as an attractive view of freedom, since he also advances it elsewhere: "The definition of a rational desire would include, first, an optimal property: that of leading to choices which maximize utility. If people very strongly desire what they cannot get, they will be unhappy; such desires, therefore, are irrational. A rational desire is one which is optimally adjusted to the feasible set. To this clause we would have to add, secondly, a condition on the process whereby this adjustment is achieved. If the adaptation of desires to possibilities is brought about by some unconscious mechanism of dissonance reduction, as exemplified in the fable of the fox and the sour grapes, we would hardly call the result a paradigm of rationality. Our intuitions would rather suggest the opposite conclusion: to be under the sway of opaque psychological forces is a mark of irrationality. To be rational, the adjustment of desires to possibilities would have to be freely and consciously willed. This course was advocated by Buddhism, the Stoa and Spinoza. It amounts to making *autonomy* part of the notion of rationality, and is thus inconsistent with any purely welfarist conception of rational choice. Acting rationally means more than acting in ways that are conducive to welfare: it also implies that the beliefs and desires behind the action have a causal history with which we can identify ourselves." See Jon Elster, "Introduction," in *Rational Choice*, ed. J. Elster, 15 (New York: New York University Press, 1986).

15. Elster describes character planning as involving preferences being shaped by meta-preferences. See *Sour Grapes*, 117. This idea is very close to Harry Frankfurt's hierarchical theory of freedom. See Frankfurt, "Freedom of the Will

and the Concept of a Person," in his *The Importance of What We Care About: Philosophical Essays*, 11–25 (New York: Cambridge University Press, 1988). For a discussion of Frankfurt, see Christian F. Rostbøll, "Freedom as Satisfaction? A Critique of Frankfurt's Hierarchical Theory of Freedom," *Sats: Nordic Journal of Philosophy* 5:1 (2004): 131–46.

16. Elster, *Sour Grapes*, 16; see also "The Market and the Forum," 9.

17. This point is similar to a common objection to Frankfurt's theory. We may ask with Gary Watson, "Can't one be a wanton, so to speak, with respect to one's second-order desires?" See "Free Agency," in *Free Will*, ed. G. Watson, 108 (Oxford: Oxford University Press, 1982).

18. Elster, *Sour Grapes*, 21.

19. Ibid., 118.

20. For a critique of Stoicism for beginning the decline of the idea of freedom as something pertaining to politics, see Hannah Arendt, "What Is Freedom?," in her *Between Past and Future: Eight Exercises in Political Thought*, 147–48 (Harmondsworth, UK: Penguin Books, 1993).

21. Elster, *Sour Grapes*, 138.

22. Epictetus, *The Handbook*, trans. Nicholas White (Indianapolis, IN: Hackett, 1983), c. 8, 13.

23. Epictetus begins *The Handbook* by emphasizing the premise that "Some things are up to us and some are not up to us," c. 1, 11. It seems that even though he uses the plural he really means "up to us individually," and not "up to us in common or together."

24. Cf. Hannah Arendt, "What Is Freedom?," 147; *The Human Condition* (Chicago: University of Chicago Press, 1958), 222, 234, 244.

25. Joshua Cohen, "Deliberation and Democratic Legitimacy," in *Deliberative Democracy: Essays on Reason and Politics,* ed. J. Bohman & W. Rehg, 78 (Cambridge, MA: MIT Press, 1997).

26. This is an issue I take up later in the discussion of Sunstein.

27. As I argue later, these conditions must be justified in deliberation.

28. S. I. Benn argues, "Someone who has escaped [a proper] socialization process would not be free, unconstrained, able to make *anything* of himself that he chose; he would be able to make nothing of himself, being hardly a person at all." See *A Theory of Freedom* (Cambridge: Cambridge University Press, 1988), 179. See also the discussion in Bernard Berofsky, *Liberation from Self: A Theory of Personal Autonomy* (Cambridge: Cambridge University Press, 1995), 112ff. For the point that to formulate an empirically feasible conception of autonomy we should not see socialization as undermining autonomy, see Gerald Dworkin, "The Nature of Autonomy," in *The Theory and Practice of Autonomy* (Cambridge: Cambridge University Press, 1988), 7–8.

29. Compare Kenneth Baynes, "Public Reason and Personal Autonomy," in *The Handbook of Critical Theory*, ed. D. Rasmussen, 243–54 (Oxford: Blackwell,

1996). Baynes argues that personal autonomy and public reason presuppose each other; either is only normatively attractive in the presence of the other, which is similar to my point. But he goes beyond my point when he argues, "The notion of individual or personal autonomy, understood as the capacity for critical or reflective self-governance, is normatively attractive only if it is taken to imply that one acts for reasons that could not reasonably be rejected by others" (245). I do not think that *my* autonomy requires that others cannot reject my reasons, but that *I myself* do not reject my reflective attitudes *in light of what I have learned in public deliberation.*

30. Sunstein, *The Partial Constitution*, 3ff.

31. Ibid., 166ff.

32. Sunstein, "Politics and Preferences," 5.

33. Ibid., 11, emphasis added. Similar definitions of autonomy are given in *The Partial Constitution*, 176, and *Designing Democracy: What Constitutions Do* (New York: Oxford University Press, 2001), 163.

34. Sunstein, "Politics and Preferences," 13, similarly, *The Partial Constitution*, 178.

35. Sunstein, "Politics and Preferences," 10, similarly, *The Partial Constitution*, 175.

36. Sunstein, *The Partial Constitution*, 163.

37. For a good discussion of social critics in the public sphere, see James Bohman, *Public Deliberation: Pluralism, Complexity, and Democracy* (Cambridge, MA: MIT Press, 1996), chap. 5.

38. For an elaboration of the distinction drawn here, see the fourth section in Chapter 6.

39. Sunstein, "Politics and Preferences," 13, similarly, *The Partial Constitution*, 178.

40. Sunstein, *The Partial Constitution*, 179ff.

41. See Peter Strawson, "Freedom and Resentment," in *Free Will*, ed. G. Watson, 66 (Oxford: Oxford University Press, 1982).

42. What the exact institutional implications of the alternative accounts would be is a complicated issue that I cannot go into here. But it is important to stress that they do have institutional implications of the sort I mention in the text.

43. Cass R. Sunstein and Richard H. Thaler, "Libertarian Paternalism Is Not an Oxymoron," *University of Chicago Law Review* 70 (Fall 2003): n22.

44. Sunstein and Thaler, "Libertarian Paternalism Is Not an Oxymoron," 1201.

45. Richard H. Thaler and Cass R. Sunstein, "Libertarian Paternalism," *The American Economic Review* 93 (May 2003): 175.

46. Generalizing from this research, Sunstein and Thaler's main empirical premise is that what people "choose is strongly influenced by details of the

context in which they make their choices, for example default rules, framing effects (that is, the wording of possible options), and starting points." See "Libertarian Paternalism Is Not an Oxymoron," 1161.

47. Thaler and Sunstein, "Libertarian Paternalism," 178.

48. Sunstein and Thaler note "that respect for autonomy is adequately accommodated by the libertarian aspect of libertarian paternalism," that is, the availability of options to opt out. See "Libertarian Paternalism Is Not an Oxymoron," n22. But autonomy for libertarians is not merely a matter of existence of choice but also of Kantian respect for others as ends; cf. Robert Nozick, *Anarchy, State, and Utopia* (New York: Basic Books, 1974), 30–31.

49. "What people choose often depends on the starting point, and hence the starting point cannot be selected by asking what people choose." See Thaler and Sunstein, "Libertarian Paternalism," 178.

50. Among deliberative democrats, Habermas has repeatedly warned against the dangers of paternalism, but to my knowledge he has never given a definition of the term. Habermas describes uncritical affirmation of the status quo and assuming a paternalistic role as the two poles political philosophy should navigate between. See " 'Reasonable' versus 'True,' " in *The Inclusion of the Other: Studies in Political Theory* (Cambridge, MA: MIT Press, 1998), 97. He also repeatedly warns against paternalism in *Between Facts and Norms,* trans. W. Rehg (Cambridge: Polity Press, 1996).

51. Gerald Dworkin, "Paternalism: Some Second Thoughts," in his *The Theory and Practice of Autonomy*, 123 (Cambridge: Cambridge University Press, 1988).

52. Cf. Gerald Dworkin, "Paternalism," *Monist* 56 (1972): 78–79.

53. Aristotle's classic discussion of *akrasia*, or incontinence, can be found in Book VII of *Nicomachean Ethics.*

54. Amy Gutmann and Dennis Thompson, *Democracy and Disagreement* (Cambridge, MA: Belknap Press of Harvard University Press, 1996), 263.

55. For such a definition, see Donald VanDeVeer, *Paternalistic Intervention: The Moral Bounds on Benevolence* (Princeton, NJ: Princeton University Press, 1986), 22.

56. Gutmann and Thompson, *Democracy and Disagreement*, 264.

57. This is one way of seeing the problem, which I return to later.

58. Gutmann and Thompson, *Democracy and Disagreement*, 261.

59. In this regard, Gutmann and Thompson do not go beyond the negative freedom tradition criticized in Chapter 1.

60. Dworkin, "Paternalism: Some Second Thoughts," 123.

61. Jon Elster notes that arguing, bargaining, and voting are the three ways in which decisions can be reached in modern societies. See his "Introduction," in *Deliberative Democracy*, ed. J. Elster, 5–6 (Cambridge: Cambridge University Press, 1998). Others have argued for the inclusion of humor, greetings, testimony, storytelling, and so on as legitimate parts of the deliberative process. These, however,

are not forms of decision making, though they do affect opinion formation. For alternative forms of communication, see Iris M. Young, *Inclusion and Democracy* (Oxford: Oxford University Press, 2000), chap. 2.

62. Cf. Habermas, *Between Facts and Norms*, 162–68, esp. 166–67.

63. This understanding of argument is indebted to Jürgen Habermas's theory of communicative action; see his *The Theory of Communicative Action*, vol. I, trans. T. McCarthy (Cambridge: Polity Press, 1984), 8–42, 273–338.

64. For a discussion of how bypassing persons' "capacities for control over their mental lives" limits their freedom, see Alfred R. Mele, *Autonomous Agents: From Self-Control to Autonomy* (New York: Oxford University Press, 1995), 166–67; also see Chapter 6, the section "Heteronomy as Bypassing Critical Reflection."

65. Such a law exists, for example, in Germany.

66. I am here assuming that this law is made for the sake of the woman's freedom only and not for the unborn baby. I also am assuming that it is not made in order to favor one decision over another. To be sure, such a law might be made for other reasons and in particular for the sake of certain outcomes. I am considering the validity of one particular argument for such a law. But many laws that are defended in paternalistic terms also can be justified in other terms.

67. I take this example from Elster, "The Market and the Forum," 13.

68. For a fuller argument to this effect, see the third section in Chapter 6 and Chapter 7, the section "The Obligation to Participate."

69. As Elster points out, this is what distinguishes action in the "forum" from market behavior. See "The Market and the Forum," 10.

70. This also is the view of validity underlying Habermas's model of deliberative democracy; see *Between Facts and Norms*, esp. 104ff.

71. We find this dimension of freedom also in Gutmann and Thompson: "Citizens who have effective opportunities to deliberate treat one another not merely as objects who are to be judged by theoretical principles but also as subjects who can accept or reject reasons given for the laws and policies that mutually bind them." See "Democratic Disagreement," in *Deliberative Politics: Essays on* Democracy and Disagreement, ed. S. Macedo, 244 (New York: Oxford University Press, 1999). See also Klaus Günther, "Communicative Freedom, Communicative Power, and Jurisgenesis," in *Habermas on Law and Democracy: Critical Exchanges*, ed. M. Rosenfeld and A. Arato, 243 (Berkeley: University of California Press, 1998).

72. Bernard Manin, "On Legitimacy and Political Deliberation," *Political Theory* 15 (August 1987): 359; see also Bernard Manin, *The Principles of Representative Government* (Cambridge: Cambridge University Press, 1997), 190.

73. See Bohman, *Public Deliberation*, 184; Manin, "On Legitimacy and Political Deliberation," 360; Mark E. Warren, *Democracy and Association* (Princeton, NJ: Princeton University Press, 2001), 92.

74. Manin, "On Legitimacy and Political Deliberation," 360.
75. Habermas, *Between Facts and Norms*, 179.

Chapter 4

1. Michael Walzer, *Politics and Passion: Toward a More Egalitarian Liberalism* (New Haven, CT: Yale University Press, 2004), 90.

2. Joshua Cohen's influential 1989 article, "Deliberation and Democratic Legitimacy," draws heavily on both Rawls and Habermas. (Reprinted in *Deliberative Democracy: Essays on Reason and Democracy*, ed. J. Bohman and W. Rehg, 67–92 [Cambridge, MA: MIT Press, 1997]). In his later articles, however, Cohen draws less on Habermas and more on Rawls (who, in his later writings, is in turn influenced by Joshua Cohen). See "Procedure and Substance in Deliberative Democracy" in ibid., 407–37, and "Democracy and Liberty" in *Deliberative Democracy*, ed. J. Elster, 185–231 (Cambridge: Cambridge University Press, 1998). For Gutmann and Thompson's theory of deliberative democracy, see *Democracy and Disagreement* (Cambridge, MA: Belknap Press of Harvard University Press, 1996), and *Why Deliberative Democracy?* (Princeton, NJ: Princeton University Press, 2004). However, there is another, more empirical literature on deliberative democracy that developed without relying on Rawls (or Habermas). See Joseph M. Bessette, *The Mild Voice of Reason: Deliberative Democracy and American National Government* (Chicago: University of Chicago Press, 1994), and James S. Fishkin, *Democracy and Deliberation: New Directions for Democratic Reform* (New Haven, CT: Yale University Press, 1991).

3. To mention just two key followers of Habermas who have endorsed deliberative democracy, see James Bohman, *Public Deliberation: Pluralism, Complexity, and Democracy* (Cambridge, MA: MIT Press, 1996), and Seyla Benhabib, *Claims of Culture: Equality and Diversity in the Global Era* (Princeton, NJ: Princeton University Press, 2002), chap. 5.

4. Even though many of the ideas that today are seen as central to deliberative democracy can be found in the earlier works of Habermas and Rawls, not until recently have they both explicitly joined the ranks of adherents. Habermas first develops an explicit theory of deliberative democracy in his 1992 *Between Facts and Norms* (trans. W. Rehg [Cambridge, UK: Polity, 1996]), but already his 1962 *The Structural Transformation of the Public Sphere* (trans. T. Burger [Cambridge, MA: MIT Press, 1989]) brings up central concerns of what later was to be called deliberative democracy, such as publicity and rational argumentation. The theory of communicative action and discourse ethics also can be seen as being prolegomena to the theory of deliberative democracy; see *The Theory of Communicative Action* I–II, trans. T. McCarthy (Cambridge, UK: Polity Press, 1984, 1987) and "Discourse Ethics: Notes on a Program of Philosophical Justification,"

in *Moral Consciousness and Communicative Action*, trans. C. Lenhardt and S. Weber Nicholsen, 43–115 (Cambridge, UK: Polity Press, 1990). The first time Rawls identifies his idea of public reason as belonging to the theory of deliberative democracy is in his 1997 "The Idea of Public Reason Revisited" (reprinted in his *Collected Papers*, ed. S. Freeman, 579–80 [Cambridge, MA: Harvard University Press, 1999]), though he also mentions the relation in "Reply to Habermas," in *Journal of Philosophy* XCII (1995): 133, n1, 177–78.

5. John Dryzek also notes and laments the merger between liberalism and critical theory. See *Deliberative Democracy and Beyond: Liberals, Critics, Contestations* (Oxford: Oxford University Press, 2000), 3–4.

6. Habermas, "Reconciliation through the Public Use of Reason," reprinted in *The Inclusion of the Other: Studies in Political Theory* (Cambridge, MA: MIT Press, 1998), 50.

7. Rawls also is a neo-Kantian of sorts, but his turn to political liberalism is a turn away from a commitment to Kantian autonomy.

8. J. Donald Moon, "Rawls and Habermas on Public Reason: Human Rights and Global Justice," *Annual Review of Political Science* 6 (2003): 257–74, also notes the very different traditions Rawls and Habermas stem from but without discussing their views of freedom.

9. This discussion was commissioned by *The Journal of Philosophy* and published in vol. XCII (1995).

10. Joshua Cohen also focuses on the relationship between ancient and modern liberties. See "Procedure and Substance," 409–12.

11. Habermas, "Reconciliation," 69ff.; " 'Reasonable' versus 'True,' or the Morality of Worldviews," in *The Inclusion of the Other: Studies in Political Theory*, ed. C. Cronin and P. De Greiff, 100–101 (Cambridge, MA: MIT Press, 1998); Rawls, "Reply to Habermas," 168–69. On this difference between Rawls and Habermas, see also Frank Michelman, "How Can the People Ever Make the Laws?," in *Deliberative Democracy: Essays on Reason and Politics*, ed. J. Bohman and W. Rehg, 145–71 (Cambridge, MA: MIT Press, 1997), and Samuel Freeman, "Deliberative Democracy: A Sympathetic Comment," *Philosophy and Public Affairs* 29:4 (Fall 2000): 413ff.

12. John Rawls, *Political Liberalism* (New York: Columbia University Press, 1996), xxxvii–viii. References to this text will be given in the text as PL, but I have used the 1993 edition except for the "Introduction to the Paperback Edition" of 1996.

13. See, e.g., Joshua Cohen, "Procedure and Substance in Deliberative Democracy," and "Democracy and Liberty."

14. Cohen, "Procedure and Substance," 408–409; Cohen, "Democracy and Liberty," 187ff.; Rawls, *Political Liberalism*, passim.

15. See PL, lecture IV, 133ff.

16. See also Rawls, "Reply to Habermas," 136.

17. In the article that marks what might be called Rawls's "political turn," Rawls connects his political liberalism to the Reformation no less than in three different places. See "Justice as Fairness: Political not Metaphysical," *Philosophy and Public Affairs* 14 (Summer 1985): 225, 245, 249.

18. William Galston distinguishes Reformation and Enlightenment liberalism, where the former is concerned with diversity and the latter with autonomy. According to Galston's definitions, autonomy is "linked with the commitment to sustained rational examination of self, other, and social practices"; diversity means "legitimate differences among individuals and groups over such matters as the nature of the good life, sources of moral authority, reason versus faith, and the like." See *Liberal Pluralism* (Cambridge: Cambridge University Press, 2002), 21. See also the third section in Chapter 6.

19. See also "Public Reason Revisited," 611.

20. Joseph Raz and Ronald Dworkin are both committed to a liberalism focusing on comprehensive autonomy. See Raz, *The Morality of Freedom* (Oxford: Clarendon Press, 1986), and Dworkin, "Liberal Community," in *Sovereign Virtue: The Theory and Practice of Equality* (Cambridge, MA: Harvard University Press, 2000) 211–36. Their views are criticized by Rawls (PL, 135, n1) and Joshua Cohen, "Democracy and Liberty," 215ff.

21. See also Cohen, "Democracy and Liberty," 188ff.

22. For Madison's discussion of faction, see Hamilton, Madison, and Jay, *Federalist Papers*, ed. C. Rossiter, no. 10, esp. 46 (New York: Mentor, 1999).

23. Rawls, "Reply to Habermas," 145.

24. As Will Kymlicka notes in a discussion of Rawls, there is in fact no agreement, no overlapping consensus, on the extent or implications of freedom of conscience, the negative freedom, which Rawls has discussed as paradigmatic; see *Contemporary Political Philosophy: An Introduction*, 2d ed. (New York: Oxford University Press, 2002), 232–33.

25. The preceding argument borrows from Habermas, " 'Reasonable' versus 'True,' " 83–85, 93.

26. Rawls, however, goes beyond the negative freedom tradition by emphasizing the economic conditions that secure "the worth of freedom." But see discussion of this idea in Chapter 5.

27. Similarly, Nadia Urbinati has argued that deliberative practices (and Mill's conception of liberty) cannot be understood in terms of Berlin's theory of two liberties. See Urbinati, *Mill on Democracy: From the Athenian Polis to Representative Government* (Chicago: University of Chicago Press, 2002), 1, 10, 12, 155ff.

28. For critical comments on the Rawlsian idea of public reason and reasonableness, see Seyla Benhabib, *Claims of Culture,* 108–12; Dryzek, *Deliberative Democracy and Beyond,* 15, 47; Gerald F. Gaus, "Reason, Justification, and Consensus: Why Democracy Can't Have It All," in *Deliberative Democracy: Essays on Reason and Politics,* ed. J. Bohman and W. Rehg, 222, 231 (Cambridge, MA: MIT Press,

1997); Jack Knight and James Johnson, "What Sort of Equality Does Deliberative Democracy Require?," in *Deliberative Democracy: Essays on Reason and Politics*, ed. J. Bohman and W. Rehg, 283–87 (Cambridge, MA: MIT Press, 1997).

29. Rawls, "Public Reason Revisited," 581.

30. Cohen, "Democracy and Liberty," 187.

31. Ibid., 194, emphasis in original.

32. This also is the idea behind Amy Gutmann and Dennis Thompson's notion of reciprocity. See *Democracy and Disagreement*, 55ff.

33. Seyla Benhabib also notes that Rawls does not see public reason as a process; see *The Claims of Culture*, 108.

34. In a Rawls-inspired account, Samuel Freeman defines deliberative democracy in terms that it "counsels voting one's deliberated judgments." See "Deliberative Democracy: A Sympathetic Comment," 377.

35. Charles Larmore identifies this ambiguity in Rawls. He suggests that we should distinguish between open discussion and decision making, and that only the latter needs to be constrained by the idea of public reason. See "Public Reason," in *Cambridge Companion to Rawls*, ed. S. Freeman, 382–83 (Cambridge: Cambridge University Press, 2003).

36. The distinction I am drawing also could be expressed as a global and local distinction, according to which we would say that the aim is reasonableness of the system as a whole, not of every part of it. Jane Mansbridge makes such a distinction when she says, "The criterion for good deliberation should not be that every interaction in the system exhibit mutual respect, consistence, acknowledgement, open-mindedness, and moral economy, but that the larger system reflect those goals." See Jane Mansbridge, "Everyday Talk in the Deliberative System," in *Deliberative Politics: Essays on* Democracy and Disagreement, ed. S. Macedo, 224 (New York: Oxford University Press, 1999).

37. Gutmann and Thompson, *Democracy and Disagreement*, 52, emphasis in original. Or, as Rawls puts it, public reason "is a view about the kind of reasons on which citizens are to rest their political cases in making their political justifications to one another when they support laws and policies that invoke the coercive powers of government concerning fundamental political questions." See "Public Reason Revisited," 603. I would group Gutmann and Thompson as Rawlsian deliberative democrats, but it should be noted that they allow greater inclusion of comprehensive views in public deliberation than Rawls does. See Dennis F. Thompson, "Public Reason and Precluded Reasons," *Fordham Law Review* 72:5 (April 2004): 2083–84.

38. Jürgen Habermas, *The Theory of Communicative Action* I, trans. T. McCarthy (Cambridge, UK: Polity Press, 1984), 24.

39. Jürgen Habermas, *The Theory of Communicative Action* II, trans. T. McCarthy (Cambridge, UK: Polity Press, 1987), 277; "Discourse Ethics," 58; Cohen and Arato, *Civil Society and Political Theory* (Cambridge, MA: MIT Press, 1992), 486.

40. Habermas, it should be emphasized, would not see a *virtue* such as reasonableness as the solution to the problem of distorted communication; see discussion later.

41. I am not able to go into a discussion of the place of rhetoric in a deliberative democracy. I have made a few comments on the issue in "On Deliberative Democracy," *Sats: Nordic Journal of Philosophy* 2:2 (2001): 176ff. According to Gutmann and Thompson (*Democracy and Disagreement*, 135ff.), rhetoric can play an important and even a valuable role in *provoking* deliberation but is not itself deliberation. A new issue may thus be brought to the public agenda in a rhetorical way, by appealing to emotion, but after that it must yield to rational argumentation. John Dryzek (*Deliberative Democracy and Beyond*) sets out by presenting his view of deliberation as one that "would allow argument, rhetoric, humour, emotion, testimony or storytelling, and gossip" (1). He seems in the end, however, to privilege argument, for two reasons. First, "emotion can be coercive, which is why in the end it must answer to reason" (53). Second, only argument can answer the question, "What is to be done?" (71). So Gutmann and Thompson and Dryzek all allow for some use of rhetoric but believe that in the end reason and rational argument must rule. Iris Young (*Inclusion and Democracy* [Oxford: Oxford University Press, 2000], 63ff.) rejects this view. According to her, all speech is inevitably rhetorical.

42. Habermas sees this as a loss in Rawls's use. See Habermas, "Reconciliation," 64ff.; " 'Reasonable' versus 'True,' " 88.

43. See also Rawls, "Reply to Habermas," 134, 149ff.

44. These definitions are all formulated in terms of reasonableness as a virtue of citizens, not as denoting assertions.

45. See, e.g., Rawls, PL, 253; "Public Reason Revisited," 577; on the right to drop out of communication, see Habermas, *Between Facts and Norms*, 120.

46. Cf. Freeman, "Deliberative Democracy: A Sympathetic Comment," 405ff. For Habermasian criticisms of content reasonableness constraints, see Seyla Benhabib, "Toward a Deliberative Model of Democratic Legitimacy," in *Democracy and Difference: Contesting the Boundaries of the Political*, ed. S. Benhabib, 74ff. (Princeton, NJ: Princeton University Press, 1996); Dryzek, *Deliberative Democracy and Beyond,* 42ff.; Habermas, *Between Facts and Norms*, 308.

47. Rawls, "Public Reason Revisited," 578.

48. Ibid., 578.

49. Knight and Johnson make a similar point. See "What Sort of Equality Does Deliberative Democracy Require?," 286–87.

50. Jean-Jacques Rousseau, *On the Social Contract*, trans. D. A. Cress (Indianapolis, IN: Hackett, 1987), bk. IV, chap. 2, p. 82.

51. Rousseau, *On the Social Contract*, bk. IV, chap. 1, p. 80.

52. This argument draws on my "On Deliberative Democracy," 173.

53. Cf. Habermas, *Between Facts and Norms*, 313: "To talk about something is not *necessarily* the same as meddling in another's affair" (emphasis added). But it can be, we may ask, and so I will in Chapter 6.

54. Rawls, "Public Reason Revisited," 577, emphasis in original.

55. This is how Larmore believes it should be used; see "Public Reason," 383.

56. I realize that this criterion is not sufficient. Some means that contribute to future deliberation might be ruled out for other reasons. I have discussed this issue in more detail in "Dissent, Criticism, and Transformative Political Action in Deliberative Democracy," *CRISPP*, forthcoming.

57. Iris Young has written a very nice article "The Activist Challenges to Deliberative Democracy," *Political Theory* 29 (2001): 670–90. I agree with her argument that a deliberative democracy should not exclude activism (see especially p. 688), but I think she neglects to consider how activist forms of politics must in the end be justified in deliberation, if they are not to be just a form of coercion. See also Archon Fung, "Deliberation before the Revolution: Toward an Ethics of Deliberative Democracy in an Unjust World," *Political Theory* 33:3 (2005): 397–419.

58. The most important work here is still *The Theory of Communicative Action*, but see also *Between Facts and Norms*, 151–68, where Habermas makes it clear that deliberative democracy cannot rely on argumentation as the only form of communication but must allow also for, for example, bargaining. See, in addition, "Three Normative Models of Democracy," in *The Inclusion of the Other*, ed. C. Cronin and P. De Greiff, 245 (Cambridge, MA: MIT Press, 1998): "The concept of deliberative politics acquires empirical relevance only when we take into account the multiplicity of forms of communication in which a common will is produced, that is, not just ethical self-clarification but also the balancing of interests and compromise, the purposive choice of means, moral justification, and legal consistency-testing."

59. In *Between Facts and Norms*, 340–41, Habermas emphasizes, "One should seek the *conditions* for a rational political will-formation not only at the individual level of the orientation and decisions of single actors but also at the social level of institutionalized processes of deliberation and decision making." And in his discussion with Rawls, Habermas, "propose[s] that philosophy limit itself to the clarification of the moral point of view and the procedure of democratic legitimation, to the analysis of the *conditions* of rational discourses and negotiations." See "Reconciliation," 72, emphases added.

60. See, e.g., Richard Bernstein, "The Retrieval of the Democratic Ethos," in *Habermas on Law and Democracy: Critical Exchanges*, ed. M. Rosenfeld and A. Arato, 287–306 (Berkeley: University of California Press, 1998).

61. For the importance of a democratic ethos for deliberative democracy, see the third section in Chapter 6.

62. Though Rawlsians like Joshua Cohen are concerned with form also, insofar as they distinguish deliberation from bargaining. See "Deliberation and Democratic Legitimacy," 67.

63. Habermas, " 'Reasonable' versus 'True,' " 101.

64. Rawls, "Reply to Habermas," 140, n13; "Public Reason Revisited," 575–76, 608; PL, 220, 249. See also Larmore, "Public Reason," 381–82.

65. Rawls, "Public Reason Revisited," 575.

66. Ibid., 576.

67. Ibid., 580.

68. The deliberations of judges are a different case, which I cannot go into here.

69. Rawls, "Reply to Habermas," 140.

70. Cass R. Sunstein, "The Law of Group Polarization," in *Debating Deliberative Democracy,* ed. J. S. Fishkin and P. Laslett, 80–101 (Malden, MA: Blackwell, 2003), gives some empirical evidence that discussion among like-minded groups will make them move toward extremes. He also notes that the right institutional arrangements can circumvent this tendency.

71. John Stuart Mill, "On Liberty," in *On Liberty and Other Writings* ed. S. Collini, chap. 3 (Cambridge: Cambridge University Press, 1989). Brian Barry makes two important points in defense of Mill's alleged perfectionism. First, even if Mill thinks autonomy is a good thing, he does not want the state to coercively mold character. Second, autonomy is not a conception of the good on par with any other, since autonomous people might hold different substantive beliefs and values. See Brian Barry, *Culture and Equality* (Cambridge, MA: Harvard University Press, 2001), 118–23.

72. For a discussion of the complexities, see Thomas E. Hill Jr., "The Kantian Conception of Autonomy," in his *Dignity and Practical Reason in Kant's Moral Theory*, 76–96 (Ithaca, NY: Cornell University Press, 1992), and for a more textual account, see Henry E. Allison, *Kant's Theory of Freedom* (Cambridge: Cambridge University Press, 1990), 94ff.

73. Christine M. Korsgaard, *Sources of Normativity* (Cambridge: Cambridge University Press, 1996), 19–20, 91, 165.

74. "Rawls's idea of public reason does not . . . depend on an account of the origin of moral duty." See Freeman, "Deliberative Democracy: A Sympathetic Comment," 401. On Kant's view as a substitute for the idea of God as lawgiver, see J. B. Schneewind, "Autonomy, Obligation, and Virtue: An Overview of Kant's Moral Philosophy," in *The Cambridge Companion to Kant,* ed. P. Guyer, 311–12 (Cambridge: Cambridge University Press, 1992).

75. In a recent article on Rawls, Joshua Cohen argues that including political liberties among the basic liberties "cannot turn on the Rousseauean or Kantian idea that autonomy is the supreme good and that we achieve a form of autonomy (call it 'public autonomy') when we have equal political liberties."

See "For a Democratic Society," in *Cambridge Companion to Rawls*, ed. S. Freeman, 106–107 (Cambridge: Cambridge University Press, 2003).

76. Joshua Cohen, "Procedure and Substance in Deliberative Democracy," 408.

77. Cohen, "Procedure and Substance," 416; cf. also Cohen, "Democracy and Liberty," 222; PL, 77ff.

Chapter 5

1. Jürgen Habermas, *The Structural Transformation of the Public Sphere* (Cambridge, MA: MIT Press, 1989), 135.

2. Jürgen Habermas, "Further Reflections on the Public Sphere," in *Habermas and the Public* Sphere, ed. C. Calhoun, 441ff. (Cambridge, MA: MIT Press, 1992); Christian F. Rostbøll, *Human Rights, Popular Sovereignty and Freedom* (Copenhagen: Copenhagen Political Studies Press, 1998), 58–59.

3. Jürgen Habermas, " 'Reasonable' versus 'True,' or the Morality of Worldviews," in *The Inclusion of the Other: Studies in Political Theory*, ed. C. Cronin and P. De Greiff, 97 (Cambridge, MA: MIT Press, 1998).

4. For a criticism of philosophers who impose their ideas on citizens from without, see Michael Walzer, "Philosophy and Democracy," *Political Theory* 9 (1981): 379–99, see also Rostbøll, *Human Rights, Popular Sovereignty and Freedom*, 98–99.

5. Jürgen Habermas, *Between Facts and Norms*, trans. W. Rehg (Cambridge, UK: Polity Press, 1996), xli.

6. John Rawls, "Reply to Habermas," *Journal of Philosophy* XCII (1995): 135–36.

7. Habermas has, of course, much to say that relates to democratic theory in his works in the thirty years between *The Structural Transformation* and *Between Facts and Norms*. But it is only with the latter work that he develops a comprehensive democratic theory.

8. Habermas, *Between Facts and Norms*, 445–46.

9. John Rawls, *Political Liberalism* (New York: Columbia University Press, 1993), 77ff. See earlier discussion in Chapter 4.

10. Habermas, " 'Reasonable' versus 'True'," 98ff.

11. An exception is James Bohman. See his *Public Deliberation* (Cambridge, MA: MIT Press, 1996), chap. 5, and " 'When Water Chokes': Ideology, Communication, and Practical Rationality," *Constellations* 7 (September 2000): 382–92. This lack of concern with ideology also is noted and regretted (but not made good) by Iris Young. See her "Activist Challenges to Deliberative Democracy," *Political Theory* 29 (2001): 686.

12. Rawls directly rejects that ideology critique has a legitimate role in public deliberation; see discussion later.

13. For a recent article that gives a good, systematic overview of the literature on ideology, see Tommie Shelby, "Ideology, Racism, and Critical Social Theory," *The Philosophical Forum* XXXIV (Summer 2003): 153–88. The best book on Habermas and ideology is, to my knowledge, Raymond Geuss, *The Idea of a Critical Theory* (Cambridge: Cambridge University Press, 1981). I have learned much from Geuss's excellent study and draw upon it later in my discussion of ideology.

14. Geuss notes that ideology critique and critical theory depend "crucially on a theory of freedom and coercion." See *The Idea of a Critical Theory*, 78.

15. Ibid., 83.

16. Karl Marx, *Capital Vol. 1*, trans. Ben Fowkes (Harmondsworth, UK: Penguin, 1990); see Part I, chap. 1, for the labor theory of value and Part III on surplus value and exploitation.

17. Sheldon S. Wolin, *Politics and Vision: Continuity and Innovation in Western Political Thought*, expanded ed. (Princeton, NJ: Princeton University Press, 2004), 418.

18. Shelby, "Ideology, Racism, and Critical Social Theory," 177. On reification, see also Jürgen Habermas, *The Theory of Communicative Action*, vol. II, trans. T. McCarthy (Cambridge, UK: Polity Press, 1987), 355.

19. See Jürgen Habermas, "Technology and Science as 'Ideology,' " in his *Toward a Rational Society*, 81–122 (Boston: Beacon Press, 1970), and *Knowledge and Human Interests* (Boston: Beacon Press, 1971), 303.

20. Habermas, "Technology and Science as 'Ideology,' " 112.

21. Ibid., 105.

22. Geuss, *The Idea of a Critical Theory*, 78.

23. Geuss, ibid., 12, gives such a definition of ideology as a form of consciousness. Bohman rejects that ideology is "false consciousness"; it is, rather, "the result of asymmetric communication"; see " 'When Water Chokes,' " 385. But to say what something is the *result* of is not to give an alternative to what it is. And, as Shelby notes, "Ideologies cannot have their peculiar and profound social impact without being received into the consciousness of human beings." See "Ideology, Racism, and Critical Social Theory," 157. Habermas also sees (saw?) ideology as a form of consciousness, "technocratic consciousness." See "Technology and Science as 'Ideology,' " 107.

24. In her empirical study of town meeting government in "Selby," Jane Mansbridge found "the absence of legal barriers leads most Selby citizens to look on participation or nonparticipation as only a matter of choice. Many townspeople believe, for instance, that holding town office depends primarily on one's willingness to take the job." See *Beyond Adversary Democracy* (Chicago: University of Chicago Press, 1983), 115. Here, of course, there might be a certain freedom ideology at play. Everyone can run for office, so what is there to complain about?

25. Robert A. Dahl, "The Concept of Power," *Behavioral Science* 2:3 (1957): 202–203.

26. Steven Lukes, *Power: A Radical View* (Houndsmills, UK: Macmillan, 1974), 23.

27. Lukes, *Power: A Radical View*, 23.

28. According to Berlin, "[T]he fundamental sense of freedom is freedom from chains, from imprisonment, from enslavement by others." See "Introduction," in his *Four Essays on Liberty*, lvi (Oxford: Oxford University Press, 1969).

29. Geuss, *The Idea of a Critical Theory*, 60; see also 58, 74.

30. John Rawls, "The Domain of the Political and Overlapping Consensus," in *Collected Papers*, ed. S. Freeman, 478 (Cambridge, MA: Harvard University Press, 1999).

31. Jack Knight and James Johnson, "What Sort of Equality Does Deliberative Democracy Require?," in *Deliberative Democracy: Essays on Reason and Politics*, ed. J. Bohman & W. Rehg, 284 (Cambridge, MA: MIT Press, 1997).

32. Michael Rosen, "*On Voluntary Servitude* and the Theory of Ideology," *Constellations* 7 (2000): 393.

33. Shelby lists features that distinguish ideological beliefs from other beliefs in "Ideology, Racism, and Critical Social Theory," 158ff.

34. For a recent discussion of this position, see Bohman, " 'When Water Chokes,' " esp. 383–84.

35. Shelby, "Ideology, Racism, and Critical Social Theory," 187–88.

36. Whether or to what extent such a separation can be upheld, I discuss in the first section in Chapter 6.

37. Rainer Forst, "Justice, Reason, and Critique: Basic Concepts of Critical Theory," in *The Handbook of Critical Theory*, ed. D. Rasmussen, 158 (Oxford: Blackwell, 1996).

38. See, esp., Habermas, *The Theory of Communicative Action II*, 343ff., 350, 355, 367ff.

39. In metaphorical language, "The imperatives of autonomous subsystems make their way into the lifeworld from the outside—like colonial masters coming into a tribal society—and force a process of assimilation upon it." See Habermas, *The Theory of Communicative Action II*, 355.

40. For an alternative account that connects a concern with bureaucratic domination to deliberative democracy, see Henry S. Richardson, *Democratic Autonomy: Public Reasoning about the Ends of Policy* (New York: Oxford University Press, 2002).

41. Habermas, *The Theory of Communicative Action II*, 325.

42. Ibid., 350.

43. Ibid., 355.

44. Ibid., 356.

45. See Herbert Marcuse, *One-Dimensional Man: Studies in the Ideology of Advanced Industrial Society* (Boston: Beacon Press, 1964).

46. Jürgen Habermas, "Dogmatism, Reason, and Decision: On Theory and Praxis in Our Scientific Civilization," in *Theory and Practice*, trans. J. Viertel (Boston: Beacon Press, 1973), 265.

47. Habermas, *The Theory of Communicative Action II*, 367; *Between Facts and Norms*, 416.

48. Habermas, "Technology and Science as "Ideology," " 111, 113; see also *The Theory of Communicative Action II*, 352.

49. Habermas, *The Theory of Communicative Action II*, 350, 343ff., 367ff., 325; *Between Facts and Norms*, chap. 9.

50. See, e.g., Ian Shapiro; also see Chapter 1.

51. Excepted from this criticism is Joshua Cohen and Charles Sabel, "Directly-Deliberative Polyarchy," *European Law Journal* 3:4 (1997): 313–42.

52. Habermas, *The Theory of Communicative Action II*, 323ff.

53. On the charge that Habermas has left the issue of meaning behind and that his acceptance of the liberal idea of the priority of the right over the good leads to a "joyless reformism," see Andreas Kalyvas, "The Politics of Autonomy and the Challenge of Deliberation: Castoriadis Contra Habermas," *Thesis Eleven* 64 (2001): 14–15; Joel Whitebook, *Perversion and Utopia: A Study in Psychoanalysis and Critical Theory* (Cambridge, MA: MIT Press, 1995), 84, 89, 214–15.

54. Cf. Geuss, *The Idea of a Critical Theory*, 13ff., 26ff. I leave out here Geuss's third possibility, functional properties.

55. On the "genetic fallacy," see ibid., 20.

56. Ibid., 69.

57. Bohman, " 'When Water Chokes,' " 385.

58. Habermas, *Legitimation Crisis*, trans. T. McCarthy (Boston: Beacon Press, 1975), 113.

59. For a good discussion of the issue of hypothetical versus actual deliberation and its relationship to the charge of authoritarianism against Habermasian discourse ethics/deliberative democracy, see Cohen and Arato, *Civil Society and Political Theory*, 360ff.

60. Geuss lists three kinds of statements about self-reflection that can be found in Habermas's writings: "1. Self-reflection 'dissolves' a) 'self-generated objectivity,' and b) 'objective illusion.' 2. Self reflection makes the subject aware of its genesis or origin. 3. Self-reflection operates by bringing to consciousness unconscious determinants of action, or consciousness." See *The Idea of a Critical Theory*, 61, notes omitted.

61. James Bohman, "Habermas, Marxism and Social Theory: The Case for Pluralism in Critical Social Science," in *Habermas: A Critical Reader*, ed. P. Dews, 80 (Oxford: Blackwell, 1999).

62. In *Knowledge and Human Interest* (310), Habermas describes self-reflection as an "emancipatory cognitive interest," which "releases the subject from dependence on hypostatized powers."

63. Cf. Geuss, *The Idea of a Critical Theory*, 73.

64. Habermas, *Legitimation Crisis*, 112–13.

65. Bohman, " 'When Water Chokes,' " 387.

66. See the first section in Chapter 1.

67. Thomas McCarthy, *The Critical Theory of Jürgen Habermas* (Cambridge, MA: MIT Press, 1978), 182–83; James Bohman, "Emancipation and Rhetoric: The Perlocutions and Illocutions of the Social Critic," *Philosophy and Rhetoric* 21 (1988): 192; Jay Bernstein, "Habermas," in *Conceptions of Liberty in Political Philosophy*, ed. Z. Pelczynski and J. Gray, 409ff. (New York: St. Martin's Press, 1984). See also my "The Different Roles of the Idea of Democratic Deliberation" (typescript, University of Copenhagen, 2007).

68. See Iris Young, *Inclusion and Democracy* (Oxford: Oxford University Press, 2000), 119, who argues that inclusive deliberation does not necessarily make agreement easier, but that it can show that we were mistaken about something we thought to be a common interest. Nancy Fraser makes a similar argument. See "Rethinking the Public Sphere: A Contribution to the Critique of Actually Existing Democracy," in *Habermas and the Public Sphere*, ed. C. Calhoun, 130 (Cambridge, MA: MIT Press, 1992).

69. Habermas, " 'Reasonable' versus 'True,' " 97.

70. In their 1995 discussion, Habermas raised the question of whose theory is most modest, Rawls or his own. See "Reconciliation through the Public Use of Reason," in *The Inclusion of the Other: Studies in Political Theory*, ed. C. Cronin and P. De Greiff, 72–73 (Cambridge, MA: MIT Press, 1998).

71. John Rawls, *Political Liberalism* (New York: Columbia University Press, 1993), 269.

72. Rawls, *Political Liberalism*, 5–6, 327.

73. Simone Chambers, "The Politics of Equality: Rawls on the Barricades," *Perspectives on Politics* 4 (March 2006): 87.

74. See Habermas, " 'Reasonable' versus 'True,' " 95.

Chapter 6

1. For this definition of perfectionism, I draw on Will Kymlicka, *Contemporary Political Philosophy: An Introduction* (Oxford: Clarendon Press, 1990), 186–87.

2. In his discourse ethics, Habermas emphasizes the openness to "any assertion whatever" and to the expression of "attitudes, desires, and needs." See

"Discourse Ethics: Notes on a Program of Philosophical Justification," in *Moral Consciousness and Communicative Action*, trans. C. Lenhardt and S. Weber Nicholsen, 89 (Cambridge: Polity Press, 1990).

3. As William Rehg notes, "Moral discourses would seem to depend on the results of ethical discourses in which participants get clear about their needs and interests." See his *Insight and Solidarity: A Study in the Discourse Ethics of Jürgen Habermas* (Berkeley: University of California Press, 1994), 55.

4. Habermas, *Between Facts and Norms*, trans. W. Rehg (Cambridge, UK: Polity Press, 1996), 153, passim.

5. Thomas McCarthy, "Legitimacy and Diversity: Dialectical Reflections on Analytic Distinctions," in *Habermas on Law and Democracy: Critical Exchanges*, ed. M. Rosenfeld and A. Arato, 127 (Berkeley: University of California Press, 1998).

6. "[S]ince for Habermas questions of justice have to be posed in terms of what is equally *good* for all, value disagreements will often translate into disagreement about what is right or just." In other words, because of the fact of pluralism, there may be conflicts about "what is 'really' in the general interest of all." See McCarthy, "Legitimacy and Diversity," 120, 150.

7. Habermas, "Reply to Symposium Participants, Benjamin N. Cardozo School of Law," in *Habermas on Law and Democracy: Critical Exchanges*, ed. M. Rosenfeld and A. Arato, 393, emphasis in original (Berkeley: University of California Press, 1998).

8. Jürgen Habermas, "Struggles for Recognition in the Democratic Constitutional State," in *Multiculturalism*, ed. A. Gutmann, 116 (Princeton, NJ: Princeton University Press, 1994).

9. Ethical-political discourses require conditions of systematically undistorted communication; see Habermas, *Between Facts and Norms*, 182. This has been a consistent concern for Habermas over the years. According to Thomas McCarthy, in (the early) Habermas "[a]utonomy requires . . . not the suppression of inclinations but their 'insertion' into, or 'formation' through, nondistorted communication." See McCarthy, *The Critical Theory of Jürgen Habermas*, 328; cf. Habermas, *Legitimation Crisis*, trans. T. McCarthy (Boston: Beacon Press, 1975), 89. In the "Discourse Ethics" (67–68), Habermas says, "The descriptive terms in which each individual perceives his interests must be open to criticism by others. Needs and wants are interpreted in the light of cultural values. Since cultural values are always components of intersubjectively shared traditions, the revision of the values used to interpret needs and wants cannot be a matter for individuals to handle monologically."

10. Habermas, *Between Facts and Norms*, 309.

11. For the difference between internal autonomy and personal autonomy, see Chapter 8.

12. Nancy Fraser, "Talking about Needs: Interpretive Contests as Political Conflicts in Welfare-State Societies," *Ethics* 99 (1989): 299.

13. Rostbøll, *Human Rights, Public Sovereignty, and Freedom* (Copenhagen: Copenhagen Political Studies Press), 59.

14. On the last points, see Pablo D. Gilabert, "The Substantive Dimension of Deliberative Practical Rationality," *Philosophy & Social Criticism* 31:2 (2005): 185–210, and "A Substantivist Construal of Discourse Ethics," *International Journal of Philosophical Studies* 13:3 (2005): 405–37.

15. Jean L. Cohen, "Democracy, Difference, and the Right to Privacy," in *Democracy and Difference: Contesting the Boundaries of the Political*, ed. S. Benhabib, 202, 203 (Princeton, NJ: Princeton University Press, 1996).

16. J. Donald Moon, *Constructing Community: Moral Pluralism and Tragic Conflicts* (Princeton, NJ: Princeton University Press, 1993), 94.

17. Moon, *Constructing Community*, 91.

18. Habermas, *Between Facts and Norms*, 313.

19. Alexis de Tocqueville, *Democracy in America*, trans. G. Lawrence, ed. J. P. Mayer (New York: HarperPerennial, 1969), 255.

20. John Stuart Mill, "On Liberty," in *On Liberty and Other Writings* (Cambridge: Cambridge University Press, 1989), 8.

21. Ibid., 15.

22. Ibid., 76.

23. Ibid., 77.

24. See Seyla Benhabib, *Claims of Culture: Equality and Diversity in the Global Era* (Princeton, NJ: Princeton University Press, 2002), 120–21, and "Models of the Public Sphere: Hannah Arendt, the Liberal Tradition, and Jürgen Habermas," in *Habermas and the Public Sphere,* ed. C. Calhoun, 84 (Cambridge, MA: MIT Press, 1992); Nancy Fraser, "Rethinking the Public Sphere: A Contribution to the Critique of Actually Existing Democracy," in *Habermas and the Public Sphere*, ed. C. Calhoun, 128ff., 131ff. (Cambridge, MA: MIT Press, 1992), and "Talking about Needs," 298ff.; Habermas, *Between Facts and Norms*, 396ff.

25. For a discussion of the effect of TV talk shows on the public and private divide, see Joshua Gamson, "Taking the Talk Show Challenge: Television, Emotion, and Public Spheres," *Constellations* 6 (1999): 190–205.

26. Herbert Marcuse, *One-Dimensional Man: Studies in the Ideology of Advanced Industrial Society* (Boston: Beacon Press, 1964), 10, 244, emphasis in original.

27. Ibid., 10.

28. Pamela Johnston Conover, Donald D. Searing, and Ivor M. Crewe, "The Deliberative Potential of Political Discussion," *British Journal of Political Science* 32 (2002): 55. I thank Don Moon for referring me to this article.

29. Richard Bernstein, "The Retrieval of the Democratic Ethos," in *Habermas on Law and Democracy: Critical Exchanges*, ed. M. Rosenfeld and A. Arato, 291, emphasis in original (Berkeley: University of California Press, 1998).

30. Habermas, "Reply," 384, emphasis in original. Habermas had earlier, in *Between Facts and Norms*, 302, acknowledged that "deliberative politics is internally connected with contexts of a rationalized lifeworld that meets it halfway."

31. Habermas, *Between Facts and Norms*, 298.

32. Habermas, "Reply," 385.

33. Ibid., 386.

34. Jürgen Habermas, "Three Normative Models of Democracy," in *The Inclusion of the Other*, ed. C. Cronin and P. De Greiff, 244, emphasis added (Cambridge, MA: MIT Press, 1998).

35. Cf. Charles Taylor, "What's Wrong with Negative Liberty," in his *Philosophy and the Human Sciences: Philosophical Papers 2*, 213 (Cambridge: Cambridge University Press, 1985).

36. Habermas, *Between Facts and Norms*, 119, emphases added.

37. I agree with Arne Johan Vetlesen, that Habermas's conception of deliberative democracy is quite demanding of citizens. He also is right to say that "Habermas' presuppositions are of an altogether non-Aristotelian kind; they do not form part of a virtue ethics; and Habermas is unwilling to grant participation in politics a prime importance for the self-realization of individuals." See "Hannah Arendt, Habermas, and the Republican Tradition," *Philosophy & Social Criticism* 21:3 (1995): 11. The last point shows that deliberative freedom has nothing to do with freedom as self-realization.

38. Immanuel Kant, "An Answer to the Question: What Is Enlightenment?," in *Perpetual Peace and Other Essays on Politics, History, and Morals*, trans. T. Humphrey (Indianapolis, IN: Hackett, 1983), 33.

39. Hannah Arendt, *The Human Condition*, 2nd ed. (Chicago: University of Chicago Press, 1998), 186.

40. Tocqueville, *Democracy in America*, 186, emphases added.

41. Ibid., 254–55.

42. Conover, Searing, and Crewe, "The Deliberative Potential of Political Discussion," 54, 58.

43. Cf. Charles Larmore, "The Foundation of Modern Democracy: Reflections on Jürgen Habermas," *European Journal of Philosophy* 3:1 (1995): 59ff.

44. Jürgen Habermas, "On the Internal Relationship between the Rule Law and Democracy," in *The Inclusion of the Other*, 261.

45. Habermas, *Between Facts and Norms*, 130, emphasis in original.

46. Ibid., 131.

47. Conover, Searing, and Crewe, "The Deliberative Potential of Political Discussion," 60.

48. The relationship between democracy and education is, of course, a difficult and much debated one. Unfortunately, I am not able to go into that discussion. For a defense of civic education from a deliberative democratic point of view, see Gutmann and Thompson, *Democracy and Disagreement* (Cambridge, MA: Belknap Press of Harvard University Press, 1996), 63ff. For a criticism of Gutmann's and Thompson's view, see William A. Galston, "Diversity, Toleration, and Deliberative Democracy: *Religious Minorities and Public Schooling*," in *Deliberative*

Politics: Essays on Democracy and Disagreement, ed. S. Macedo, 44ff. (New York: Oxford University Press, 1999). See also Galston's argument in favor of giving more authority to parents in matters of education and of exempting minorities for parts of the curriculum on religious grounds, in *Liberal Pluralism: The Implications of Value Pluralism for Political Theory and Practice* (Cambridge: Cambridge University Press, 2002), chap. 8.

49. According to Habermas, bargaining must necessarily also be part of the political process, but its rules must be justified in a process of argumentation; see *Between Fact and Norms*, 151ff. Similarly, I see argumentation as the fundamental, but not the only, form of deliberation. See also Chapter 3, the section "Can Deliberation Be Paternalistic?"

50. Jürgen Habermas, *The Theory of Communicative Action*, vol. I, trans. T. McCarthy (Cambridge: Polity Press, 1984), 24.

51. Habermas, *The Theory of Communicative Action II*, 486.

52. Habermas, "Discourse Ethics," 58.

53. Immanuel Kant, *The Critique of Judgment*, trans. J. C. Meredith (Oxford: Clarendon Press, 1952), part I, p. 152. See also Klaus Günther, "Communicative Freedom, Communicative Power, and Jurisgenesis," in *Habermas on Law and Democracy: Critical Exchanges*, ed. M. Rosenfeld and A. Arato, 237, n16 (Berkeley: University of California Press, 1998).

54. Joseph Raz identifies independence as freedom from coercion and manipulation by others. Coercion limits options, while manipulation perverts preference formation. See *The Morality of Freedom* (Oxford: Clarendon Press, 1986), 372–73, 377–78. Looking at independence this way, I agree that freedom requires independence. But Raz is identifying only one form of independence, while I argue that not all forms of independence are required for deliberative freedom.

55. For a description and critique of this view, see Christine Swanton, *Freedom: A Coherence Theory* (Indianapolis, IN: Hackett, 1992), 124.

56. Similarly, Nadia Urbinati notes that J. S. Mill "realized that a discursive approach to politics demands a kind of liberty whose foundation is interaction and cooperation without necessarily excluding interference." See *Mill on Democracy: From the Athenian Polis to Representative Government* (Chicago: University of Chicago Press, 2002), 1.

57. On procedural independence, see Gerald Dworkin, *The Theory and Practice of Autonomy*, (Cambridge: Cambridge University Press, 1988), 18–19; Lawrence Haworth, *Autonomy: An Essay in Philosophical Psychology and Ethics* (New Haven, CT: Yale University Press, 1986), 20–21; Bernard Berofsky, *Liberation from Self: A Theory of Personal Autonomy* (Cambridge: Cambridge University Press, 1995), 111, 122ff.

58. Dworkin, *The Theory and Practice of Autonomy*, 18.

59. Ibid.

60. Bohman, *Public Deliberation*, 27; cf. Gutmann and Thompson, *Democracy and Disagreement*, 58.

61. Cf. Bohman, *Public Deliberation*, 55–56.

62. Berofsky, *Liberation from Self*, 111.

63. "The concept of communicative freedom . . . refers to one of the most obvious aspects of 'freedom': the possibility to say 'no'." See Günther, "Communicative Freedom, Communicative Power, and Jurisgenesis," 236–37.

64. On the last point, see Albrecht Wellmer, "Models of Freedom in the Modern World," *The Philosophical Forum* 21:1–2 (Fall–Winter 1989–1990): 241.

65. According to Thomas Hobbes, liberty of subjects lies in the silence of the laws. See *Leviathan* (Oxford: Oxford University Press, 1996), 141, 146. Isaiah Berlin agrees. See "Two Concepts of Liberty," in his *Four Essays on Liberty*, 148 (Oxford: Oxford University Press, 1969).

66. John Christman distinguishes the psychological condition of autonomy and autonomy as right. He argues that autonomy as right is a right against actions that undercut, or do not respect one's capacity for autonomy. See John Christman, "Introduction," in *The Inner Citadel: Essays on Individual Autonomy*, ed. J. Christman, 5–6 (New York: Oxford University Press, 1989).

67. For a philosophical discussion of how bypassing persons' "capacities for control over their mental lives" limits their freedom, see Alfred R. Mele, *Autonomous Agents: From Self-Control to Autonomy* (New York: Oxford University Press, 1995), 166–67.

68. Habermas, *The Theory of Communicative Action II*, 183.

69. Bohman, " 'When Water Chokes'," 386.

70. See, e.g., John S. Dryzek, *Deliberative Democracy and Beyond: Liberals, Critics, Contestations* (Oxford: Oxford University Press, 2000), 2.

71. Benjamin R. Barber, *Superman and Common Men: Freedom, Anarchy, and the Revolution* (New York: Praeger, 1971), 67.

72. See Jay Bernstein, "Habermas," 397; Bohman, *Public Deliberation*, chap. 5.

73. See Simone Chambers, *Reasonable Democracy* (Ithaca, NY: Cornell University Press, 1996), 7.

74. Philosophers sometimes distinguish advice, as something that is directed toward a person's rational faculties, on the one hand, and persuasion, manipulation, indoctrination, and so on as forms of influence that bypass a person's reason, on the other hand; see R. M. Hare, "Freedom of the Will," in his *Essays on the Moral Concepts*, 2ff. (Berkeley: University of California Press, 1973), and Swanton, *Freedom*, 125ff. According to Robert P. Wolff, the autonomous person "may listen to the advice of others, but he makes it his own by determining for himself whether it is good advice." See *In Defense of Anarchism* (Berkeley: University of California Press, 1998), 13.

75. I return to this point in Chapter 7, the section "Diversity and Tolerance."

76. For an argument concerning "empirical possibility" of a concept of autonomy, see Gerald Dworkin, "The Nature of Autonomy," in his *The Theory and Practice of Autonomy*, 7–8 (Cambridge: Cambridge University Press, 1988).

77. "If realizing our freedom partly depends on the society in which we live, then we exercise a fuller freedom if we can help determine the shape of this society and culture." See Charles Taylor, "Atomism," in *Philosophy and the Human Sciences: Philosophical Papers 2*, 208 (Cambridge: Cambridge University Press, 1985).

78. Taylor, "What's Wrong with Negative Liberty," 213.

Chapter 7

1. For an objection to deliberative democracy along these lines, see Lynn M. Sanders, "Against Deliberation," *Political Theory* 25:3 (June 1997): 347–76.

2. See Andrew Sabl, *Ruling Passions: Political Offices and Democratic Ethics* (Princeton, NJ: Princeton University Press, 2002), 310–11.

3. James Bohman, "Deliberative Democracy and Effective Social Freedom: Capabilities, Resources, and Opportunities," in *Deliberative Democracy: Essays on Reason and Politics*, ed. J. Bohman and W. Rehg, 334 (Cambridge, MA: MIT Press, 1997).

4. Bohman, "Deliberative Democracy and Effective Social Freedom," 335.

5. One source of this unfortunate dichotomy seems to be Habermas's categorical distinction between communicative action (where the participants are solely concerned with reaching understanding) and strategic action (where they are oriented toward obtaining an end). See *The Theory of Communicative Action*, vol. I, trans. T. McCarthy (Cambridge, UK: Polity Press, 1984), 85–86, 294–95. Bohman has himself earlier criticized this distinction as being untenable. See "Emancipation and Rhetoric: The Perlocutions and Illocutions of the Social Critic," *Philosophy and Rhetoric* 21 (1988): 185–204.

6. I find Gutmann and Thompson's use of the term *impartiality* somewhat unfortunate and at odds with its ordinary use, but that need not concern us here. For an understanding of impartiality that is close to what Gutmann and Thompson call "reciprocity," see Brian Barry, *Justice as Impartiality* (Oxford: Oxford University Press, 1995).

7. Gutmann and Thompson, *Democracy and Disagreement* (Cambridge, MA: Belknap Press of Harvard University Press, 1996), 52ff.

8. Cf. Habermas, *Between Facts and Norms,* trans. W. Rehg (Cambridge: Polity Press, 1996), 119.

9. Habermas, *Between Facts and Norms*, 153; "Three Normative Models of Democracy," in *The Inclusion of the Other*, ed. C. Cronin and P. De Greiff, 243 (Cambridge, MA: MIT Press, 1998).

10. Knight and Johnson, "What Sort of Equality Does Deliberative Democracy Require?," in *Deliberative Democracy: Essays on Reason and Politics*, ed. J. Bohman and W. Rehg, 290, emphasis in original (Cambridge, MA: MIT Press, 1997).

11. See Nancy Fraser, "Rethinking the Public Sphere: A Contribution to the Critique of Actually Existing Democracy," in *Habermas and the Public Sphere*, ed. C. Calhoun, 130 (Cambridge, MA: MIT Press, 1992); Thomas McCarthy, *The Critical Theory of Jürgen Habermas* (Cambridge, MA: MIT Press, 1978), 327–28; Habermas, *Legitimation Crisis*, trans. T. McCarthy (Boston: Beacon Press, 1975), 89.

12. Habermas, "Three Normative Models of Democracy," *Constellations* 1:1 (1994): 5, emphasis in original.

13. Cf. Jürgen Habermas, "Struggles for Recognition in the Democratic Constitutional State," in *Multiculturalism*, ed. A. Gutmann, 116 (Princeton, NJ: Princeton University Press, 1994); Young, *Inclusion and Democracy*, 16–17, 29–30, 35–36.

14. Barry, *Justice as Impartiality*, 77.

15. Cohen, "Deliberation and Democratic Legitimacy," 75.

16. Cf. Habermas, "Three Normative Models," 6.

17. Nadia Urbinati divides deliberative democrats into two camps, the rational consensus model and the agonistic model. The latter is concerned more with process than with outcome. See "Representation as Advocacy: A Study of Democratic Deliberation," *Political Theory* 28:6 (December 2000): 773–74. It is true that there are different views among deliberative democrats regarding the emphasis on either process or outcomes, but I think they all share a belief that deliberation tends to improve political outcomes. The epistemic and instrumental value of deliberation also is accepted by those proponents of deliberative democracy who see themselves as less rationalistic. See, e.g., Bernard Manin, "On Legitimacy and Political Deliberation," *Political Theory* 15 (1987): 363; Iris M. Young, *Inclusion and Democracy* (Oxford: Oxford University Press, 2000), 16–17, 29–30, 35–36.

18. I write "tendency" because deliberative democrats do not believe deliberative procedures infallibly lead to true and therefore uncriticizable outcomes.

19. Bohman, *Public Deliberation*, 26–27; David Estlund, "Beyond Fairness and Deliberation: The Epistemic Dimension of Democratic Authority," in *Deliberative Democracy: Essays on Reason and Politics*, ed. J. Bohman and W. Rehg, 173–204 (Cambridge, MA: MIT Press, 1997); Joshua Cohen, "An Epistemic Conception of Democracy," *Ethics* 97:1 (1986): 26–38. Manin sees as the end of deliberation not the rational but the reasonable and the justifiable. See "On Legitimacy and Political Deliberation," 363.

20. The formulation "what the will of the people is" is perhaps not the most appropriate insofar as some deliberative democrats reject that we can speak

of the will of the people; cf. Manin, "On Legitimacy and Political Deliberation," 352.

21. Jane Mansbridge, "Everyday Talk in the Deliberative System," in *Deliberative Politics: Essays on* Democracy and Disagreement, ed. S. Macedo, 211 (New
York: Oxford University Press, 1999). I will disregard here Mansbridge's main
point in this article, that a full deliberative system must involve what she calls
everyday talk and not just deliberation.

22. See, e.g., Anne Phillips, *The Politics of Presence* (Oxford: Clarendon
Press, 1995), 145ff.; Iris Young, *Justice and the Politics of Difference* (Princeton, NJ:
Princeton University Press, 1990), 106–107. (Young is not criticizing delibera-
tive democracy as such here, but one of its proponents, Habermas; see Young,
Inclusion and Democracy, 42ff.)

23. Phillips, *The Politics of Presence*, 151, emphasis in original; cf. Young,
Inclusion and Democracy, 112ff.

24. Young, *Inclusion and Democracy*, 76–77, 112ff.

25. On deliberation as a means of gathering information about people's
needs, interests, and opinions, see James D. Fearon, "Deliberation as Discussion," in
Deliberative Democracy, ed. J. Elster, 45ff. (Cambridge: Cambridge University Press,
1998); Diego Gambetta, " 'Claro!': An Essay on Discursive Machismo," in *Deliberative
Democracy*, ed. J. Elster, 22; Roberto Gargarella, "Full Representation, Deliberation,
and Impartiality," in *Deliberative Democracy* ed. J. Elster, 261; Seyla Benhabib, "Toward
a Deliberative Model of Democratic Legitimacy," in *Democracy and Difference: Contesting the Boundaries of the Political*, ed. S. Benhabib, 71 (Princeton, NJ: Princeton
University Press, 1996); Manin, "On Legitimacy and Political Deliberation."

26. Cf. Gutmann and Thompson, *Democracy and Disagreement*, 48.

27. "[T]he discovery that I can offer no persuasive reason on behalf of a
proposal of mine may transform the preferences that motivate the proposal." See
Joshua Cohen, "Deliberation and Democratic Legitimacy," in *Deliberative Democracy: Essays on Reason and Politics,* ed. J. Bohman and W. Rehg, 77 (Cambridge,
MA: MIT Press, 1997).

28. The division into objective world, social world, and subjective world
is taken from Habermas. For his definition of these three worlds, see *The Theory
of Communicative Action* I, 52.

29. On self-knowledge as required for autonomy, see Richard Double, *The
Non-reality of Free Will* (New York: Oxford University Press, 1991), 39ff.

30. Double, *The Non-reality of Free Will,* 40.

31. This section draws on Jon Elster, "Deliberation and Constitution Making," in *Deliberative Democracy*, ed. J. Elster, 100–101 (Cambridge: Cambridge
University Press), and Adam Przeworski, "Deliberation and Ideological Domination," in ibid., 142ff. They both argue that policy preferences are derived from
values and beliefs. Elster also shows that even if people share values, they might
not have the same policy preferences because they do not share beliefs about
how to meet their values.

32. Mill, "Considerations on Representative Government," in *Utilitarianism, On Liberty, Considerations on Representative Government* (London: Everyman, 1993), chap. 3.

33. Ibid., 218.

34. Ibid., 225.

35. Robert Gargarella argues that "decisions are often 'partial' because of ignorance concerning the actual interests and preferences of others," and that deliberation, therefore, may help impartiality. See "Full Representation, Deliberation, and Impartiality," 261.

36. I am grateful to Andreas Kalyvas for provoking me to consider this issue.

37. "Letter to Langriche," quoted in Pitkin, *The Concept of Representation*, 173.

38. Sanders, "Against Deliberation," 357ff.

39. Jon Elster, "Introduction," in *Deliberative Democracy*, ed. Jon Elster, 3 (Cambridge: Cambridge University Press, 1998). Burke advanced more than one concept of representation, as Hanna Pitkin has pointed out, virtual representation being only one of them; see *The Concept of Representation* (Berkeley: University of California Press, 1967), chap. 8. Elster's reference is to a different view of representation in Burke, but one that is no less elitist.

40. See Diego Gambetta, " 'Claro!': An Essay on Discursive Machismo," 22; James D. Fearon, "Deliberation as Discussion," 45ff.

41. The following discussion is indebted to Jean Cohen and Andrew Arato, *Civil Society and Political Theory* (Cambridge, MA: MIT Press, 1992), and Jürgen Habermas, *Between Facts and Norms*, chaps. 7 and 8.

42. Habermas, *Between Facts and Norms*, 307. Of course, it could be said that not all deliberations in formal assemblies are oriented toward decisions; some are aimed at selling the decisions already made. In fact, today most deliberation aimed at decisions takes place behind closed doors, while the public deliberations in parliament are mere show. The latter form of deliberation is not really deliberation but corresponds to what Habermas calls "representative publicness," that is, acting "before" the people. See his *The Structural Transformation of the Public Sphere,* trans. T. Burger (Cambridge, MA: MIT Press, 1989), 5ff., 200. The first to make this point seems to have been Carl Schmitt. See his *The Crisis of Parliamentary Democracy* (Cambridge, MA: MIT Press, 1985). This point, however, does not affect my overall argument about the constraints on formal deliberations.

43. Elster is right to emphasize the importance of time constraints, but he fails to differentiate between the degree of importance of this constraint in formal or institutionalized deliberations and the deliberations in the informal public sphere; see "The Market and the Forum," 14.

44. Habermas, *Between Facts and Norms*, 356ff.

45. Ibid., 314.

46. Cf. Habermas, *The Structural Transformation of the Public Sphere*, 37.

47. Habermas, *Between Facts and Norms*, 307, emphasis in original.

48. Ibid., 359.

49. Cohen and Arato, *Civil Society and Political Theory*, esp. chap. 10.

50. Jürgen Habermas, "Popular Sovereignty as Procedure," 485, emphasis added.

51. Nancy Fraser rejects "a sharp separation between (associational) civil society and the state." See "Rethinking the Public Sphere," 136. James Bohman thinks "too strong a distinction between will-forming and opinion-forming institutions undermines any actual democratic sovereignty." See *Public Deliberation*, 185.

52. Habermas, *Between Facts and Norms*, 171, 362.

53. Isaiah Berlin fears that conceptions of freedom that are related to reason will lead to the repression of the irrational in name of rationality. This is his objection to Kant. See "Two Concepts of Liberty," in his *Four Essays on Liberty*, 152–53 (Oxford: Oxford University Press, 1969).

54. John Locke, *A Letter Concerning Toleration* (Indianapolis, IN: Hackett, 1983), 27.

55. Susan Neiman, *The Unity of Reason: Rereading Kant* (New York: Oxford University Press, 1994), 118.

56. For an excellent comparison of Kant and Habermas, see Pablo D. Gilabert, "Considerations on the Notion of Moral Validity in the Moral Theories of Kant and Habermas," *Kantstudien* 97 (June 2006): 210–27.

57. Berlin, "Two Concepts of Liberty," 153.

58. Habermas, *Between Facts and Norms*, 107.

59. Simone Chambers, *Reasonable Democracy* (Ithaca, NY: Cornell University Press, 1996), 203. Habermas sometimes explicitly says that in deliberation (or discourse) there are only participants, and that no one has a privileged access to truth. But at other times, he does seem to give a privileged position to the critical social theorist and to see discourse in hypothetical terms, e.g., in *Legitimation Crisis*, 113. For a discussion of this tension in Habermas, see Cohen and Arato, *Civil Society and Political Theory*, 360ff.

60. For this distinction, see Immanuel Kant, *The Metaphysics of Morals*, trans. and ed. M. Gregor, 20 (Ak 6: 219) (Cambridge: Cambridge University Press, 1996).

61. Kant's universal law of right is a clear formulation of a negative view of freedom: "Let your external actions be such that the free application of your will can co-exist with the freedom of everyone in accordance with a universal law." See Immanuel Kant, "Metaphysics of Morals," in *Kant's Political Writings*, ed. H. Reis, 2d ed., 133 (Cambridge: Cambridge University Press, 1991).

62. For the point that to have moral worth an action must be done not only in accordance with duty but "from duty," see Immanuel Kant, *Grounding for*

the Metaphysics of Morals, trans. J. W. Ellington, 3rd ed. (Indianapolis, IN: Hackett, 1993), Ak. 397–99.

63. Kant, *Grounding,* Ak. 444.

64. Seyla Benhabib, *Situating the Self: Gender, Community, and Postmodernism in Contemporary Ethics* (New York: Routledge, 1992), 5.

65. Cf. Young, *Inclusion and Democracy*, 28–29; Thomas McCarthy, *The Critical Theory of Jürgen Habermas*, 327–28; Habermas, *Legitimation Crisis,* 89.

66. Deliberation includes and generates many other forms of knowledge too, such as knowledge about the objective world and about causal relationships, e.g., of consequences of alternative public policies (cf. Chapter 7, the section "Learning and the Epistemic Dimension of Public Deliberation"). To have these kinds of knowledge is an essential part of self-rule.

67. Jean-Jacques Rousseau, "On Thee Social Contract," in *The Basic Political Writings*, trans. D. A Cress (Indianapolis, IN: Hackett, 1987), bk. II, chap. 3, p. 155.

68. Ibid., bk. IV, chap. 2, p. 206.

69. Estlund, "Beyond Fairness and Deliberation," 183ff. Cf. Christian F. Rostbøll, "On Deliberative Democracy," *Sats: Nordic Journal of Philosophy* 2 (2001): 168–69.

70. Gutmann and Thompson, *Democracy and Disagreements*, 9; cf. 16, and *Why Deliberative Democracy?* (Princeton, NJ: Princeton University Press, 2004), chap. 3.

71. Bernard Manin, *The Principles of Representative Government* (Cambridge: Cambridge University Press, 1997), 174.

72. Manin, "On Legitimacy and Political Deliberation," 359; see also Manin, *Principles of Representative Government*, 190.

73. Tim Gray, *Freedom* (Houndmills: Macmillan, 1991), 46.

74. For this definition of manipulation, see Christine Swanton, *Freedom: A Coherence Theory* (Indianapolis, IN: Hackett, 1992), 125.

75. John Christman, "Introduction," in *The Inner Citadel: Essays on Individual Autonomy*, ed. J. Christman, 9, emphasis in original (New York: Oxford University Press, 1989).

76. For an argument about autonomy as history-bound, see Alfred R. Mele, *Autonomous Agents: From Self-Control to Autonomy* (New York: Oxford University Press, 1995), chap. 9. Mele connects manipulation and history at 145–46.

77. For a rejection that history and origins should matter for autonomy, see Bernard Berofsky, *Liberation from Self: A Theory of Personal Autonomy* (Cambridge: Cambridge University Press, 1995), 211ff. Politically, Berofsky's argument is a dangerous one—it can justify forcing others to be free.

78. I am here speaking of what deliberation ideally is. In actual deliberation, of course, there might be strategic uses of argument and manipulation. As theory, the aim of deliberative democracy should be to show the difference be-

tween manipulated speech and free deliberation; in practice, the way to overcome manipulation is through ongoing discussion and learning as well as dismantling the conditions that make it possible for some to manipulate others. See further Christian F. Rostbøll, "Dissent, Criticism, and Transformative Political Action in Deliberative Democracy," *CRISPP*, forthcoming.

79. As Andrew Knops argues, "Explicitness in language [is] the key emancipatory mechanism in deliberation." See "Delivering Deliberation's Emancipatory Potential," *Political Theory* 34 (October 2006): 595.

80. After criticizing theories of deliberative democracy for requiring too much unity, Young holds that her own model of communicative democracy implies much thinner conditions. The conditions that all must accept on Young's model are significant interdependence, commitment to equal respect for others as discussion partners, and procedural rules of fair discussion. See Iris M. Young, "Communication and the Other: Beyond Deliberative Democracy," in *Democracy and Difference: Contesting the Boundaries of the Political*, ed. S. Benhabib, 126–27 (Princeton, NJ: Princeton University Press, 1996). But clearly her conditions and her advocacy for egalitarian, participatory democracy would not be recognized by cultures that are neither egalitarian nor democratic.

81. "A principal tenet of that religion is that its adherents remain separate and apart from the modern world. This concept of separation emanates from Christian biblical directions to "be not conformed to this world" (see Romans 12:2); "Be ye not unequally yoked together with unbelievers" (see II Corinthians 6: 14); *Minnesota v. Hershberger* 444 N.W.2d. 282 (Minn. 1989), 284.

82. Will Kymlicka, *Multicultural Citizenship* (Oxford: Oxford University Press, 1995), 154.

83. Ibid.

84. William Galston, *Liberal Pluralism: The Implications of Value Pluralism for Political Theory and Practice* (Cambridge: Cambridge University Press, 2002), 20ff. Brian Barry says, "Neither of the above." See *Culture and Equality* (Cambridge, MA: Harvard University Press, 2001), 119.

85. Galston, *Liberal Pluralism*, 21

86. The fear that those who criticize autonomy liberalism have is that it, by positing autonomy as the fundamental value, promotes a particular version of the good life. This fear is to be found not only in a value pluralist such as Galston, but it also lies behind Rawls's opposition between political liberalism and comprehensive liberalism. See Galston, *Liberal Pluralism*, 21, and Rawls, *Political Liberalism* (New York: Columbia University Press, 1993), 11ff. See also Joshua Cohen, "Democracy and Liberty," in *Deliberative Democracy*, ed. J. Elster, 185–231 (Cambridge: Cambridge University Press, 1998). Galston, in contrast to Rawls and Cohen, sees liberalism as comprehensive; see *Liberal Pluralism*, chap. 4.

87. Galston, *Liberal Pluralism*, 120. The passage in *Democracy and Disagreement* is on 62–63.

88. William Galston, "Diversity, Toleration, and Deliberative Democracy: *Religious Minorities and Public Schooling*," in *Deliberative Politics: Essays on* Democracy and Disagreement, ed. S. Macedo, 40 (New York: Oxford University Press, 1999). On the importance of not being required to justify one being different, see Ira Katznelson, *Liberalism's Crooked Circle: Letter to Adam Michnik* (Princeton, NJ: Princeton University Press, 1996), 171ff.

89. See my "Impartiality, Deliberation, and Multiculturalism," paper delivered at the conference *What's the Culture in Multiculturalism? What's the Difference of Identities?*, organized by the Danish Network on Political Theory in collaboration with the Research Group on Cultural Encounters, University of Aarhus, Denmark, May 22–24, 2003, http://www.politicaltheory.dk/conference/res/papers/5202003144147Rostboll-%20Multi%20DK03%20-%20Impart%20delib.pdf, accessed 14 November 2007. Note here that negative liberties are only given regarding issues we regard as significant; cf. Charles Taylor, "What's Wrong with Negative Liberty," in his *Philosophy and the Human Sciences: Philosophical Papers 2* (Cambridge: Cambridge University Press, 1985), 217ff.

90. Galston, "Diversity, Toleration, and Deliberative Democracy," 44.

91. As Jeremy Waldron has pointed out, in deliberation an individual "cannot expect any special weight to be attached to his opinion simply because of its connection with his identity. His opinion will be responded to in civic debate on the basis of its content. Has he made a good argument? Are his facts right?," and so on. See "Cultural Identity and Civic Responsibility," manuscript 7, in *Waldron Reader*, for the class, "L8675: Multiculturalism," at Columbia University (Fall 1998), 82.

92. For an argument about privacy rights as a result of learning in public deliberation, see Jean Cohen, *Regulating Intimacy: A New Legal Paradigm* (Princeton, NJ: Princeton University Press, 2002), 53–54, 74–75.

93. Gutmann and Thompson, *Democracy and Disagreement*, 62–63.

94. Peter Jones, "Respecting Beliefs and Rebuking Rushdie," *British Journal of Political Science* 20 (October 1990): 429, emphasis in original.

95. Waldron, "Rushdie and Religion," in *Liberal Rights: Collected Papers 1981–91* (Cambridge: Cambridge University Press, 1993), 138.

96. Cohen, "Deliberation and Democratic Legitimacy," 81.

97. Ibid.

98. Sabl, *Ruling Passions*, 310–11.

99. Taylor, "What's Wrong with Negative Liberty," 213ff.

100. This value of deliberation is perhaps most clearly expressed in the early Habermas. In *Legitimation Crisis*, Habermas describes it as a requirement for forming a common interest without deception that it be formed in a practical discourse. The interest "is free of deception because even the interpretation of needs in which *each individual* must be able to recognize what he wants become the object of discursive will-formation" (108, emphasis in original). In *Structural*

Transformation, Habermas lists two requirements for an opinion to be public: (1) Consciously formed, (2) formed in discussion (221).

101. Bohman stresses that deliberation is an activity, and that this has consequences for how we should view equality and autonomy. See *Public Deliberation*, 250, n13.

102. The empirical study by Conover, Searing, and Crewe, cited in Chapter 6, also indicates that even though most people are adverse to having their views challenged, they are open to listening to others, to gaining information, and to understanding different perspectives; see Pamela Johnston Conover, Donald D. Searing, and Ivor M. Crewe, "The Deliberative Potential of Political Discussion," *British Journal of Political Science* 32 (2002): 52. From this they conclude, "Citizens are willing to learn from discussions so long as it feels as though they are *educating themselves*, but they do not want to be pushed by others to accept ideas that challenge them. Thus to facilitate more deliberative discussions, our schools must teach students that political discussion is a means for citizens to *educate one another*" (ibid., 60).

103. Habermas, " 'Reasonable' versus 'True,' or the Morality of Worldviews," in *The Inclusion of the Other*, ed. C. Cronin and P. De Greiff, 99, emphasis in original (Cambridge, MA: MIT Press, 1998).

Chapter 8

1. Cf. Gerald F. Gaus, "The Place of Autonomy within Liberalism," in *Autonomy and the Challenges to Liberalism: New Essays*, ed. J. Christman and J. Anderson, 273 (Cambridge: Cambridge University Press, 2005).

2. For Mill's ideal of autonomy, see "On Liberty," chap. 3. For his argument about the effects on character of political participation, see "Considerations on Representative Government," chap. 3; also see Carole Pateman, *Participation and Democratic Theory* (Cambridge: Cambridge University Press, 1970), 28ff.

3. This is Kant and some Kantians' view of moral autonomy. For a recent discussion, see Jeremy Waldron, "Moral Autonomy and Personal Autonomy," in *Autonomy and the Challenges to Liberalism: New Essays*, ed. J. Christman and J. Anderson, 307–29 (Cambridge: Cambridge University Press, 2005).

4. Gerald Dworkin emphasizes this second aspect of moral autonomy but also notes that living according to one's own moral principles can mean a number of different things. See his "Moral Autonomy," in *The Theory and Practice of Autonomy* (Cambridge: Cambridge University Press, 1988), 34–35.

5. Practical reason and morality are only part of the concern of public deliberation. Collective self-legislation cannot be reduced to a matter of collective moral autonomy insofar as positive law cannot be reduced to moral law.

6. John Christman argues that in the liberal tradition of Locke, Rousseau, and Kant, as well as in Rawls and Habermas, the authority of the state

"is a collective manifestation of their own autonomy." See his "Autonomy, Self-Knowledge, and Liberal Legitimacy," in *Autonomy and the Challenges to Liberalism: New Essays*, ed. J. Christman and J. Anderson, 341 (Cambridge: Cambridge University Press, 2005).

7. Berlin, "Two Concepts of Liberty," in his *Four Essays on Liberty*, 158 (Oxford: Oxford University Press, 1969).

8. As mentioned previously, Berlin confusingly sees positive freedom as referring to a number of different ideas. In one of its individual versions, positive freedom is a matter of holding off internal obstacles to freedom. Here I am concerned with the collective version of positive freedom.

9. Cf. Jürgen Habermas, *Between Facts and Norms: Contributions to a Discourse Theory of Law and Democracy*, trans. William Rehg (Cambridge, UK: Polity Press, 1996), secs. 7.3, 8.2.

10. John Christman has in a recent article noted that for Kantians, public deliberation itself, and not merely its results, is of moral significance. See "Autonomy, Self-Knowledge, and Liberal Legitimacy," 341–42, 349.

11. For the distinction between passive matter and active makers of political society, I am indebted to Charles R. Beitz, *Political Equality: An Essay in Democratic Theory* (Princeton, NJ: Princeton University Press, 1989), 97ff. Beitz uses this distinction to argue for a complex theory of political equality. I am indebted to Beitz also in my characterization of citizenship as complex.

12. I take the notion of "web of relationships" from Hannah Arendt but without following her exact use. See *The Human Condition*, 2nd ed. (Chicago: University of Chicago Press, 1998), 181ff.

13. On the relationship between deliberative democracy and social complexity, see James Bohman, *Public Deliberation: Pluralism, Complexity, and Democracy* (Cambridge, MA: MIT Press, 1996), 155ff.

14. For the distinction between an opportunity and an exercise concept of freedom, see the third section in Chapter 6.

15. On deliberative forums, see the third section in Chapter 8.

16. For the notion "real freedom," see Philippe Van Parijs, *Real Freedom for All: What (if Anything) Can Justify Capitalism?* (Oxford: Oxford University Press, 1995). The phrase, "the worth of freedom," is Rawls's; see Chapter 4 in this book.

17. This fear we find, of course, in Isaiah Berlin. A more recent and popular account of this fear can be found in Fareed Zakaria, *The Future of Freedom: Illiberal Democracy at Home and Abroad* (New York: Norton, 2003).

18. This is not meant as an argument against property rights but as opening up a possible argument against seeing any form of redistribution as a violation of individual freedom.

19. I do not claim that my conception of freedom and deliberation should be the *sole* normative basis of critique.

20. Cf. Gaus, "The Place of Autonomy within Liberalism," 298–99.

21. For a discussion of the "appropriate division of labor between theorist and citizenry," see Nancy Fraser, "Social Justice in the Age of Identity Politics: Redistribution, Recognition, and Participation," in Nancy Fraser and Axel Honneth, *Redistribution or Recognition? A Political-Philosophical Exchange* (London: Verso, 2003), 70ff.

22. Those who try to uphold an idea of negative freedom as the totality of freedom often positively affirm the status quo as a just or neutral baseline.

23. As Archon Fung recently put it: "Deliberative democracy is a revolutionary political ideal. . . . It has been thought to require dramatically more egalitarian political, social, and economic conditions than exist in contemporary society." See "Deliberation before the Revolution: Toward an Ethics of Deliberative Democracy in an Unjust World," *Political Theory* 33:3 (June 2005): 397–98.

24. Gianpaolo Baiocchi, "Participation, Activism, and Politics: The Porto Alegre Experiment," in *Deepening Democracy: Institutional Innovations in Empowered Participatory Governance*, ed. A. Fung and E. O. Wright, 52ff. (London: Verso, 2003); Archon Fung, "Deliberative Democracy, Chicago Style: Grass-roots Governance in Policing and Public Education," in *Deepening Democracy*, 111–43.

25. My argument about ideology in Chapter 5 is that economic conditions can have detrimental effects on freedom and deliberation, but I argue that changes in economic conditions must go hand in hand with practices of public deliberation.

26. I consider this issue in more detail in "Dissent, Criticism, and Transformative Political Action in Deliberative Democracy," *CRISPP*, forthcoming. See also the discussion in Fung, "Deliberation before the Revolution."

27. For an overview of experiments with deliberative forums, see Archon Fung and Erik Olin Wright, eds., *Deepening Democracy: Institutional Innovations in Empowered Participatory Governance* (London: Verso, 2003), and John Gastil and Peter Levine, eds. *The Deliberative Democracy Handbook: Strategies for Effective Civic Engagement in the 21st Century* (San Francisco: Jossey-Bass, 2005). See also the home pages of the Deliberative Democracy Consortium, http://www.deliberative-democracy.net, and of the National Coalition for Dialogue and Deliberation, http://www.thataway.org.

28. Fung, "Deliberative Democracy, Chicago Style," 132.

29. Arendt's concern is that the U.S. Constitution "had given all the power to the citizens, without giving them the opportunity of *being* republicans and of *acting* as citizens." See *On Revolution* (Harmondsworth, UK: Penguin Books, 1990), 253, emphasis in original.

30. See Joseph M. Bessette, *The Mild Voice of Reason: Deliberative Democracy and American National Government* (Chicago: University of Chicago Press, 1994); Jürg Steiner, André Bächtiger, Markus Spörndli, and Marco R. Steenbergen, *Deliberative Politics in Action: Analyzing Parliamentary Discourse* (New York: Cambridge

University Press, 2004); and my review of the latter in *Political Science Quarterly* 120:4 (Winter 2005–2006): 697–98.

31. Bessette, *The Mild Voice of Reason*, 1–2; see also 212ff.

32. See, for example, Jean Cohen and Andrew Arato, *Civil Society and Political Theory* (Cambridge, MA: MIT Press, 1992), esp. chaps. 1, 8–11; Habermas, *Between Facts and Norms*, chap. 8; Mark Warren, *Democracy and Association* (Princeton, NJ: Princeton University Press, 2001), chaps. 4, 6, and 7.

33. See *The Deliberative Democracy Handbook* for a discussion of these and other experiments. Joshua Cohen and Charles Sabel also find promising, from the perspective of deliberative democracy, the new democratic experiments that are neither public nor private. See "Directly-Deliberative Polyarchy," *European Law Journal* 3:4 (1997): 316.

34. For studies and discussions of these three experiments, see T. M. Thomas Isaac and Patrick Heller, "Democracy and Development: Decentralized Planning in Kerala," in *Deepening Democracy*, 77–110; Fung, "Deliberative Democracy, Chicago Style"; Baiocchi, "Participation, Activism, and Politics."

35. For a similar typology, see Mark Button and David Michael Ryfe, "What Can We Learn from the Practice of Deliberative Democracy?," in *The Deliberative Democracy Handbook*, 23ff.

36. Cohen and Sabel, "Directly-Deliberative Polyarchy," 337.

37. See Habermas, *Between Facts and Norms*, 363–64; Cohen and Arato, *Civil Society and Political Theory*, 486–87; Warren, *Democracy and Association*, 52.

38. On this, see Ned Crosby and Doug Nethercut, "Citizens Juries: Creating a Trustworthy Voice of the People," in *The Deliberative Democracy Handbook*, 114–15.

39. Carolyn J. Lukensmeyer, Joe Goldman, and Steven Brigham, "A Town Meeting for the Twenty-first Century," in *The Deliberative Democracy Handbook*, 157.

40. See also Archon Fung and Erik Olin Wright. "Thinking about Empowered Participatory Governance," in *Deepening Democracy*, 35.

41. For discussions and case studies of "deliberative governance," see the chapters in part 3 of *The Deliberative Democracy Handbook*.

42. As I have argued earlier, the different dimensions of freedom are not necessarily in harmony but must be balanced against each other.

43. Peter Levine, Archon Fung, and John Gastil, "Future Directions for Public Deliberation," in *The Deliberative Democracy Handbook*, 275.

44. This can be done by a national broadcast, they think. For a short, recent description of deliberative polling, see James Fishkin and Cynthia Farrar, "Deliberative Polling: From Experiment to Community Resource," in *The Deliberative Democracy Handbook*, 68–79. See also James S. Fishkin, *Democracy and Deliberation: New Directions for Democratic Reform* (New Haven, CT: Yale University Press, 1991).

Bibliography

Ackerman, Bruce. *We the People: Vol. I: Foundations.* Cambridge, MA: Belknap/ Harvard University Press, 1991.

Allison, Henry E. *Kant's Theory of Freedom.* Cambridge: Cambridge University Press, 1990.

Arato, Andrew. "Procedural Law and Civil Society: Interpreting the Radical Democratic Paradigm." In *Habermas on Law and Democracy: Critical Exchanges*, edited by M. Rosenfeld and A. Arato, 26–36. Berkeley: University of California Press, 1998.

Arendt, Hannah. *The Human Condition.* 2nd ed. Chicago: University of Chicago Press, 1998.

———. *On Revolution.* Harmondsworth: Penguin Books, 1990.

———. *The Origins of Totalitarianism.* New York: Harcourt Brace, 1979.

———. "What Is Freedom?" Chap. 4 in *Between Past and Future: Eight Exercises in Political Thought.* Harmondsworth: Penguin Books, 1993.

Aristotle. *Ethics.* Translated by J. A. K. Thomson. Revised by T. J. Saunders. Harmondsworth: Penguin, 1976.

———. *The Politics.* Translated by T. A. Sinclair. Revised by T. J. Saunders. Harmondsworth: Penguin, 1992.

Baiocchi, Gianpaolo. "Participation, Activism, and Politics: The Porto Alegre Experiment." In *Deepening Democracy: Institutional Innovations in Empowered Participatory Governance*, edited by A. Fung and E. O. Wright, 45–76. London: Verso, 2003.

Barber, Benjamin. *Strong Democracy: Participatory Politics for a New Age.* Berkeley: University of California Press, 1984.

Barber, Benjamin R. *Superman and Common Men: Freedom, Anarchy, and the Revolution.* New York: Praeger, 1971.

Barry, Brian. *Culture and Equality.* Cambridge, MA: Harvard University Press, 2001.

———. *Justice as Impartiality.* Oxford: Oxford University Press, 1995.

Baynes, Kenneth. "Public Reason and Personal Autonomy." In *The Handbook of Critical Theory*, edited by D. Rasmussen, 243–54. Oxford: Blackwell, 1996.

————. "Rights as Critique and the Critique of Rights." In *Political Theory* 28:4 (August 2000): 451–68.

Beitz, Charles R. *Political Equality: An Essay in Democratic Theory.* Princeton, NJ: Princeton University Press, 1989.

Benhabib, Seyla. *Claims of Culture: Equality and Diversity in the Global Era.* Princeton, NJ: Princeton University Press, 2002.

————, ed. *Democracy and Difference: Contesting the Boundaries of the Political.* Princeton, NJ: Princeton University Press, 1996.

————. "Models of the Public Sphere: Hannah Arendt, the Liberal Tradition, and Jürgen Habermas." In *Habermas and the Public Sphere*, edited by C. Calhoun, 73–98. Cambridge, MA: The MIT Press, 1992.

————. *Situating the Self: Gender, Community and Postmodernism in Contemporary Ethics.* New York: Routledge, 1992.

————. "Toward a Deliberative Model of Democratic Legitimacy." In *Democracy and Difference: Contesting the Boundaries of the Political*, edited by S. Benhabib, 67–94. Princeton, NJ: Princeton University Press, 1996.

Benn, S. I. *A Theory of Freedom.* Cambridge: Cambridge University Press, 1988.

Berlin, Isaiah. "Introduction." In *Four Essays on Liberty*, ix–lxiii. Oxford: Oxford University Press, 1969.

————. "Two Concepts of Liberty." Chap. 3 in *Four Essays on Liberty*, 118–72. Oxford: Oxford University Press, 1969.

Bernstein, Jay. "Habermas." In *Conceptions of Liberty in Political Philosophy*, edited by Z. Pelczynski and J. Gray, 397–425. New York: St. Martin's Press, 1984.

Bernstein, Richard. "The Retrieval of the Democratic Ethos." In *Habermas on Law and Democracy: Critical Exchanges*, edited by M. Rosenfeld and A. Arato, 287–306. Berkeley: University of California Press, 1998.

Berofsky, Bernard. *Liberation from Self: A Theory of Personal Autonomy.* Cambridge: Cambridge University Press, 1995.

Bessette, Joseph M. *The Mild Voice of Reason: Deliberative Democracy and American National Government.* Chicago: University of Chicago Press, 1994.

Blaug, Ricardo. "New Theories of Discursive Democracy: A User's Guide." *Philosophy and Social Criticism* 43 (1996): 49–80.

Boesche, Roger. "Thinking about Freedom." *Political Theory* 26 (December 1998): 855–73.

Bohman, James. "The Coming of Age of Deliberative Democracy." *The Journal of Political Philosophy* 6 (1998): 400–25.

————. "Deliberative Democracy and Effective Social Freedom: Capabilities, Resources, and Opportunities." In *Deliberative Democracy: Essays on Reason and Politics*, edited by J. Bohman and W. Rehg, 321–48. Cambridge, MA: MIT Press, 1997.

————. "Emancipation and Rhetoric: The Perlocutions and Illocutions of the Social Critic." *Philosophy and Rhetoric* 21 (1988): 185–204.

———. "Habermas, Marxism, and Social Theory: The Case for Pluralism in Critical Social Science." In *Habermas: A Critical Reader*, edited by P. Dews, 53–86. Oxford: Blackwell, 1999.

———. *Public Deliberation: Pluralism, Complexity, and Democracy*. Cambridge, MA: MIT Press, 1996.

———. " 'When Water Chokes': Ideology, Communication, and Practical Rationality." *Constellations* 7:3 (September 2000): 382–92.

Bohman, James, and William Rehg, eds. *Deliberative Democracy: Essays on Reason and Politics*. Cambridge, MA: MIT Press, 1997.

Brown, Vivienne. "Self-Government: The Master Trope of Republican Liberty." *Monist* 84:1 (2001): 60–76.

Burke, Edmund. "Equality in Representation." From *Reflections on the Revolution in France*, excerpted in *Equality*, edited by D. Johnston, 65–68. Indianapolis, IN: Hackett, 2000.

———. *Reflections on the Revolution in France*. Edited by J. G. A. Pocock. Indianapolis, IN: Hackett, 1987.

———. "Speech at Mr. Burke's Arrival in Bristol." In *The Portable Edmund Burke*, edited by I. Kramnick, 155–57. New York: Penguin, 1999.

Bush, George W. "President Discusses Iraq in State of the Union Address—January 20, 2004." http://www.whitehouse.gov/news/releases/2004/01/20040120-12.html (accessed March 17, 2004).

Button, Mark, and David Michael Ryfe. "What Can We Learn from the Practice of Deliberative Democracy?" In *The Deliberative Democracy Handbook: Strategies for Effective Civic Engagement in the 21st Century*, edited by J. Gastil and P. Levine, 20–33. San Francisco: Jossey-Bass, 2005.

Canovan, Margaret. *Hannah Arendt: A Reinterpretation of Her Political Thought*. Cambridge: Cambridge University Press, 1992.

Carter, Ian. *A Measure of Freedom*. New York: Oxford University Press, 1999.

Chambers, Simone. *Reasonable Democracy*. Ithaca, NY: Cornell University Press, 1996.

Chambers, Simone. "Deliberative Democratic Theory." *Annual Review of Political Science* 6 (2003): 307–26.

———. "The Politics of Equality: Rawls on the Barricades." *Perspectives on Politics* 4 (March 2006): 81–89.

Christiano, Thomas. "The Significance of Public Deliberation." In *Deliberative Democracy: Essays on Reason and Politics*, edited by J. Bohman and W. Rehg, 243–78. Cambridge, MA: MIT Press, 1997.

Christman, John. "Autonomy, Self-Knowledge, and Liberal Legitimacy." In *Autonomy and the Challenges to Liberalism: New Essays*, edited by J. Christman and J. Anderson, 330–57. Cambridge: Cambridge University Press, 2005.

———. "Introduction." In *The Inner Citadel: Essays on Individual Autonomy*, edited by J. Christman, 3–23. New York: Oxford University Press, 1989.

Cohen, G. A. "Capitalism, Freedom, and the Proletariat." In *Liberty*, edited by D. Miller, 163–82. Oxford: Oxford University Press, 1991.

Cohen, Jean L. "Democracy, Difference, and the Right to Privacy." In *Democracy and Difference: Contesting the Boundaries of the Political*, edited by S. Benhabib, 187–217. Princeton, NJ: Princeton University Press, 1996.

———. *Regulating Intimacy: A New Legal Paradigm*. Princeton, NJ: Princeton University Press, 2002.

Cohen, Jean L., and Andrew Arato. *Civil Society and Political Theory*. Cambridge, MA: MIT Press, 1992.

Cohen, Joshua. "Deliberation and Democratic Legitimacy." In *Deliberative Democracy: Essays on Reason and Politics*, edited by J. Bohman and W. Rehg, 67–92. Cambridge, MA: MIT Press, 1997.

———. "Democracy and Liberty." In *Deliberative Democracy*, edited by J. Elster, 185–231. Cambridge: Cambridge University Press, 1998.

———. "An Epistemic Conception of Democracy." *Ethics* 97:1 (1986): 26–38.

———. "For a Democratic Society." In *Cambridge Companion to Rawls*, edited by S. Freeman, 86–138. Cambridge: Cambridge University Press, 2003.

———. "Procedure and Substance in Deliberative Democracy." In *Deliberative Democracy: Essays on Reason and Politics*, edited by J. Bohman and W. Rehg, 407–37. Cambridge, MA: MIT Press, 1997.

———. "Reflections on Habermas on Democracy." *Ratio Juris* 12:4 (December 1999): 385–416.

Cohen, Joshua, and Charles Sabel. "Directly-Deliberative Polyarchy." *European Law Journal* 3:4 (1997): 313–42.

Cohen, Joshua, and Joel Rogers. "Power and Reason." In *Deepening Democracy: Institutional Innovations in Empowered Participatory Governance*, edited by A. Fung and E. O. Wright, 237–55. London: Verso, 2003.

Connolly, William E. *The Terms of Political Discourse*. 3rd ed. Oxford: Blackwell, 1993.

Conover, Pamela Johnston, Donald D. Searing, and Ivor M. Crewe. "The Deliberative Potential of Political Discussion." *British Journal of Political Science* 32 (2002): 21–62.

Constant, Benjamin. "The Liberty of the Ancients Compared to That of the Moderns." In *Political Writings*, edited by B. Fontana, 307–28. Cambridge: Cambridge University Press, 1988.

Cook, Maeve. "Habermas, Feminism, and the Question of Autonomy." In *Habermas: A Critical Reader*, edited by P. Dews, 178–210. Oxford: Blackwell, 1999.

Crick, Bernard. "Freedom as Politics." In *Philosophy, Politics and Society*, third series, edited by P. Laslett and W. G. Runciman, 194–214. Oxford: Blackwell, 1967.

Crosby, Ned, and Doug Nethercut. "Citizens Juries: Creating a Trustworthy Voice of the People." In *The Deliberative Democracy Handbook: Strategies for Effec-*

tive Civic Engagement in the 21st Century, edited by J. Gastil and P. Levine, 111–19. San Francisco: Jossey-Bass, 2005.

Dagger, Richard. "Autonomy, Domination, and the Republican Challenge to Liberalism." In *Autonomy and the Challenges to Liberalism*, edited by J. Christman and J. Anderson, 177–203. Cambridge: Cambridge University Press, 2005.

Dahl, Robert A. *Democracy and Its Critics*. New Haven, CT: Yale University Press, 1989.

Deliberative Democracy Consortium. http://www.deliberative-democracy.net.

Double, Richard. *The Non-reality of Free Will*. New York: Oxford University Press, 1991.

Downs, Anthony. *An Economic Theory of Democracy*. New York: HarperCollins, 1957.

Dryzek, John S. *Deliberative Democracy and Beyond: Liberals, Critics, Contestations*. Oxford: Oxford University Press, 2000.

DuBois, W. E. B. *The Souls of Black Folk*. New York: Dover, 1994.

Dworkin, Gerald. "Moral Autonomy." Chap. 3 in *The Theory and Practice of Autonomy*, 34–47. Cambridge: Cambridge University Press, 1988.

———. "The Nature of Autonomy." Chap. 1 in *The Theory and Practice of Autonomy*, 3–20. Cambridge: Cambridge University Press, 1988.

———. "Paternalism." *Monist* 56 (1972): 64–84.

———. "Paternalism: Some Second Thoughts." Chap. 8 in *The Theory and Practice of Autonomy*, 121–29. Cambridge: Cambridge University Press, 1988.

———. *The Theory and Practice of Autonomy*. Cambridge: Cambridge University Press, 1988.

Dworkin, Ronald. "Do Liberal Values Conflict?" In *The Legacy of Isaiah Berlin*, edited by M. Lilla, R. Dworkin, and R. B. Silvers, 73–90. New York: New York Review Books, 2001.

———. "Liberal Community." Chap. 5 in *Sovereign Virtue: The Theory and Practice of Equality*, 211–36. Cambridge, MA: Harvard University Press, 2000.

———. "Political Equality." Chap. 4 in *Sovereign Virtue*, 184–210. Cambridge, MA: Harvard University Press, 2000.

———. "What Is Equality? Part 1: Equality of Welfare." *Philosophy and Public Affairs* 10 (1981): 185–246.

Elster, Jon. "Deliberation and Constitution Making." In *Deliberative Democracy*, edited by J. Elster, 97–122. Cambridge: Cambridge University Press, 1998.

———, ed. *Deliberative Democracy*. Cambridge: Cambridge University Press, 1998.

———. "Introduction." In *Deliberative Democracy*, edited by J. Elster, 1–18. Cambridge: Cambridge University Press, 1998.

———. "Introduction." In *Rational Choice*, edited by J. Elster, 1–33. New York: New York University Press, 1986.

———. "The Market and the Forum: Three Varieties of Political Theory." In *Deliberative Democracy: Essays on Reason and Politics*, edited by J. Bohman and W. Rehg, 3–33. Cambridge, MA: MIT Press, 1997.

———. *Sour Grapes: Studies in the Subversion of Rationality*. Cambridge: Cambridge University Press, 1983.

Elster, Jon, and Rune Slagstad, eds. *Constitutionalism and Democracy: Studies in Rationality and Social Change*. Cambridge: Cambridge University Press, 1988.

Epictetus. *The Handbook*. Translated by N. White. Indianapolis, IN: Hackett, 1983.

Estlund, David. "Beyond Fairness and Deliberation: The Epistemic Dimension of Democratic Authority." In *Deliberative Democracy: Essays on Reason and Politics*, edited by J. Bohman and W. Rehg, 173–204. Cambridge, MA: MIT Press, 1997.

Fearon, James, D. "Deliberation as Discussion." In *Deliberative Democracy*, edited by J. Elster, 44–68. Cambridge: Cambridge University Press, 1998.

Fishkin, James, and Cynthia Farrar. "Deliberative Polling: From Experiment to Community Resource." In *The Deliberative Democracy Handbook: Strategies for Effective Civic Engagement in the 21st Century*, edited by J. Gastil and P. Levine, 68–79. San Francisco: Jossey-Bass, 2005.

Fishkin, James S. *Democracy and Deliberation: New Directions for Democratic Reform*. New Haven, CT: Yale University Press, 1991.

Fishkin, James S., and Peter Laslett, eds. *Debating Deliberative Democracy*. Malden, MA: Blackwell, 2003.

Fleischacker, Samuel. *A Third Concept of Liberty: Judgment and Freedom in Kant and Adam Smith*. Princeton, NJ: Princeton University Press, 1999.

Forst, Rainer. "Justice, Reason, and Critique: Basic Concepts of Critical Theory." In *The Handbook of Critical Theory*, edited by D. Rasmussen, 138–62. Oxford: Blackwell, 1996.

———. "Political Liberty." University of Frankfurt. Typescript. n.d.

———. "The Rule of Reasons: Three Models of Deliberative Democracy." *Ratio Juris* 14:4 (December 2001): 345–78.

Frankfurt, Harry. "Freedom of the Will and the Concept of a Person." Chap. 2 in *The Importance of What We Care About: Philosophical Essays*, 11–25. New York: Cambridge University Press, 1988.

Fraser, Nancy. "Rethinking the Public Sphere: A Contribution to the Critique of Actually Existing Democracy." In *Habermas and the Public Sphere*, edited by C. Calhoun, 109–42. Cambridge, MA: MIT Press, 1992.

———. "Social Justice in the Age of Identity Politics: Redistribution, Recognition, and Participation." In Nancy Fraser and Axel Honneth, *Redistribution or Recognition? A Political-Philosophical Exchange*, 7–109. London: Verso, 2003.

————. "Talking about Needs: Interpretive Contests as Political Conflicts in Welfare-State Societies." *Ethics* 99 (January 1989): 289–313.

Freeman, Samuel. "Deliberative Democracy: A Sympathetic Comment." *Philosophy and Public Affairs* 29:4 (Fall 2000): 371–418.

Friedman, Milton. *Capitalism and Freedom.* Chicago: University of Chicago Press, 2002.

Fung, Archon. "Deliberation before the Revolution: Toward an Ethics of Deliberative Democracy in an Unjust World." *Political Theory* 33:3 (2005): 397–419.

————. "Deliberative Democracy, Chicago Style: Grass-roots Governance in Policing and Public Education." In *Deepening Democracy: Institutional Innovations in Empowered Participatory Governance*, edited by A. Fung and E. O. Wright, 111–43. London: Verso, 2003.

Fung, Archon, and Erik Olin Wright. "Countervailing Power in Empowered Participatory Governance." In *Deepening Democracy: Institutional Innovations in Empowered Participatory Governance*, edited by A. Fung and E. O. Wright, 259–89. London: Verso, 2003.

————, eds. *Deepening Democracy: Institutional Innovations in Empowered Participatory Governance.* London: Verso, 2003.

————. "Thinking about Empowered Participatory Governance." In *Deepening Democracy: Institutional Innovations in Empowered Participatory Governance*, edited by A. Fung and E. O. Wright, 3–42. London: Verso, 2003.

Gallie, W. B. "Essentially Contested Concepts." *Proceedings of the Aristotelian Society* 56 (1955–1956): 167–98.

Galston, William A. "Diversity, Toleration, and Deliberative Democracy: Religious Minorities and Public Schooling." In *Deliberative Politics: Essays on Democracy and Disagreement*, edited by S. Macedo, 39–48. New York: Oxford University Press, 1999.

————. *Liberal Pluralism: The Implications of Value Pluralism for Political Theory and Practice.* Cambridge: Cambridge University Press, 2002.

Gambetta, Diego. " 'Claro!': An Essay on Discursive Machismo." In *Deliberative Democracy*, edited by J. Elster, 19–43. Cambridge: Cambridge University Press, 1998.

Gamson, Joshua. "Taking the Talk Show Challenge: Television, Emotion, and Public Spheres." *Constellations* 6 (1999): 190–205.

Gargarella, Roberto. "Full Representation, Deliberation, and Impartiality." In *Deliberative Democracy*, edited by J. Elster, 260–80. Cambridge: Cambridge University Press, 1998.

Gastil, John, and Peter Levine, eds. *The Deliberative Democracy Handbook: Strategies for Effective Civic Engagement in the 21st Century.* San Francisco: Jossey-Bass, 2005.

Gaus, Gerald F. "Backwards into the Future: Neorepublicanism as a Postsocialist Critique of Market Society." *Social Philosophy & Policy* 20 (2003): 59–91.

———. "The Place of Autonomy within Liberalism." In *Autonomy and the Challenges to Liberalism: New Essays*, edited by J. Christman and J. Anderson, 272–306. Cambridge: Cambridge University Press, 2005.

———. "Reason, Justification, and Consensus: Why Democracy Can't Have It All." In *Deliberative Democracy: Essays on Reason and Politics*, edited by J. Bohman and W. Rehg, 205–42. Cambridge, MA: MIT Press, 1997.

Geuss, Raymond. *The Idea of a Critical Theory: Habermas and the Frankfurt School.* Cambridge: Cambridge University Press, 1981.

Gilabert, Pablo. "Arguing for the Expressive-Elaboration Model." Concordia University. Typescript, 2003.

———. "Considerations on the Notion of Moral Validity in the Moral Theories of Kant and Habermas." *Kantstudien* 97 (June 2006): 210–27.

———. *Substance and Procedure in Discourse Ethics and Deliberative Democracy*, Ph.D. diss., Graduate Faculty, New School University, May 2003.

———. "The Substantive Dimension of Deliberative Practical Rationality." *Philosophy & Social Criticism* 31:2 (2005): 185–210.

———. "A Substantivist Construal of Discourse Ethics." *International Journal of Philosophical Studies* 13:3 (2005): 405–37.

Gilabert, Pablo, and Christian F. Rostbøll. "Beyond Libertarianism and Republicanism: The Deliberative Conception of Political Freedom." Paper presented at the 11th Annual Critical Theory Roundtable, Stony Brook University, October 24–26, 2003.

Gray, John N. "On the Contestability of Social and Political Concepts." *Political Theory* 5:3 (August 1977): 331–48.

———. "On Liberty, Liberalism, and Essential Contestability." *British Journal of Political Science* 8:4 (October 1978): 385–402.

Gray, Tim. *Freedom.* Houndmills, UK: Macmillan, 1991.

Günther, Klaus. "Communicative Freedom, Communicative Power, and Jurisgenesis." In *Habermas on Law and Democracy: Critical Exchanges*, edited by Michael Rosenfeld and Andrew Arato, 234–54. Berkeley: University of California Press, 1998.

Gutmann, Amy, and Dennis Thompson. *Democracy and Disagreement.* Cambridge, MA: Belknap Press of Harvard University Press, 1996.

———. "Democratic Disagreement." In *Deliberative Politics: Essays on Democracy and Disagreement*, edited by S. Macedo, 243–79. New York: Oxford University Press, 1999.

———. *Why Deliberative Democracy?* Princeton, NJ: Princeton University Press, 2004.

Habermas, Jürgen. *Between Facts and Norms: Contributions to a Discourse Theory of Law and Democracy.* Translated by William Rehg. Cambridge: Polity Press, 1996.

———. "Discourse Ethics: Notes on a Program of Philosophical Justification." In *Moral Consciousness and Communicative Action*, translated by C. Lenhardt and S. Weber Nicholsen, 43–115. Cambridge: Polity Press, 1990.

———. "Dogmatism, Reason, and Decision: On Theory and Praxis in Our Scientific Civilization." In *Theory and Practice*. Translated by J. Viertel, 253–82. Boston: Beacon Press, 1973.

———. "Equal Treatment of Cultures and the Limits of Postmodern Liberalism." *The Journal of Political Philosophy* 13 (2005): 1–28.

———. "Further Reflections on the Public Sphere." In *Habermas and the Public Sphere*, edited by C. Calhoun, 421–61. Cambridge, MA: MIT Press, 1992.

———. *Knowledge and Human Interests*. Translated by J. J. Shapiro. Boston: Beacon Press, 1971.

———. *Legitimation Crisis*. Translated by T. McCarthy. Boston: Beacon Press, 1975.

———. "The New Obscurity: The Crisis of the Welfare State and the Exhaustion of Utopian Energies." Chap. 2 in *The New Conservatism: Cultural Criticism and the Historians' Debate*, translated by S. Weber Nicholsen, 48–70. Cambridge, MA: MIT Press, 1989.

———. "On the Internal Relationship between the Rule of Law and Democracy." In *The Inclusion of the Other: Studies in Political Theory*, edited by C. Cronin and P. De Greiff, 253–64. Cambridge, MA: MIT Press, 1998.

———. "On the Pragmatic, the Ethical, and the Moral Employments of Practical Reason." In his *Justification and Application*, translated by C. P. Cronin, 1–17. Cambridge: Polity Press, 1995.

———. "Popular Sovereignty as Procedure." In *Between Facts and Norms*, translated by W. Rehg, 463–90. Cambridge: Polity Press, 1996.

———. " 'Reasonable' versus 'True,' or the Morality of Worldviews." In *The Inclusion of the Other: Studies in Political Theory*, edited by C. Cronin and P. De Greiff, 75–101. Cambridge, MA: MIT Press, 1998.

———. "Reconciliation through the Public Use of Reason." In *The Inclusion of the Other: Studies in Political Theory*, edited by C. Cronin and P. De Greiff, 49–74. Cambridge, MA: MIT Press, 1998.

———. "Reply to Symposium Participants, Benjamin N. Cardozo School of Law." In *Habermas on Law and Democracy: Critical Exchanges*, edited by Michael Rosenfeld and Andrew Arato, 381–452. Berkeley: University of California Press, 1998.

———. "Richtigkeit versus Wahrheit. Zum Sinn der Sollgeltung moralischer Urteile und Normen." Chap. 5 in *Wahrheit und Rechtfertigung*, 271–318. Frankfurt a.M.: Suhrkamp, 1999.

———. *The Structural Transformation of the Public Sphere*. Translated by T. Burger, with F. Lawrence. Cambridge, MA: MIT Press, 1989.

———. "Struggles for Recognition in the Democratic Constitutional State." In *Multiculturalism*, edited by A. Gutmann, 107–48. Princeton, NJ: Princeton University Press, 1994.

———. "Technology and Science as 'Ideology.' " In *Toward a Rational Society*, translated by J. J. Shapiro, 81–122. Boston: Beacon Press, 1970.

———. *The Theory of Communicative Action*, vol. 1. Translated by T. McCarthy. Cambridge: Polity Press, 1984.

———. *The Theory of Communicative Action*, vol. 2. Translated by T. McCarthy. Cambridge: Polity Press, 1987.

———. "Three Normative Models of Democracy." *Constellations* 1:1 (1994): 1–10.

———. "Three Normative Models of Democracy." In *The Inclusion of the Other*, edited by C. Cronin and P. De Greiff, 239–52. Cambridge, MA: MIT Press, 1998.

Hamilton, Alexander, James Madison, and John Jay. *The Federalist Papers*. Edited by C. Rossiter. New York: Mentor, 1961.

Hare, R. M. "Freedom of the Will." Chap. 1 in *Essays on the Moral Concepts*, 1–12. Berkeley: University of California Press, 1973.

Haworth, Lawrence. *Autonomy: An Essay in Philosophical Psychology and Ethics*. New Haven, CT: Yale University Press, 1986.

Held, David. *Models of Democracy*. 2nd ed. Cambridge: Polity Press, 1996.

Hill, Jr. Thomas E. "The Kantian Conception of Autonomy." Chap. 5 in *Dignity and Practical Reason in Kant's Moral Theory*, 76–96. Ithaca, NY: Cornell University Press, 1992.

Hirschmann, Nancy J. *The Subject of Liberty: Toward a Feminist Theory of Freedom*. Princeton, NJ: Princeton University Press, 2003.

Hobbes, Thomas. *Leviathan*. Oxford: Oxford University Press, 1996.

Holmes, Stephen. *Passions and Constraint: On the Theory of Liberal Democracy*. Chicago: University of Chicago Press, 1995.

Honohan, Iseult. *Civic Republicanism*. London: Routledge, 2002.

Isaac, T. M. Thomas, and Patrick Heller. "Democracy and Development: Decentralized Planning in Kerala." In *Deepening Democracy: Institutional Innovations in Empowered Participatory Governance*, edited by A. Fung and E. O. Wright, 77–110. London: Verso, 2003.

Jones, Peter. "Political Theory and Cultural Diversity." *CRISPP* 1:1 (Spring 1998): 28–62.

———. "Respecting Beliefs and Rebuking Rushdie." *British Journal of Political Science* 20 (October 1990): 415–37.

Kalyvas, Andreas. "The Politics of Autonomy and the Challenge of Deliberation: Castoriadis Contra Habermas." *Thesis Eleven* 64 (2001): 1–19.

Kant, Immanuel. "An Answer to the Question: What Is Enlightenment?" In *Perpetual Peace and Other Essays on Politics, History, and Morals*, translated by T. Humphrey, 41–48. Indianapolis, IN: Hackett, 1983.

———. *The Critique of Judgment*. Translated by J. C. Meredith. Oxford: Clarendon Press, 1952.

———. *Grounding for the Metaphysics of Morals*. Translated by J. W. Ellington.
Indianapolis, IN: Hackett, 1993.

———. *The Metaphysics of Morals*. Translated and edited by Mary Gregor. Cambridge: Cambridge University Press, 1996.

———. "Metaphysics of Morals." In *Kant's Political Writings*, 2nd ed., edited by
Hans Reis, 131–75. Cambridge: Cambridge University Press, 1991.

———. "On the Common Saying: 'This May Be True in Theory, but It Does
Not Apply in Practice.'" In *Kant's Political Writings*, 2nd ed., edited by Hans
Reis, 61–92. Cambridge: Cambridge University Press, 1991.

Katznelson, Ira. *Liberalism's Crooked Circle: Letter to Adam Michnik*. Princeton, NJ:
Princeton University Press, 1996.

Knight, Jack and James Johnson. "Aggregation and Deliberation: On the Possibility
of Democratic Legitimacy." *Political Theory* 22:2, (May 1994): 277–96.

———. "What Sort of Equality Does Deliberative Democracy Require?" In
Deliberative Democracy: Essays on Reason and Politics, edited by J. Bohman
and W. Rehg, 279–319. Cambridge, MA: MIT Press, 1997.

Knops, Andrew. "Delivering Deliberation's Emancipatory Potential." *Political Theory*
34 (October 2006): 594–623.

Korsgaard, Christine M. *Sources of Normativity*. Cambridge: Cambridge University
Press, 1996.

Kristjánsson, Kristján. *Social Freedom: The Responsibility View*. Cambridge: Cambridge University Press, 1996.

Kymlicka, Will. *Contemporary Political Philosophy: An Introduction*. Oxford: Clarendon Press, 1990.

———. *Contemporary Political Philosophy: An Introduction*, 2nd ed. New York:
Oxford University Press, 2002.

———. *Multicultural Citizenship*. Oxford: Oxford University Press, 1995.

Larmore, Charles. "A Critique of Philip Pettit's Republicanism." *Philosophical
Issues 11* (2001): 229–43.

———. "The Foundations of Modern Democracy: Reflection on Jürgen Habermas." *European Journal of Philosophy* 3:1 (1995): 55–68.

———. "Liberal and Republican Conceptions of Freedom." In *Republicanism:
History, Theory and Practice*, edited by D. Weinstock and C. Nadeau, 96–119.
London: Frank Cass, 2004.

———. "Public Reason." In *Cambridge Companion to Rawls*, edited by S. Freeman,
368–93. Cambridge: Cambridge University Press, 2003.

Lefort, Claude. "Politics and Human Rights." Chap. 7 in *The Political Forms of
Modern Society*, 239–72. Cambridge, MA: MIT Press, 1986.

Levine, Peter, Archon Fung, and John Gastil. "Future Directions for Public Deliberation." In *The Deliberative Democracy Handbook: Strategies for Effective Civic*

Engagement in the 21st Century, edited by J. Gastil and P. Levine, 271–88. San Francisco: Jossey-Bass, 2005.

Locke, John. *A Letter Concerning Toleration*. Indianapolis, IN: Hackett, 1983.

———. "The Second Treaties of Government." In *Political Writings of John Locke*, edited by D. Wootton, 261–387. New York: Mentor/Penguin, 1993.

Lukensmeyer, Carolyn J., Joe Goldman, and Steven Brigham. "A Town Meeting for the Twenty-First Century." In *The Deliberative Democracy Handbook: Strategies for Effective Civic Engagement in the 21st Century*, edited by J. Gastil and P. Levine, 154–63. San Francisco: Jossey-Bass, 2005.

Lukes, Steven. *Power: A Radical View*. Houndmills, UK: Macmillan, 1974.

MacCallum, Gerald C. "Negative and Positive Freedom." In *Liberty*, edited by D. Miller, 100–22. Oxford: Oxford University Press, 1991.

Macedo, Stephen, ed. *Deliberative Politics: Essays on* Democracy and Disagreement. New York: Oxford University Press, 1999.

———. "Introduction." In *Deliberative Politics: Essays on* Democracy and Disagreement, edited by S. Macedo, 3–14. New York: Oxford University Press, 1999.

MacKinnon, Catharine A. *Toward a Feminist Theory of the State*. Cambridge, MA: Harvard University Press, 1989.

Macpherson, C. B. *The Life and Times of Liberal Democracy*. Oxford: Oxford University Press, 1977.

Manin, Bernard. "On Legitimacy and Political Deliberation." *Political Theory* 15:3 (August 1987): 338–68.

———. *The Principles of Representative Government*. Cambridge: Cambridge University Press, 1997.

Mansbridge, Jane. *Beyond Adversary Democracy*. Chicago: University of Chicago Press, 1983.

———. "Everyday Talk in the Deliberative System." In *Deliberative Politics: Essays on* Democracy and Disagreement, edited by S. Macedo, 211–39. New York: Oxford University Press, 1999.

———. "Practice-Thought-Practice." In *Deepening Democracy: Institutional Innovations in Empowered Participatory Governance*, edited by A. Fung and E. O. Wright, 175–99. London: Verso, 2003.

———. "Using Power/Fighting Power." In *Democracy and Difference. Contesting the Boundaries of the Political*, edited by S. Benhabib, 67–94. Princeton, NJ: Princeton University Press, 1996.

Marcuse, Herbert. *One-Dimensional Man: Studies in the Ideology of Advanced Industrial Society*. Boston: Beacon Press, 1964.

Marx, Karl. *Capital,* Vol. 1. Translated by Ben Fowkes. Harmondsworth: Penguin, 1990.

———. "On the Jewish Question." In *The Marx-Engels Reader*, 2nd ed., edited by R. Tucker, 26–52. New York: Norton, 1978.

Marx, Karl, and Friedrich Engels. "Manifesto of the Communist Party." In *The Marx-Engels Reader*, 2nd ed., edited by R. Tucker, 469–500. New York: Norton, 1978.

McBride, William L. " 'Two Concepts of Liberty' Thirty Years Later: A Sartre-Inspired Critique." *Social Theory and Practice* 16:3 (Fall 1990): 297–322.

McCarthy, Thomas. *The Critical Theory of Jürgen Habermas*. Cambridge, MA: MIT Press, 1978.

———. "Legitimacy and Diversity: Dialectical Reflections on Analytic Distinctions." In *Habermas on Law and Democracy: Critical Exchanges*, edited by Michael Rosenfeld and Andrew Arato, 115–53. Berkeley: University of California Press, 1998.

McCormick, John P. "Machiavelli against Republicanism: On the Cambridge School's 'Guicciardinian Moments'." *Political Theory* 31 (2003): 615–43.

McMahon, Christopher. "The Indeterminacy of Republican Policy." *Philosophy & Public Affairs* 33 (2005): 67–93.

Mele, Alfred R. *Autonomous Agents: From Self-Control to Autonomy*. New York: Oxford University Press, 1995.

Michelman, Frank. "Conceptions of Democracy in American Constitutional Argument: The Case of Pornography Regulation." *Tennessee Law Review* 56 (1989): 291–319.

———. "How Can the People Ever Make the Laws?" In *Deliberative Democracy: Essays on Reason and Politics*, edited by J. Bohman and W. Rehg, 145–71. Cambridge, MA: MIT Press, 1997.

Mill, James. "Essay on Government." In *Utilitarian Logic and Politics*, edited by Jack Lively and John Rees, 53–95. Oxford: Clarendon Press, 1978.

Mill, John Stuart. "Considerations on Representative Government." In *Utilitarianism: On Liberty and Considerations on Representative Government*, edited by G. Williams, 187–428. London: Everyman, 1993.

———. "On Liberty." In *On Liberty and Other Writings*, edited by S. Collini, 1–115. Cambridge: Cambridge University Press, 1989.

Miller, David. "Introduction." In *Liberty*, edited by D. Miller, 1–20. Oxford: Oxford University Press, 1991.

Minnesota v. Hershberger 444 N.W.2d. 282 (Minn. 1989).

Moon, J. Donald. *Constructing Community: Moral Pluralism and Tragic Conflicts*. Princeton, NJ: Princeton University Press, 1993.

———. "Rawls and Habermas on Public Reason: Human Rights and Global Justice." *Annual Review of Political Science* 6 (2003): 257–74.

National Coalition for Dialogue and Deliberation. http://www.thataway.org.

Neiman, Susan. *The Unity of Reason: Rereading Kant*. New York: Oxford University Press, 1994.

Neumann, Franz. "The Concept of Political Freedom." In *The Democratic and Authoritarian State: Essays in Political and Legal Theory*, edited by H. Marcuse, 160–200. Glencoe, IL: The Free Press, 1957.

Nino, Carlos S. *The Constitution of Deliberative Democracy*. New Haven, CT: Yale University Press, 1996.

Nozick, Robert. *Anarchy, State, and Utopia*. New York: Basic Books, 1974.

Nunberg, Geoffrey. "More Than Just Another Word for Nothing Left to Lose." *New York Times*, March 23, 2003.

Offe, Claus. *Modernity and the State: East, West*. Cambridge, MA: MIT Press, 1996.

O'Neill, Shane. "The Politics of Inclusive Agreement: Towards a Critical Discourse Theory of Democracy." *Political Studies* 48 (2000): 503–21.

Oppenheim, Felix E. "Social Freedom and Its Parameters." *Journal of Theoretical Politics* 7:4 (1995): 403–20.

Pateman, Carole. *Participation and Democratic Theory*. Cambridge: Cambridge University Press, 1970.

Pettit, Philip. "Deliberative Democracy and the Discursive Dilemma." *Philosophical Issues* 11 (2001): 268–99.

———. "Deliberative Democracy, the Discursive Dilemma, and Republican Theory." In *Debating Deliberative Democracy*, edited by J. S. Fishkin and P. Laslett, 138–62. Malden, MA: Blackwell, 2003.

———. "Democracy, Electoral and Contestatory." In *Designing Democratic Institutions*, edited by Ian Shapiro and Stephen Macedo, 105–44. *Nomos* XLII. New York: New York University Press, 2000.

———. "Depoliticizing Democracy." *Ratio Juris* 17:1 (March 2004): 52–65.

———. "Discourse Theory and Republican Freedom." In *Republicanism: History, Theory and Practice*, edited by D. Weinstock and C. Nadeau, 72–95. London: Frank Cass, 2004.

———. "Keeping Republican Freedom Simple: On a Difference with Quentin Skinner." *Political Theory* 30:3 (June 2002): 339–56.

———. "Liberty and Leviathan." *Politics, Philosophy & Economics* 4:1 (2005): 131–51.

——— "Republican Freedom and Contestatory Democratization." In *Democracy's Value*, edited by Ian Shapiro and Casiano Hacker-Cordón, 163–90. Cambridge: Cambridge University Press, 1999.

———. *Republicanism: A Theory of Freedom and Government*. Oxford: Oxford University Press, 1997.

———. "Reworking Sandel's Republicanism." *The Journal of Philosophy* 95:2 (February 1998): 73–96.

———. *A Theory of Freedom: From the Psychology to the Politics of Agency*. New York: Oxford University Press, 2001.

Phillips, Anne. *The Politics of Presence*. Oxford: Clarendon Press, 1995.

Pitkin, Hanna F. "Are Freedom and Liberty Twins?" *Political Theory* 16:4 (1988): 523–52.

———. *The Concept of Representation*. Berkeley: University of California Press, 1967.

Plato. *Republic*. Translated by G. M. A. Grube. Indianapolis, IN: Hackett, 1992.

Pocock, J. G. A. *The Machiavellian Movement*. Princeton, NJ: Princeton University Press, 1975.

Przeworski, Adam. "Deliberation and Ideological Domination." In *Deliberative Democracy*, edited by J. Elster, 140–60. Cambridge: Cambridge University Press, 1998.

———. *Democracy and the Market: Political and Economic Reform in Eastern Europe and Latin America*. New York: Cambridge University Press, 1991.

———. "Minimalist Conception of Democracy: A Defense." In *Democracy's Value*, edited by I. Shapiro and C. Hacker-Cordón, 23–55. Cambridge: Cambridge University Press, 1999.

Raaflaub, Kurt. "Democracy, Oligarchy, and the Concept of the 'Free Citizen' in Late Fifth-Century Athens." *Political Theory* 11:4 (November 1983): 517–44.

Rawls, John. "The Domain of the Political and Overlapping Consensus." In *Collected Papers*, edited by S. Freeman, 473–96. Cambridge, MA: Harvard University Press, 1999.

———. "The Idea of Public Reason." In *Deliberative Democracy: Essays on Reason and Politics*, edited by J. Bohman and W. Rehg, 93–141. Cambridge, MA: MIT Press.

———. "The Idea of Public Reason Revisited." In *Collected Papers*, edited by S. Freeman, 573–615. Cambridge, MA: Harvard University Press, 1999.

———. "Introduction to the Paperback Edition." In *Political Liberalism*, xxxvii–lxii. New York: Columbia University Press, 1996.

———. "Justice as Fairness: Political not Metaphysical." *Philosophy and Public Affairs* 14 (Summer 1985): 223–51.

———. *Politcal Liberalism*. New York: Columbia University Press, 1993.

———. "Reply to Habermas." *Journal of Philosophy* XCII (1995): 132–80.

———. *A Theory of Justice*. Rev. ed. Cambridge, MA: Belknap Press of Harvard University Press, 1999.

Raz, Joseph. *The Morality of Freedom*. Oxford: Clarendon Press, 1986.

Rehg, William. *Insight and Solidarity: A Study in the Discourse Ethics of Jürgen Habermas*. Berkeley: University of California Press, 1994.

Renick, Timothy M. "Response to Berlin and McBride." *Social Theory and Practice* 16:3 (Fall 1990): 323–35.

Richardson, Henry S. *Democratic Autonomy: Public Reasoning about the Ends of Policy*. New York: Oxford University Press, 2002.

Riker, William. *Liberalism against Populism*. Prospect Heights, IL: Waveland Press, 1982.

Rosen, Michael. "*On Voluntary Servitude* and the Theory of Ideology." *Constellations* 7 (2000): 393–407.

Rostbøll, Christian F. "The Different Roles of the Idea of Democratic Deliberation." University of Copenhagen. Typescript, 2007.

———. "Dissent, Criticism, and Transformative Political Action in Deliberative Democracy." *CRISPP*, forthcoming.

———. "The Divergent Roles of the Idea of Democratic Deliberation." Annual Meeting of the American Political Science Association, Washington, DC, September 1–4, 2005, and Critical Theory Roundtable, Dartmouth College, Hanover, NH, November 4–6, 2005.

———. "Freedom as Satisfaction? A Critique of Frankfurt's Hierarchical Theory of Freedom." *Sats: Nordic Journal of Philosophy* 5:1 (2004): 131–46.

———. "Freedom and Rationality: On the Consequences of the Epistemic Dimension of Deliberative Democracy." Paper delivered at the 2002 Annual Meeting of the American Political Science Association, August 29–September 1, 2002, Boston.

———. "Hannah Arendt: Magt som handling i fællesskab." In *Magtens tænkere: Politisk teori fra Machiavelli to Honneth* ["Hannah Arendt: Power as Acting in Concert." In *The Theoreticians of Power: Political Theory from Machiavelli to Honneth*], edited by Carsten Bagge Laustsen and Jesper Myrup, 293–314. Frederiksberg: Roskilde University Press, 2006.

———. *Human Rights, Popular Sovereignty and Freedom*. Copenhagen: Copenhagen Political Studies Press, 1998.

———. "Humanitet, pluralitet og ret—Arendts svar på erfaringerne med totalitarismen." In *Ondskabens banalitet—Om Hannah Arendts "Eichmann i Jerusalem"* ["Humanity, Plurality, and Law—Arendt's Response to the Experience with Totalitarianism." In *The Banality of Evil—On Hannah Arendt's Eichmann in Jerusalem*], edited by C. B. Laustsen og J. Rendtorff, 61–90. Copenhagen: Museum Tusculanum, 2002.

———. "Impartiality, Deliberation, and Multiculturalism." Paper delivered at the conference *What's the Culture in Multiculturalism? What's the Difference of Identities?* Organized by the Danish Network on Political Theory in collaboration with the Research Group on Cultural Encounters, University of Aarhus, Denmark, May 22–24, 2003. http://www.politicaltheory.dk/conference/res/papers/5202003144147Rostboll-%20Multi%20DK03%20-%20Impart%20delib.pdf (accessed 14 November 2007).

———. "On Deliberative Democracy." *Sats: Nordic Journal of Philosophy* 2:2 (2001): 166–81.

———. Review of Jürg Steiner, André Bächtiger, Markus Spörndli, and Marco R. Steenbergen, *Deliberative Politics in Action: Analyzing Parliamentary Discourse*. New York: Cambridge University Press, 2004, *Political Science Quarterly* 120:4 (Winter 2005–2006): 697–98.

Rousseau, Jean-Jacques. "Discourse on the Origin of Inequality." In *The Basic Political Writings*, translated by D. A Cress, 83–109. Indianapolis, IN: Hackett, 1987.

———. "On the Social Contract." In *The Basic Political Writings*, translated by D. A Cress, 141–227. Indianapolis, IN: Hackett, 1987.

Ryan, Alan. "Two Concepts of Politics and Democracy: James and John Stuart Mill." In *Machiavelli and the Nature of Political Thought*, edited by M. Flischer, 76–113. London: Croom Helm, 1972.

Sabl, Andrew. *Ruling Passions: Political Offices and Democratic Ethics*. Princeton, NJ: Princeton University Press, 2002.

Sandel, Michael. *Democracy's Discontent: America in Search of a Public Philosophy*. Cambridge, MA: Harvard University Press, 1996.

Sanders, Lynn M. "Against Deliberation." *Political Theory* 25:3 (June 1997): 347–76.

Schauer, Frederick. "Talking as a Decision Procedure." In *Deliberative Politics: Essays on* Democracy and Disagreement, edited by S. Macedo, 17–27. New York: Oxford University Press, 1999.

Scheuerman, William E. "Between Radicalism and Resignation: Democratic Theory in Habermas's *Between Facts and Norms*." In *Habermas: A Critical Reader*, edited by P. Dews, 153–77. Oxford: Blackwell, 1999.

Schneewind, J. B. "Autonomy, Obligation, and Virtue: An Overview of Kant's Moral Philosophy." In *The Cambridge Companion to Kant*, edited by P. Guyer, 309–41. Cambridge: Cambridge University Press, 1992.

Schumpeter, Joseph A. *Capitalism, Socialism and Democracy*. New York: Harper Torchbooks, 1976.

Shapiro, Ian. "Enough of Deliberation: Politics Is about Interests and Power." In *Deliberative Politics: Essays on* Democracy and Disagreement, edited by S. Macedo, 28–38. New York: Oxford University Press, 1999.

———. "Optimal Deliberation." In *Debating Deliberative Democracy*, edited by J. S. Fishkin and P. Laslett, 121–37. Malden, MA: Blackwell, 2003.

———. "The State of Democratic Theory." Paper presented at the annual meeting of American Political Science Association, Washington, DC, 2000.

———. *The State of Democratic Theory*. Princeton, NJ: Princeton University Press, 2003.

Shelby, Tommie. "Ideology, Racism, and Critical Social Theory." *The Philosophical Forum* XXXIV (Summer 2003): 153–88.

Simon, William H. "Three Limitations of Deliberative Democracy: *Identity Politics, Bad Faith, and Indeterminacy*." In *Deliberative Politics: Essays on* Democracy and Disagreement, edited by S. Macedo, 49–57. New York: Oxford University Press, 1999.

Skinner, Quentin. *Liberty before Liberalism*. Cambridge: Cambridge University Press, 1998.

———. "Machiavelli on the Maintenance of Liberty." *Politics* 18 (1983): 3–15.

———. "The Paradoxes of Political Liberty." In *Liberty*, edited by D. Miller, 183–205. New York: Oxford University Press, 1991.

———. "A Third Concept of Liberty." *Proceedings of the British Academy* 117 (2002): 237–68.

Steiner, Jürg, André Bächtiger, Markus Spörndli, and Marco R. Steenbergen. *Deliberative Politics in Action: Analyzing Parliamentary Discourse.* New York: Cambridge University Press, 2004.

Stokes, Susan. "Pathologies of Deliberation." In *Deliberative Democracy*, edited by J. Elster, 123–39. Cambridge: Cambridge University Press, 1998.

Strawson, Peter. "Freedom and Resentment." In *Free Will*, edited by G. Watson, 59–80. Oxford: Oxford University Press, 1982.

Swanton, Christine. *Freedom: A Coherence Theory.* Indianapolis, IN: Hackett, 1992.

———. "On the 'Essential Contestedness' of Political Concepts." *Ethics* 95:4 (July 1985): 811–27.

Sunstein, Cass R. *After the Rights Revolution.* Cambridge, MA: Harvard University Press, 1990.

———. *Designing Democracy: What Constitutions Do.* Oxford: Oxford University Press, 2001.

———. "Health-Health Trade-offs." In *Deliberative Democracy*, edited by J. Elster, 232–59. Cambridge: Cambridge University Press, 1998.

———. "The Law of Group Polarization." In *Debating Deliberative Democracy*, edited by J. S. Fishkin and P. Laslett, 80–101. Malden, MA: Blackwell, 2003.

———. *The Partial Constitution.* Cambridge, MA: Harvard University Press, 1993.

———. "Preferences and Politics." *Philosophy and Public Affairs* 20 (1991): 3–34.

Sunstein, Cass R., and Richard H. Thaler. "Libertarian Paternalism Is Not an Oxymoron." *University of Chicago Law Review* 70 (Fall 2003): 1159–1202.

Taylor, Charles. "Atomism." In *Philosophy and The Human Sciences: Philosophical Papers 2*, 187–210. Cambridge: Cambridge University Press, 1985.

———. "Cross-Purposes: The Liberal-Communitarian Debate." In *Philosophical Arguments*, 181–203. Cambridge, MA: Harvard University Press, 1995.

———. "What's Wrong with Negative Liberty." Chap. 8 in *Philosophy and The Human Sciences: Philosophical Papers 2*, 211–29. Cambridge: Cambridge University Press, 1985.

Thalberg, Irving. *Misconceptions of Mind and Freedom.* Lanham, MD: University Press of America, 1983.

Thaler, Richard H., and Cass R. Sunstein. "Libertarian Paternalism." *The American Economic Review* 93 (May 2003): 175–79.

Thompson, Dennis F. "Public Reason and Precluded Reasons." *Fordham Law Review* 72:5 (April 2004): 2073–88.

Tocqueville, Alexis de. *Democracy in America.* Translated by G. Lawrence. Edited by J. P. Mayer. New York: HarperPerennial, 1969.

Urbinati, Nadia. *Mill on Democracy: From the Athenian Polis to Representative Government.* Chicago: University of Chicago Press, 2002.

———. "Representation as Advocacy: A Study of Democratic Deliberation." *Political Theory* 28:6 (December 2000): 758–86.

VanDeVeer, Donald. *Paternalistic Intervention: The Moral Bounds on Benevolence.* Princeton, NJ: Princeton University Press, 1986.

Van Parijs, Philippe. *Real Freedom for All: What (if Anything) Can Justify Capitalism?* Oxford: Oxford University Press, 1995.

Vetlesen, Arne Johan. "Hannah Arendt, Habermas, and the Republican Tradition." *Philosophy & Social Criticism* 21:3 (1995): 1–16.

Waldron, Jeremy. "Cultural Identity and Civic Responsibility." Manuscript in *Waldron Reader*, for the class "L8675: Multiculturalism," Columbia University, Fall 1998.

———. "Is the Rule of Law an Essentially Contested Concept (in Florida)?" *Law and Philosophy* 21 (2002): 137–64.

———. "Moral Autonomy and Personal Autonomy." In *Autonomy and the Challenges to Liberalism: New Essays*, edited by J. Christman and J. Anderson, 307–29. Cambridge: Cambridge University Press, 2005.

———. "Rushdie and Religion." Chap. 6 in *Liberal Rights: Collected Papers 1981–91*, 134–42. Cambridge: Cambridge University Press, 1993.

Wall, Steven. "Radical Democracy, Personal Freedom, and the Transformative Potential of Politics." In *Democracy*, edited by E. F. Paul, F. D. Miller Jr., and J. Paul, 225–54. Cambridge: Cambridge University Press, 2000.

Walzer, Michael. "Deliberation, and What Else?" In *Deliberative Politics: Essays on Democracy and Disagreement*, edited by S. Macedo, 58–69. New York: Oxford University Press, 1999.

———. "Philosophy and Democracy." *Political Theory* 9 (1981): 379–99.

——— *Politics and Passion: Toward a More Egalitarian Liberalism.* New Haven, CT: Yale University Press, 2004.

Warren, Mark E. *Democracy and Association.* Princeton, NJ: Princeton University Press, 2001.

Watson, Gary. "Free Agency." In *Free Will*, edited by G. Watson, 96–110. Oxford: Oxford University Press, 1982.

Weinstock, Daniel M. "Introduction." In *Republicanism: History, Theory, and Practice*, edited by D. Weinstock and C. Nadeau, 1–4. London: Frank Cass, 2004.

Wellmer, Albrecht. *Critical Theory of Society.* Translated by J. Cumming. New York: Herder and Herder, 1971.

———. "Models of Freedom in the Modern World." *The Philosophical Forum* 21:1–2 (Fall–Winter 1989–1990), 227–52.

Whitebook, Joel. *Perversion and Utopia: A Study in Psychoanalysis and Critical Theory.* Cambridge, MA: MIT Press, 1995.

Wolff, Robert P. *In Defense of Anarchism.* Berkeley: University of California Press, 1998.

Wolin, Sheldon S. *Politics and Vision: Continuity and Innovation in Western Political Thought.* Expanded ed. Princeton, NJ: Princeton University Press, 2004.

Wood, Gordon S. *Creation of the American Republic: 1776–1787.* Chapel Hill: University of North Carolina Press, 1998.

Woolf, Virginia. *Three Guineas. San Diego: Harcourt, 1966.*

Young, Iris M. "Activist Challenges to Deliberative Democracy." *Political Theory* 29 (2001): 670–90.

———. "Communication and the Other: Beyond Deliberative Democracy." In *Democracy and Difference: Contesting the Boundaries of the Political*, edited by S. Benhabib, 120–35. Princeton, NJ: Princeton University Press, 1996.

———. *Inclusion and Democracy.* Oxford: Oxford University Press, 2000.

———. *Justice and the Politics of Difference.* Princeton, NJ: Princeton University Press, 1990.

Zakaria, Fareed. *The Future of Freedom: Illiberal Democracy at Home and Abroad.* New York: Norton, 2003.

Index